BRITISH
SPECIAL FORCES

BRITISH
SPECIAL FORCES

WILLIAM SEYMOUR

FOREWORD BY DAVID STIRLING
MAPS BY W.F.N. WATSON

PEN & SWORD MILITARY CLASSICS

This book is dedicated to all those who have served, and still serve, with such distinction and courage in the British Special Forces in an attempt, however inadequate, to repay the incalculable debt that I, and many others, owe them.

BY THE SAME AUTHOR
Battles in Britain
Ordeal by Ambition
Lands of Spice and Treasure
Sovereign Legacy
Yours to Reason Why

First published in Great Britain in 1985 by Sidgwick and Jackson Limited
Published in this format in 2006 by
Pen & Sword Military Classics
An imprint of
Pen & Sword Books Ltd
47 Church Street
Barnsley
South Yorkshire
S70 2AS

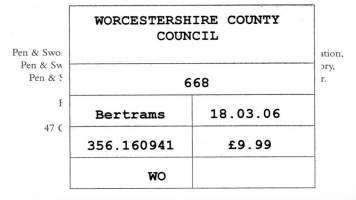

Pen & Swo:
Pen & Sw
Pen & S

F

47 C

ation,
ory,
r.

Foreword

This deeply researched and authoritative book has long been awaited by all those interested in the wartime exploits of the British Special Forces. For the first time readers will be able to understand the origin, inter-relationship and special functions of all the main units within the Special Forces throughout the Second World War and after it. William Seymour identifies the principal leaders and tells of their triumphs, failures and frustrations, all set against the backcloth of the main strategic events in the Western Desert, Italy, the Eastern Mediterranean, Western Europe and the Far East. With rare good sense, and never risking the overall balance, he brings to the fore many hitherto unsung acts of heroism and achievement.

At the end of the war all Special Forces units as defined in this book were disbanded, though the special role of each has been knitted into today's defence forces. The function of the Commandos and the SBS is covered by the Marines, Airborne Forces and to some extent by regular Army battalions – thanks to the latter's greatly improved standards of training and equipment and to their general sophistication. The role of the other Special Forces, essentially a strategic one, has been incorporated into the reconstituted SAS Group which now enjoys full Army Corps status.

Just how effectively the roles of the Special Forces have been thus absorbed was brilliantly exemplified during the Falklands War. This claim is further consolidated by the activities carried out since 1945 by the SAS, ranging from extensive training missions in jungle and desert to grappling with Mount Everest, together with their sustained campaigns which are well documented in the final chapters of this book.

The British, as William Seymour notes, have demonstrated a unique aptitude for Special Forces. During the Second World War no other country produced men of such calibre as the Special Forces leaders, with one major exception – Otto Skorzeny of Germany. After the war he told me that he read all the available German Intelligence reports on the exploits and organization of the Commandos and the SAS, and on the basis of these he planned his part in the famous Mussolini operation. Despite the disapproval of the High Command and the Wehrmacht, Hitler backed Skorzeny and his team, enabling him to carry out highly effective operations such as the abduction of Admiral Horthy, and his deception activities in the Ardennes, when Skorzeny's men posed as Allied staff officers. On Skorzeny's own evidence, therefore, we can say that the 'one major exception' derived from British rather than German military thinking.

The author has analysed the qualities required by the SAS but there is one often neglected factor which I would like to emphasize – the importance of the two SAS Territorial regiments. At the start of the Second World War, and during its early stages, it was the ideas and initiatives of these amateur soldiers which led to the creation of at least two units within the Special Forces and gave a particular élan to others. When, however, a specialist unit becomes part of the military establishment, it runs the risk of being stereotyped and conventionalized. Luckily the modern SAS looks safe from this danger; it is constantly experimenting with innovative techniques, many of which stem from its Territorial regiments, drawn as they are from every walk of civilian life.

As a wartime soldier only, with no writing experience, I had qualms about writing this Foreword. William Seymour, on the other hand, was a professional soldier from 1934 to 1949, and he served in the Special Forces during the Second World War. Since his retirement he has led a distinguished civilian career and he is now a professional author. All this is reflected in his excellent book, which in my opinion should be regarded as indispensable for military students and war historians, and as the definitive work for everyone else with a non-professional interest in this fascinating subject.

David Stirling
January 1985

Contents

Foreword by David Stirling   *v*
Maps   *viii*
Author's Note   *1*

1	Commandos: In the Beginning . . .	5
2	Commandos: Combined Operations, North-West Europe	15
3	Commandos: North Africa, Sicily and Italy	31
4	Commandos: Adriatic, Aegean and Far East	48
5	Commandos: Operations in the Middle East, 1940–1941	64
6	Commandos: Operations in the Middle East, after Crete	83
7	The Special Boat Section, 1940–1945	93
8	Combined Operations Pilotage Parties	109
9	The Long Range Desert Group: The Formative Months	125
10	The Long Range Desert Group: Freedom of the Desert	136
11	The Long Range Desert Group: A Different Kind of War	150
12	Popski's Private Army	167
13	The Special Air Service: The Desert, 1941–1943	187
14	The Special Boat Squadron and Raiding Forces	206
15	Royal Marines' Special Forces: Force Viper and the Royal Marine Boom Patrol Detachment	228
16	The Special Air Service: Europe, 1943–1945	249
17	The Special Air Service: Malaya and Borneo, 1950–1976	268
18	The Special Air Service: South Arabia, 1958–1976	285
19	The Special Air Service: Recent Years	303

Bibliography   *318*
Index   *325*

Maps

Contemporary British usage is followed for place-names throughout the text; modern equivalents are given in the list below (bracketed) for reference.

Abyssinia (Ethiopia)
Ada Ugri (Adi Ugri)
Agedabiah (Ajdabiyah)
Alghena (Elghena)
Arsa (Rasa)

Banba (Bunbah)
Barce (Al Marj)
Bardia (Bardiyah)
Beda Fomm (Baydafumm)
Billiton (Belitung)
Bir Hakeim (Bir Hukayyim)
Bishara (Matan Bisharah)
Bizerta (Bizerte)
Bone (Annaba)
Bouerat (Al Buaryat)
British Somaliland (Somalia)

Cape Bon (Ras el Tib)
Castelorizzo (Kastellorizon)
Cos (Kos)
Cyclades (Kikladhes)
Cyrene (Shahhat)

Derna (Darnah)
Dhofar (Dhufa)
Dodecanese (Sporadhes)
Durazzo (Durres)

El Agheila (Al Uqaylah)
Euboea (Evvoia)

Fayoum (El Faiyum)
Fiume (Rijeka)
French Somaliland (Djibouti)

Gazala (Ayn al Ghazalah)
Ghadames (Ghudamis)
Grand Sea Erg (Grand Erg Oriental)

Himara (Himare)
Homs (Al Khums)

Icaria (Ikaria)
Istria (Istra)
Italian Somaliland (Somalia)

Johore (Johor)
Johore Bahru (Johor Baharu)

Kalansho Sand Sea (Calanscio Sand Sea)
Kalymnos (Kalimnos)
Kastrou (Kastron)
Kufra (Al Kufrah)

Leghorn (Livorno)
Lemnos (Limnos)
Lesbos (Lesvos)
Lussin (Losinj)

Mechili (Al Makili)
Mersa Brega (Qasr al Burayqah)
Mersa Taklai (Marsa Taklai)
Msus (Zawiyat Masus)
Mudhros (Moudhros)
Murge (Minervino)
Murzak (Marzuq)
Mykonos (Mikonos)

Philippeville (Skikda)
Pola (Pula)

Quarnero Gulf (Kvarner)

Retimo (Rethimnon)

Salonika (Thessaloniki)
Santorini (Thira)
Sarra (Matan as Sarra)
Scarpanto (Karpathos)
Senj (Sinj)
Sheikh Othman (Shaykh Uthman)
Siam (Thailand)
Sirte (Surt)
Solluch (Suluq)
Sollum (Salum)
South Yemen (People's Democratic Republic of Yemen)
Sphakhia (Sfakion)
Stampalia (Astipalaia)

Timbaki (Timbakion)
Tmimi (At Tamimi)
Tobruk (Tubruq)
Traghen (Traghan)
Trucial Oman States (United Arab Emirates)

Vaagso Island (Vågsoy)

Yemen (Yemen Arab Republic)

Zara (Zadar)
Zella (Zillah)
Zuara (Zuwarah)

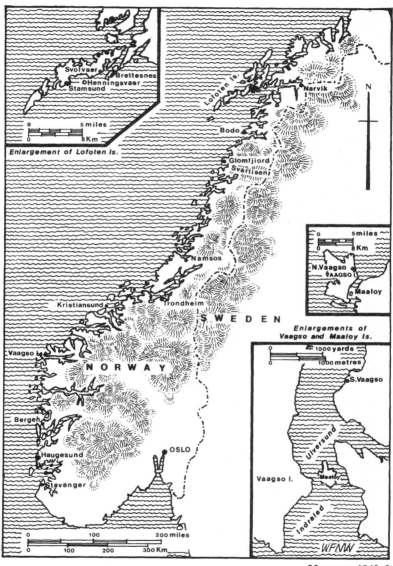

Enlargement of Lofoten Is.

Svolvaer
Brettesnes
Henningsvaer
Stamsund

5 miles
8 Km

Lofoten Is.
Narvik
Bodo
Glomfjiord
Svartisen

Namsos

Kristiansund
Trondheim

SWEDEN

NORWAY

Vaagso I.

Bergen

Haugesund
Stavanger

OSLO

N

5 miles
8 Km

N.Vaagso
VAAGSO I.
Maaloy

**Enlargements of
Vaagso and Maaloy Is.**

1000 yards
1000 metres

S.Vaagso

Ulversund

Vaagso I.

Maaloy

Indreled

WFNW

100   200 miles
100   200   300 Km

Norway 1940–2

Enlargement of Channel Is.

0   5   10 miles
0   10   20 Km

Alderney

Race of Alderney

Cherbourg

Guernsey
St. Peter
Port
Herm

Sark

Jersey
St. Helier

ENGLAND

ENGLISH CHANNEL

Berneval
Dieppe
Varengeville

Channel Is.

Cherbourg
St. Vaast

COTENTIN

St. Laurent
St. Honorine
Arromanches
Courseulles
Ouistreham

Bruneval
Le Havre

Caen
Canal

Caen

R. Orne

R. Seine

Brest

St. Brieuc

St. Malo

BRITTANY

Rennes

F   R   A   N   C

St. Nazaire

R. Loire

Tours

Nantes

Indre

Vienne

BAY

OF

BISCAY

Limoges

Le Verdon
Pte. aux Oiseaux

Gironde

Blaye

Garonne

Bordeaux

France and Belgium 1940–5

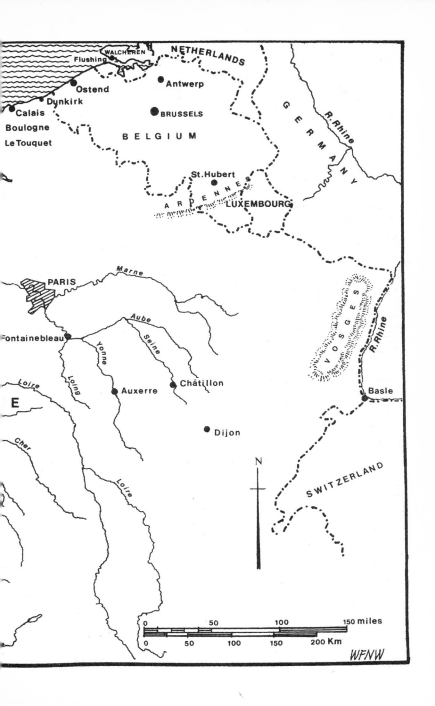

NETHERLANDS

WALCHEREN
Flushing

Ostend

Dunkirk

Calais

Boulogne

Le Touquet

Antwerp

BRUSSELS

BELGIUM

GERMANY

R. Rhine

St. Hubert

ARDENNES

LUXEMBOURG

Marne

PARIS

Aube

Fontainebleau

Yonne

Seine

Loing

Auxerre

Châtillon

Loire

E

VOSGES

R. Rhine

Basle

Dijon

Cher

Loire

N

SWITZERLAND

0	50	100	150 miles
0	50	100	150	200 Km

WFNW

Enlargement of Pisa – R.Po area

Italy, Sicily and the Adriatic 1943–5

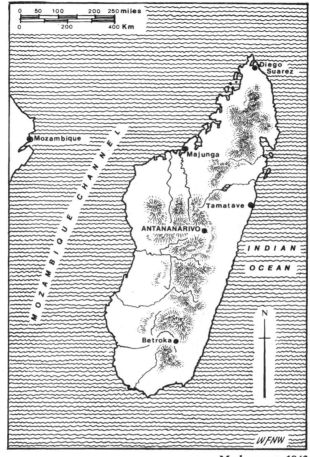

Madagascar 1942

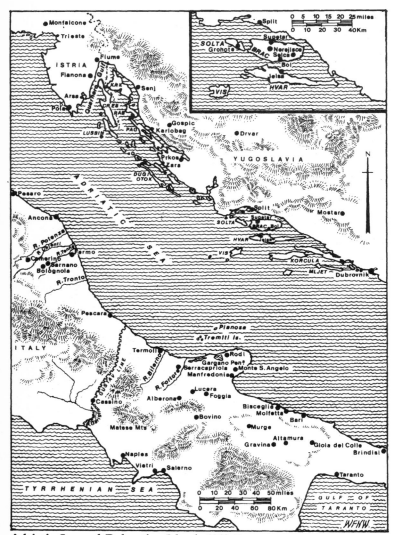

Adriatic Sea and Dalmatian Islands 1943–5

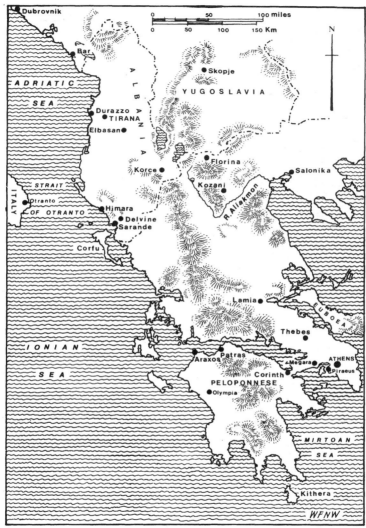

Greek Mainland and Albania 1941–5

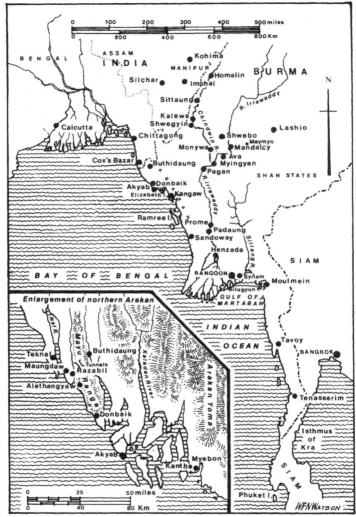

Burma 1942–5

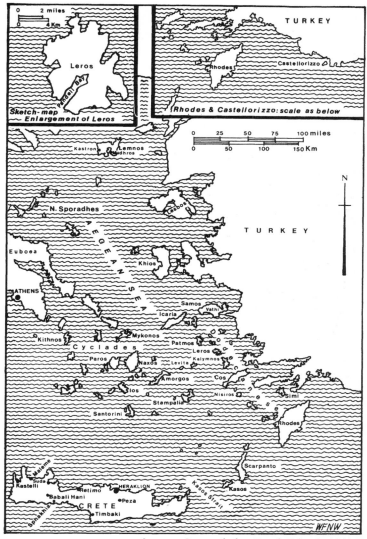

Aegean Sea and the Greek Islands 1941–5

Belgium, the Netherlands and North-West Germany 1940–5

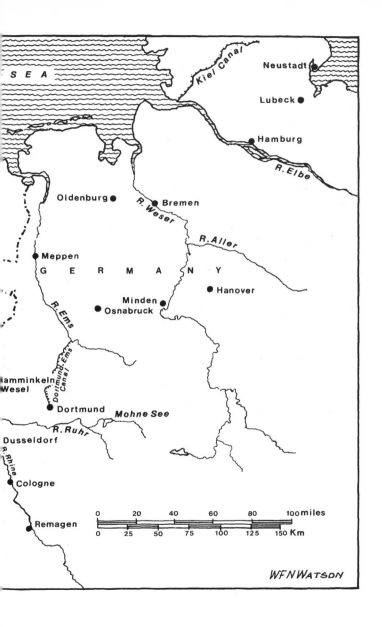

Enlargements 1. ALGIERS

C. Matifou

Fort
Sidi Ferruch
Algiers

Fort
d'Estrées

Maison Blanche

0   5   10 miles
         (approx.)
0   10   20 Km

2. NORTHERN TU

Bize

C. Serrat

Sedjenane

Tabarka
Beja

Tuni

Medjez-el-Bab

0   20   40   60mi
0   30   60   80 Km

SPAIN

Sicily

Algiers

Blida

Philippeville Bone

Oran

Tunis

Pantellaria

Sousse

Malta

Tebessa

Lampedusa

A L G E R I A

Sfax

Gafsa

Tozeur   Gabes

Matmata
Hills

Mareth

Ben Gardane

Bir
Soltane

Zuara

Qaret Ali

TUNISIA

Tripoli

Grand

Gebel Nefusa

Sea

Bouerat

Erg

Ghadames

T R I P O L I T A N

Hon

N

L

Murzak   Traghen

F E Z Z A N

Fort Lamy 650 miles

Wadi Tamin

Ta

0   100   200   300   400   500 miles
0   200   400   600   800 Km

N I G E R   CHA

North Africa and the Middle East 1940–3

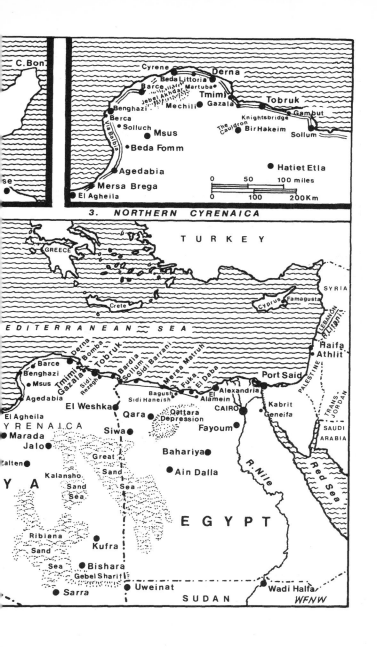

C. Bon

se

Cyrene
Beda Littoria
Derna
Barce
Martuba
Jebel Akhdar
Tmimi
Benghazi
Mechili
Gazala
Tobruk
Berca
Mersa
Knightsbridge
Gambut
Solluch
Msus
The
Cauldron
Bir Hakeim
Sollum
Beda Fomm

Agedabia
Hatiet Etla

Mersa Brega
El Agheila

0		50		100 miles
0		100		200 Km

3. NORTHERN CYRENAICA

GREECE

T U R K E Y

SYRIA

Crete

Cyprus
Famagusta

M E D I T E R R A N E A N ～ S E A

LEBANON

PALESTINE

Haifa
Athlit

Derna
Bomba
Tobruk
Barce
Bardia
Sidi Barrani
Benghazi
Gazala
Sollum
Mersa Matruh
Msus
Sidi
Rezegh
Bagush
Fuka
El Daba
Port Said
Agedabia
El Weshka
Sidi Haneish
El
Alamein
Alexandria

TRANS-
JORDAN

C Y R E N A I C A
Qara
Kabrit
Geneifa
CAIRO

Marada
Qattara
Depression
Fayoum
SAUDI
ARABIA

Jalo
Siwa

alten

Bahariya

Great
Kalansho
Sand

Sand
Sea
Ain Dalla

L I B Y A

E G Y P T

R. Nile

Red Sea

Ribiana

Sand
Kufra

Sea
Bishara
Gebel Sharif

Sarra
Uweinat
Wadi Halfa
WFNW

S U D A N

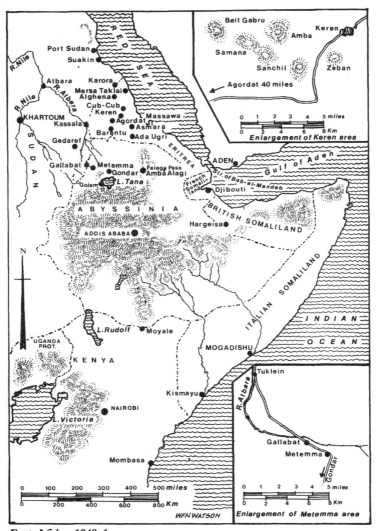

Beit Gabru
Keren
Amba
Samana
Sanchil
Zeban

Agordat 40 miles

0 1 2 3 4 5 miles
0 2 4 6 8 Km
Enlargement of Keren area

Port Sudan
Suakin
R. Nile
R. Atbara
Atbara
Karora
Mersa Taklai
Alghena
Cub-Cub
Keren
L. Massawa
KHARTOUM
Kassala
Agordat
Asmara
Gedaref
Barentu
Ada Ugri

R. Nile

S U D A N

ERITREA

ADEN
Gulf of Aden
Str. of Bab-el-Mandeb

Gallabat
Metemma
Gondar
Falaga Pass
Amba Alagi
Golam
L. Tana

A B Y S S I N I A

French
Somali-
land
Djibouti

BRITISH SOMALILAND

Hargeisa

ADDIS ABABA

N

ITALIAN SOMALILAND

L. Rudolf
Moyale

MOGADISHU

I N D I A N

O C E A N

UGANDA
PROT.
K E N Y A

Kismayu

R. Atbara
Tuklein

L. Victoria
NAIROBI

Gallabat
Metemma
Gondar

Mombasa

0 100 200 300 400 500 *miles*
0 200 400 600 800 Km

0 1 2 3 4 5 miles
0 2 4 6 8 Km
Enlargement of Metemma area

WFN WATSON

East Africa 1940–1

Phuket I.

SOUTH CHINA SEA

SIAM

PERLIS

Khota Bahru

KEDAH

Kroh

Belum Valley

PENANG

KELANTAN

PERAK

TRENGGANU

Ipoh

MALAYA

Telok Anson

PAHANG

Kuantan

SELANGOR

Kuala Lumpur

NEGRI SEMBILAN

Morib beaches

Seremban

Port Dickson

MALACCA

MALACCA STRAIT

JOHORE

SUMATRA

Johore Bahru

Singapore

0   50   100   150 miles

0   100   200 Km

WFNW

Malaya 1950–8

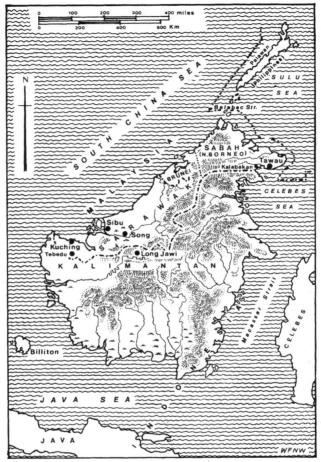

Borneo 1962–6

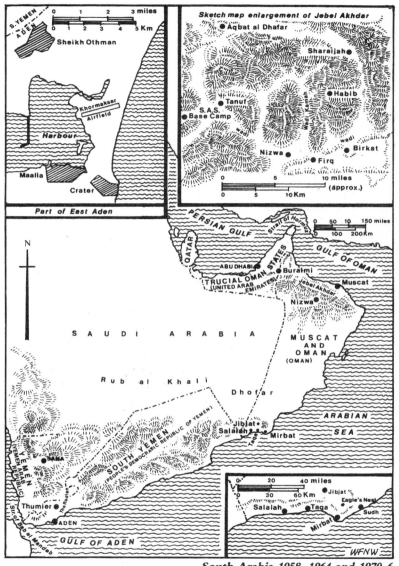

Part of East Aden

Sketch map enlargement of Jebel Akhdar

0 1 2 3 miles
0 1 2 3 4 5 Km

Sheikh Othman

S. YEMEN
ADEN

Khormaksar Airfield

Harbour

Maalla

Crater

Aqbat al Dhafar

Sharaijah

Habib

Tanuf

S.A.S. Base Camp

Nizwa

Firq

Birkat

wadi

wadi

0 5 10 miles
0 5 10Km
(approx.)

N

PERSIAN GULF

Strait of Hormuz

QATAR

GULF OF OMAN

ABU DHABI

Buraimi

TRUCIAL OMAN STATES
(UNITED ARAB EMIRATES)

Jebel Akhdar

Muscat

Nizwa

S A U D I   A R A B I A

MUSCAT
AND
OMAN
(OMAN)

Rub al Khali

Dhofar

ARABIAN
SEA

SOUTH YEMEN
(PEOPLE'S DEMOCRATIC REPUBLIC OF YEMEN)

Jibjat

Salalah
Taqa
Mirbat

SANA

YEMEN
(YEMEN
ARAB
REPUBLIC)

Thumier

The Radfan

Strait of Bab el Mandeb

ADEN

GULF OF ADEN

0 50 10 150 miles
0 100 200Km

0 20 40 miles
0 30 60 Km

Salalah
Taqa

Jibjat

Eagle's Nest

Sudh

Mirbat

WFNW

South Arabia 1958, 1964 and 1970–6

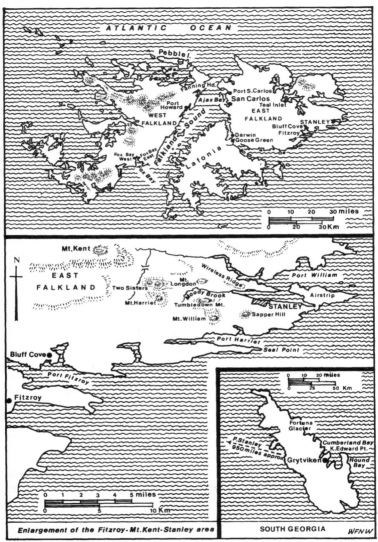

ATLANTIC OCEAN

Pebble I.

Fanning Hd.

Port S.Carlos
Ajax Bay
San Carlos
Teal Inlet

Port
Howard

WEST
FALKLAND

EAST
FALKLAND

STANLEY
Bluff Cove
Fitzroy

Falkland Sound

Darwin
Goose Green

Fox Bay
West
Fox Bay
East

Lafonia

0   10   20   30 miles
0   20   30 Km

Mt.Kent

N

EAST
FALKLAND

Wireless Ridge

Port William

Two Sisters

Mt.
Longdon

Moody Brook

Airstrip

STANLEY

Mt.Harriet

Tumbledown Mt.

Sapper Hill

Mt.William

Port Harriet

Seal Point

Bluff Cove

Port Fitzroy

Fitzroy

0   10   20 miles
0   25   50 Km

Fortuna
Glacier

P.Stanley
950 miles approx

Cumberland Bay
K.Edward Pt.

Grytviken

Hound
Bay

0   1   2   3   4   5 miles
0   5   10 Km

Enlargement of the Fitzroy-Mt.Kent-Stanley area

SOUTH GEORGIA

WFNW

The Falkland Islands and South Georgia 1982

Author's Note

During the last war there was a good deal of misunderstanding, and a certain amount of resentment, associated with 'private armies' – a pejorative term applied by their detractors to some of the special forces that were raised in the early 1940s. The great specialist value to the modern army of the two survivors of the Second World War (the SAS and SBS) has helped to dispel the accusation that they were all a waste of manpower which could have been better, or at least as well, used in a properly trained regular formation.

It is probably true to say that in the war too many special forces were formed and a certain amount of duplication took place. But there was then, and perhaps will be even more so in any future war, a need to raise a force specially trained and equipped to fulfil a particular purpose for which regular formations may not be suitable or cannot be spared – the Long Range Desert Group is just one example. The criteria must be that such a force should not be large, should be kept well under control, should be used only for the special purpose for which it was raised and should be well disciplined.

In the course of my research for this book (coupled with some practical experience) it has been possible to find that where occasional cases of indiscipline have not been speedily dealt with they have damaged the performance and reputation of the force. There is no place in special forces for scallywags in search of adventure of a piratical nature, but there is plenty of opportunity for men with courage, intelligence, initiative and self-discipline. Throughout the story of the special forces mentioned in this book, the quality of courage runs as a golden thread through the rich

1

tapestry of a colourful type of warfare; and for the most part these men showed intelligence and initiative in bringing to a successful conclusion the many difficult and dangerous enterprises they were called upon to perform.

All this I have tried to show, and at the same time I have tried to bear in mind Sir Lewis Namier's precept, 'What matters in history is the great outline . . . what must be avoided is the deadly mass of irrelevant detail.' However, in attempting to write compendiously on a vast subject this has not been easy, for certain details as to recruitment, organization, equipment, training and purpose are important if the composition and performance of the various forces are to be properly understood. As the bibliography shows, almost all of the special forces outlined in this book have had their story told, mostly by men who commanded or fought in those forces. Therefore many of the tales of daring and resource here recounted can be found in greater detail elsewhere. But to those who may say that this book merely repeats much of what has already been written in other books, I can only reply that as far as I know the story of the special forces in those memorable years of audacity and excitement has never been put under one umbrella – and that is the main purpose of this work.

Inevitably (owing to shortage of space, lack of information or security), some of the forces have been treated less fully than others, some have been mentioned only in chapters dealing with a unit to which they were attached or with whom they had close associations, and some – for there were a few which sprang up and died down quite quickly – may have been omitted altogether, in which case I apologize. But I make no apologies for devoting over 2,000 words to Force Viper, a small and relatively unknown force that was raised, went into action and was disbanded all in the space of less than six months. In the first place I consider this was an excellent example of the use of a special force; and in the second their story highlights some of the appalling dangers and difficulties that faced those soldiers swamped by the tidal wave of a victorious Japanese army in a retreat that has not always received the attention it deserves.

A notable omission in the wartime force is the Chindits, and in the peacetime forces the Royal Marines SBS. The former was intentional, for in my opinion they were not an irregular force, but regular formations doing an irregular job; and in the latter there is simply not enough information available to devote a whole chapter to their activities. Nor have I attempted to cover the widespread and invaluable work of the Special Operations

Executive (SOE), which existed principally for clandestine work in enemy countries. It was not a special force, as I define the latter, although on occasions – as I have mentioned – the work of its members had to be carefully co-ordinated with that of a special force operating in the same area.

In a work of this kind the making of every paragraph often requires the reading of many books and documents, but there is much that cannot be gleaned from the printed page. Considerable correspondence with the possessors of facts was necessary, and I owe a big debt of gratitude to a large number of people who have been most generous with their time in reading those chapters describing events with which they were concerned, and making a number of useful comments and corrections; the mistakes that remain are entirely my own. To all of those kind people (some of whom wished to remain anonymous) I am extremely grateful, and in particular I would mention: Henry Brown, Esq., MBE; Lt-General Sir Edward Burges, KCB, OBE; Brigadier J.M. Calvert, DSO; Captain Nigel Clogstoun-Willmott, RN (retd), DSO, DSC; H.L. Collins, Esq.; Lt-Colonel Peter Davis, RM (retd), DSC; J.P. Foot, Esq., MBE; Lt-Colonel L.E.O.T. Hart, OBE; Lt-Colonel H.G. Hasler, RM (retd), DSO, OBE; J.D. Ladd, Esq.; Major-General David Lloyd Owen, CB, DSO, OBE, MC; W.H.A. Pritchard-Gordon, Esq.; Colonel B.G.B. Pugh; Lt-Colonel S.M. Rose, OBE (whose kindness in allowing me to make use of his extensive research into the Middle East Commandos proved quite invaluable); Lt-Colonel Anthony Sellon; Colonel A.D. Stirling, DSO, OBE; Colonel David Sutherland, OBE, MC; Captain Arthur Swinburn, DCM; Miss A.J. Ward; S. Weatherall, Esq.; Brigadier M. Wingate-Gray, OBE, MC; Lt-Colonel J.M. Woodhouse, MBE, MC; and Brigadier Peter Young, DSO, MC.

Colonel Watson has masterminded my maps on previous occasions, and once again his skill has embellished the work and contributed very greatly to any success the book may have. I am also greatly indebted to the staffs of the London Library, the Ministry of Defence Library, the Public Records Office and the Imperial War Museum for their willing and efficient assistance on very many occasions.

The idea of this book belongs to General Sir John Hackett, GCB, CBE, DSO, MC, who passed it to my publisher who, in turn, passed it to me; I trust they will not think that a good suggestion has been badly handled. Finally, my sincere thanks must go to my wife for her encouragement throughout, and for reading the manuscript and offering advice; and to my hard-working secretary, who besides assisting in the research has had the task of typing and retyping the chapters more often than she cares to remember.

1

Commandos: In the Beginning . . .

Until the Second World War the British Army had occasionally dabbled with, but never given serious thought to, the employment of small élite forces formed, trained and equipped for special operations. These demand a particular skill, exceptional courage, a certain amount of imagination (but not too much), and the will-power to go on to the end, come what may; all of which are well suited to the British character with its love of adventure, willingness to accept hardship and risk, and propensity for individualism.

Neither the Germans nor the Italians made much use of irregular troops. Apart from Otto Skorzeny's brilliant operations, and from individual feats such as the Italian swimmers' with their 'human torpedoes', little attempt was made by the enemy to use the opportunities presented by the desert and the various coastlines, for deep penetration or hit-and-run raids. Perhaps it is an island race whose men have the blood of seafaring folk coursing through their veins – and thickened over the centuries by some successful buccaneering – who are more likely to respond to the call of maritime adventure than those who have never had to look to their moat for salvation. Certainly in recent years the British have made more use of special forces than any other major military power, and by their undoubted genius for this particular art of war they have given the lead to the armies of many other nations.

Military history is patterned with the successful, and sometimes unsuccessful, use of special forces, and many deeds of great daring by such troops glimmer in the distant shadows of time. Homer takes us back to the twelfth century BC to make Agamemnon's

5

horse the archetypal undercover (quite literally) special service operation. Alexander had his élite troops and so did the Persians and the Romans, but these were mostly regular formations; however General Davidoff's Cossacks, who harassed the retreat of Napoleon's Grand Army from Moscow so successfully, operated as irregulars, and guerrilla warfare has come to symbolize in part the cruelty and turbulence of Spanish history. Boer commandos (from whom the name originated) helped keep a quarter of a million British troops at bay for three years, and in 1918 German Stormtroopers successfully menaced the Allied lines of communication.

Perhaps the nearest the British came to employing special forces before 1940 was first the raising by Colonel Coote Manningham in 1800 of an Experimental Corps of Riflemen (soon to become a famous regiment of the Regular Army) as a skirmishing and reconnaissance force armed with a new precision rifle. But it was more than a hundred years later that the authorities gave official blessing to T.E. Lawrence's raiders, and later still (in much the same area although on a smaller scale) that they seconded a British officer, Orde Wingate, to lead a *mélange* of irregulars in his Special Night Squads.

Although Wingate had the opportunity to put his ideas into practice he was not the only officer serving between the wars who realized the potential of small bodies of men specially trained to operate against selected targets. In 1935 a subaltern in the Durham Light Infantry, H.E. Fox-Davies, wrote a paper which showed the value of such operations in creating damage out of all proportion to the numbers of men used.* This paper found its way to the desk of General Wavell – then commanding at Aldershot – and that most perspicacious general gave Fox-Davies a chance to prove his point on manoeuvres, and a few years later, when still under Wavell's command but now in Egypt, Fox-Davies was chosen to command a Middle East Commando.

Another, more elderly officer but with similar thoughts, and experience in the Irish troubles of the 1920s, was J.F.C. Holland, a major in the Royal Engineers who, working on the research side of Military Intelligence, was to bring to fruition many practical ideas for subversion warfare.

---

* At this stage it is reasonable to suppose that Fox-Davies' thoughts in regard to numbers were more akin to those later developed by David Stirling: a handful of men, rather than a full-sized Commando involving beach protection etc. Wavell in his reply mentioned the possible uses of the motorized guerrilla, which was even more forward-looking.

The immediate precursor of the Commandos was the Independent Companies. These were the direct result of Major Holland's earlier thinking; ten of them were formed in the spring of 1940, recruited mainly from Territorial divisions, and each Company comprised 20 officers and 270 men.* Nos. 1 to 5 went to Norway, under Lt-Colonel (later Major-General Sir Colin) Gubbins, when the Germans invaded that country. Although trained and armed principally to carry out sabotage raids on the enemy's line of communications, they were mostly employed in the role of ordinary infantry. There was some excuse for this in that there was a dire shortage of troops, but it was not to be the last time that special forces were misused in this way, largely through the failure of higher command to appreciate or understand their proper role. These Companies, which were to be finally disbanded in November 1940, contained men ready-made for special service work, and many of these were to volunteer for the Special Service battalions which at that time were being formed.

The man who did more than anyone to get the Commando idea off the ground was Dudley Clarke, a Gunner colonel, serving in 1940 as Military Assistant to General Dill, the Chief of the Imperial General Staff.

Pondering on the unhappy turn of events immediately following Dunkirk, Clarke's mind traversed through the Boer commandos along similar lines to that of Fox-Davies a few years previously; but Clarke, unlike Fox-Davies, was in a position of influence at the right time. Both the CIGS and the Prime Minister were already thinking in terms of immediate offensive action, if for no other reason than to bolster the nation's confidence; and the Commando plan, when put to the CIGS by Clarke, and by the CIGS to the Prime Minister, met with immediate approval.

Permission was given for Clarke to proceed on the understanding that he was not to plunder the new Home Forces Command of men and weapons. The Commandos,† therefore, conceived in confidence, were born under difficulties that were to pursue them for some time, since in June 1940 every man was needed to guard England's shores, and her arsenals were woefully short of arms with which to equip these men. But the Commandos were

---

* This may have been a paper establishment, for in July 1940 No. 2 Independent Company's strength was 17 officers and 252 other ranks.
† The official designation of Commando was not easily won, for the mandarins of the War Office considered it misplaced, and the CIGS had to give a ruling. Even then the singularly inappropriate Special Service (SS) crept in from time to time.

nothing if not resourceful, and very soon good men, with an assortment of shared weapons, were undergoing training for the first of two more or less impromptu raids that Clarke was urged to carry out. These were centred on a German aerodrome near Le Touquet, and on Guernsey. Both these raids were poor harbingers of what was to come, but they taught valuable lessons and the publicity they achieved was good for recruiting.

When Dudley Clarke made his original selection of raiders from the Independent Companies, and a little later when a handful of officers had been chosen to form the first Commando, men were carefully hand picked by these same officers to serve in their own troops. Later, volunteers were supplied on demand direct from units, through the Commando Base Depot or Young Soldiers' Battalions. In every case, however, and throughout the whole of the Commandos' existence, the same very high standard of recruit was required.

A good Commando soldier had to be a protean figure. Every worthwhile soldier needs to have courage, physical fitness and self-discipline, but those who served in the Commandos needed these virtues more abundantly, for they would be called upon to perform feats well beyond the normal run of duty, and often to work longer hours and enjoy less rest than their counterparts in a regiment. A high standard of marksmanship had to be attained, as did the ability to cross any type of country quickly, to survive a rough passage at sea in a small boat and arrive the other side ready to scale a cliff, to use explosives, to think quickly and if needs be to act independently, and to be prepared to kill ruthlessly. A man would learn some of these skills in his training, but vitality and a zest for adventure must be the well-spring of every one of his actions. Those who could not make the grade – and for one reason or another there were quite a few – had to be returned to their units; a sufficient punishment in itself.

It is easy to understand that some commanding officers were unwilling to part with such paragons, and it has often been argued that by taking men of this calibre the regular regiments were deprived of potential junior leaders of above-average quality. But when figures are compared, and the small number of men who volunteered and were accepted for special service (for it was not only the Commandos that demanded these standards) against those who made up the rest of the army, such arguments hold little water. On the whole, as the results show, the special forces got the men they wanted; but inevitably there were some misfits and not all regiments played fair. Every man was a volunteer all

Commandos: In the Beginning . . .

right, but in some cases the motive was to avoid the long arm of
the Company Sergeant Major, and occasionally these volunteers
were the first to be sent. It was a waste of time because sooner or
later – usually sooner – they were all back in their regiments.

All new formations must endure growing pains, and when
these formations are raised in a hurry the pains are liable to be
more severe. Many changes were to occur between June 1940 and
March 1941 in composition and designation of the Commandos.
The first Commando into the field was No. 3,* and its commander was a regular Gunner called John Durnford-Slater, who later
rose to be a brigadier. In late June 1940 he was commissioned to
raise the Commando to be formed at Plymouth from volunteers
serving in Southern Command. By 5 July the task was accomplished, and in the middle of that month some of his men joined
those of No. 11 Independent Company (who had carried out the
first cross-Channel raid) in the Guernsey adventure already mentioned.

In 1940 the official war establishment for 'An Irregular Troop'
gave the strength as one captain, two subalterns, four sergeants,
eight corporals, twelve lance-corporals and twenty-three privates;
there were at that time ten troops. In addition there was a small
headquarters, consisting of a Lt-Colonel commanding, one major
(second-in-command), four subalterns (adjutant, administrative
officer, signals and intelligence officers) two warrant officers, two
sergeants, one corporal, two lance-corporals and twenty privates:
a total, all ranks, of 533.

When Clarke first received authority to raise a special raiding
force he started work in close co-operation with the navy through
Captain G.A. Garnons-Williams, and soon a small secretariat was
set up in the Admiralty under Lt-General Sir Alan Bourne,
Adjutant-General of the Royal Marines, to co-ordinate raids and
assist in organization. During the summer of 1940 six more
Commandos (Nos. 4, 5, 6, 7, 8 and 9) were formed, mostly from
the remnants of the Independent Companies. Since Norway Nos.
1 to 5 of these had languished in tented camps around western
Scotland, while Nos. 6 to 9 were in the Land's End zone. In

* No. 2 was originally designated No. 2 (Para) Commando, but was disbanded
with many of the men forming the nucleus of the airborne forces. The identity of
No. 1 was submerged in the Group of Independent Companies formed in July
1940 from the original ten Companies, and soon to become a part of the Special
Service Battalions. Not until March 1941 did Nos. 1 and 2 Commandos emerge
under their true colours.

9

October of that year Brigadier J.C. Haydon was appointed to command the Special Service Brigade.

It was under his leadership* that the Commandos were amalgamated into Special Service Battalions. Apart from the unfortunate nomenclature of 'Nos. 1 to 5 SS Battalions', these five formations, each of no fewer than 70 officers and a little over 1,000 other ranks, were hopelessly unwieldy, and in March 1941 they were disbanded. The existing Commandos had kept their identity within the Special Service Battalions and were reformed as such, and there was now to be a total of eleven Commandos. They were numbered 1 to 12, with No. 10 missing – this was formed in January 1942 as an Inter-Allied Commando with troops of six different nationalities. Nos. 7, 8 (plus A Troop of No. 3) and 11 Commandos sailed for the Middle East early in 1941 and will be heard of later as Layforce – the eponymous force of Colonel (later Major-General) R.E. Laycock who had originally raised No. 8 Commando.

The remaining Commandos were now to be organized into a headquarters and six rifle troops, each of three officers and sixty-two other ranks.† Sixty-five soldiers could be fitted into two assault landing craft and leave five spare spaces for signal and medical personnel or others; this new organization also made it easier for headquarters to control the Commando. Each troop was to have two sections consisting of an officer and thirty other ranks, and each section was to have a section headquarters (one officer and two orderlies) and two subsections of a lance-sergeant and thirteen men. There was to be one Bren gun and one Thompson submachine gun per subsection, and one anti-tank rifle per section.

Commando training was initially carried out under the best available arrangements that could be made by each commanding officer. But in August 1940 Admiral Keyes, who by then had become Director of Combined Operations, improved upon these rather unsatisfactory arrangements by concentrating his Commando force at the Combined Training Centre at Inveraray, the seat of the Dukes of Argyll. The CTC was commanded by Vice-Admiral Hughes-Hallett and the facilities on and around Loch Fyne were excellent. Moreover, the large naval presence of 50 officers and 300 ratings, with a boatshed to accommodate sixty

---

* Although not of his doing, and indeed it was largely through Brigadier Haydon's insistence that a few months later they reverted to Commandos.
† The 6th Troop later became the Heavy Weapons Troop with a 3 in. Mortar section (two mortars) and a Machine Gun section (two Vickers).

landing craft, proved invaluable for one of the most important parts of a Commando's training.

In February 1942 the Commandos were to get their own training headquarters with the establishment of a Depot – later to be known as the Commando Basic Training Centre – under its formidable and extremely efficient Commandant, Lt-Colonel C.E. Vaughan, and situated at Achnacarry, the home of another Scottish chieftain, Cameron of Lochiel. It has to be remembered that the men who volunteered for the Commandos were all trained soldiers specially selected for the high quality of their performance, and therefore much of their training was to sharpen them up so that they were able to carry out the normal operational duties of an infantryman quicker and better than the ordinary soldier.

This, and much else, was achieved during a twelve-week course, which was perhaps the toughest and most exacting that the British Army had ever devised. Every exercise was conducted with live ammunition and explosives. A man was expected to march 7 miles in the hour, climb a cliff, fire a gun accurately on the run and know how to kill silently with knife or garrotte. The assault course – part of which was known as the Death Ride – became legendary, and training included living off the land (cooking and eating rats!). Much of a Commando's work would be done in the hours of darkness, and training at Achnacarry was aimed to produce a creature of the night and mist who through stealth would strike swiftly and silently at the foe. And never was a man allowed to forget that as well as all this, if he wished to wear the green beret (introduced after Dieppe in 1942), he must cultivate cleanliness, smartness, self-discipline and an honourable pride in his unit.

But the ultimate purpose of all this training was to perfect the Commando soldier in the art of amphibious warfare, to make him familiar with boat drill and to ensure that he could land on a hostile beach ready for immediate, swift and tough fighting. In the course of the war the Commandos had at their disposal a large assortment of sea-going craft. At the top of the scale were the assault carrier ships, and typical of these were the converted fast passenger-carrying cargo ships of the Holt Line, the *Glenroy*, *Glenearn*, *Glengyle* and *Breconshire*; they had a range of 12,000 miles and could carry more than a full Commando, and for comparatively short distances two could be lifted.

Assault landing craft came in different shapes and sizes. LCI Landing Craft Infantry (Large) could carry 200 troops and for assault purposes had a range of 500 miles. There was also an LCI (Small) – a wooden ship with armour plate in scales – which carried only 100 soldiers and could be used for long distance raids with a range of 700 miles. There were occasions when these infantry landing craft were supported by an LCS (Landing Craft Support) which carried two 5 in. Vickers machine guns, two Bren guns and a 4 in. mortar for smoke, to give close support after a group had come ashore from an LCI. LCP or Landing Craft Personnel (Large), called Eurekas, were wooden ships mounting two machine guns and able to carry about twenty fully equipped soldiers. They were designed for short runs to carry troops from ship to shore, but could be used – and at Dieppe were – for trips of 70 miles or more. Another largely unarmed ship was the LCA (Landing Craft Assault), which had a range of rather over 50 miles and could carry thirty-five soldiers. There were many other types of landing craft of different calibres carrying tanks and heavy vehicles.

These craft, except in an emergency, were not the direct concern of the raiders once they had mastered the techniques of boarding and disembarking down gangways or ramps, but smaller boats played a vital part in special service operations. Chief among these were the dories, of which the prototype – the CNI – was built in June 1941, though a number of modifications and improvements were made later. They were powered boats 18 ft long with a light plywood frame. Dories were used extensively on small-scale raids when men were transferred to them from Motor Torpedo Boats (MTBs), or other larger craft, some 3 miles off the selected landing site.

Another small boat used for close approach to the target was the Goatley, named after its designer Mr Fred Goatley of Saro Laminated Woodwork Ltd. This was a collapsible craft of 11 ft 6 in. overall length; with its canvas sides it was a flimsy vessel fairly easily swamped in rough water. Both types of craft could take about eight men. Even more alarming to operate were the various types of canoe used principally by the Special Boat Section and often launched from a submarine. The German-type Folbot was covered with a rubberized fabric skin stretched on a wooden frame: it held two people and could be folded into a pack. Later developments of this craft resulted in the Cockle boats Mks I and II, the second of which is described in Chapter 15.

The founding fathers of the Commando movement laid it down that there should be no administrative tail, and that every man in the unit should be a front-line fighter. A Commando had one medical officer and five orderlies and they were every bit as much front-line personnel as riflemen; because a Commando often fought in fairly small groups it was very important that the orderlies were well trained – and they invariably were. Willing landladies and the average soldier's aptitude for foraging enabled the early Commandos to dispense with barrack accommodation; officers were given an allowance of 13s. 4d. a day and other ranks 6s. 8d. (later increased to 7s. 6d.) with which to secure board and lodging, and furthermore to secure it at short notice and in widely separated places. There was no transport and great stress was placed on individual initiative; men would be dismissed in one place and told to be on parade the next day perhaps 100 miles away.

Travelling light with minimum rations and no transport was admirable as long as Commandos were employed in their original role, which was for short, sharp raids on enemy lines of communication or specially selected targets which could not be destroyed by more orthodox methods. For these the system worked, in spite of what has been said to the contrary. But from 1943 onwards Commandos were used more and more in roles not very different from that of an ordinary infantry battalion, and then they had to have a certain amount of transport and a small non-combatant tail. Inevitably, when operating as part of a larger force, as in Italy and North-West Europe, their war establishment had to be on a footing more approaching that of a battalion of the line.

During the summer and autumn of 1940 the principal emphasis in the Commando camp was on organization and training, but a number of small raids across the Channel did take place; the two already mentioned were followed by a slightly more successful one carried out in September in the areas of St Vaast and Courseulles on the Normandy coast. But it is open to question whether the handful of Germans killed and the experience gained in these raids (for they certainly had no tactical and only marginal strategic value) justified the reprisals sometimes meted out to the local inhabitants. But little more could be done at this time with the weapons available.

Night and day in embattled Britain modern machinery in the factories was at full stretch, and the forges were roaring and the hammers descending to beat out implements of slaughter. Commando leaders were constantly and strenuously importuning the service ministries for sufficient arms and small craft to enable their troops to adopt the strong offensive role for which they were designed, but opposition from the regular army was fierce.

However, a few days after the Guernsey raid in July an event took place which was to prove of great significance for the future of all special service operations. A Director of Combined Operations (DCO), in the person of Admiral of the Fleet Sir Roger Keyes, was appointed. Keyes replaced General Bourne, who had been in charge of raiding, and who unselfishly agreed to stay on as Keyes's second-in-command.

Between the wars lip service had been paid to the need for a combined operations organization, but little had been done. In 1937 the War Office set up a committee to study inter-service exercises and the need to develop special equipment, and in 1938 the Inter-Services Training and Development Centre came into being at Fort Cumberland near Portsmouth. Shortly afterwards it submitted a report, and some of its recommendations were under consideration when war broke out in 1939. But it was left to Winston Churchill's customary breadth of view to translate theory into practice, and to establish a Combined Operations Headquarters (COHQ) which would devise and control the complete integration of planning, experimenting and operating within the three services.

2

Commandos: Combined Operations, North-West Europe

When Admiral Keyes was appointed DCO, Combined Operations was looked upon as an Admiralty Division. In August 1940 he moved his headquarters out of the Admiralty to offices at 1A Richmond Terrace, but the complete fulfilment of Churchill's ideal lay a little way into the future. Keyes at sixty-eight was still a man of immense vitality and enthusiasm, who believed in personal contact conveyed by example and never by precept. He worked unceasingly, and with considerable success, to put the Commandos on the map, and because he had the ear of those in high places he was able to make some headway in procuring the tools of the trade. But even he found it difficult to overcome certain strands of red tape, and plans for cross-Channel raids were inhibited by Home Forces' insistence that each army commander should be responsible for all raids launched from his sector of the coast.

This meant that COHQ had unfettered control of operations only against enemy posts on the Norwegian coast, and it was not until Lord Louis Mountbatten had succeeded Admiral Keyes that the Chief (as he was then called) of Combined Operations became the Mounting Authority for all raids in North-West Europe. Although Keyes continued to direct detachments of his 'private army' against the French coast, obviously Norway was an easier target administratively, and it was in Norwegian waters that the first major Commando raid took place in March 1941.

Five hundred men from Nos. 3 and 4 Commandos, fifty-two Royal Engineers and fifty-two men from the Free Norwegian Forces, all under the command of Brigadier Haydon, were to raid the Lofoten Islands, which are situated 850 miles from Scapa

Flow. These islands were of great importance to the Germans, for vast quantities of herring and cod were processed into oil there. This oil was exported to Germany and used for, among other things, the production of nitro-glycerine for explosives.

The plan envisaged simultaneous landings on the four key ports of Henningsvaer, Svolvaer, Stamsund and Brettesnes, and the object was to destroy the factories in these ports and the ships around them, and to bring back prisoners and any Norwegians who wished to volunteer for their free forces. Personnel involved in the raid proceeded to Scapa Flow for final exercises, and set sail from there in two converted Channel ferries with assault landing craft on their davits. A formidable naval escort was allotted to the carrier vessels and at 4 a.m. on 4 March the guiding submarine brought the troops opposite their objectives. It was expected that opposition would not be great, for there was thought to be only a handful of German soldiers on the islands and winter conditions greatly impeded enemy air interference.

It was a well-chosen 'soft' target, and if the operation was successful it would give the Commandos a fillip much needed at that time, for many earlier operations had been planned, only to be cancelled. It would also be a most valuable contribution to the war effort. And it was very successful: none of the landings was opposed, and the troops were greeted enthusiastically by the local inhabitants – who, it was learned later, did not on this occasion suffer severe reprisals. Commando demolition parties did a fine job destroying factories, oil and electrical installations (800,000 gallons of oil and petrol were left burning), and sinking some 20,000 tons of shipping. Some 216 Germans and 60 Norwegian quislings were captured, and 315 Norwegian volunteers were brought home. The only British casualty was an officer who accidently discharged a pistol bullet into his thigh! This raid was to put British Commandos firmly on the world map, and even though there was – to everyone's disappointment – no fighting, it had proved how a small number of determined men put ashore boldly and secretly could achieve considerable damage to valuable installations.

In October 1941 Admiral Keyes, who had done so much for the Commandos, was in disagreement with a new directive which among other things lowered his status from Director to Adviser of Combined Operations. But he had been at variance with the Chiefs of Staff for some time because he felt that the Commandos, who had been restricted mainly to small reconnaissance raids, were not being used in their proper role. Keyes was now nearly seventy and there were some (Sir Geoffrey Congreve for one*) who, while full of admiration for him, thought that age was beginning to tell and that he had lost his drive. Moreover, some of the ideas he had for using his force were suspect – his projected assault on Pantelleria for example. His place was taken by the much younger sailor Lord Louis Mountbatten – advanced from Captain to Commodore – with a wide brief and massive powers. A part of his directive was the development of special craft suitable 'for all forms of combined operations from small raids to a full-scale invasion of the Continent'.

Mountbatten was a man of action and ambition, clever and audacious, and with connections even more impressive than Keyes's. His dominant personality, well fitted for the contentions of the time, soon gained him most of what he required to mount three large-scale raids at Vaagso, St Nazaire and Dieppe. But the ground had been well prepared for him by the thundering attack on the War Office's iniquitous treatment of the Commandos launched by Keyes in Parliament on his retirement. Under Lord Louis, Combined Operations Headquarters was greatly expanded with a Chief of Staff (Brigadier G.E. Wildman-Lushington, a Royal Marine); a scientific branch under Professor J.D. Bernal; a Planning Staff; an Intelligence Staff; and several committees one of which, the Search Committee, was responsible for seeking out targets.

The Chief of Combined Operations (CCO) was now to have the power to promote raids launched from any of the Home Forces commands, but the commanders-in-chief in any area affected were to comment on the outline plan prepared at COHQ. A force commander was then appointed to work out details of the plan and to co-ordinate it with the Navy and Air Force, and the CCO had to have it approved by the Chiefs of Staff Committee. The Intelligence Staff of COHQ received considerable help from that secretive organization the Special Operations Executive (SOE). It had been originally decided in 1940 that SOE would handle all small coastal raids, but this never materialized. However, its co-operation with COHQ proved most fruitful, particularly in the field of equipment and weapon research.

Each of the many small raids that had been undertaken in the summer of 1941 brought little bits of information which when pieced together made an important whole, and on every raid new lessons were learned and later implemented. But Mountbatten

* Commander Sir Geoffrey Congreve, RN, personal papers with Commandos.

was anxious to promote raids on a larger scale, and the first of these, on Vaagso, was scheduled for the end of December 1941. The raid had a strategic and tactical object. Strategically it was hoped that the scale of the raid would determine the Germans to strengthen their coastal defences with troops that could have been better employed elsewhere; the tactical object was to destroy all military targets, factories and shipping in the port of South Vaagso, and the neighbouring island of Maaloy, and to liquidate their garrisons.

South Vaagso is a Norwegian port on the east side of Vaagso Island some four miles from the open sea up the Vaags Fjord and Indraled channel. The small island of Maaloy guards the entrance to the Ulvesund (part of the Indraled channel) in a narrow neck of water about 1,000 yards south of the port. Brigadier Haydon was again in command of the Commando force, which included the whole of No. 3 Commando and detachments from Nos. 2, 4 and 6 with some Norwegian Army troops and the Brigade Signalling Section – a total of 576 all ranks. Lt-Colonel Durnford-Slater (OC No. 3 Commando), who had done most of the planning, was to command the troops ashore. A strong naval force under Rear-Admiral (later Admiral Sir Harold) Burrough accompanied the two LSIs which carried the raiders, and No. 50 Squadron RAF flew Hampdens in close support of the raid. The principal difference between this raid and the one staged earlier on the Lofoten Islands was knowledge that fairly stiff opposition would be encountered. On Maaloy the Germans had a battery of Belgian 75s, anti-aircraft and machine guns, while South Vaagso was defended by troops of their 181st Division with battle experience in the Norway campaign.

The Force was to be divided into five groups; three were to land on Vaagso Island (Group 1 at the south tip, Group 2 just south of the town and Group 5 north of it to prevent reinforcements coming from North Vaagso). Group 3 had the battery on Maaloy as its objective, and Group 4 was a floating reserve. Naval guns were to bombard Maaloy Island. This opening cannonade, from which some 400 shells crashed into the tiny island, took the Germans completely by surprise, and the Commando troops landing in its wake had little difficulty in capturing the place despite its strong garrison. No. 1 Group also landed virtually unopposed, but the fighting in and around South Vaagso was extremely heavy. The German garrison defended every building, and snipers were cunningly placed. Street fighting is one of the most difficult and dangerous tasks a soldier has to perform: there is the continual feeling of being lapped about by the enemy, and bullets come whizzing and whining by from no particular direction in a hideously frightening manner. To be successful, troops must be well led and imbued with the offensive spirit – the outcome of sound training, physical fitness and good teamwork.

Colonel Durnford-Slater's men possessed these important requirements, and the results of the raid were eminently satisfactory. As was hoped, the Germans did increase their outlying garrisons in Norway to a very considerable extent; and in the raid itself they suffered heavy material damage to shipping, oil installations and factories, important documents were burned, four field guns and a tank were destroyed, 120 Germans were killed and 98 taken prisoner – the largest German bag of the war so far. The Commandos lost two officers and fifteen other ranks killed, and five officers and forty-eight other ranks wounded: the Navy lost two ratings killed and two officers and four ratings wounded.

A few days before the Vaagso raid the Lofoten Islands had been revisited by No. 12 Commando, some Norwegian troops and certain details of SOE, all under command of Lt-Colonel S.S. Harrison. Operation Anklet, as it was called, was mounted as a curtain raiser to the larger raid, for which it was also to act as a diversion. A formidable naval force, under the overall command of Rear-Admiral Hamilton, accompanied the Commando troops who landed unopposed on 26 December. Some enemy shipping was destroyed, but the force had to retire after two days with little accomplished when it was learned that a large German air strike was imminent. However, a good deal was learned about the difficulties of operating in the winter in high latitudes.

The St Nazaire raid, brilliantly conceived and executed, had as its primary objective the blocking of what was at that time the largest dock in the world – the Forme Écluse. Bombers having made Brest too uncomfortable for German capital ships, St Nazaire was the only port left on the French coast capable of taking a ship like the *Tirpitz*, which could play such a damaging part in the Battle of the Atlantic. Subsidiary objectives were the destruction of various locks and bridges that controlled the entrances of the three harbours – Avant Port, Bassin de St Nazaire and Bassin de Penhouet.

HMS *Campbeltown*, one of the fifty lease-lend American destroyers, was selected for the part played by the *Vindictive* at Zeebrugge twenty-five years earlier, and she was accompanied by a strong naval force under the command of Commander R.E.D. Ryder. The size of the military component was dictated by the number of MLs (Motor Launches) available, and had to be restricted to 44 officers and 233 other ranks, who were split into three groups to be landed at different points. The main force was found almost entirely from No. 2 Commando under their Commanding Officer, Lt-Colonel A.C. Newman, but the demolition parties came from Nos. 1, 3, 4, 5, 9 and 12 Commandos.

The thrilling and heroic story of this raid, which took place in March 1942 and in which no fewer than five Victoria Crosses were won, has often been told in all its triumphant detail. It is only necessary here to record the complete success of the primary objective, for the *Cambeltown* was well and truly rammed into the entrance to the huge dock and in due course her charges went off, destroying part of the dock and completely blocking it. Despite great efforts the Germans were unable to repair the damage, and the dock remained unserviceable until 1950.

The sabotage parties were somewhat less successful owing to heavy losses to the MLs, caught in a devastating crossfire as they made their way up the Loire. Troops could not in all cases be landed at the right places, and a thoroughly roused and numerous enemy resisted the attack strenuously. Although a great deal of damage was done by the demolition parties, in the savage fighting casualties on both sides were heavy, and with the destruction of so many MLs many Commandos and naval men could not get away. The Commando lost 59 men killed and 153 taken prisoner. Out of the total force committed almost two-thirds failed to return; a high price to pay, which could be justified only by the great success of the venture with its important bearing on the Battle of the Atlantic.

Dieppe was easily the largest operation so far promoted by the CCO. By now Mountbatten's position had been greatly strengthened, for in March 1942 he had been promoted from Commodore to Vice-Admiral, given a seat on the Chiefs of Staff Committee, and made the holder of honorary senior ranks (Lt-General and Air Marshal) in the Army and Air Force. He was, therefore, more readily able to requisition his every requirement for almost any martial enterprise – although on this particular occasion the original COHQ directive was drastically changed by Home Forces Command when, for political reasons, it was decided to use Canadian troops. The plan in its final form stipulated that the main attack was to be a frontal assault on the port with two flank attacks to silence batteries. The attack was to go in at first light without any preliminary bombardment from sea or air (to obtain surprise), against the advice of COHQ.

The purpose of the raid was a trial run against a defended port as a preliminary to the detailed planning that would be necessary before a full-scale invasion of the Continent could be mounted – a 'reconnaissance in force', as Churchill called it. There were, of course, subsidiary objectives involving destruction of defences and installations, capture of prisoners and sinking of ships. The main assault was to be made by two brigades of the 2nd Canadian Division and the 14th Canadian Army Tank Regiment under command of Major-General J.H. Roberts. Two outer flank attacks on batteries at Berneval and Varengeville were to be made by No. 3 Commando under Lt-Colonel Durnford-Slater and No. 4 under Lt-Colonel Lord Lovat. Each Commando had with it a party from the 1st United States Rangers.

The whole force embarked on the evening of 18 August 1942 at four ports. The two Commandos (with whom we are most concerned) met with varying fortunes. No. 3 sailed from Newhaven in twenty unarmed landing craft (Eurekas), not really designed for a long cross-Channel trip. Shortly before 4 a.m. their craft were intercepted and scattered by armed enemy trawlers, and their Commanding Officer's landing craft was among those that never made land off Berneval. A party from four boats which did arrive on the correct beach, but behind schedule, met with very stiff opposition and failed to break through; only one Lance-Corporal from this party managed to reach the landing craft in time to be taken off later in the morning. However, another party of eighteen men, under Major Peter (later Brigadier) Young fought their way with great gallantry and resolution through to a position from where they could engage the enemy battery with such withering fire as to prevent the Germans from bringing their guns to range on the main anchorage. Had the Commando been able to land in full strength the battery would surely have been destroyed.

Meanwhile, on the western flank, four troops of Lord Lovat's No. 4 Commando landed as planned on two beaches either side of the German battery position near Varangeville, and proceeded to carry out the archetypal Commando raid in its fearful fulfilment – dash, daring, determination and destruction. The Commando sailed from Southampton, not in Eurekas but in an LSI, and met with no interference at sea. In the early hours, while it was still dark, their assault craft were launched, and the two groups landed a little before 5 a.m. The plan was to take out the battery in a pincer movement. The group under Major Derek Mills-Roberts had the task of pinning down the battery with mortar fire, while

Lord Lovat's larger force, which had landed farther to the west, worked their way round and attacked the battery from the rear. Like all good plans it was simple, and also like most plans it was subjected to unforeseen interruptions. But the Commando was trained to deal with the unexpected. The final assault was a short, sharp and bloody affair of fixed bayonets and hand-to-hand grapple. No. 4 Commando suffered forty-five casualties in the battle, of whom two officers and ten other ranks were killed. They wiped out some thirty Germans, wounded as many more and silenced a potentially dangerous battery.

Tactically it was perhaps the only happy result of that unhappy day, for the main attack was a shambles. Canadian troops, lacking battle experience, were asked to tackle strong German defences manned by resolute men without any preliminary softening up. The measure of their courage is in the 68 per cent casualties their large force suffered. Dieppe was a costly failure brought about principally through faulty planning, but in the womb of disaster was the embryo of later success. It became very obvious that to seize a defended port, even with the aid of a preliminary bombardment, was not practicable; and the solution to the problem was to be the Mulberry Harbour. Furthermore, the Germans felt that a port seizure would be tried again on a larger scale, and made preparations accordingly.

For each of these large-scale raids there were many smaller ones launched, for Mountbatten was anxious to keep the pressure up and the Commandos in fighting trim. These could be of a purely sabotage-cum-reconnaissance nature, or raids against specially selected targets of strategic importance, which could be best handled by a small party of determined men. Some of these small raids were carried out by an offshoot of the Commandos, the Small-Scale Raiding Force, founded by three Commando officers – Major G. March-Phillips, Major J.G. Appleyard and Captain G. Hayes. They had their headquarters in Anderson Manor, near Wareham, and they carried out intensive training in the Dorset countryside and the waters of Poole Harbour. They were also parachute trained.

The SSRF were operationally under the Chief of Combined Operations, but some of their work was of a secret nature and they were jointly controlled by the CCO and SOE. They raided in small parties of around eight to ten men against targets chosen at random, with the broad objective of killing Germans. But in October 1942 it was decided their role should be more selective, and although they still came from the sea (using chiefly Goatley boats) the 'hand of steel which plucks the German sentries from their posts' was to be employed also in bringing back prisoners for identification and certain technical equipment for examination. Their independent role ceased at the beginning of 1943.

In 1942 SSRF carried out a number of very daring raids, including one on Sark which was to have unfortunate repercussions for future Commando prisoners. On the night of 7/8 September March-Phillips, Appleyard and Hayes with nine other ranks took part in a raid on St Honorine on the Normandy coast. They encountered a much stiffer defence position than had been expected, and so the party had to withdraw. On the way back to their boat they ran into two patrols, one of which they destroyed; but in the fierce fight that developed March-Phillips and three others were killed. Hayes swam along the coast, was sheltered by some French people and later made his way to Spain, where he was caught by the Spanish police and handed over to the Germans. Nine months later, after a long period of solitary confinement, he was shot. Appleyard had remained in the MTB, for he had an injured leg, and got back to Portsmouth; he was killed the next year in the Middle East when working with 2 SAS Regiment.

Perhaps the prize for the tidiest, most successful and least costly raid undertaken by components of all three services should go to the men who planned and carried out the attack on the radar station at Bruneval. In February 1942 aircraft of Bomber Command dropped two parties of parachutists from C Company 2nd Parachute Battalion, under Major (later Major-General) J.D. Frost, who in less than two hours had overcome the defenders of the radar station, carried away much needed scientific evidence before destroying the plant, killed about thirty Germans and taken three prisoners. They then withdrew and were taken off the beach by the Navy. This important operation was accomplished for the loss of one man killed and seven wounded.

Bruneval was not a raid in which the Commandos played a large part, although thirty-two men from No. 12 Commando armed with four Bren guns, and brought in by six LCAs, gave valuable supporting fire. But another most effective raid, also directed at a vitally important strategic target, which on account of its proximity to friendly civilians could not be bombed, was successfully carried out by a small party from No. 2 Commando.

Two officers and eight other ranks, accompanied by two Norwegian corporals, left the Clyde in a Free French submarine on 11 September 1942. Their target was the hydro–electric power station at Glomfjord on the Norwegian coast, which supplied a major aluminium plant. They arrived at a point south of Glomfjord on 15 September and landed from folding boats. They then had a long and extremely hazardous march to their objective across the formidable Svartisen glacier, much of it traversed by a narrow path that clung to the frozen face of the steep mountainside with a sheer drop into a lake. This had to be negotiated in the dark and in silence – no easy task with plenty of loose stones ready to be dislodged into the water – for it brought the party within a short distance of the power station.

After a detailed reconnaissance the party divided, six men forming two demolition squads, one for the power station and one for the pipeline that supplied it, while the other six were to deal with the guards. On the night of 20/21 September they went into action; one sentry was quickly overpowered but the other got away to raise the alarm. Both demolitions were successfully accomplished, but on the way to the Swedish frontier these intrepid raiders clashed with an enemy patrol sent out to intercept them. One soldier and one of the Norwegian corporals were killed. After this skirmish the party split; three soldiers and the remaining Norwegian corporal reached Sweden and were repatriated, but the other six were caught, both officers having been wounded. It was later learned that they were shot in accordance with Hitler's infamous order condemning all Commandos to be 'ruthlessly destroyed'.

Not all of these small raids were successful; inevitably there were some failures or at best raids with little or no positive gains. Some of these were caused by faulty planning, others by the weather, and some by unforeseen hazards – such as estuary sandbars at the mouth of a river making landing impossible. Furthermore, the number of these hit-and-run affairs tended to put enemy defences very much on the alert, and failure to gain surprise could result in men having to withdraw with nothing achieved.

An example of this was the raid against a radar station at St Cécily Plage by half of No. 1 Commando in June 1942. The navigational ML failed to make the rendezvous and in consequence the party made land at quite the wrong place, and found the enemy well prepared. They managed to get ashore without casualties, but achieved virtually nothing in the hour they spent wandering about looking for targets; and then they found that as the LCAs were unable to come close on shore they had to swim for it. One object of the raid was to tempt the Luftwaffe to take to the air and the RAF were briefed to shoot anything afloat at first light, and so two non-swimmers had to be left behind.

After Operation Torch, the landing in North Africa in November 1942, the principal Commando scene shifts to the Mediterranean, to where Nos. 7, 8 and 11 Commandos had sailed in the early part of 1941. Their activities, and those of other Commandos serving in that theatre, will be described later. However, throughout 1942 and the summer of 1943 raids continued against targets on the French and Norwegian coasts, and particularly active in these was No. 10 (Inter-Allied) Commando.

Formed in January 1942, the Commando was commanded by Lt-Colonel Dudley Lister, who had as his second-in-command Major Peter Laycock. The troops comprised men from almost every nation that was at war with Germany, all very fine men and eager to play their part in the fight for freedom, and of course of great value when operating in their native countries. There was even a German troop, whose men for obvious reasons operated under false names and with false papers. Their early training, which on account of the heterogeneity of the force took rather longer than normal, was carried out in North Wales. Towards the end of 1943 some troops were attached to Special Service Brigades in various theatres of war, and others served under Peter Laycock in Layforce II.

Mention must also be made of No. 14 Commando, which under Lt-Colonel E.A.M. Wedderburn had a short but hectic career. They were formed on 11 December 1942 and disbanded on 31 August 1943. They were to operate against German bases in the frozen Arctic wastes, and part of their training was with the Commando Mountain and Snow Warfare Camp at Braemar. They carried out at least two raids off the coast of Norway in the spring of 1943; one of which, at Haugesund, ended in total disaster, for the landing made in canoes from MGBs (Motor Gun Boats) in those fast-moving grey seas was a particularly hazardous undertaking, and the canoe party was lost without trace.

In October 1943 Lord Louis Mountbatten left COHQ to become 'Supremo' of South-East Asia Command. His place was taken by Major-General R.E. (later Sir Robert) Laycock who had formed No. 8 Commando in the very early days, and who had recently been commanding the Special Service Brigade, which at this time was replaced by the Special Service Group. Laycock did not inherit Mountbatten's almost unfettered power, nor his massive empire which in the course of two years had multiplied and diversified beyond the wildest dreams of Admiral Keyes.* In that summer the Admiralty had taken back control of almost all the naval responsibilities of COHQ, which certainly lightened the CCO's burden, but abolished the hitherto uncomplicated line of communication to the Board of Admiralty.

When Laycock took over the days of defeat had almost passed, and the tide of victory (except in the Far East) flowed strongly for the Allies; but many stern battles lay ahead in three widely separated theatres of war, and plans in preparation for D-Day in Europe were going forward amain. Commandos were serving in every theatre, for by now they were in great demand, but the era of small raids was giving way to fighting of a more orthodox kind. Laycock, who knew so much about Commando warfare, was always anxious that these troops should be used so far as possible in ways for which they had been specially trained, but inevitably there were occasions when Commandos spent long periods in the line.

Between 1942 and 1944 nine Royal Marine Commandos were formed to serve in the four Special Service Brigades that were created towards the end of 1943.† No. 40 (RM) Commando – originally formed as RM A Commando – had taken part in the Dieppe raid and suffered heavy casualties; later, reformed, they had done excellent work in Italy. They, like the men in the army Commandos, were all volunteers doing a job – amphibious operations – that formed an important part of a Royal Marine's normal duty, and their Commando role was entirely understandable. Indeed, earlier there had been a slight feeling of resentment among some Marines that the Commandos had usurped one of their main functions. Now it was the turn of some of the Commando officers and men to feel that the new Marine Commandos, most of whose men – unlike No. 40 – were not volunteers and had had no Commando training, nor Commando battle experience, were an unnecessary intrusion. However, with firm and tactful handling by Major-General R.G. (later General Sir Robert) Sturges, RM, commanding the newly formed Special Service Group, his Deputy and the Brigade commanders, helped by the Royal Marine Headquarters office being prevailed upon to select some of their best men for the exacting tasks that lay ahead, relationships gradually improved. Later Army Commando offi-

---

* There were 100 officers on the strength of COHQ alone, and the total, all ranks, in Combined Operations was no fewer than 50,000.
† A year later thankfully redesignated Commando Brigade.

cers were to serve in Royal Marine Commandos and then, close-knit by hardship and danger, a real comradeship was developed between these two élite forces.

Two Special Service (later Commando) Brigades were to take part in the D-Day landings and subsequent fighting in France, Belgium, Holland and Germany. One was the 1st Special Service Brigade commanded by Brigadier Lord Lovat, consisting of Nos. 3, 4 and 6 Army Commandos and 45 (RM) Commando. No. 4 Commando (Lt-Colonel R.W.P. Dawson) had Nos. 1 and 8 Troops of Free French from No. 10 (Inter-Allied) Commando when they landed on D-Day, and later for their attack on Flushing had a Dutch troop attached. No. 3 Commando was recalled from the Mediterranean, where it had been campaigning in Sicily and Italy.

No. 4 Special Service Brigade was originally all Royal Marines (No. 4 Commando was to join it later) and was commanded by one of their officers, Brigadier B.W. ('Jumbo') Leicester. He had under him Nos. 41, 46, 47 and 48 Commandos, and like the 1st Brigade he had to await the return of one Commando (No. 41) from Italy before being complete for D-Day. As the war went on Commando recruiting had presented some problems, for the high standard required of volunteers was never relaxed, but Colonel Vaughan continued to do an excellent job at Achnacarry and these two brigades landed in the third wave on 6 June pretty well up to strength with first-class fighting men.

In this short account of the Commandos it is not possible to do justice to the magnificent fighting record achieved by Nos. 1 and 4 Brigades in North-West Europe. Little more can be done here than mention some of the principal landmarks in their bloody but triumphant progress from the beaches of Normandy to the Baltic.

The role of the 1st Special Service Brigade after the initial landing was to hold, in conjunction with the 6th Airborne Division, a perimeter on the left flank of the Allied bridgehead. The Brigade would land on the extreme left of the British sector and fight their way through enemy defences for some 5 miles to bridges over the River Orne and Caen Canal, where they would link up with brigades of the 6th Airborne Division that had dropped the previous night. No. 4 Commando was to operate separately against the Ouistreham garrison and battery and then rejoin the Brigade. It was indeed a formidable task and all ranks were well aware that the struggle would be heavy and the losses cruel. The role of No. 4 Special Service Brigade was no less hazardous. They were to go ashore in the Arromanches-

Courseulles area, and operating as individual Commandos to capture a number of strongpoints and then link up with the 1st Brigade on the left flank.

The landings of both Brigades were accomplished with less loss than had been feared, although a number of craft – including the one carrying the Heavy Weapons Troop of 3 Commando – were hit and losses incurred. The men of 1st Special Service Brigade went ashore in two waves: Nos. 4 and 6 Commandos in the first, and 3 and 45 (RM) in the second. The beaches were crossed without too much difficulty, but inland the defence was stubborn and the fighting very fierce. Nevertheless, the 1st Brigade (and the detached No. 4 Commando) by assaults and stratagem dislodged their enemy and, headed by the cycle troop of No. 6 Commando, reached the Orne by 2 p.m. and joined up with a Parachute battalion. No. 4 Brigade had some difficult and dangerous house-to-house clearing before their D-Day tasks were accomplished. Before joining the 1st Brigade their No. 41 Commando successfully demolished an underground radar station. The casualties in both Commando brigades had been grievous in this early fighting, and in 1 Brigade three officers of the finest calibre, who had been with the Commandos from the start, were killed. Losses such as these were irreplaceable.

There followed a period of intensive patrolling during static warfare. On 12 June Lord Lovat was severely wounded and command of the 1st Brigade went to Derek Mills-Roberts, who had been commanding No. 6 Commando; he was to lead it for the remainder of the war. A solicitor by profession, he had quickly proved himself to be a brave, resourceful and clear-sighted commander. The long sought break-through did not come until July and Caen, which it had been hoped to take on D-Day, or very soon after, did not fall until 9 July. There were to be further bouts of intensive activity for the 1st Brigade before they were pulled out for a rest after eighty-three continuous days of hard slogging and fierce fighting; since D-Day their casualties had been 77 officers and 890 other ranks, a very high percentage of the total force. On 7 September the Brigade was withdrawn to England to train for operations in the Far East, but a month later No. 4 Commando returned to France, having been transferred to 4 Commando Brigade in exchange for No. 46 (RM) Commando.

No. 4 Brigade played its part in the capture of Le Havre and then, after a period of well-deserved rest, it commenced intensive training for the assault on the heavily-fortified island of Walcheren. Its capture was vital, for it commanded the approaches to the important port of Antwerp which had recently been seized intact by the 11th Armoured Division. The attack was launched in three phases: the first two involved flooding and heavy bombardment, and in the third the three Royal Marine Commandos were to assault the island in amphibious vehicles through the gap blown in the dyke at Westkapelle. They were then to move along the sand dunes towards Zoutelande, clearing pillboxes and beach defences. No. 4 Commando was to take the town of Flushing in an independent operation, and then link up with the rest of the Brigade.

The month of November is not likely to be a pleasant one for an amphibious operation against a strongly-defended coast. And so it proved, for damp and drizzling weather with no horizon and sea and sky merging in grey mist prevented the proposed bomber attack, and later kept the tank-landing craft from beaching. But the Royal Marines, displaying those extra ounces of hidden courage which come to men with a long tradition behind them, stormed their way through the gap, took the village, a battery and a radar station and went on into the dunes. By nightfall 4 Commando, with equal courage and *élan*, had taken Flushing; a performance as polished as their seizure of the battery at Varengeville. Further severe fighting and mopping-up continued for several days before the gateway to Antwerp was in safe hands. The scarred, pitted and corpse-strewn island was a tragic witness to the heavy casualties the 4th Commando Brigade and other units had suffered in this fight.

For the remaining months of the war No. 4 Brigade was to carry out intensive patrolling and reconnaissance work in the South Beveland area and on the Maas front, all these arduous and dangerous duties being performed in the highest tradition of the Commando offensive spirit. Meanwhile, by mid-January pleasant thoughts of screeching bullock carts and sun-baked stones in Burma had been rudely shattered for the men of the 1st Commando Brigade, when orders were received to change direction to snow-covered Europe, where winter had set in with bleak intensity. Before the end of hostilities they were required to play a major part in four important river crossings – the Rhine, Weser, Aller and Elbe – and for good measure lead the attack on Osnabrück.

These formidable river crossings, made with the full strength of the now very considerable Allied air and ground forces, went according to plan. Inevitably there was to be extremely hard fighting, and heavy casualties, for the German soldiers' redoubtable qualities did not fail them in adversity. Heavy air bombardment was of inestimable value and much appreciated by the Commandos who, splashing into the rivers in amphibious Buffaloes, spearheaded the attacks, and together with British and American airborne forces were to become savagely engaged in the towns and fields on the other side.

Once across the Rhine armoured troops swept in devastating fury towards what was left of the riches of the Ruhr. And after the last great river, the Elbe, had been negotiated the way to the Baltic was no longer barred by obstacle or serious German resistance. The Nazi dyke had been burst and triumphant British soldiers flowed through in a deluge. The 1st Commando Brigade reached Neustadt, and a few days later one of the toughest, most destructive and least rewarding European wars had fought itself to a finish.

3

Commandos: North Africa, Sicily and Italy

The first Commandos to sail for the Mediterranean were Nos. 7, 8 and 11. They eventually became Layforce and will be treated in another chapter. But Nos. 1 and 6 had an important role in the North Africa landings (Operation Torch) and subsequent fighting. These two Commandos had had plenty of raiding experience, and now they hoped they would be able to operate as a team. But it was not to be, and they landed on 8 November 1942 as a composite force (No. 1 was actually split in two halves) with troops from the 168th US Infantry Regimental Combat Team (RCT).* They were armed, like their American comrades, with the Garand rifle, which they retained until the end of the war.

No. 1 Commando had sailed from Scotland in two ships, and with their supporting American RCT Companies landed in two groups: the right half under their Commanding Officer Lt-Colonel T.H. Trevor at Villa des Dunes, west of Algiers, and the left half under Major K.R.S. Trevor east of the port. The men of No. 6 Commando were more fortunate in being together in one ship, HMT *Awatea*, but their landing was a much messier affair than that of No. 1, because the landing craft navigation was hopelessly at fault, and some of the boats proved unseaworthy in the swirling turmoil of Mediterranean rollers. Three craft made landfall on the rocky and strongly defended Ilot de la Marine, with the result that the second-in-command of the Commando (Major A.S. Ronald) was killed, and many men wounded and captured. Other craft grounded on the wrong beaches and hours late, but

---

* An American Combat Team was an infantry regiment of three battalions with artillery, engineers and usual ancillary troops.

eventually the Commando, together with the four American RCT companies that had sailed with them, were united some three miles west of Algiers. Fortunately, with the exception of the Ilot de la Marine, the Commando's reception had been friendly.

This was the general pattern with regard to the French army (but not their navy) in the vicinity of the landings, although the left half of No. 1 Commando met strong resistance in their attack on the Batterie de Lazaret and Fort d'Estrée. The latter surrendered only after a heavy bombardment. But the right half had no trouble in taking Fort Sidi Ferruch, and after some parleying Blida capitulated on 10 November. Here prompt action in taking over French trucks secured the airfield and greatly facilitated Allied air operations. This accomplished, both halves of No. 1 were united at Maison Blanche, south of Algiers, from where they were shortly to be transferred by rail to Bône, and joined there a week later by No. 6.

From here, operating in the triangle Tabarka-Bizerta-Beja, both Commandos, together with the Americans, carried out a number of fighting and reconnaissance patrols, and one or two small operations in support of 36 Infantry Brigade, which clearly demonstrated that the sea could no longer be considered a safe barricade, and that a small force operating on the enemy's flank and in his rear while a main attack is in progress can inflict relatively high casualties and disrupt supply routes.

No. 1 Commando's Operation Bizerta was a typical example. Six British and four American troops were ordered to support the Brigade's attack by turning the enemy's sea flank, cutting his lines of communication and harrying his withdrawal. Split again into two halves, they landed in high seas from nine LCMs and four LCAs at 1 a.m. on 30 November. The only casualties in the landings were among the eight donkeys brought along to carry the mortars – five managed to swim ashore, but only two were found to be serviceable after this ordeal. The Commando group then had to operate in exceptionally difficult terrain, for the hills and valleys were covered with the tall Mediterranean heather and tracks were few and far between. For the next three days the Commando held two important road junctions, cut the roads between them, destroyed enemy transport and generally dominated the area.

Throughout the period they had been constantly engaged in stiff fighting, and existing on very slender rations – one tin of bully and one packet of biscuits (sodden from the sea) per man for three days. Living off the country in the prevailing circumstances was difficult, but one troop did manage to buy a calf. During their withdrawal to Cap Serrat they were able to embarrass the right flank of the enemy who were being engaged frontally by 36 Brigade. Apart from demonstrating the vulnerability of a flank resting on the sea, the chief value of the raid was the denial to the enemy for three important days of the supply road to his forward troops. For this a heavy price had been paid, for the casualties were four British officers and fifty-six other ranks, and two American officers and seventy-two other ranks.

While No. 1 was employed in this Commando-style raid, No. 6 was engaged in a very different type of battle – a straightforward assault on a 900-ft stronghold known as Green Hill. It could have been undertaken by any regular battalion – and indeed had been by the Argyll and Sutherland Highlanders, many of whose bodies strewed the hill. Matters were made no easier for the Commando by the urgency of the order. The mood was valiant when they stormed into the attack but the ground was treacherous and unstudied, and the plan hastily formed.

The German positions were cleverly sited and well protected by sangars and slit trenches, from which they poured a withering fire on the Commando as they tried to rush the positions. A call for artillery support was quickly and accurately answered, but the enemy positions survived this cannonade almost unscathed. In the final attempt one troop was ambushed by a party of Germans in Arab clothing, and although two other troops penetrated the enemy defences they had not the strength to capture the hill. This impregnable position – which never fell to direct assault – had cost the Commando eighty casualties.

The comparatively high casualties suffered by both Commandos in the fighting so far necessitated a degree of contraction within troops, for it inevitably took time to acquire suitable replacements. Sixty-five of the Americans volunteered to stay with them, although these were withdrawn at the end of January 1943. Meanwhile No. 6 Commando was given a brief rest period at Sejenane before, on 5/6 January, being involved in a further attack on the now notorious Green Hill. This time they acted as flank guard to the 36th Brigade's central hammer blow, with the additional role of harassing the enemy's rear. They seized the dominating feature Djebel Azag, and despite fierce and constant attempts to dislodge them held it for two days, keeping considerable numbers of the enemy from joining the main battle. The attack on the hill failed, but No. 6 Commando's performance was highly creditable.

Throughout February and March both Commandos (No. 6 now under the inspiring leadership of Lt-Colonel Derek Mills-Roberts) carried out raids, patrols and minor operations too numerous to be described, in the Baja–Medjez-el–Bab area of mountain and valley. In all these activities against German and Italian troops there were savage clashes and considerable slaughter. At the end of February No. 6 Commando with 250 officers and men found themselves confronted by no less a foe than two Jäger parachute battalions of the Hermann Goering Division; a desperate battle developed under the steel flail of armour brought up by both sides, in which the Commando suffered 40 per cent casualties, but the main German attack had been held up and vital time gained.

At the beginning of April these tough, battle-hardened men of Nos. 1 and 6 Commandos were withdrawn to Algiers for a well deserved rest, and on the 24th they sailed for home. They, and their American comrades who for many weeks had fought so stoutly alongside them, had done a magnificent job not only when used in their proper Commando role, but also on the frequent occasions when necessity had forced the Army Commander to put them in the line. Here they suffered from lack of heavy weapons, which was soon to be rectified by the introduction of the heavy weapons troop.

Even before the German surrender in Tunis planning was under way for the invasion of Sicily (Operation Husky), and Commandos were earmarked for an important part in the assault. Those selected were two Royal Marine Commandos, Nos. 40 and 41, and No. 3 Commando. Both 3 and 40 had suffered severe casualties at Dieppe but had been brought up to strength, Colonel Durnford-Slater having procured 120 ex-police volunteers from the Commando Depot, which he said were the best single intake No. 3 ever received. The two Royal Marine Commandos set about training for the operation in Scotland and sailed on 28 June for the Mediterranean. But No. 3 had been sent to Gibraltar in February to relieve No. 9, whose role was to carry out seaborne raids on Spanish targets should Germany decide to occupy that country. After a few weeks there they went to Suez – via Oran, Algiers and Alexandria – to train for the landing, and were replaced in Gibraltar by No. 2 Commando. Brigadier Laycock, commanding the Special Service Brigade, now having four Commandos in the Mediterranean, managed to get permission to form a Commando brigade. An active man, who disliked being spancelled to a desk, he was quick to take command of the brigade, leaving Lord Lovat as his deputy in England.

On the night of 9/10 July the British Eighth Army was to land in the south-east corner of Sicily, and the American Seventh on the southern and western coasts. The Royal Marine Commandos were to land on the left flank of the Canadians and No. 3 Commando on the north-east extremity of the invasion. The Marines had the usual landing problems, ending up late and on the wrong beach; but the Italian opposition was negligible, and No. 41, after a very wet landing in the wrong place, fairly quickly captured all the objectives of both Marine Commandos.

No. 3 Commando was allotted two tasks initially, to clear the machine-gun posts known to be overlooking the 5th Division's beach, and to silence a battery north-west of Casibile. To accomplish these Colonel Durnford-Slater took three troops to attack the battery, leaving Major Young with the remainder of the Commando to assault the beach defences. Everything went wrong for his party at sea, largely due to the incompetence of the RNVR officer commanding the landing craft flotilla. They eventually made an unopposed landing, together with the brigade whose safe landing it should have been their task to ensure. But Durnford-Slater's men took the battery in just five minutes under the ninety he had told General Dempsey was the time he required from the moment of landing. The Italians had put up a fairly stiff resistance, but faced with the bayonet in the hands of stern, unflinching men they broke before the storm.

That evening both groups were reunited in Casibile and the following morning Major Young with one troop, under Captain Lash, successfully cleaned up a strongly defended farmhouse called Torre Cuba, and on 13 July the Commando made ready for what was to be its most successful engagement in Sicily.

The Eighth Army had got the enemy moving back nicely, and General Montgomery was anxious to increase the pressure and ensure that two bridges – Primasole and Ponte dei Malatti – on the only road from Syracuse to Catania were taken and held before they could be destroyed, thus impeding the advance of the 50th (Northumbrian) Division. Airborne troops were to be dropped to deal with the bridge at Primasole, and 3 Commando was to execute a right hook by landing at Agnone, some 10 miles north of 50 Division, at 10 p.m. on 13 July. This allowed little enough time for planning, but Intelligence reports indicated (wrongly as it turned out) that the Commando would not meet stiff German opposition.

Owing to the shortage of landing craft the landing was to be made in two flights, and Colonel Durnford-Slater's plan was for the first flight to comprise four troops, the bulk of which would push ahead immediately while the landing craft returned for the remaining two troops. The landing was opposed, and by a German force, which caused some confusion and called for stiff fighting to penetrate the beach defences and commence the march – over thick difficult country – inland towards the bridge. The first flight battled their way to the bridge, and arriving at about 3 a.m. succeeded in taking the defences on its northern side. A troop was then sent to investigate the southern end, but got held up under the bridge, where at least it was able to remove the demolition charges. However, this and another troop sent to the south-west of the position suffered heavy casualties.

Meanwhile, the second flight under Captain Pooley did not reach the beach until 2 a.m., and like the first party met with stiff opposition both there and on the Agnone railway line, but as dawn was breaking they reached the bridge and joined the main party, who were now threatened by German armour moving south to reinforce their line facing 50 Division. General Dempsey had told Durnford-Slater that if the 50th Division had not put in an appearance by dawn the Commando should clear off. They were now in a difficult position astride the enemy's lines of communication and engaged by armour with little in the way of natural or artificial defences, and so the Colonel gave orders for the Commando to disperse in small bodies and make their way to Augusta.

This was not easily accomplished, for the 3rd Battalion of the Hermann Goering Parachute Regiment was by now in the area, and every party had some hair-raising adventures and many casualties. Shortly afterwards, when the German position was overrun, some prisoners got free and some of the wounded who had laid up were recovered, but the Commando suffered the loss of five officers and twenty-three other ranks killed, four officers and sixty-two other ranks wounded, and eight officers and fifty-one other ranks missing or prisoners. On the credit side they had saved the bridge intact, and in recognition of their fortitude, endurance and competence a Distinguished Service Order, four Military Crosses and four Military Medals were awarded for this operation, and General Montgomery immediately ordered that a stone should be let into the masonry of the Ponte dei Malatti bearing the words '3 Commando Bridge'.

No. 3 Commando was now down to 270 officers and other ranks, and as no reinforcements were immediately available it was reorganized into a headquarters and four troops. In August Peter Young, now commanding, was ordered to carry out a number of reconnaissance raids on the toe of Italy. Information gained at places like Bova Marina had an important influence on the planning of the invasion, for which there was to be a regrouping of the Commando forces.

No. 2 Commando had arrived from Gibraltar on 22 July, and in the middle of August carried out the last Commando raid in Sicily, when unsuccessfully attempting to cut off the fast-retreating Germans from Messina, their embarkation port. Brigadier Laycock then had under his command two Royal Marine and two Army Commandos. He decided to split the Brigade, giving Durnford-Slater a separate brigade command of Nos. 3 and 40 (RM) Commandos and the Special Raiding Squadron.* There were to be two operations for the invasion of Italy: Baytown, an assault across the Messina Straits; and Avalanche against Salerno. Durnford-Slater's Special Service Brigade was to form part of Operation Baytown, while Nos. 2 and 41 (RM) Commandos with Laycock and Brigade Headquarters spearheaded the 10th British Corps' landing on the left of the American 5th Army. Their orders were to destroy the coast defence batteries at a place called Marina some 2 miles west of Salerno, and then to move inland to hold the defile at La Molina.

Durnford-Slater's men met with few difficulties. The SRS landed in advance and seized Bagnara Calabria, holding it for twenty-four hours until relieved by the 15th Infantry Brigade, while the two Commandos landed on 9 September at Porto San Venere in the face of little opposition. But at Salerno, although the Commandos' landing was unopposed, thereafter it was quite a different matter.

Brigade Headquarters and No. 2 Commando moved into Vietri at dawn on 9 September, and two troops were then despatched to operate against the western approaches to Salerno. The German build-up was rapid, and the fighting soon became very fierce for the Royal Marines in the defile and for two troops of 2 Commando, who shinned up a 1,300-ft near-precipice above Vietri to deal with German machine-gun positions. By D plus 3 the total strength of the Special Service Brigade was down to 619 all ranks and no reinforcements were available. On the morning of 13

---

* On 19 March 1943 the Special Air Service (SAS) Regiment was reorganized into two parts: the Special Boat Squadron under Major Earl Jellicoe and the Special Raiding Squadron under Major Mayne.

September 2 Commando was heavily engaged around the village of Dragone; here the clash was extremely savage and the slaughter heavy, but through stubborn resistance and some splendid artillery support the enemy was first held and then beaten back. It was the Germans' last major attack down the valley of La Molina towards Vietri. However, the price paid was a heavy one: 2 Commando that morning lost five officers killed and one wounded and seventeen other ranks killed and forty-nine wounded, while 41 (RM) Commando, which had already suffered cruelly in the defile, had a further forty-nine casualties.

Withdrawn for a brief respite, the two Commandos were soon on the move again, this time to Mercatello, a small place east of Salerno. Here they were again sternly engaged, storming three strong points in the area of Pigoletti village known as Whitecross Hill, The Pimple and what became 41 Commando Hill. For three days amid scenes of utmost valour this strife and struggle continued, until on 18 September the Brigade was withdrawn to Sicily to lick its wounds and rebuild its strength. Their total casualties of 367 all ranks represented 48 per cent of the two Commandos as they had landed in Italy on 9 September. In due course 2 Commando managed a successful recruiting campaign, but for all special forces replacements were never readily available, and casualties were cumulative and increasingly a liability.

Meanwhile the British Eighth Army, with which Durnford-Slater's brigade had been operating, advanced 200 miles in three weeks up the western coast of Calabria to relieve the pressure on Salerno. Thereafter they were to fight their way up the Adriatic coast while the American Fifth Army kept to the western half of the long, narrow and mountainous Italian peninsula. For the next twenty months in bitter cold, searing heat, pouring rain, snow and slush these two armies were to inch their way across rivers and up mountains, pinning down many German divisions which could otherwise have been used elsewhere, and fighting some of the finest soldiers of the Third Reich under a general (Kesselring) whose martial ability was second to none. With them for much of the time went two Royal Marine and two Army Commandos (a third, No. 3, was withdrawn after Operation Devon on Termoli) taking their place in the line, or raiding from the sea parts of those lovely coasts hitherto unscourged by the horrors of war.

Among their more notable engagements could be numbered Termoli, the Garigliano, Anzio and Lake Comacchio. Termoli is a small port on the Adriatic coast 2 miles north of the River Biferno, where the retreating Germans had decided to make a stand.

Durnford-Slater's force – Nos. 3 and 40 (RM) Commandos and the SRS – was to land west of the town, capture it and link up with the forward elements of the 78th Division. No. 3 Commando (commanded by Captain Arthur Komrower, for Peter Young was recovering from jaundice) were to land first and form a bridgehead through which the Marines and SRS would pass, the former to take the town and harbour, the latter a road junction south-east of the town where two main highways met. Termoli was not thought to be strongly held, but on account of its importance a counter-attack seemed inevitable.

Sailing from Manfredonia, a distance of 120 miles from Termoli, on 2 October, the small, unescorted flotilla of LCIs towing assault craft made a correct pinpoint landing at 2.15 a.m. on 3 October which was unopposed. The bridgehead established, the Marines went through to take the town after a sharp skirmish, and by 8 a.m. all objectives were secure. By midday a perimeter defence had been set up round the town, and that afternoon troops of the 78th Division were in Termoli, and Lt-Colonel Chavasse of the 56th Reconnaissance Regiment took over command of the force. The expected German counter-attack erupted in full fury on the morning of 5 October, headed by the 16th Panzer Division with Mk IV tanks. The Commandos and SRS were right in the thick of the bitter fighting that followed, and Colonel Durnford-Slater admitted later that the situation around Termoli was so critical that for the first time in all his battles he felt defeat was possible.

In the confused jumble of battle when units are split, and often soldiers are fighting tenaciously in isolated small pockets, it is invidious to single out any for special praise. All those who helped to defeat the counter-attack and retain the prize of Termoli fought magnificently, but the stubborn outer defence by 3 Commando led Durnford-Slater to say that he thought it was their finest performance of the war. A valuable harbour had been won for the Eighth Army, but again the toll, coming as it did so soon after Sicily, had been serious. Casualties in the two Commandos and the SRS amounted to 11 officers and 120 other ranks. Now they truly deserved a rest, and General Montgomery gladly granted them one. 'Take them away to Bari for a good holiday, there's plenty of everything down there,' he told Durnford-Slater. And so they went to Molfetta near Bari, and to Army reserve.

Towards the end of 1943 there were to be important changes in the Commando organization. On 23 October Brigadier Laycock became Chief of Combined Operations, and it was decided that the Special Service Brigade was too small a set-up to control the many Commandos now in the field. A Special Service Group, comparable in strength to an infantry division, was created under the command of General Sturges (see Chapter 2), with Colonel Durnford-Slater as his deputy whose brief was, among other things, to look after the Army side of the Group. As already mentioned, there were to be four Special Service Brigades each comprising two Royal Marine and two Army Commandos, with a combined RM and Army headquarters of some fifty personnel. There was also to be a Brigade signal troop of seventy men, acting as a separate unit.

The Brigade which was to carry out operations in the Mediterranean during 1944 and 1945 was No. 2, commanded by Brigadier T.B.L. Churchill, and it was made up of Nos. 2, 9, 40 (RM) and 43 (RM) Commandos with Belgian and Polish troops of No. 10 (IA) Commando.* The SRS, Nos. 3 and 41 (RM) Commandos were returned to the United Kingdom, in the place of Nos. 9 and 43 (RM). Detachments of No. 9 were sent to reconnoitre the Adriatic islands of Pianosa and Tremiti, but they were found to be free of enemy forces. The first major operation of the Brigade was to assist 10 Corps' crossing of the Garigliano river at the end of December 1943.

Brigade Headquarters was at Molfetta, and No. 9 Commando under Lt-Colonel (later Brigadier) R.J.F. Tod was sent across Italy for the operation, codenamed Partridge. Italy was a country that greatly favoured the defenders, and the Allied advance had become bogged down in front of the Garigliano, where the Germans gained great advantage from the cheerless, snow-covered hills that dominated the position to the north-east. The Commando was placed under 201 Guards Brigade and was to create a diversion in the boggy reaches of the river downstream from the Guards Brigade's main attack.

The Commando's plan was pleasantly simple, but it was evident that complications could arise during the withdrawal and elaborate precautions were taken. The landing was timed for 11 p.m. on 29 December, under the guidance of US patrol boats

* These two troops arrived in Italy in December 1943 to join 2 Special Service Brigade. They were at first in the line with the Eighth Army, constantly patrolling in very difficult mountainous country. On 20 January the Belgian troop was with 2 Special Service Brigade in the attack on Monte Ornito, and on 17 March it went to Vis as Brigade HQ protection troop. The Polish troop was with 10 Corps on the west coast of Italy until 15 February, when it joined the Polish Corps and ceased to be under 2 Special Service Brigade.

fitted with radar. It was to be on the coast north of the river, and after it the Commando would divide into three forces, X, Y and Z. X Force (No. 5 Troop less one section) was to clear a spit of land immediately north-west of the river mouth and form a bridgehead at the river mouth through which the rest of the Commando could withdraw. Y Force (Nos. 1 and 2 Troops) was to attack a hill called Monte D'Argento and withdraw not later than 4 a.m. through X Force. Z Force (Nos. 4 and 6 Troops plus one section of 5 Troop) was to attack and seize the western side of a broken bridge across the river, and 5 Troop's section was to hold a crossroads 500 yards west of the bridge. Having cleared the area, Z Force was to attempt to withdraw across the river or, should that prove impossible, to fall back through the bridgehead. An RE minelifting detachment was added to X Force for clearing the beach, and 9 DUKWs (amphibious troop-carrying trucks) were put under command of Colonel Tod to assist in the final evacuation from the spit.

Despite the radar navigational devices the landing craft got lost, and the landing was one and a half hours late. Furthermore, one craft – carrying a section of 5 Troop – never made land owing to faulty steering gear. This was 9 Commando's first major action, and it was executed very successfully under most difficult conditions. The loss of time in landing meant that Y and Z Forces were hard pressed to achieve their objectives before daylight. X Force soon established a bridgehead. Y Force had a difficult approach march to its objective over mine-sown ground, but captured the hill for the loss of two officers and two men wounded. In their withdrawal a new route was followed in order to avoid the minefield, and this took Y Force close to Z Force. At night when all cats are grey and every eye seeks to pierce the darkness accidents can occur, but 9 Commando was a Scottish one and each troop went into battle with its own piper, and here was an occasion when the pipes were purposeful as well as pleasurable. Z Force had a stiff fight but, helped by a timely artillery stonk, cleared the west bank, and then managed to withdraw across the fast-flowing, icy river by rope and a toggle bridge, with the loss of only one man drowned. The other two Forces crossed the river near its mouth with the aid of the DUKWs.

For the loss of eight killed and twenty-one wounded the Commando had destroyed two defensive positions, taken twenty-eight prisoners, killed at least sixteen Germans and persuaded the enemy to reinforce that sector of his front, which was the principal object of the operation.

Just behind the Garigliano was the formidable Gustav Line, stretching the breadth of Italy with strong defensive positions many miles deep. German policy was to stand firm south of Rome. Winter had cast her mantle across the land; the mountains – beautiful, yet savage beyond belief – presented a snow-covered panorama; in the valleys the wind and sleet swept like a curtain, turning all to mud and slush. The troops had become disillusioned and a general weariness had set in. Allied policy was to break through somehow and reach Rome quickly. There were three routes to Rome: Highways 6, 7 and 16. The Allies did not have the overwhelming superiority to achieve a straight breakthrough. There was, however, also a fourth route – by sea, or by sea and air combined.

After much planning and counter-planning Operation Shingle was finally decided upon. The plan was to land two divisions, Ranger and Commando battalions, and a Tank and Parachute regiment at Anzio to synchronize with a major offensive by the British X Corps and American II Corps against the Gustav Line. The whole plan was based on a successful body punch and left hook. No. 9 Commando was to visit Anzio twice, the first time briefly when with 43 (RM) Commando they landed in the second wave of this ill-starred operation, and then again they were there with 40 (RM) Commando at the end of February.

At Anzio, not for the first time, the Commandos were operating alongside the American Rangers. This force was raised along Commando lines at the end of May 1942, and the 1st Rangers, recruited from American troops in Northern Ireland, were trained at Achnacarry before taking a part in the Dieppe raid. It was not long before Commandos and Rangers were working closely together, and a comradeship arose between these two bodies of hard fighting men who had learnt to know and respect one another. Before the end of the war there were six Ranger battalions.

During the night of 20/21 January 1944 ships crammed with troops sailed from Naples, Salerno and two other ports for the Anzio beaches. At 2 a.m. on the 23rd the landings commenced. The two Commandos (9 and 43) of No. 2 Special Service Brigade went ashore six miles north-west of Anzio, with instructions to block the highway above the town, while the 1st, 3rd and 4th Rangers were landed near the harbour to gain immediate control of the port. The landings were unopposed and both special forces achieved their objectives with little difficulty, but whereas the Rangers were soon to be engaged in some very tough fighting both Commandos were withdrawn to Naples after only three days on the beachhead.

The immediate success of the initial landings was not fully exploited. It is very doubtful whether the Allied plan of a quick breakthrough to Rome could ever have been achieved, but that is a controversial matter that cannot be discussed here. As it was, the German build-up was extremely rapid and General Lucas's VI Corps was soon bogged down. Meanwhile, in early February 9 and 43 (RM) Commandos were fighting in support of the 46th Division of X Corps immediately after the troops had at last managed to get across the Garigliano. In the battle round Monte Ornito the Brigade casualties amounted to 11 officers and 172 other ranks. After a fortnight to rest and reorganize, 9 Commando, this time with 40 (RM) Commando, was back in the Anzio beachhead.

The fighting in this difficult and trappy country with its dry watercourses, bogs and rivulets was some of the toughest, most dangerous and beastliest of the whole war. The Commandos were lucky to have only three weeks of it. During that time they carried out many patrols, and No. 9 (led again by Colonel Tod, who had been wounded at Monte Ornito) mounted a full-scale attack on a German forming-up position in three ravines. Like so many of these beachhead forays, the result was inconclusive and the cost – nineteen killed and fifty wounded – after some extremely stiff fighting was very heavy. Shortly after this, in the last week of March, both Commandos were sent to Molfetta for a month's recuperation.

The next operation undertaken by No. 9 Commando was Operation Darlington II to rescue Allied ex-prisoners of war, who having escaped were hiding some 70 miles behind the German front line on the east coast of Italy near the mouth of the River Tenna. It was arranged that A Force,* which had borrowed 9 Commando for this operation, would concentrate these ex-prisoners at a given rendezvous, and a method of signalling had been arranged. In the event the signal light was eventually spotted by the troop carrying out the operation some two miles from the pre-arranged position, but thereafter everything went according to plan and 120 men were successfully rescued.

A month later a party of 73 all ranks from the Commando was

---

* This force was originally established in Cairo under Dudley Clarke, and ran an organization helping evaders in the Middle East, Italy and the Greek islands. On occasion it would borrow troops to help rescue these people.

involved in Operation Astrolabe, in which it was to give protection to thirty men of 'Popski's Private Army' (see Chapter 12). This strange force, with twelve armed jeeps, was to land south of the River Tenna from an LCT, then establish a base inland from which to carry out raids. The LCT beached safely at 11 p.m. on 15 June, and the Commando men went ashore to hold the bridgehead. However, on landing Popski received information that the enemy was too active in the area for the operation to succeed, and the troops re-embarked. It was then found that the LCT was hard aground and could not be shifted. Only after the most hazardous ferrying were the personnel and some of the equipment transferred to the escorting ML. The LCT and jeeps had to be blown up.

In contrast to this débâcle, on the night of 9/10 August 109 men from the Commando sailed from Ancona in three MTBs and one MGB to carry out a most successful raid on a swing bridge that connected two islands in the extreme north of the Adriatic – Cherso and Lussin. The bridge, guarded by Italian soldiers who did not stay to fight, was destroyed, thoroughly blocking the channel and thereby forcing enemy shipping to make a long and dangerous detour.

During 1944 the four Commandos comprising No. 2 Special Service Brigade became widely dispersed. No. 2 was sent to the Adriatic island of Vis in January, where it was joined by 43 (RM) the next month, and by 40 (RM) in May, while No. 9 stayed in Italy until September when it went to Kithera, and from there to Salonika. Brigade headquarters remained at Molfetta until March when it too went to Vis. The exploits of the Brigade in the Adriatic and Aegean seas are dealt with in Chapter 4, but by the end of February 1945 the unit – now No. 2 Commando Brigade under Brigadier R.J.F. Tod – was back in Italy concentrated in Ravenna, and in order to complete the Commando story in Italy their last action will be related here.

Field-Marshal Kesselring's sorely tried but remarkably tough and stubborn soldiers had given way only slowly, and, always making clever use of the favourable terrain, had taken up positions along the line of the River Po. No. 2 Commando Brigade, which had recently spent several weeks in the line, was given the task of driving back the extreme left of the enemy position in the low lying marshy land round Lake Comacchio, and in particular to dislodge some 1,200 troops holding the narrow spit that divides the lake from the sea. It was a strange aquatic operation in which Nos. 2 and 9 Commandos were to enter the German position via the back door provided by the lake, while 43 (RM) Commando attacked north up the tongue of land. No. 40 (RM) Commando was to carry out a feint in the south, and then clear the line of the River Reno at the point where it runs close to the edge of the lake.

The greatest problem facing those Commandos attacking from the lake was launching their stormboats into water of sufficient depth first for floating and then for operating their outboard engines. A stormboat weighs ¾ ton and some eighty of them had been brought to the lakeside two nights before the attack. Now, with a recent long drought having lowered the level of the lake, they had to be manhandled for more than a mile across deep slush and mud. It says much for the determination and patient endurance of the British soldier that after hours of sweating and heaving in a frenzy of desperation the boats were afloat. But by then the night being well advanced, and the two Commandos (Nos. 2 and 9) hopelessly intertwined, their commanders sought permission to postpone the assault. But Brigadier Tod quite rightly refused to agree, for to call off a carefully-synchronized large-scale operation at this late stage, with no likelihood of improved conditions, would have been most unwise.

The lake was soon alive with stormboats towing assault craft in various directions, for navigation was difficult in this flat, featureless country (even though Coppists – see Chapter 8 – had put out markers) and some craft were being paddled in quite the wrong direction. Nevertheless, the struggles and torments of these two Commandos were finally rewarded when, admirably covered by the smoke and noise of a heavy bombardment, they landed on the spit of land. Somewhat surprisingly – after all the noise, chaos and confusion – the enemy, whose defences were facing east and south, were taken completely unawares. By the evening of this traumatic day – some recalled it was April 1st – the Brigade had consolidated its positions.

On the morrow the advance continued northwards, supported by armour. No. 43 (RM) Commando went up the coast with No. 2 on their left. There was some very stiff fighting in the open ground north of Scaglioca, where Corporal Hunter of 43 Commando won a posthumous Victoria Cross, but the Valetta canal was too strongly held, and the Brigade halted on a line 400 yards to its south. On the night of 4 April it was relieved. The operation was entirely successful in that the enemy had been dislodged from a difficult position and had suffered extremely heavy casualties.

It was nearly the end of the war in Italy, but the Brigade was called upon to fight one further action in the Argenta gap – that piece of marshy country that lies between the River Reno and Lake Comacchio. On the night of 10 April No. 40 (RM) Commando was ordered to advance along a narrow strip of bog land in order to secure an important road bridge across the Menate Canal and destroy a pumping station situated at the junction of the canal and Lake Comacchio. Their approach march, which had to be carried out at considerable speed, was beset with difficulties, chief among them being 150 mines which had to be lifted through the skill and heroism of the 2nd Field Company RE. They were then hotly engaged when trying to take the bridge by assault, and only a lucky bullet that severed the connecting wires of the demolition charges saved it from being blown. However, the enemy brought up reinforcements and the battle raged fiercely on the morning of 11 April, before the Germans surrendered and the bridge was captured intact. This action had cost 40 Commando a quarter of its strength.

A few days later No. 9 Commando was to fight its final battle – one of its toughest – when it came under command of 24 Guards Brigade, who were to execute a right hook across the flooded area south of Lake Comacchio. The Commando's objective was the bridge over the Fossa Marina, a waterway about 5,000 yards north of Argenta. From 13 to 15 April, together with the 2nd Battalion Coldstream Guards, 1st Battalion Scots Guards and 1st Battalion the Buffs, they were engaged in the most desperate fighting in an attempt to force this canal.

The first attack over the waters of the Strada della Pioppa was only a partial success and severe casualties were suffered, especially by the Buffs in the stranded Fantail amphibious landing vehicles. On 14 April the Commando was ordered to pass through the Buffs, to clear houses south-east of the Fossa and to reconnoitre the canal. On the night of the 15th, in a fierce battle alongside the Scots Guards against fanatical German resistance, they failed to achieve the crossing. The Commando was relieved the next day, and although the Guards Brigade finally overcame the obstacle the following night, the fighting, and particularly the information gained on the nature of the canal, by 9 Commando (who lost two officers and forty-nine men in this battle) proved invaluable.

Meanwhile, Nos. 2 and 43 Commandos had been fighting strenuously to clear the enemy south-west of Argenta, and the combined efforts of the four Commandos had contributed greatly to driving the Germans from this watery maze. Once across the Fossa Marina the 56th (London) Division was able to outflank

Argenta, and before long Alexander's avenging armies had swept on to final victory.

The casualties suffered by 2 Commando Brigade during its eighteen months of almost continuous fighting in the Mediterranean were 136 officers and 1,444 other ranks. After service with the occupation forces the Brigade was disbanded in 1946, but it had – like its component units – left its mark on military history.

4

Commandos: Adriatic, Aegean and Far East

By the time of the Italian surrender in September 1943 Marshal Tito's partisans were a very formidable guerrilla force. Possessed of a curious assortment of arms, equipment and clothing, they were nevertheless a well disciplined, utterly ruthless and determined body of men with a bitter hatred of the Germans and a stoic philosophy of enduring, fighting and dying. They were tying down large numbers of German troops, and although no match for these in open combat, in the hills they were a deadly menace to German detachments and lines of communication. But their problems increased when it came to capturing and holding the vitally important Dalmatian islands.

At the end of December 1943 Brigadier Fitzroy Maclean, who was head of the Allied Mission to Tito, arrived in Italy to solicit help for the partisans in their efforts to keep the Germans out of the Adriatic. It was a request that had a strategic appeal to the higher command, for the islands in enemy hands could prove a serious threat to the right flank of the Allied advance into Italy; and it also appealed to Brigadier T.B.L. Churchill, commanding No. 2 Special Service Brigade, as the type of operation ideally suited to Commandos.

As a result of these confabulations an expedition was sent to the island of Vis consisting of a party of Americans from their Special Operations Group,* a part of the Raiding Support Regiment,† the Yugoslav troop of No. 10 (IA) Commando, No. 2 Commando

---

* These were 12 officers and 120 men, mostly second-generation Yugoslavs and Greeks. They spoke the language and could be used as interpreters.
† The Raiding Support Regiment was a part of Raiding Forces (see Chapter 14). It had a headquarters and five batteries manned by paratroopers.

under Lt-Colonel J.M.T.F. Churchill – the Brigade Commander's brother – and some regular army units. These troops, numbering in all about a thousand men, were a part of Force 133, a military and diplomatic organization for supplying aid to all partisan forces in seven Baltic countries. In addition to the troops, MTBs and MGBs of the Royal Navy under Lt-Commander Morgan Giles, were based on the island and gave invaluable assistance to the Commandos in their many raids.

Vis is an island eighteen miles long by eight miles wide situated halfway up the Adriatic off the Dalmatian coast; it had a strong partisan garrison under a Colonel Millic, which gave a very warm welcome to the Force. Unfortunately the comradely partnership did not survive the many difficulties – language, dual command, misrepresentation, suspicion and the like – that are apt to arise between two allies who are constantly involved in dangerous and difficult operations, and who possess different outlooks and military backgrounds. But in the beginning there were no unpleasant incidents and everything went very well.

The principal role of the garrison was to defend the island against attack, for the Germans were now established in the three neighbouring islands of Solta, Brac and Hvar; for this purpose the partisans had observation posts throughout the island, and various strongpoints were manned by them and troops of Force 133. But Colonel Churchill's philosophy – like that of most successful commanders – was that attack was the best method of defence, and raiding commenced on 27 January when he himself led three troops of No. 2 Commando and thirty members of the American Group in a raid on the neighbouring island of Hvar. In this raid four prisoners were taken, who on interrogation revealed that the islands were garrisoned by troops of the 118th Jäger Division, and that they were strongly held. This determined Churchill to resort to bluff, and to step up his harassing raids in which his troops were given considerable help from the partisans.

There was one extraordinary, and undoubtedly very gallant, exploit that occurred about this time, which may have been inspired by a similar action with a less successful conclusion that had taken place in North Africa some two years earlier. It is mentioned only briefly because in the opinion of some senior Commando officers (an opinion shared by the author) it was not the role of a Commando, even in total war, to go slaughtering enemy generals in cold blood. They should be allowed to take their chance along with everyone else in the course of battle.

However, a young subaltern of No. 2 Commando disguised

himself as a shepherd on the island of Brac, and with the help of partisans secured a flock of sheep, a mule and a muleteer. Somehow bluffing the German sentries, he entered the headquarters compound, discarded his disguise, retrieved his Sten gun which had been concealed on the mule under a load of faggots, made his way into the house and shot the German commandant of the island while he was eating his dinner. The Germans thereupon shot fifty civilians as a reprisal.

At the end of February Brigade Headquarters and No. 43 (RM) Commando joined No. 2 on Vis. In addition Allied Force Headquarters (AFHQ) allotted the rest of the Raiding Support Regiment and some administrative officers. Force 133 in Bari was now separated from Force 133 in Cairo and redesignated Force 266, of which the Brigade formed a part. At the time of their arrival, or a little before, reconnaissance patrols had landed on the small island of Solta to spy out the land for a raid later in March by two troops of No. 2 Commando, the Heavy Weapons Troop of No. 43 (RM), a battery of anti-tank guns, and some of the American Special Operations Group (SOG). The plan was to surround the small town of Grohote on the south of the island, where the German garrison was centred, and to await a dawn air strike before assaulting.

The Navy was in charge of the landings which went according to plan, and the troops scrambled up a steep hill to surround the town. Surprise was not achieved, but following the air strike, which came in exactly on time, the assault was made and the German commandant, who was captured, did not need much persuasion to order his troops to surrender. For the loss of two men killed and fourteen slightly wounded this small force had killed four Germans and captured 104 – the perfect success story of a miniature combined operation.

A week later, on 23 March, a joint venture with the partisans against the garrison of Jelsa, a port on the north coast of the long, narrow island of Hvar, was successfully undertaken, and further raids on a less ambitious scale against other islands took place in April. All this time the garrison on Vis was being strengthened, for there were signs that the Germans had become restless as a result of the constant harassment and would try to evict the Allied force. In May 40 (RM) Commando arrived on the island, and the Royal Air Force had constructed an airfield which the RAF Regiment guarded. Towards the end of that month German parachutists landed near Drvar in Bosnia, and although their attempt to capture Tito at his headquarters failed, it caused considerable consternation throughout the whole partisan organization, and the Marshal asked his followers in Vis to create a major diversion.

The Germans had withdrawn some of their island garrison, leaving only small parties in strongly-protected posts on inaccessible hills, but on Brac they still had about 1,200 troops, which could be used to reinforce mainland units. In order to prevent this, and to comply with Tito's call for help, it was decided that an operation by some 6,000 partisans and Allied troops should be launched against the enemy on Brac.

Although the German force manning Brac was numerically inferior to the raiding party, their positions were cleverly sited, making full use of the island's hills and natural defences. They also had an OP (observation post) on a hill above the beaches which could direct fire on to the assault craft. The plan was to assault the enemy strongpoints with four separate raiding forces. The main landing would take place in the early hours of 2 June 1944, but on the previous night two forces – North and OP – were to land and lie up close to their objectives, and a few hours before the main landing North Force was to cut the road running north from Nerezisce (where the main German force was) to Supetar, while the other Force wiped out the OP. The main – or West – Force would come ashore on three beaches in the south-west of the island. East Force was to land some 5 miles to the east at the harbour of Bol and cut the road from Nerezisce to Selca, and then take Selca.

North Force (500 partisans) and OP Force (one company of the 2nd Highland Light Infantry) got ashore and to their target area unseen. North Force cut the road, but the Highlanders were prevented from rushing the OP by a cleverly-laid minefield, although they did stop the observers from directing the German batteries. West Force (43 (RM) Commando, two troops of 40 (RM) Commando and 1,300 partisans under Lt-Colonel Jack Churchill commanding Special Service Brigade in his brother's absence) landed safely and after the air strike attacked the German battery, but here again minefields prevented them from reaching their objectives. East Force (partisans, and artillery support for both East and West Forces) also landed unopposed and were successful in taking Selca, killing 150 Germans and capturing several guns and 100 prisoners.

On D plus 1 Colonel Churchill carried out a personal reconnaissance of the area and decided that the capture of Point 622 – a major feature just south of Nerezisce – would ensure the fall of the main position. Three more troops of No. 40 (RM) Commando together with 300 partisans had reached the island that morning, and Churchill planned to attack the strongpoint with both Marine Commandos that night. But – as can happen with the best-laid plans – things went wrong. Orders went out by wireless for the attack, and for some reason were incorrectly received by the Commando signallers, who understood that only 43 Commando would make the attack. Furthermore the Brigade G3 staff officer was misled by his guide and delivered orders to No. 40 Commando fifteen minutes after No. 43 had left their start line for the attack. It is never easy to rectify such errors once troops have left the start line, and the result was an uncoordinated effort, which may have arisen partly through lack of experience.

Both Commandos reached the summit but separately and from different directions, and neither was able to hold it. No. 40 had been led into the attack by their commanding officer, Lt-Colonel J.C. Manners, and Colonel Churchill – playing his bagpipes. Their fight on the hilltop was extremely fierce, and by the time Lt-Colonel Manners fell mortally wounded not many Marines remained alive. Before they were finally beaten back, emptying magazines into the enemy as they went, Colonel Churchill had been stunned by a grenade and taken prisoner.

The next day nothing further could be done and the Force, now under Lt-Colonel R.W.B. Simonds (of 43 Commando), withdrew. No. 2 Commando played only a small part in this operation. Three officers and twelve men under the adjutant went to cover the withdrawal of the last troops, and then they volunteered to stay behind on the island in the hope of being able to rescue their commanding officer. But despite their efforts, and those of the Royal Navy, the Germans managed to get their prisoners off the island. The Commandos had lost 16 officers and 111 other ranks in this assault, which had failed as a tactical operation; but the strategic objective had been achieved, for the Germans, far from withdrawing troops to the mainland, reinforced the island.

Ten days after the withdrawal from Brac Marshal Tito agreed to inspect No. 2 Commando (for they had been the longest on the island) and personally thanked them for their efforts on behalf of the Yugoslav people. This was a timely and much appreciated gesture, for by now the spirit of comradeship which had been such a feature of the early days between partisans and Commandos was, for a number of reasons, beginning to look a little tattered. At this time it was agreed with Tito that standing patrols of two officers and twenty or thirty men should be maintained on a number of the Dalmatian coast islands. Later in the summer No. 43 (RM) Commando helped the partisans to recapture Brac and Solta. No. 2 Commando returned to Italy on 15 July for a short rest and to re-equip before being sent to Albania.

The object of their first operation in Albania was to reopen the coastline in the neighbourhood of Himara so that stores could be sent to the Albanian partisans, who although increasing in strength were desperately short of equipment. To achieve this it was first necessary to destroy the small German garrison holding four strongpoints north-east of Spilje.

Lt-Colonel Fynn, commanding No. 2 Commando, landed on the night of 28/29 July at the head of a mixed force of 712 men. To assist the 350 men of his Commando, Land Force Adriatic (LFA) had allotted him C Company of the 2nd Highland Light Infantry, 180 men from the Raiding Support Regiment with four 75 mm guns, four anti-tank guns, six medium machine guns and six 3 in. mortars; in addition there were small parties from 9 Commando and 40 (RM) Commando and the Long Range Desert Group. The Royal Navy supplied the LCIs and two destroyers for bombardment.

The plan to attack the four strongpoints was extremely complicated, involving a carefully co-ordinated naval and artillery bombardment, and a preliminary air strike. The operation got off to a bad start, largely because Albanian quislings had warned the Germans, and so although the landing was unopposed there was never any element of surprise, and there was also a failure in communications. The FOO (forward observation officer) directing the destroyers' fire took a toss ascending a steep hill and his wireless set was put out of action (which led to some casualties from destroyer shells to troops advancing to the start line), and many of the other sixty-four sets that had been landed failed to work properly in the thick olive groves – the trees got in the way of the whip aerials.

Thereafter the gallantry of the troops did much to retrieve these earlier misfortunes, but the enemy had been reinforced and was stronger than anticipated. Repeated attacks against the four strongpoints never succeeded in dislodging the Germans, and before Colonel Fynn ordered the force to carry out a very difficult withdrawal they had lost twenty killed and sixty wounded. But the damage inflicted on the enemy had been very considerable, and only thirty Germans stayed to face the partisans – the others were either dead or wounded, or had fled to the hills. Within two days the Albanians had cleared the last remaining positions, captured many weapons, and were in the outskirts of Spilje.

Shortly afterwards No. 2 Commando was back in Italy for almost two months while various plans for the further employment of 2 Special Service Brigade were formulated and then discarded. It was eventually decided that this Commando and troops from the RSR with four 75 mm guns should return to Albania. This time they were to land near Sarande, a town opposite the island of Corfu. The Albanian partisans were anxious to wipe out the German garrison at Borsh and extend their bridgehead, but before they could accomplish this the Sarande garrison, which was available to reinforce Borsh, had to be isolated. The Commando force was therefore ordered to land north of Sarande on 22 September in order to render the Sarande-Delvine road unusable, and generally to harass the Sarande garrison so as to prevent their going to the assistance of their friends in Borsh.

It was originally intended that this should be a 36-hour raid, for it was thought that the Albanians could probably take Sarande unaided. However, it was soon discovered that the garrison was far stronger than expected, and having made a personal reconnaissance Brigadier Churchill realized that more troops would be needed, for Sarande must be taken and not just isolated.

Therefore, while the existing force advanced a short distance over exceptionally unpleasant and difficult country to take up a waiting position, LFA was asked to despatch reinforcements. On 24 September Brigade Headquarters, 40 (RM) Commando and a second troop of the RSR with 75 mm guns sailed. The Marines arrived next day, but the guns took a week, and for a fortnight the troops lay up in appalling conditions of persistent, soaking rain. But by 7 October No. 1 Parachute Company of the RAF Levies, a battery of the 111th Regiment RA and 150 Pioneers (invaluable for off-loading supplies among other things) had increased the force still further, and Brigadier Churchill was now ready to attack.

At 4 a.m. on 9 October the gunners and RSR mortars commenced a noisy cannonade. The main attack on Sarande followed closely with No. 2 Commando on the left and 40 (RM) on the right. The Marines were given two preliminary objectives (Italian Bay and Point 261), and then Sarande itself. No. 2 Commando had to clear a ridge. Churchill had good reasons for believing the enemy garrison in Delvine would not attempt to reinforce Sarande, and as long as it did not he reckoned he had sufficient troops to take that town. In this he was right; the Marines, who had the lion's share of some very tough fighting, were in the western outskirts of Sarande twelve hours after the first shots of the battle had been fired, and after a bitter bout of street fighting the last of the enemy surrendered. Meanwhile 2 Commando had swept along the ridge and captured both their objectives.

The whole operation had been a great success, and co-operation with the Albanian partisans had proved a pleasant and profitable affair. With the capture of Sarande, Corfu – which the Germans had already begun to evacuate – fell like a ripe plum without any fighting. But for 2 Special Service Brigade there was to be a sad sequel to the fighting in Albania. They were to lose their popular and extremely competent commander, Brigadier Churchill. Ordered by his superiors, sitting in LFA many miles away, to pursue the retreating Germans with the utmost vigour, he clearly saw that for a number of excellent reasons he was unable to comply, and when his objections had been overruled he offered his resignation, which was very foolishly accepted. In due course Lt-Colonel Tod was given command of the Brigade, and Major J.M. Dunning-White succeeded Tod in command of No. 9.

On 16 September 1944 No. 9 Commando left Italy to land on Kithera, an island off the south coast of Greece, which the Germans had evacuated and where it was planned to establish a naval base to operate against enemy shipping supplying the Aegean. They had under command a squadron of the Greek Sacred Regiment,* patrols of the SBS and one officer and seven men of the LRDG. This composite force was named Foxforce, and it remained in existence until a few days after the triumphal return to Athens on 14 October. That day the whole Force, amid uproarious acclamation, landed at the port of Piraeus and in the afternoon No. 9 Commando made a ceremonial march into Athens.

Previously the Commando had been engaged trying to keep the peace between Greek and Greek in the Peloponnese; an uncongenial task that occupied them for a further four months after Foxforce had been disbanded, and one they performed with firmness, fairness and forbearance. Not for the first time, nor for the last, did British soldiers faced with a difficult and dangerous situation prove themselves exemplars of the civilized virtues, to uphold which was principally why they fought.

---

* Formed by officers of the Royal Hellenic Army who had escaped after the invasion of Greece. It was the Regiment's third revival – others had been in 370 BC and 1821, when they had died to a man in defence of freedom. This time there was to be a happier ending.

While 9 Commando returned to Italy to rejoin 2 Commando Brigade for the final fighting there, 3 Brigade, commanded first by Brigadier W.I. Nonweiler and later by Brigadier C.R. (later General Sir Campbell) Hardy, and comprising Nos. 1, 5, 42 (RM) and 44 (RM) Commandos, was operating in the Far East. The Brigade had sailed on 15 November 1943, but enemy air action in the Mediterranean damaged one of the transports so severely that Nos. 1 and 42 Commandos were held up in Alexandria for weeks, and the Brigade was not united in Ceylon until the following September. Meanwhile, Brigade Headquarters and Nos. 5 and 42 Commando reached Bombay on 22 January, and were operating in Burma some six weeks later.

The men of No. 5 Commando were no strangers to the Indian Ocean, for in May 1942 they had landed in Madagascar with 5 Division to seize the island from the French before it could fall into Japanese hands. Landing took place off Diego Suarez, which surrendered after only slight resistance, and the Commando was later involved in the taking of Tamatave and some islands. Madagascar was not completely secured until early November, but 5 Commando had returned home long before. The fighting for the Commando had not been of a very severe nature, and they suffered few casualties, but the experience they gained was useful for the far tougher role they were called upon to play in Burma.

The Japanese initial thrust into Burma had taken them across to the Arakan where, like the Germans in Italy, they found that the ground greatly favoured defence. The coastal area from Cox's Bazar down to Akyab – a distance of around 100 miles – consists of numerous rivers separated by jungle-covered ridges running north and south, which the Japanese honeycombed with strong defences. Below Akyab, and along the coast southwards to Sandoway, were many islands and small islets, some of which were only separated from the mainland by mud and mangrove swamps at the mouth of chaungs* and rivulets. Although inferior in numbers the Japanese were clever jungle fighters, and unsurpassed in their contempt of death.

The monsoon lasted in this area from May until October, and the initial attempts of the British to recapture the Arakan were made in the dry season. The Burma coast was ideal for combined operations, but in 1942 and 1943 there was a great shortage of

---

* Coastal creeks. These treacherous waterways, familiar to all who fought in Burma, are overhung with impenetrable foliage and fouled by green mats of slime and mangrove roots.

landing craft, and so operations to take the important port of Akyab were confined to landward thrusts and the earlier attempts ended in disaster.

Shortly before the first two Commandos arrived in India XV Corps, commanded by Lt-General Christison, had reached the main Japanese defensive line of the Maungdaw-Tunnels-Buthidaung road. It was an extremely strong position, known by the Japanese as the Golden Fortress. At the end of December 1943 Christison launched his attack on this position, which was interrupted in February, after some very stiff fighting without much gain, by the Japanese offensive under General Hanaya. Operation HA-GO was aimed at Imphal and Kohima, but despite the Imperial Army Headquarters' ukase that these two towns were to be captured, and the Japanese soldiers' devotion to dying, the attack was defeated. At the beginning of March, by which time the two Commandos were ready to operate, Christison resumed his offensive.

Training in India could not simulate the peculiar conditions of the Arakan with its numerous chaungs, spiny ridges and jungle swamps, and so there was a further short period at Teknaf (a small town near the mouth of the Naf river) before the Commandos' first major operation. Here they were introduced to some members of the famous V Force and its energetic and inspiring leader Major Denis Holmes. Holmes was greatly impressed by the superb fitness and enthusiasm of the two Commandos under their commanding officers (Lt-Colonel David Shaw for No. 5 and Lt-Colonel Cyril Horton for No. 44), and they in their turn were soon to appreciate the enormous value to them, and indeed to the whole XIVth Army, of V Force. A brief digression must be made to give an outline background of this Force.

In the early days of the Burmese fighting, when General Alexander was leading a bedraggled and bewildered army to the safety of India, the Commander-in-Chief, General Wavell, saw the need for a small select force who knew the country and could operate behind the enemy lines. Wavell was always far in advance of his contemporaries in appreciating the value of irregular forces. V Force was conceived as a guerrilla force, formed of hillmen from the mountainous Burma-Assam-India frontier with a view to harassing the enemy lines of communication if they should invade India. This did not happen, but V Force personnel did excellent work in helping the thousands of refugees to safety.

Later, when it was the XIVth Army's turn to advance, the Force was reconstituted and its principal role ceased to be one of harassment (although whenever opportunity occurred Japanese sentries were liable to be swiftly and silently dispatched with the knife) and they acted as a screen to the army, constantly supplying information of enemy activity. They also ran a fleet of sampans for the use of Allied troops crossing chaungs. Under the direction of Lt-Colonel A.A. Donald, and expertly guided by such intrepid British officers as Denis Holmes and Anthony Irwin, this polyglot band of endearing thugs did magnificent work. In the Arakan they were XV Corps' eyes and ears. Most of the scouts were tough, uneducated peasants, but the principal agents working well behind the Japanese lines possessed considerable intelligence, and every man in the Force needed – and had – unrivalled nerve and guts. *

Operation Screwdriver was to be launched on the night of 11 March when the 5th Indian Division of XV Corps was to assault Razabil, which lies just south of the Maungdaw-Tunnels road and west of the Mayu Range. This attack was aimed at dominating the whole coastal strip up to the foothills of the Mayu Range. The Royal Marine Commando, with Brigadier Nonweiler's advance HQ, was to land on the enemy's left flank a little south of Alethangyaw, establish a beachhead, capture the village and advance three miles inland to take a feature called Hill 250. No. 5 Commando was held in reserve to relieve the Marines after a few days. The landing at 11.30 p.m. on 11 March was made in three flights from landing craft that were barely seaworthy.

This was 44 (RM) Commando's first action, and they were allowed to make an unopposed landing – although they got very wet from the high surf. But once ashore they were quickly involved in some of the most difficult fighting that can fall to any soldier. It was a dark night, for the moon had not yet risen; the vegetation was dense; communications were difficult; and there was an alert enemy in well sited positions. The Japanese were masters of deception and up to every kind of dirty trick, but they were at best of times poor shots and in the dark their aim was very wild; this was as well, for it undoubtedly saved the Marines many casualties. Even so, a slightly too ambitious plan and the Commanding Officer's difficulty in maintaining contact with the forward troops resulted in considerable early confusion. Alethangyaw was not completely taken on the first night, and an advance into the hills was not possible by day. The Commando therefore consolidated in a 'box' – a square formed with pickets at the

* Their story has been well told in *The Raiders of Arakan* by Brigadier Lucas Phillips.

corners, and very much used in this type of dense jungle fighting – and Colonel Horton made a fresh plan.

On the second night only a little progress was made, but on the third – operating in most trying conditions, such as wading thigh-deep through a chaung fringed by dripping and dense jungle – the Commando gained its objective. The following night (14 March) they were ordered to withdraw, an operation skilfully carried out through enemy-held territory.

That same night 5 Commando, with attachments of V Force, landed from river craft on the banks of a large chaung south of Alethangyaw. Here a defensive position was established from which the Commando carried out active patrolling during the next five days and nights, and engaged in some very severe close-quarters fighting. In the course of these many scraps the enemy invariably came off worst, but inevitably there were casualties and the Commando lost fourteen men killed; there were also twenty-nine wounded who had to be evacuated under extreme difficulties to the Alethangyaw beach. But by 21 March, when the Commando was relieved by No. 44 – after an exceptionally tricky and dangerous withdrawal – they had dominated the area of operations, and both Commandos had fulfilled their mission of occupying the attention of considerable Japanese forces while the main attack was in progress.

Before 3 Commando Brigade was moved to Silchar in Manipur State, No. 5 was dispatched at short notice on an operation well suited to Commando tactics. A battery of mountain artillery was in danger of being overwhelmed. The second-in-command led two troops, Nos. 4 and 5, in a very spirited action over rough open ground. No. 5 Troop, under Captain Kerr, came under withering fire from unlocated positions and suffered casualties, but their momentum was scarcely checked, and soon the troops were at grips with the enemy and it became a matter of hack and cut, turn and trample. Fighting on through the short eastern twilight the Japanese eventually gave way, leaving many dead on the ground, and the battery was safe. Captain Kerr lost an arm in the engagement, and his troop had no fewer than twenty-two men killed and fourteen wounded. Men from No. 4 Troop performed many feats of gallantry in rescuing the wounded under intense fire.

The big Japanese thrust in the centre of Burma failed. By April it was clear that they had hopelessly overreached themselves, and with an extended line of communication constantly under threat failure was inevitable. Many died of starvation and the rest beat a confused retreat across the Chindwin. Brigadier Nonweiler's two Commandos were therefore able to leave for Ceylon, where in due course they were joined by the rest of the Brigade. But by the beginning of November the whole Brigade was back in what was for Nos. 5 and 44 the familiar area of Teknaf. XV Corps had now got the Japanese on the move, and before long many places whose names had been symbols of stubborn resistance and gallantry unrewarded were to be seized from the enemy.

Colonel Peter Young, formerly CO of No. 3 Commando in North-West Europe, joined the Brigade as deputy commander at the end of October. When, soon after his arrival, Brigadier Nonweiler was sent home ill, Young took command until the arrival of Brigadier Hardy in mid-December. He found the brigade to be below the standard he expected and took immediate steps to rectify this. During the last two months of the year the Commandos did a spell in the line and were constantly on patrol; occasionally they were engaged in quite large-scale raids. Most of these adventures of inroad and foray were successful in gaining information, and keeping the enemy constantly on edge.

By the end of December the big push for Rangoon was under way. A large amphibious landing to take Akyab proved unnecessary, for the Japanese, hastening to reach the passes of the Arakan Yoma before their retreat was cut off, had abandoned the place. No. 3 Commando Brigade therefore made an unopposed entry, but another amphibious operation – this time against the Myebon Peninsula – was soon to be launched, and in this and its sequel the Brigade was to see plenty of action.

Brigadier Hardy, with a small party, reconnoitred the landing area from an RIN (Royal Indian Navy) Sloop whereby he gained useful knowledge of the beaches to supplement details supplied by Combined Operations Pilotage Parties (COPPs – see Chapter 8). The creeks and chaungs were even more labyrinthine than higher up the coast. They varied in width but not in the thick glutinous mud that was everywhere, nor in the rocks and mass of tangled mangrove roots which at low tide made any form of navigation impossible. The Brigadier had chosen the best beach from a bad lot, and the fact that it had been protected by stakes (which a COPP party had destroyed) meant that the Japanese considered it to be passable. It was also found to be mined.

The assault took place at 8.30 a.m. on 12 January, and was preceded by a large and completely successful air strike. The Japanese had apparently been taken by surprise, for although the landing was difficult it was unopposed, and by evening the

Brigade had formed a bridgehead. The night was peaceful, nor was there any counter-attack at dawn. By midday on D plus 1 three Sherman tanks of the 19th Lancers had somehow managed to find sufficient firm sand to get ashore, and during the following days, when they were in close support of the advance, they caused consternation among the enemy who had no long-range anti-tank guns. On the 18th the 74th Indian Brigade relieved the Commandos, who had taken two strongpoints and the village of Kantha, and advanced some four or five miles north of their landing place. Their losses had been four killed and thirty-eight wounded.

Aerial reconnaissance clearly showed that the Japanese were holding a strong line from Kangaw village to the Myebon Peninsula, which was obviously intended to cover their withdrawal down the Kalandan valley and would therefore be held at all costs. The Commando Brigade was to be part of the force whose task it was to turn the left of this line, and they were to make a second landing close to Kangaw. This involved a 5-mile approach up the Daingbon Chaung, and the dual objectives of Hill 170 – a wooded feature rising steeply out of paddy fields and mango swamps – and Kangaw village. The landing was to take place about noon on 22 January; No. 1 Commando would seize the hill, supported in due course by No. 5, while No. 42 would land on, and hold, both banks of the chaung. On D plus 1 it was reckoned that No. 44 Commando should be able to advance to the capture of the village.

The Daingbon Chaung is around 100 yards wide with densely-clad banks, and had these been manned the small flotilla would have been easy prey. But again the Japanese seemed to be taken by surprise and were facing the wrong way. No. 1 Commando succeeded in taking Hill 170 and had dug themselves in by nightfall. This was one of the line's key positions, and it was not likely that the Commando would be left in peace for long. Indeed that night there was a determined attack on the two forward troops but it was beaten off, leaving nine Japanese dead. No. 44 Commando had also made good progress and taken a hill not far from Kangaw, but on this they were heavily shelled and then attacked. Before the Japanese were thrown back the Commando had suffered sixty-one casualties, and the Brigadier relieved them with the 8/19th Hyderabad Regiment, which had recently arrived to reinforce the Brigade.

The fighting went on at a comparatively low level until the enemy had been reinforced; but then at 5.45 a.m. on 1 February, after a particularly heavy stonk, the Japanese began a series of suicidal attacks to regain this key position. An avalanche of men, determined to destroy No. 1 Commando or else themselves, stormed up the hill; platoon after platoon was beaten back by No. 4 Troop under its heroic commander, George Knowland, whose fine leadership and great personal courage saved the hill from capture. He was to be awarded a posthumous Victoria Cross. Almost the first casualties were two of the 19th Lancers' Sherman tanks, destroyed by a party of twenty-one desperados from the Japanese 154 Assault Regiment. These men rushed the position and, in words of their official report, 'OC Kodama Tai and six men clung to the two tanks and bravely blew themselves up with the tanks.' Ten others of the party did the same with the trucks. The surviving Sherman continued to give valuable support.

All that day the battle raged with various degrees of intensity. At times there were brief lulls, and then attack and counter-attack in some of the fiercest fighting of the campaign, under a sizzling midday sun which seared even the hardened Japanese. Brigadier Hardy threw in two troops from No. 42 to help the hard-pressed No. 1 drive the enemy from the position. Eventually, at about 5 p.m., it was possible to pass No. 5 Commando through No. 1, for the latter had done enough. Shortly afterwards Major Robin Stuart (who had taken over from the wounded commanding officer of No. 5) sought permission to thrust forward in a final push to clear the hill. When he did so he found the Japanese had gone. Under cover of darkness they had cut a loop track in the jungle by which their main body slipped away.

The ground was littered with their dead. In an area of 100 square yards 340 bodies were counted, and it is estimated that 450 Japanese fell in their final attack on Hill 170. In the words of Colonel Young, who thought it was the worst slaughter he had seen in all of his many fights, 'You could hardly tread on the ground without touching a dead body.' It had taken two blood-stained days to capture Hill 170, and the Commando Brigade lost forty-five men killed and ninety wounded.

It was several more days before Kangaw fell, by which time 3 Commando Brigade was back at Akyab, having fought its last battle. It was indeed a battle to be proud of, for they had shattered and scattered a vast horde of some of the toughest and most daring soldiers in the world. In a special order of the day General Christison wrote of the Commandos: 'The battle of Kangaw has been the decisive battle of the whole Arakan campaign and that it was won was due very largely to your magnificent courage on Hill 170.'

The 3rd Commando Brigade was moved from Burma to India in the spring of that year, where they carried out a refresher course in jungle warfare prior to a further campaign in Malaya. They were on the point of leaving when the atomic bomb descended on Hiroshima, and their destination was eventually switched to Hongkong. Here in 1946 the Brigade was disbanded along with Nos. 1 and 5 Commandos, but the Royal Marine Commandos were to be reformed as a brigade with Nos. 40, 42 and 45.

At the beginning of June Colonel Young returned to the United Kingdom to command No. 1 Commando Brigade, which like the other Commando brigades was disbanded the following year. As a member of the Committee of the Commando Association formed to discuss a memorial to those Commandos who had fallen during the war, it was he who suggested Westminster Abbey as the most suitable location. The then Dean of Westminster gave the idea his enthusiastic support, and in May 1948 the Commando Memorial was unveiled in the West Cloister of the Abbey by Winston Churchill. The Dean chose the inscription from the second book of Samuel: 'They performed whatsoever the King commanded' – a fitting epitaph to a remarkable story of comradeship, self-sacrifice and devotion to duty.

5

Commandos: Operations in the Middle East, 1940–1941

In the summer and autumn of 1940 three Commandos were formed in the Middle East. These three were entirely separate from those raised in the United Kingdom, although three of the latter (Nos. 7, 8 and 11) were in due course to operate in the same theatre of war. The Middle East Commandos' war establishment was different, and much of their training was aimed to fit them for operations in conditions of climate and country not likely to be encountered by those operating from British shores. No. 50* (ME) Commando was the first to be raised in August 1940; it was therefore almost contemporaneous with those being formed in England. Nos. 51 and 52 were formed near the end of that year.

An opportunity to brigade these three Middle East Commandos was never taken, perhaps because with the exception of General Wavell (who had many other more important matters on his mind) there existed an opaque ignorance in the upper echelons of GHQ Middle East as to what Commandos were capable of doing and how they should be handled. Moreover, despite the Commander-in-Chief's willingness and the Prime Minister's promptings it is possible to presume that, at a time when there was a grave shortage of men, weapons and shipping, there lurked an entirely understandable reluctance to siphon troops away from their units to perform tasks that were not clearly understood. And so in the early months after their formation these three Commandos were frittered away in independent and somewhat unsatisfactory roles.

---

* Numbering was started at 50 so as to allow an ample margin between those Commandos to be raised in Great Britain and those in the Middle East.

At the time of their formation the overall war situation in North and East Africa was in its initial stages. In September the Italians, who had entered the war in June 1940 and were at this time the principal Middle East enemy, had advanced into Egypt from their bases in Libya and taken Sidi Barrani. The British and Dominion troops were greatly outnumbered in the area. But the cautious advance by the Italians had of course considerably extended their lines of communication, and this offered the good opportunities for seaborne raids by Commandos that Churchill had foreseen back in July. One operation was attempted, but at the eleventh hour naval support had to be withdrawn. When General Wavell launched his great offensive on 8 December Italian fortunes tumbled from illusory success to ineluctable disaster, and soon two of the Middle East Commandos were operating a long way from the sea.

The Italians also held the strategic Dodecanese islands in the southern Aegean, from which they could control the shipping routes in the eastern Mediterranean, and also pose a threat to Crete should Greece enter the war. These were ideal, and important, targets for Commando raids, and indeed it was intended to mount a large operation (Cordite) against Rhodes – the principal island of the group – in which the Middle East Commandos and the three UK-raised ones forming Layforce were to play a part. However, the need to send assistance to Greece made this impossible. Later in the war Raiding Forces played havoc in these waters, but in the early days of the Middle East Commandos there was an acute shortage of suitable landing craft (troops rowed ashore in whalers), and what raids could be carried out had to be on an improvised and experimental basis.

In East Africa Italian troops in Ethiopia, Eritrea and Italian Somaliland posed a threat to the Sudan, Kenya, British Somaliland and the entrance to the Red Sea through which so many important convoys had to sail. In June 1940 their overall strength in this theatre was considerably greater than that which the three British commanders had at their disposal. But strategically the Italians were in a very poor condition; supply by air was difficult and by sea virtually impossible. Furthermore Ethiopia was a perpetual headache to the Viceroy, the Duke of Aosta, whose troops were principally employed in internal security. Nevertheless, while Graziani maundered over a vanishing army in Libya, Aosta never despaired, and his soldiers performed considerably better than did their compatriots farther north.

Personnel for 50 and 52 Middle East Commando were recruited

from units then serving in Egypt and Palestine, with the exception of the Royal Engineers, armoured regiments and technical corps (other than RAMC) whose members were not permitted to volunteer. A fruitful field for recruitment was the Yeomanry regiments in Palestine, many of whose members felt they were in a backwater and leaped at the opportunity of seeing action in the near future. Other than some administrative details all personnel were to be volunteers, and the supply greatly outnumbered the demand, which resulted in one or two regiments filling their quota with the less desirable of their volunteers. This was unwise, for it caused considerable trouble and in due course they got most of these misfits back.

An out-of-the-ordinary enrolment for No. 50 Commando was a party of some seventy Spaniards. They were men who had been on the losing side in the Spanish civil war and had crossed the Pyrenees into France. Here they enlisted in foreign service battalions and eventually found themselves in Syria. On the collapse of France these mercenaries left Vichy Syria and made their way to Palestine, where they agreed to continue in service if commanded by British officers. They were a rough and tough lot but malleable material, and their powers of endurance and ability to bear pain were very considerable. There were initial language difficulties, and for this reason they were not taken on the early raids. Most of them were to be captured in Crete, but posing as Gibraltarians they survived as prisoners of war.

All three Middle East Commandos were trained at Geneifa, on the Suez Canal. The war establishment was on a somewhat *ad hoc* basis and underwent a number of changes, and each Commando differed slightly in composition. No. 50 Commando, the first to be raised, had a headquarters of 80, four companies each of 105 all ranks divided into four troops, and the 70 Spaniards made up a small extra company. The Commando totalled 570 all ranks. No. 52 started with only three companies and a total of 405, but this was increased later. The composition of No. 51 will be dealt with later. On the personnel side the principal weakness was the administration; there was no quartermaster (the adjutant doubling for that duty), only one CQMS and no storeman.

Middle East Commandos were well equipped with small arms. Each troop normally had a Bren gun, and the soldiers were armed with rifle and bayonet – other than Nos. 1 and 2 on the Bren, who like the officers carried pistols. There were also Thompson submachine guns, Mills grenades and explosives to be used according to the type of operation. But the Commandos, unlike an infantry battalion, did not have any mortars, anti-tank weapons, or Bren carriers. Their transport was insufficient and their wireless sets both insufficient and inadequate. Every man carried a fighting knife known as a 'Fanny'. This had a nine-inch blade with a brass handle which contained two rings for two fingers. The outside of the rings had blunt spikes so that the knife could also be used as a knuckle-duster. A miniature replica of this ferocious weapon became the Commandos' cap badge.

Geneifa was ideally situated for specialized training, with the Great Bitter Lake at hand for boatwork and the Sweet Water Canal for rafting. At the back of the camp there stretched for many miles barren areas of sand, scrub, hill and rock, where demolition work could be practised and a variety of tactical exercises to include very long, exhausting marches carrying full equipment and the man's daily ration. This ration was made up of 6 oz of bully beef, 4 oz of dates, 2 oz of rice and sugar, ¾ oz of tea, 4 oz of biscuits, two packs of chewing gum and four limes, as well as the normal water bottle.

Nos. 50 and 52 Commandos had only about six weeks in which to train before being considered operational. This was just sufficient time, because every man on joining was physically fit and well versed in basic training, and so nearly all the work was of a specialized nature – periods spent on camelcraft might even be described as esoteric! The men of both Commandos left the training area in peak physical condition and fully trained, except that time allowed for only the officers and NCOs to become qualified in elementary demolition work. The soldiers had to receive this training at a later stage. No. 51 Commando needed a longer period in which to train, on account of its heterogeneous composition. But they appear to have made the best of it, for Captain Lapraik's Arab troop set up what was then considered to be a marching record for the British Army, of 51 miles in 15¾ consecutive hours over rough, hilly and rocky country.

The first operation planned for 50 (ME) Commando was a raid upon the Italian seaplane base at Bomba. The Gulf of Bomba lies between Tobruk and Derna, and the Commando was to sail at the end of October in two destroyers (HMS *Decoy* and *Hereward*). After a great deal of intensive training, rehearsals and operational planning the troops duly embarked for their objectives. But when the destroyers were drawing close to their target on the night of 29/30 October 1940 they were ordered to return to Alexandria immediately.

The cause for this cancellation of a raid was the Italian attack on

Greece, but unfortunately it was not an isolated case either in home or Mediterranean waters. It cannot be emphasized too strongly how much damage is done to morale when troops are keyed to highest expectancy after months of training only to be confronted with the anticlimax of abandonment, or merely of postponement, of an operation. Especially this is so with new units, which having no long tradition and battle honours behind them are anxious to gain recognition through their deeds. On occasions (and this was one of them) such action cannot be avoided, but there were others when with more forethought it could have been.

The importance of the Dodecanese islands has already been noted, and so it was no surprise that shortly after this abortive operation 50 Commando was sent to Crete, from where it could carry out raids. At this time the capture of Scarpanto and Rhodes was still a viable plan for the spring, and the Commanders-in-Chief Middle East wished to capture the islands of Kasos and Castelorizzo as good jumping-off grounds for the larger operation. And possession of Kasos meant domination of Scarpanto airfield by naval coastal guns, and control of both sides of the U- and E-boat-infested Kasos Straits.

Accordingly 50 Commando was ordered to make two visits of reconnaissance to report upon suitable landing beaches, exits and the general terrain on the north and south coasts of Kasos. These were carried out under immense difficulties with faulty equipment and lack of information. The Commando had been given no indication of the strength of the Italian garrison nor of its locations, and no air photographs were available. HMS *Derby*, in which the troops detailed for the reconnaissance sailed, had no special davit mountings for extra whalers, and no scrambling nets. On the first attempt, in January 1941, some of the boats on reaching the water sprang leaks from damage inflicted when being handled over improvised davits. On the second, a month later, tide times were mistaken and local Greek guides failed to appear. Although a few men did get ashore the reconnaissance was not successful; the failure highlighted the equipment problem in these early days of improvisation.

The decision to capture Kasos was then shelved in favour of an attempt against Castelorizzo. This island is at the extreme east of the Dodecanese chain, within easy reach of what was then the big Italian base at Rhodes, but far distant from the British military and air base at Cyprus. Admiral Cunningham wanted it for an advance MTB base, but it seems a curious choice. And anyway, once taken how could it possibly be held for sufficient time to establish the base by only one company of infantry without AA or coastal gun support? It was an ill-conceived operation, and as far as the Royal Navy was concerned disastrous in execution.

Operation Abstention (or Pitch as it was sometimes called) was scheduled for the fourth week of February 1941. No. 50 Commando was to seize the island and be relieved after twenty-four hours by troops from Cyprus. The Commando sailed at 1 a.m. on 24 February in two destroyers (HMS *Decoy* and *Hereward*). For some reason they sailed west from Suda instead of east through the Kasos Straits, which added 160 miles to their journey, and caused them to run short of fuel at a critical stage of the operation. While at sea the senior soldier in both ships opened the sealed orders and learned the destination and objectives. No doubt this was a good security precaution, but it made a co-ordinated plan difficult – and as at the Kasos landings no information nor aerial photographs had been given to the Commando.

The destroyers arrived some 200 yards off shore in the early hours of 25 February, and the first flight was in the whalers by 3 a.m. But there was considerable delay in getting the troops ashore, largely because the naval officer in charge of the first flight misread his chart and passed the landing beach. However, eventually most of the Commando landed in the right place; the few who had got ashore in the first flight shot up an Italian patrol, and the rest of the landing was unopposed.

The principal resistance came from Paleocastro Fort into which most of the small garrison had withdrawn. Here the Italians put up a stout resistance but the Commando, supported by HMS *Ladybird*, which had sailed into the harbour at first light, had the fort by about 10 a.m. They were then virtually in possession of the island, although throughout that day they had to endure continuous bombing and low-level machine-gunning which was far more noisy than dangerous, but inevitably caused some casualties.

What should have been a quiet night, pending relief in the morning, was rudely disturbed when an Italian warship sailed into the harbour and scattered armour-piercing shells into buildings occupied by the troops. The enemy ship landed a few armed men to rescue Italian nationals from possible danger of avenging Greeks, but no serious counter-attack came until the morning of the third day. Meanwhile, in the early hours of the second and third mornings, the Commando made the prearranged signals at the landing beach to inform the Navy that it was safe to approach;

but they got no response. And again throughout these days the troops were subjected to heavy air attack.

About midday on the 27th two Italian destroyers and some MTBs sailed into the harbour and landed a strong and well-armed force, including a detachment of mountain artillery, which was supported by CR 42 fighters and the two destroyers. It was a tense situation and some very hard fighting resulted, but by the end of the day the Commando was still intact, although there had been a number of casualties and it now occupied only a small part of the island. The troops were also running very short of ammunition and food, for this had been meant to be only a 24-hour operation. The initial planning for Operation Abstention had been rushed and the intelligence faulty, but the principal muddle occurred in bringing in troops from Cyprus who were to form the garrison. The Commando understood that the 1st Battalion The Sherwood Foresters were coming, but in the event only B Company, under Major L.C. Cooper, was sent. The Company was due to land from the Armed Boarding Vessel *Rosaura* at 3 a.m. on 26 February. The ABV sailed from Famagusta on the morning of the 25th, to rendezvous with the 3rd Cruiser Squadron commanded by Rear-Admiral E. de F. Renouf, who was in charge of the operation.

One unfortunate incident succeeded another. HMS *Hereward*, sent forward to arrange the landing, failed to carry out her orders after being unnecessarily alarmed by a badly-signalled message from the shore. The signal she then sent the Admiral, together with enemy activity in the area, and very rough weather which was causing much seasickness among the troops, decided him to postpone the landing until 10 p.m. on the 26th. But before this could happen the destroyers ran short of fuel and had to return to Alexandria, where they arrived at 10 p.m., the time they should have been off Castelorizzo. Here the Sherwood Foresters were transferred from *Rosaura* to *Hero* and *Decoy*. Meanwhile, there had been a complete lack of communication between the Royal Navy and the small Commando force, which had had to fend for itself with totally inadequate weapons against a superior Italian one supported by naval and air bombardment.

Eventually, on the night of 27/28 February, a platoon of B Company landed, but too much of the island had been lost to contemplate recapture in daylight next day. It was therefore decided to abandon the operation and withdraw all British troops. After a difficult and dangerous withdrawal all the wounded and twelve prisoners were evacuated. But a few men from the

Commando who had become separated from the main body had to be left behind. Some of these set off to swim to the Turkish coast, a distance of just over 3 miles. Only three of them made it; the rest drowned. The survivors were succoured by the Turks and in due course passed through various channels to Egypt.

In the subsequent enquiries and post-mortems the gravamen against the Navy was that they failed to isolate the island and prevent Italian reinforcements arriving, but from start to finish there had been a number of bad decisions and wrong thinking. Admiral Cunningham characteristically took the blame for this embarrassing failure, but Admiral Renouf, who was a sick man at the time, was shortly afterwards relieved of his command. It was almost the only time in the many operations in which the Royal Navy co-operated with the special forces that things went so sadly awry, and the troops were seriously let down. For this reason, perhaps, little has been heard of this operation, in which at least the soldiers of 50 (ME) Commando acquitted themselves with distinction (quite contrary to what Evelyn Waugh wrote in his diary*).

Some two months before 50 Commando entered upon this raid, 52 (ME) Commando was ordered to the East Africa front, where General Wavell was shortly to launch his two-pronged attack into Eritrea from the Sudan and Kenya. The Commando arrived at Tuklein, an uninhabited place on the River Atbara a short distance from the Sudan–Abyssinia frontier post at Gallabat, on Christmas Eve 1940. Here they came under Brigadier Mayne's 9th Indian Infantry Brigade (a part of the 5th Indian Division), which was holding that sector of the front with two battalions forward, dug in just short of Gallabat, which the Italians still held.

The Brigadier had not much previous knowledge of how Commandos were armed and what they could do, and there was a natural temptation to put companies in the line after some preliminary patrol activity. This did in fact occur, and the whole Commando was used in its proper role on only one occasion, although companies carried out a number of useful patrols inflicting casualties and gaining information.

Previous to the Commando's arrival there had been two daringly deep penetrations in this area by Colonel Sandford's 101 Mission, and by a band of local patriots known as Gideon Force, and commanded by that enigmatic, unpredictable Englishman

---

* *The Diaries of Evelyn Waugh*, edited by Michael Davie, Weidenfeld & Nicolson, 1976, p. 494.

Orde Wingate. Sandford had been made personal adviser to the Emperor Haile Selassie on military matters, and the principal object of these expeditions was to secure a stronghold in preparation for the Emperor's immediate return. Later an expanded Gideon Force was to be engaged in some tough fighting to clear the way for the Emperor's return to his capital.

But this was a different form of fighting to the raids and patrols carried out by 52 Commando against the Italian lines of communication in Abyssinia. By the time the Commando had completed its kindergarten patrols and had become familiar with this (to them) new type of country, the Italians were in the process of thinning out their forward positions and the Brigade Commander was anxious to maintain strong pressure and harass their withdrawal. Operations were therefore conceived in which the regular battalions of the brigade engaged the enemy frontally, while the Commando did what damage it could behind the lines.

The only full Commando raid was designed to destroy troops and transport withdrawing down the Metemma-Gondar road – no more than an earth track but quite passable for transport in the dry weather. The Commando was behind the enemy lines for five days, operating from a forward base which contained the only water supply. Lack of water restricted the scope of this operation and the time that could be spent on the road, and only minor damage was done with casualties received and inflicted during the two short, sharp fights.

It was, however, typical of the type of work individual companies had to perform during the time spent on the Gallabat front. Raids of this kind were ideal employment for a Commando, but as was so often the case insufficient thought had been given to the type of equipment and support required to ensure success. To arrive at the target area the soldiers usually had a very long march across difficult country humping their every requirement, for the Italians had complete control of the air and supply drops were impossible. Moreover, the only four wireless sets had a range of no more than 5 miles, and so companies were very soon unable to communicate with the base camp.

Mules would have been the answer for carrying ammunition and rations, but these were not available. Towards the end of January the Commando was allotted some camels, but they were incredibly slow and at times could be maddeningly contrary. The author, when commanding a small patrol some twelve miles behind the enemy lines, had to abandon one. Its Sudanese keeper had been severely wounded in a skirmish, and when other members of the patrol tried to persuade the beast to stand up it merely ground its teeth and slobbered.

No. 51 (ME) Commando was also actively employed in the East African campaign. The two Commandos met in Gedaref, where No. 52 had arrived on 10 February after marching 90 miles in three days from its Tuklein camp. Both were destined for Kassala, but whereas No. 52 was shortly to return to Egypt No. 51 went on to fight at Keren, Amba Alagi and Gondar.

This Commando had a strange history and composition. It was originally raised, at Sarafand in Palestine, in January 1940, as No. 1 Company Palestinian Auxiliary Military Pioneer Corps. The Company was commanded by Major H.J. Cator of the Royal Scots Greys, and he had five Palestinian officers and a British Company Sergeant Major and Company Quartermaster Sergeant. The total strength of the Company was 650 men, three-quarters of whom were Jews and a quarter Arabs. The Jews came originally from no less than eleven European countries, and the Arabs were of Sudanese, Egyptian, Iraqi and Palestinian extraction – so there was quite a confusion of tongues.

On 22 January they sailed from Haifa and disembarked at Marseilles on 28 February. They did not come into direct contact with German troops during the latter's advance through Belgium and France, but Cator was convinced they would have acquitted themselves well, and he was sure they would make a good fighting unit. To achieve this end he campaigned vigorously with many senior officers and civilians in France, and later in England; but he was not successful until the unit's return to the Middle East in September. Here General Wavell had already sanctioned the formation of No. 50 (ME) Commando, and the Palestinians were to become No. 51.

At the beginning of October Cator (by now a Lt-Colonel) selected some 300 of the best men to form the Commando, and he was given British officers as troop and section commanders. The establishment further allowed for a British adjutant, medical officer, RSM and Orderly Room Sergeant, but no quartermaster. Training at Geneifa was very tough and realistic, and included work with submarines, and practice landings from destroyers. British non-commissioned officers who served with the force speak very highly of the men's enthusiasm and discipline at this time, and mention has already been made of their fine marching performance.

By the beginning of December the Commando was sufficiently well trained to be moved to Alexandria, where seaborne raids on places such as Sollum, Bardia and the pipeline at Buq Buq were planned. But, as with 50 Commando, rough weather and shortage of shipping caused these raids to be either cancelled at sea, or postponed indefinitely. In early January 1941, by which time Sollum had been taken, the Commando found itself being used as a dock labour force there, but by the middle of the month it was back at Geneifa.

At the end of January the Commando sailed for Port Sudan, and was in camp at Gedaref until 21 February, when it moved to Kassala. From there, two days later, it motored 190 miles to the wild and mountainous country south-west of Keren in Eritrea. Here, as an independent force, it was attached to General Beresford-Pierce's 4th Indian Division, and very soon it was sending troops and sections into the mountains on probing patrols and the laying of ambushes.

The Commando's main task at this stage was to harass the enemy defences along the northern periphery of the Keren ring, and to take possession of the high ground on the Division's left flank. This involved long marches and a number of short, sharp engagements. For transport it was well served by Sudani camelmen in charge of some sixty beasts, and a few mules. The greatest problem was the scarcity of water. General Beresford-Pierce thought very highly of the men's performance, and told Cator that the Commando had succeeded in drawing two battalions and a battery of guns to face them. It was a hard, and at times a dangerously unpleasant life, but – as their colonel wrote in his diary – there were compensations in the splendour of the surroundings, and the abundance of beautiful birds and game of every kind.

Keren was undoubtedly the most fiercely contested fight of the East African campaign. The town stands over 4,000 ft above sea level and is protected by a ring of formidable mountains. The Italians manned this natural fortress with 23,000 men (which included some of their finest fighting troops) and 120 guns. This was some 10,000 men and 20 guns more than could be mustered by the two Indian divisions. The flanks of the position could not be turned. Great gallantry was shown by Indian and British troops in their attempts to assault the position, which in February were repulsed, with equal gallantry, by the Italians. General Platt*

---

* General Sir William Platt was GOC Sudan, and at this time had under his command the 4th and 5th Indian Divisions. He, with General Sir Alan Cunningham (GOC Kenya), had been designated to command the assault on Italian East Africa.

opened his second offensive on the night of 15/16 March, and some very bitter fighting followed. On 25 March the final assault went in, and on the night of the 26th the Italian Commander-in-Chief, General Frusci, admitted defeat and withdrew his troops and guns. During the 53 days of the siege the Italians lost 3,000 soldiers killed; the British casualties were 536 killed and 3,229 wounded.

In the preliminary manoeuvring before this great battle, and during the main assault, men of 51 Commando fought with much distinction on the feature known as Mount Samanna, which was one of the principal bastions on the left flank of the Keren ring. While they were patrolling from their base at Beit Gabru, Colonel Cator was ordered to send a troop back to Division Headquarters for an independent job attached to the 11th Brigade. Captain H.S. Frost's No. 3 Troop was selected and ordered to gain a footing on Mount Samanna. In this the troop was unsuccessful, but before being forced off the mountain the men had given a very good account of themselves. On the night of 4/5 March, after a stiff climb, they wiped out a well-defended outpost, but farther up they came under heavy mortar and machine-gun fire. Realizing they were in immediate danger of being surrounded by a superior force and becoming short of ammunition, Frost had no alternative but to order his men to withdraw. He remained behind himself, with his sergeant, to hold the enemy at bay; an action which in the ensuing fierce fight cost him his life.

The Commando's second action on Mount Samanna, in which Colonel Cator was badly wounded in the leg, took place on 23 March. They were given the task of infiltrating and over-powering machine-gun posts on the left flank of the main assault. Hill fighting is always difficult, and the going round Keren was appallingly rough, but towards the end of the battle they managed to cut off a substantial number of Italians and ended with more than 1,000 prisoners.

Keren held the key to Asmara and Massawa, which fell with little trouble to General Platt's troops on 1 and 8 April respectively. The Duke of Aosta now realized that he had no hope of holding Eritrea, and at the end of March he ordered what was left of the Eritrean army to withdraw to another naturally strong position at Amba Alagi. The British were not slow in following and 51 Commando – now under Lt-Colonel S.D. Miller – found itself part of a mixed force known as Fletcher Force.

The Commando played a prominent and highly successful part in Fletcher Force's diversionary attacks on the outposts of the

Falaga pass defences, where they captured an important hill feature. Aryah Shay, one of the Commando's German Jews, tells us that after climbing 'steep and forbidding cliffs' they killed the sentries with their Fanny knives, tumbled the officers out of their beds and quickly overran the whole position. They did, however, incur a number of casualties, as did other units of Fletcher Force, and the Force did not take part in the main attack on the Amba Alagi position.

After the Italians surrendered at Amba Alagi on 19 May the Commando appears to have pulled back to Adi Ugri, and been held in reserve. Here it was visited by General Platt, who took the salute at a big parade and distributed decorations and awards. By the late summer of 1941 the Italian East African empire was fast crumbling, but although isolated and invested the soldiers at Gondar – the last major position to hold out – still managed to put up a stiff resistance.

General Platt's troops were at the siege of Gondar for some time, and one section of 51 Commando was detached to act as escort to Colonel Wingate at Gojam, but they were back before the final assault in November. The Commando never entered Gondar, for their role was to deal with some of the enemy outposts. This they seem to have accomplished efficiently, for according to Aryah Shay the Italian commandant in Gondar was greatly consternated by frequent alarming signals telling him how 'big black apes jumped on his soldiers noiselessly from all sides and opened an infernal fire from a range of but a few metres'.

Gondar was 51 Commando's last fight. On returning to Egypt they were sent on leave, and then the unit was disbanded. Some men volunteered for service in the new Middle East Commando, others went back to Palestine. Between Tel Aviv and Jerusalem in the Volunteer Forest there is a bronze plaque commemorating this fine Commando, whose story is so little known. Their invaluable contribution to the victory at Keren is in itself worthy of a permanent place in the annals of the British Army, and it is sad that no one thought fit to award them that battle honour.

On its return to Egypt 52 (ME) Commando was ordered to amalgamate with No. 50, recently back from Crete, to form the fourth battalion of Layforce. Colonel Laycock had arrived from England in March 1941 at the head of Nos. 7, 8 and 11 Commandos, which respectively formed A, B and C Battalions of his eponymous force; the Middle East Commandos became D Battalion. Originally earmarked for Operation Cordite (the attack on Rhodes), Layforce was brigaded with

22 Guards and 16 Infantry Brigades, as part of General Evett's 6th Division. But when that operation was cancelled Layforce became GHQ troops.

It is a great pity that someone, for security reasons, decided that on their arrival in Egypt the three UK-raised Commandos – Nos. 7, 8 and 11 – should be designated Layforce. It is extremely unlikely that it misled the enemy for a minute, but for forty-three years it has confused the story of Commando operations in the Middle East. The fact that the identity of these three Commandos, and of course that of 50/52 as well, was obliterated by lettered battalions has tended to obscure for posterity their fine perform-ance as Commandos. It has also made it difficult to distinguish between the Middle East Commandos (Nos. 50 and 52) and those Commandos that served in the Middle East – and there was a considerable difference. In order to try to overcome this confusion once and for all, it is proposed in this chapter to revert to the original and proper nomenclature. A battalion Layforce will be called No. 7 Commando, B battalion No. 8, C battalion No. 11 and D battalion No. 50/52.

Command of the two Middle East Commandos went to Lt-Colonel Young (recently of 52 Commando), who greatly benefited from being able to select the best from both Comman-dos. The joint unit was largely composed of regular officers, NCOs and men who had pre-war service in India and the Middle East. Their organization was slightly different to that of the UK-raised Commandos in that they had a headquarters (complete with quartermaster, whom they had lacked previously) and five companies each of two troops, whereas Nos. 7, 8 and 11 had a headquarters and ten smaller troops; but the total strength of around 550 was the same for all four units.

In early May No. 11 Commando was sent to Cyprus. The others together with Brigade Headquarters remained at Sidi Bishr, near Alexandria, from where No. 7 carried out Layforce's first operation: a raid on Bardia, said to be held by about 2,000 Italian soldiers. The object was to attack the town and barracks, to destroy some coast defence guns, a bridge and a pumping station, and to harass the enemy lines of communication.

The Commando sailed from Alexandria on 19 April in HMS *Glengyle*,* escorted by a cruiser and three destroyers. Roger Courtney, the SBS leader, had left earlier in a submarine to fix a

---

* Layforce had sailed from Scotland in three Glen ships, which were to be used for raids, landings and evacuations.

navigation marker, but his Folbot became damaged in launching and he never reached the intended islet. Nevertheless, the landings, which commenced at 10.30 p.m., were in the main carried out successfully – one craft could not be launched and one detachment ended up on the wrong beach – and the Commando was ashore for a little over three hours. The bridge was destroyed and the coastal defence guns blown up,* but the pumping station could not be reached in the time available. An officer was mortally wounded by a bullet intended for an enemy, and in the withdrawal one troop got lost and was later captured.

The raid was a failure, for far from there being 2,000 Italian soldiers in Bardia, the town was deserted. Colonel Laycock was justifiably very annoyed that a Glen ship, a cruiser, three destroyers and a submarine had been put at considerable risk entirely through bad intelligence on the part of GHQ Middle East.

It was, however, notable for being the first of many occasions when that indomitable warrior, Admiral Sir Walter Cowan, accompanied a Commando on a raid. At the ripe age of 71 this courageous sailor was a man on whom action worked like a tonic; he stood little over 5 ft tall, and later at Tobruk the German tank he assaulted with his pistol must have seemed very large. Maybe he sought an honourable death upon the battlefield, but if so he was to be disappointed, for although on occasions it brushed his cheek, always it went upon its way.

Layforce's most important action was undoubtedly fought in Crete, where Nos. 7 and 50/52 Commandos conducted a highly successful rearguard action from the north to the south of the island, despite the fact that as Commando troops they were not armed for a fight of this kind, and they lacked any artillery or air support. Their resolute and skilful performance enabled many troops to be taken to safety through the heroic and costly endeavours of the Royal Navy, but most of 7 Commando and virtually all of 50/52 could not be evacuated.

On 6 April 1941 the Germans invaded Greece. Apart from Britain's age-old and chivalrous policy of aiding a small nation in distress, there were sound international reasons – although precious few military ones – for sending a force to that country. Outnumbered by superbly-equipped and fresh German units, the British faced an inevitable outcome – another withdrawal from the

* The Brigade Intelligence Officer (Evelyn Waugh) has put it on record that these guns had been put out of action by the British on evacuating the town some weeks previously.

European continent together with a heavy loss of valuable equipment. This was to have a bearing on the disaster in Crete, for many of the troops who fought in Greece were evacuated to Crete with only personal weapons and a sadly shaken morale.

The importance of Crete was principally the naval base at Suda, where British ships could refuel for the protection of Malta. The Prime Minister put much pressure on General Wavell to ensure that the island was adequately protected. The Commander-in-Chief did his best to supply General Freyberg's requirements, but it was not easy for him; Rommel was knocking at his front door, and other German forces were at his back door in Iraq.

At the time of the invasion there were some 30,000 troops in Crete, and they were lamentably short of armour (nine 'I' tanks and sixteen light ones), field and anti-aircraft guns and transport; nor had they hope of much air support. Against this weak force General Student was preparing to hurl the hitherto untouched 11th Air Corps, which consisted of a parachute division, a glider regiment, a mountain division and 700 motorcycle riflemen of the 5th Tank Division.

On the morning of 20 May the attack began – principally directed on the Maleme airfield area – with bombing and machine-gunning of unprecedented severity, which was followed by the landing of gliders. At about 8 a.m. the tensely waiting British and Commonwealth troops watched, fascinated and fearful, a meticulously-prepared air descent, in which hundreds of Junkers spewed out their loads of parachutists weaving to and fro in the Cretan sky like some crazy and macabre aerial ballet.* Meanwhile Stukas kept up a steady stream of dive bombing.

The German attack was utterly reckless and totally regardless of losses, which were enormous. The main weight of their attacks, after the initial landings, was in the Suda-Maleme area. Here they captured the airfield on the third day, forcing the 5th New Zealand Brigade to withdraw. They could now pour in troop carriers, and bring pressure to bear on the hitherto less heavily engaged troops in the Retimo-Heraklion part of the island. The Prime Minister kept urging the Commanders-in-Chief to throw in more troops, despite the cruel naval losses. And so the two Commandos of Layforce were ordered to sail at a time when, unknown to those in Egypt, the island was already doomed.

* Six thousand parachutists landed on the first day (a further 10,000 were to be dropped), and these were supported by 750 gliders. The seaborne invasion was not a success, thanks to the sterling work of the Navy.

No. 50/52 Commando, a part of No. 7 and Brigade Headquarters sailed from Alexandria on 24 May bound for the south of the island, from where they were to march north to join the battle round Maleme. Rough weather prevented this landing, and the troops returned to port to be re-embarked in the minelaying cruiser HMS *Abdiel* and two destroyers. This time their destination was Suda, and although fires were burning in the outskirts of the town only the sound of distant gunfire disturbed the disembarkation, after an uneventful journey, around midnight of 26/27 May.

But once ashore Brigade Headquarters were quickly made aware by 7 Commando's advance party of the gravity of the situation. The deadness of despair seemed to be setting in everywhere, and even the GOC felt that the arrival of reinforcements at this late hour was little better than lighting candles in a Stygian night. Here was a very different picture from what the Commandos were expecting, and soon they were to be engaged in a very different sort of fight from that for which they had been trained. The first order was to dump in the sea everything which could not be carried on the man, which meant among other things the loss of the new wireless sets that they had so hardly come by. The battalions then moved to an assembly area some 4 miles from Suda down the Spakhia road.

Creforce, as it was called, was now pulling out of the Maleme-Heraklion strip and heading south for Spakhia from where the Navy would carry out yet another evacuation. General Freyberg told Colonel Laycock that his Force was to form a part of the rearguard as from the following day, 28 May. Meanwhile the troops were subjected throughout the 27th to some very heavy bombing and strafing from the air. The noise was terrible, but the damage to these disciplined troops much less so. Colonel Laycock's initial plan was for one Commando to pass through the other, and so while No. 7 held the first position, 50/52 was to reconnoitre a good defence line farther south, and move into it on the night of the 27th.

By now any form of movement had become extremely difficult, for the countryside of hill and valley was rugged and rough, while the road to Spakhia was cluttered with thousands of refugees. And not only refugees – for soldiers, their ranks ragged, their faces grimy with dirt and sweat, battle-weary men now without discipline or cohesion, were trudging along intent only to escape the torment of shot and shell. Such was the ugly face of defeat. However, during the afternoon of 27 May Lt-Colonel

Young, commanding 50/52 Commando, chose a defensive position just north of Babali Hani village some 12 miles south of Suda Bay, and despite the congestion and confusion on the road the Commando, less one company (the mixed British and Spanish one), withdrew in good order to this line during the night.

The company (together with two companies of Maoris) ordered by Creforce headquarters to remain behind to cover the road junction, where the main road south leaves the coastal road, had a bad position liable to outflanking from the west. In the early hours of 28 May 7 Commando withdrew through them, and shortly afterwards they were heavily attacked from the air. Then, at about 8 a.m., they were engaged by strong enemy forces coming down the road, and by others on their exposed flank. They held their own for a while, but were eventually surrounded and only a few men from this company were able to extricate themselves and rejoin 50/52 Commando.

The latter had now set about preparing as good a defensive position as was possible without digging tools. The olive groves gave some protection from air observation, and stones were available for constructing sangars. The Commando had to sacrifice depth in order to cover as wide a front as possible, and had all four remaining companies forward just north of the Babali Inn crossroads. The right flank was reasonably secure where the hills joined the valley, but the left was open and very vulnerable.

In this position, with one troop of 7 Commando under command and one 'I' tank, which performed magnificently, they withstood heavy mortar and machine-gun fire, and two determined attacks by two and four battalions respectively of the élite 5th Mountain Division. The second attack, which began about 3.30 p.m. and which was principally directed against the two companies holding the vulnerable left flank, was a close-run thing. All spare HQ personnel were rushed to the scene and the Germans were held only when troops from the Australian battalion in reserve gave timely assistance. The defenders had had the best of the fight. 50/52 Commando had only three killed and fifteen wounded, while the Germans had lost around eighty men. As the main body had now passed through the rearguard the battalion was ordered to pull out that evening. It then marched through the night and much of the next day to Askipho about 3 miles north-east of Spakhia, where it arrived on the afternoon of the 29th.

Meanwhile 7 Commando had had a pretty rough time in two sharp brushes with the enemy when withdrawing from their first position and taking up an intermediary one some 8 to 10 miles farther south. In these two fights they suffered some casualties, but held their own and withdrew through 50/52. Thereafter they were not directly engaged by enemy ground troops, but had their fair share of the continual bombing and strafing from the air.

The rest of the Crete story can be sadly and simply told. Both Layforce Commandos were ordered to form the beachhead defence in the hills above Spakhia, from where the last evacuation was to be on the night of 31 May. At about 10 p.m. on that night orders were received from Colonel Laycock to make for the beach. The last coherent body of troops to pass through the Layforce defence line were the remnants of the New Zealand Maori battalion, whose discipline was perfect to the end. For the rest it was mostly one enormous uncoordinated shambles, and the 3-mile descent to the beach was so congested that 50/52 Commando and most of No. 7 did not arrive until after the last boats had sailed. In all more than 8,000 troops had to be left on Crete.

Colonel Laycock, who still had two Commandos of his brigade outside Crete, was ordered to evacuate his headquarters, and they left in HMS *Nizam* on her last sailing about midnight of 31 May/ 1 June. Lt-Colonel Young, as the senior officer left on the island, and in compliance with orders received from the GOC – Major-General Weston – contacted the enemy and surrendered on 1 June. And so the best part of two Commandos went into captivity after a long and courageously-contested withdrawal which, lacking proper weapons, had begun on a note of uncertainty but had achieved, through its performance, something of an epic quality.

6

Commandos: Operations in the Middle East, after Crete

The loss of one complete Commando and the greater part of a second in Crete adumbrated the demise of Layforce, but before this happened at the end of July, No. 11 Commando, still based on Cyprus, was to co-operate in a successful adventure against French troops in Syria. When the Vichy French there became wholly committed to the Germans and the latter's airforce, using Syrian bases, posed a dangerous threat to the Suez Canal, it was decided to send a force under General Wilson to occupy the country. Accordingly in the first week of June 1941 the 7th Australian Division, a motorized cavalry division and Free French troops moved north from Palestine into Syria.

The first major obstacle to this advance was the east-west running Litani river in the Lebanon. To assist the Australians the Commando was to make three landings north of the river, with the object of falling on the enemy's rear and causing such confusion as to allow the main body to cross the river. Once again the fickle Mediterranean weather dealt a shabby hand to the Commandos. The sea was so tempestuous that, much against the wishes of the Commanding Officer (Lt-Colonel R.R.H. Pedder), the landings had to be postponed, but not before HMS *Glengyle* had been seen by the enemy. Surprise was therefore lost, and in the early hours of 9 June the troops were landed in the face of strong opposition, with a near-full moon setting behind them and a rising sun in their front.

Nevertheless, two of the three landings were immediately successful. The troops fell upon the enemy's rear, put out of action a fair proportion of artillery and cut communications. However, the main advance was less rapid than expected and the French were able to turn much of their attention to the Commando, whose troops in daylight conditions were very exposed, and the fighting was extremely severe. Moreover, X Force under the second-in-command, Major Geoffrey Keyes, and comprising Nos. 2, 3 and 9 Troops, had been landed south of the river. But Keyes, a resourceful as well as courageous officer, was not put off by such a mishap. With the help of the Australians, who lent him some boats, he succeeded in getting Lieutenant Garland and fourteen men across fairly quickly, and they soon captured a redoubt on the far bank, taking prisoner thirty-five Algerian Tirailleurs, some of whom were used to man the boats for further crossings.

Before they broke off this action 11 Commando had done an excellent job, capturing besides many prisoners a 6 in. Howitzer, several French 75 mm field guns, a pack mountain gun, two heavy machine guns and a number of LMGs and rifles. They had also taken a barracks, and reinforcements attempting to reach the enemy had been held up. But their casualties had been grievous. Five officers, including the commanding officer, and over 100 other ranks had been killed.

No. 11 Commando was to remain in Cyprus for a little while longer; but it must not be confused with the Cyprus Commando. This was raised in June 1941 and consisted mainly of Greeks and Turks, led by Englishmen and centred on Wolseley Barracks, Nicosia. There were five squads each of eleven men and, although they trained energetically day and night, they do not seem to have seen any action before being disbanded on 7 January 1942.

No. 8 Commando sent detachments to besieged Tobruk, from where they carried out a number of raids. One in particular must be mentioned. On the night of 17/18 July a party of three officers and forty other ranks, under Captain Kealy, carried out a most successful raid against an Italian strongpoint just outside the Tobruk perimeter, which dominated the forward positions of the 18th Indian Cavalry. The night was dark enough to enable the Commando men to infiltrate through the Italian forward positions, and to come at them from the rear at the same time as the Indians staged a diversionary frontal attack. The Commando completely surprised the enemy and inflicted many casualties, while Australian sappers, who had accompanied the party, blew up two ammunition dumps. The Commando lost one man killed and had four wounded. It was the perfect example of a well-planned, reconnoitred and executed raid against a tactically-important enemy post.

This was virtually the last raid that Layforce, as such, undertook – although individuals figured in many more. The force had suffered a total of 800 casualties, and replacements were not readily available. Moreover, lack of suitable shipping at this time restricted seaborne raids, and the emphasis now switched to commando-type raids across the desert, for which the original Commandos were considered unsuitable on account of their size.

Layforce was officially disbanded at the end of July 1941, and a fair proportion of the soldiers opted to return to their regiments. About 120 volunteered for guerrilla work in the Far East. Some 300 wished to stay in special service in the Middle East and in due course were drafted into various formations, either those already formed such as the SBS and LRDG, or shortly to be so like the SAS and No. 1 Special Service Regiment.

On 23 July 1941 the Prime Minister minuted General Ismay for the Chiefs of Staff Committee: 'I wish the Commandos in the Middle East to be reconstituted as soon as possible.'* A month later on a visit to General Auchinleck – then Commander-in-Chief in the Middle East – he reinforced this wish personally. Winston Churchill had always been a great believer in the type of raid that Commandos could carry out, and he was convinced there was a further use for them in this theatre.

Nevertheless, for reasons already mentioned, it seems doubtful whether there was a good case for resuscitating a Middle East Commando as such. Apart from the shortage of suitable shipping for coastal raids and the desirability of smaller formations than a full-scale Commando, Major Bagnold had already been given authority to raise a force for desert reconnaissance (which inevitably would be extended to disrupt enemy lines of communication), and shortly after the Prime Minister's visit Auchinleck was to give Lieutenant Stirling permission to recruit men for small-scale airborne raids well behind the enemy lines.

Notwithstanding these two still embryo formations it was decided that the Middle East Commando Depot – which had existed from the early days of 50, 51 and 52 (ME) Commandos – should spawn another Commando. It was true there were men available from the existing pool to form a strong nucleus, for the LRDG started with New Zealanders and Stirling's demands were at first modest, and so commanding officers were not unduly importuned to release more men for special service. But of the

* *The Second World War*, Vol.3, p.721.

two major raids that took place during the new Commando's brief existence the first was carried out by men whose principal allegiance was still to No. 11 Commando (C Battalion Layforce), and the second was a combined operation – although troops from the Middle East Commando formed the greater part of the land force.

The new Commando was composed of squadrons – although in the various war establishments both troops and companies are laid down. On paper the squadrons were further divided into six small troops, each of two sections. Major C.L. Campbell had five officers, Squadron Sergeant-Major Arthur Swinburn (later Captain Swinburn, DCM), eight sergeants and 105 other ranks under him. But squadron strengths varied, probably in accordance with operation requirements and availability of suitable men. At the time of the Commando's inception B Squadron under Major P.A. Seleri had a strength of four officers and only thirty-nine other ranks.

In December 1941 there was a war establishment for the Middle East Commando of an HQ, four British and three foreign squadrons. The 'foreigners' were mainly those Palestinian Jews and Arabs who on the disbandment of 51 (ME) Commando elected to serve in the new formation, but in addition there were some French and Polish soldiers. However, the nominal rolls indicate that these men never formed squadrons or companies of their own. At some period, not precisely known but quite soon after it was formed, this Middle East Commando became known as No. 1 Special Service Regiment.

In June 1942 Lt-Colonel J.M. Graham, who was then in command, sent two patrols and the Heavy Section in twelve 15-cwt trucks and five 3-tonners against Marua fort. Each patrol had a sabotage party in addition to its regular personnel. The party left Siwa on 4 June, and on the 9th arrived before the fort, which was found to be held by 200 Italians. The patrols were not strong enough to dislodge the Italians, and during the time they spent in the vicinity were frequently strafed from the air. They did, however, bring back useful information regarding tracks, and the condition and construction of the fort.

No doubt there were similar raids for which details no longer exist, but the two most famous Commando operations in the Middle East after the official disbandment of Layforce concern men who were originally in 11 Commando, and some forty specially selected from D Squadron, No. 1 Special Service Regiment. The first, a raid on Field-Marshal Rommel's headquarters, took place in November 1941, and the second in September 1942 was a combined operation against enemy-held Tobruk.

The story of the raid led by Lt-Colonel Geoffrey Keyes (who was accompanied by Colonel Laycock in the role of observer) is well known and need only be outlined here. For some time past Field-Marshal Rommel had been the charismatic leader of a military machine of smooth-flowing and implacable power. Someone in high authority conceived the idea that his demise would greatly lighten the British burden. He may have been right, but it did not require a full colonel and a lieutenant-colonel to prove him so. However, on the night of 10 November a party of six officers and fifty-three other ranks set sail from Alexandria in two submarines, *Torbay* and *Talisman*.

The landings off the coast of the Jebel Akhdar on the night of 13/14 November in a very rough sea were pretty disastrous, and Laycock and Keyes found themselves ashore with too few men to attack more than two of the original four objectives. Keyes and his raiders set off on an 18-mile hike over most difficult country with a climb of more than 1,800 ft. The weather was appalling, the men being both frozen and drenched. After three nights of toil in these vile conditions the party reached a cave some 5 miles from what was thought to be Rommel's headquarters at Beda Littoria. Here they paused to dry out, and for Keyes to make a brief reconnaissance. At 6 p.m. he gave out his orders for the attack, which was to take place at midnight on 17/18 November, and he detailed Lieutenant Cook and some of the men to attack an Italian headquarters near Cyrene and to blow up a communication pylon.

Keyes's men had another five hours of arduous marching in pouring rain along treacherous tracks, but by 11.30 p.m. he had them within a few yards of the house. In itself this approach march had been a magnificent feat of leadership. The wire surrounding the building was successfully cut, but two Italian sentries patrolling the perimeter, alerted by the barking of the inevitable village pye-dog, had to be bluffed into silence by Campbell's fluent German. Most of the sentries round the house itself had sought shelter from the rain; Keyes silently killed the only one that appeared, and then kicked open the front door. But here he encountered a stout-hearted German who grappled with him, and surprise was lost.

Thereafter the action was fast, furious and suicidal. Campbell shot the German, and the six men of the assault party stormed into the house. The second room they entered was found to contain about ten startled Germans into whom Keyes emptied his revolver and Campbell hurled a grenade, but in the ensuing uproar Keyes received a mortal wound. Shortly afterwards Campbell, while running to the rear of the house, forgot the password and was so badly wounded by men of the covering party that he had to be left.

Sergeant Terry then took charge of those who were still fit and, having destroyed the generator, which plunged the house in darkness, led them back to a wadi near the beach, where Laycock was awaiting them. Here they waited for the second party, and for the return of *Torbay*. But Cook's men, having successfully destroyed the pylon, had been captured; and the submarine signalled that it was too rough to come in that night. Before the next night the raiders had been discovered, and engaged first by Arabs and then by Italians. Laycock was therefore forced to order twenty-two remaining men to split up and make for the hills. Eventually, after forty-one days of incredible hardship, he and Terry alone reached British forces in the vicinity of Cyrene.

The mission, in which many deeds of heroism were performed, had failed. It had been carried out with considerable dash and a degree of skill, and Colonel Keyes undoubtedly deserved the posthumous Victoria Cross awarded to him. But it was wasteful. The lives of many valuable officers and men were put at risk, and lost, in an attempt to achieve something which, through wrong information, could not have succeeded, for the house at Beda Littoria never had been Rommel's headquarters.

The raid on Tobruk, like that on Rommel's headquarters, has been well told in great detail,* but as an important combined operation it requires some mention here. The land force was a mélange of special forces – LRDG, SAS, SIG – but the kernel came from D Squadron, No. 1 Special Service Regiment. These men were carefully hand-picked by Major Robin Campbell and Squadron Sergeant-Major Swinburn, who selected five officers and thirty-two other ranks. Y1 Patrol of the LRDG, under Captain Lloyd Owen, was detailed to guide the Commando men to Tobruk, and then to prevent enemy reinforcements from entering the eastern perimeter. They also had the task, depending upon the success of the main enterprise, of removing a vital piece of equipment from a radio direction finder before it was destroyed.†

* See Gordon Landsborough, *Tobruk Commando*.
†In the event this was not done, for all contact was lost with the main force after they had entered the perimeter.

The key to entering the Tobruk perimeter was to be provided by Captain Buck's Special Identification Group (SIG). This near-suicidal group of Palestinian Jews of German extraction performed deeds of great daring, usually – as in this case – disguised as Germans. They were to form the 'German' escort bringing 'prisoners' (the Commando men) into Tobruk. The land force was completed by a party from the SBS (shortly to be taken over by the SAS) under Lieutenant Langton, the medical officer (Captain Gibson), one or two specialist officers and Pilot Officer Scott, who had attached himself to the Commando. These troops (a total of 81) were designated Force B and the whole was under the command of Lt-Colonel John Haselden. Haselden, a cotton broker from El Minya, had been born and bred in Egypt. At the outbreak of war he immediately offered his services and, being a fluent Arabic speaker, well known to the desert tribes, he could and did pass himself off as an Arab in his many missions behind the enemy lines.*

The Tobruk raid (Operation Daffodil) was the most ambitious of the three planned for September 1942 (the others, against Benghazi and Barce, will be described later) and had a fairly considerable Royal Navy involvement. The plan was for Force B to enter the perimeter as prisoners of war, and to establish a bridgehead outside Tobruk harbour, allowing troops to be landed from MTBs (Force C) who were to link up with Force B. These troops were to hold the enemy on the south shore of the bay while destroyers landed marines (Force A) north of the harbour. Tobruk was to be held for twelve hours during which time demolition squads would destroy the large underground fuel storage tanks and wreck harbour installations, while the Navy dealt with enemy ships. The troops were then to be taken off by the Navy. As a diversion the town and areas outside the operational zone were to be subjected to a very heavy air bombardment.

Force C, under Captain Norman MacFie, comprised his company of Argyll and Sutherland Highlanders, a platoon of the 5th Fusiliers (with machine guns) and two sub-sections of 295 Field Company RE. They were to be conveyed from Alexandria in eighteen MTBs. Force A was made up from 22 officers and 360 men of the 11th Battalion Royal Marines, which had been formed as a Commando for the operation, under Lt-Colonel Unwin. In addition there was a sub-section of 296 Field Company RE, thirty

---

* Haselden had been on the shore to give the all clear signal for Keyes's men to land for the Rommel raid the previous November.

men and one officer from 261 HAA Battery and attached RAMC and Signals personnel. They were to sail from Haifa in two destroyers (HMS *Sikh* and *Zulu*) escorted by the cruiser HMS *Coventry*.

Force B assembled at Kufra, and here men of the SIG transformed the vehicles by painting out the British markings and substituting those of the Afrika Corps. Both Lloyd Owen and Haselden were extremely worried by the fact that all three raids seemed to be the talk of Cairo, but it was too late to do anything about it now. There is reason to believe that the enemy was expecting some form of seaborne attack on Tobruk, but the land raid came as a complete surprise. On 6 September, led by Y1 Patrol, the party started on their long run, and on the 10th arrived at a place, a day's drive from Tobruk, called on the map Hatiet Etla, but which was merely a scrub area that afforded fairly good cover.

At Hatiet Etla the party rehearsed often, and with meticulous care for detail, the exceptionally dangerous task of getting past the German perimeter guard as captured prisoners whose escort held the necessary documents. On the morning of 13 September, again led by the LRDG, they moved off on the last lap. Near the perimeter that evening the LRDG peeled off to deal with an inquisitive Italian patrol, and the Commando crammed into the three trucks that were to pass through the enemy lines. There were several very nasty moments when the convoy was stopped and scrutinized, or some unexpected obstacle across their path was encountered, but the ruse worked and with the coming of night the men of Force B debussed at Mersa umm Sciausc, the appointed place for the forming of the bridgehead, south-east of Tobruk town and along the southern shore.

The fierce fighting that took place, with fluctuating fortunes, that night and in the early hours of the morning was confused. On debussing the troops divided into two parties. Haselden with the SIG men, the RA detachment, and three sections under Lieutenants Taylor, Sillito and Macdonald were to take a small house and gun positions on the west side of the bay, while Campbell with the rest of the Squadron was to take positions on the east side. After success signals denoting completion of these tasks other positions had been allocated farther east which were to be taken and held until the MTB party was ashore.

Haselden's party met with early success, for the house was occupied by a number of Italians who were far too frightened to give any trouble, and willingly submitted to being made prisoner.

Furthermore they were full of information about the gun positions, but these were mostly found to be unoccupied despite the fact that the air raid had now started. At the next strongpoint – a concrete hut – a fight developed and Lieutenant Taylor was badly wounded. Thereafter the action was brisk and the Commando men set about routing the numerous Italians in charge of that sector. It was not long before the far shore of Sciausc Bay had been cleared and a bridgehead established outside the harbour. The first success signal was fired.

But Campbell's party was not so fortunate. To begin with he himself was suffering from a bad go of dysentery although he had insisted on fighting, and the party was delayed by a minefield immediately after debussing. They then met with opposition, and cleared a German Spandau post and put out of action a small wireless station. But owing to the initial delay they were not able to send up their success signal until 1.30 a.m., and Langton was late in reaching the position from which he was to signal in the MTBs. This task was to be undertaken by Pilot Officer Scott on the west promontory and Langton on the east. The MTBs were due in at 2 a.m.

From now on things began to go very wrong. The MTBs were off the shore at approximately the right time, and the heavy air raid distracted the attention of the shore defences; but there were navigation problems in getting into the bay, and only two MTBs landed their troops (and they were late) before the enemy realized something was afoot and lit up the whole bay with searchlights, thus making further landings almost impossible. In what soon became a disastrous operation Force A was the greatest sufferer. The two destroyers *Sikh* and *Zulu*, disguised as Italian ships, were 2 miles offshore at the appointed time (3 a.m.), and after considerable difficulty the first flight of Marines was dispatched. But the heavily-laden lighters proved quite unable to cope with the high sea: many broke up, drowning their occupants, and none was able to make the return journey.

Captain Micklethwait, unaware of this, brought *Sikh* closer in so as to shorten the return trip of the lighters, and came under heavy fire from the shore batteries. His ship received what proved to be a mortal blow, and many of the remaining Marines were burnt to death; *Zulu*, herself under constant fire, managed with great skill to get the crippled *Sikh* in tow and, as Operation Daffodil had clearly failed, both ships, covered by *Coventry*, made for the open sea and home.

Meanwhile on land Colonel Haselden also realized that the

game was up, but so long as the MTBs were trying – under heavy fire – to get in he knew the beachhead must be held, and not until almost daylight did the Commando start to shoot its way out. The captured guns were spiked, and the SIG men managed to destroy the telltale trucks and exchange their German uniforms for those taken from dead comrades. Inevitably men got split up, and in the desperate fighting that ensued there were casualties, chief among them Colonel Haselden, killed while leading a counter-attack. Langton and four others put to sea in an assault craft but were forced back by enemy fire. They then, by a combination of skill and good fortune, negotiated a minefield, got through the perimeter wire and made for the hills.

Out of the whole Force B, the men who had landed from Force C and the handful of Marines who had also got ashore, just ten managed to get clear of the perimeter and make the attempt to walk 300 miles through enemy-held territory to safety. They were in two parties led by two young officers from the Brigade of Guards; David Lanark (Scots Guards) had two men with him and Tommy Langton (Irish Guards) had six. Both parties were heading in the same direction, but unknown to each other. After two months of the same sort of appalling hardship and incredible adventure that Laycock and his men had experienced after the Rommel raid, Langton and three of his party reached the British lines on 13 November;* five days later Lanark, the sole survivor of three, was picked up by a British armoured car.

The opposition in Tobruk had proved much greater than expected, and Operation Daffodil was a very costly, although most gallant, failure. The Royal Navy lost three ships (*Coventry, Sikh* and *Zulu*) besides six of the small boats, nearly all of which were hit during the long, perilous run down the African coast from Sciausc Bay to Alexandria. Of the 382 men of the Royal Marines only 90 returned to base. By the time the last man of the land force had been plucked from the desert No. 1 Special Service Regiment had ceased to exist.

---

* One of these was Private Watler, who later served in S detachment of the Special Boat Squadron, where his charmed life continued. Captured on Cos and confined in the castle there, he escaped and was recaptured, escaped again and after swimming two miles down the coast was sheltered by friendly Greeks, and eventually rejoined his detachment.

The Special Boat Section, 1940–1945

The Commandos were the progenitor of many of the British special forces that came into being during and after 1940. They may not have directly engendered such bodies as the Special Air Service and the Long Range Desert Group, but the men who founded these, and other élite formations, had either been Commando officers, or got their inspiration from the Commando movement. And one at least – the Special Boat Section (SBS) – was originally hived off from its parent Commando.

The Commandos used boats of many shapes and sizes to put them ashore to perform their deadly business. The sea was important to them, but they did not need that special intimacy with wave and tide without which men of the SBS – and of certain other amphibious raiding and reconnaissance forces – could not succeed in the many hazardous enterprises they undertook. For them, striving to keep a tiny craft afloat, the moan of the wind and the fret of the unresting sea were frequent companions of lonely nights spent off hostile shores, or up treacherous chaungs, under the very noses of the enemy.

Roger Courtney was a big man in every sense of the word, and by nature an adventurer. Before the war he had been a white hunter in Africa, had canoed down the Nile from Lake Victoria and had seen service in the Palestine Police. It was therefore to be expected that he would be among the first to join the Commando ranks; moreover, as a young officer at the Combined Training Centre, he startled authority by suggesting the use of collapsible Folbots for the purpose of killing Germans and destroying shipping. In the face of official scepticism, even ridicule, he proved his point by boarding the previously alerted *Glengyle* at her anchorage in the Clyde, and after removing her after pompom cover left unobserved. He then brought the evidence (still wearing dripping-wet swimming trunks) to a high-level conference attended by the captain of that ship – who was not amused.

However, it had the desired effect. Admiral Keyes was sufficiently impressed, after a further test against a submarine depot ship, to give Courtney authority in July 1940 to form the first special boat section – initially known as the Folbot Troop. Courtney selected twelve men, and with ten canoes started intensive training off the Isle of Arran. His ideas, which later became accepted and were developed under the auspices of CCO, were for small parties to operate in Folbots of all kinds from submarines in order to carry out inshore reconnaissance and sabotage. Reconnaissance parties could supply useful data (of a kind not always available from air photographs) regarding the nature of enemy strongpoints, and defensive systems above and below water in the locality of beaches. Sabotage parties were to disrupt communications inland, destroy dumps and attack enemy shipping with limpet mines. SBS units could also be used for the landing and recovery of agents.

The Folbot Troop was attached to No. 8 Commando, which found most of its original personnel. Throughout the lifetime of the Special Boat Section (a name which it acquired on arrival in Egypt) the personnel were nearly all military, for their principal work required a high degree of training in and understanding of land warfare. The first operation carried out by Courtney, in November 1940, was to be against targets on the Dutch coast. The party was taken close to its destination in MTBs, but the weather prevented the launching of Folbots. This abortive raid did at least teach Courtney that for future raids submarines were to be preferred as carriers. In February 1941 the Section sailed with No. 8 Commando for the Middle East, where the Mediterranean was to prove a more productive hunting ground.

On arrival the men carried out a period of training at Kabrit on the Great Bitter Lake, and were then attached to the 1st Submarine Flotilla in HMS *Medway* at Alexandria. Between March and August many operations were undertaken, most of which were a great success. The first of these, at the end of March, closely involved Lt-Commander Nigel Clogstoun-Willmott (of whom much will be heard in Chapter 8). General Wavell had planned the capture of Rhodes, and vital information regarding inshore defences and the beaches – the presence of sandbanks and shallows, density of sand and so on – was necessary before landing craft and troops could be committed. Clogstoun-Willmott had spent many hours secretly surveying the beaches from a submarine, and was convinced a much closer inspection was necessary. At GHQ he was put in touch with Courtney and his newly-arrived Special Boat Section.

Here were two strangely contrasting characters: Courtney was bluff, brave and inclined to impetuosity, while Clogstoun-Willmott was a man of wisdom as well as valour, more painstaking and attentive to detail. But both men thrived on the adrenalin of risks. At the end of two months' strenuous training they were ready to commence operating from HM Submarine *Triumph*, and in the course of three successive nights they closely reconnoitred three beaches – one of them in front of the main hotel. Mostly it was Clogstoun-Willmott who swam ashore while Courtney had the lonely task of waiting in the canoe and hoping not to meet with enemy surface craft; but on their last night Courtney went ashore to experience the tense moments of slipping past sentries undetected, or playing possum when torch or searchlight lit up beach or road.

In the course of their lengthy reconnaissance both inshore and through the submarine's periscope, Courtney and Clogstoun-Willmott were able to make useful sketches of enemy batteries; report on beaches; test the wire defences; and, most importantly, stress the Italians' total unpreparedness for attack, because throughout their time on the island both men had found a complete lack of vigilance. But sadly the information they imparted was never to be used, for the invasion of Rhodes had to be cancelled when ships and landing craft became needed for the evacuation of Greece.

However, the efforts of these two intrepid men were not wasted. Swimming and other equipment had been tested and improvements found to be clearly necessary, and the return from beach to canoe and canoe to submarine had been hazardously but on the whole satisfactorily accomplished. This part of the operation, known as 'homing', was always to be the most dangerous; it depended upon good navigation and a detailed and strictly governed timetable aided by a transmitter gadget known as 'RG'.* Courtney could be well pleased that the operation had proved the feasibility of the type of work he had advocated for the SBS, and in Clogstoun-Willmott's fertile mind there was conceived the

---

* An Aldis-type lamp which sent a beam of infra-red light visible only when a special receiver was used.

need for assault pilotage and intensive beach reconnaissance – the germ that was shortly to produce the Combined Operations Pilotage Parties (COPPs).

Before Major Courtney was ordered back to England at the end of 1941 to form a second Section, his folbotiers – trained to work from ship, submarine and aircraft – had carried out a number of raids from Alexandria and Malta. The group based on Malta was mainly occupied in train wrecking in Italy and Sicily, while the Alexandria group operated against targets on the Libyan and Cyrenaican coasts. The first SBS demolition raid was made at the end of June 1941, when Lieutenant Wilson and his canoe partner, Marine Hughes (with whom, until the end of that year, he carried out many successful operations), sailed from Malta in the submarine HMS *Urge* to the coast of Sicily.

The submarine surfaced 4 miles off the coast to enable the men to assemble their canoe and load it with explosives, then she crept in to some 2,000 yards from the shore and the canoeists slipped their boat into the water. The target was a railway tunnel on the line between Taormina and Catania. When the explosives had been firmly packed on the single track inside the tunnel, and the pressure switch connected, the two men made their way back undetected to their carefully-concealed canoe. Not long after they had regained the submarine they were able to see a train enter the tunnel and to hear the explosion, which blew up the train and put the line out of action for several days.

An unusual, but particularly valuable, operation was conducted by Corporal Bremner of the London Scottish, who between the loss of Crete and the following December contacted and helped to evacuate 125 British, Australian, New Zealand and Greek soldiers who had not surrendered. Landing from a submarine (there were three used in all) and with the help of Cretans he organized a grass line* from submarine to shore by which the men hauled themselves aboard. Other operations during this period included the sinking of a ship in Benghazi harbour; on the way back the Folbot sank and the two men were subsequently captured. There were also landings of agents on the Greek mainland and islands, and preliminary reconnaissances for larger raids by Commandos, such as the one on Rommel's headquarters.

When Courtney got home to form No. 2 SBS he found he had

* So called because it looked and floated like native grass rope. At this time it was made of coir (coconut fibre) and had only a quarter the strength of a hemp rope of similar size. Later, nylon was used.

to hand some ready-made material in the shape of 101 Troop under Captain G.C.S Montanaro. This troop, hived off from No. 6 Commando, had been formed in Scotland in April 1941, and in September of that year it moved to Dover. During November 1941 members of the troop made two beach reconnaissances off the French coast. The first, under Lieutenant Smith and Corporal Woodhouse, was unsuccessful. The canoe was swamped and both canoeists were later captured. But shortly afterwards, on the night of 22/23 November, two Folbots from the troop were safely launched off the coast near Houlgate, and their occupants brought back valuable information required for a Commando raid on a coastal gun battery planned for the following night.

By February 1942 COHQ had become intensely interested in Special Boat Sections, and within little more than a year Courtney was to find himself the father of a substantial force whose tentacles reached into almost every theatre of war. The SBS war establishment – like most *ad hoc* formations – underwent changes as Courtney's empire expanded. An initial one was laid down in April 1942 of one major (commanding), five captains (one for HQ Section and one for each of four operational groups), one administrative officer, four subalterns, and four subaltern instructors, making a total of fifteen officers. One CSM, one CQMS, eleven sergeants, eight corporals, two clerks, two storemen and seven drivers brought the total of the Section to forty-seven all ranks. The Section's armament comprised pistols, tommy guns and rifles; later in the year thirty-six of the Folbot-type canoe known as Cockle Mk I were issued. In 1943 the establishment was revised and each SBS was to consist of a headquarters (a Lieutenant-Colonel, two majors, three captains and four subalterns) and ten groups. Each group was to be self–contained and capable of providing eight canoe teams each of two men, or two dory teams each of eight men. There was no difficulty in providing volunteers from special service units but qualified instructors were another matter, and initially it became necessary to bring back men from the Middle East for that purpose.

Major Courtney, with Captain Montanaro* as his second-in-command, formed 2 SBS on 1 March 1942 from headquarters at Ardrossan, and intensive training was to take place on the Clyde and the west coast of Scotland. Before joining the SBS all ranks would have completed their basic training with their units. There

---

* Captain Montanaro, a Sapper by profession, was shortly transferred for work of a secret nature, and was granted the rank of Commander RN.

then followed a seventeen-week course along Achnacarry lines, but omitting much of the battle side, which had little bearing on their future tasks. This course specialized in Folbot-submarine management, navigation, map reading, weapon training, field-craft, signal training and report writing. And after that there was parachute training. No wonder it was recognized by those in charge that a Special Boat Section man was himself a very special person whose life was not to be unnecessarily hazarded.

Before he left No. 2 SBS Montanaro, together with Trooper Preece of the Royal Armoured Corps, carried out an extremely successful and daring operation against enemy shipping in Boulogne harbour. The target was a large German tanker (later learnt to contain 5,000 tons of copper ore), and the canoeists were taken from Dover, in a Royal Navy MTB, and launched their canoe about a mile from the harbour. After paddling through the harbour defences, the intrepid pair attached limpets to the enemy ship which subsequently sunk her. On the return journey they just managed to reach the MTB before their waterlogged canoe disappeared beneath the waves. For this exploit Montanaro was awarded the DSO, and Preece the DCM.

When Roger Courtney quitted the Mediterranean in December 1941 he left behind fifteen officers and forty-five other ranks of No. 1 SBS under Major Kealy, who continued to operate in that theatre until the autumn of 1942. But on Courtney's departure No. 1 SBS lost its independence and was attached to David Stirling's SAS; it was absorbed into that unit in November 1942.

Meanwhile, the training of No. 2 SBS in Britain was in preparation – although at the time they did not know it – for Operation Torch, the landings in North Africa, in which they played an important part both before and during the operation. Two out of the many other exploits of the contingent based on Gibraltar emphasize the varied and hazardous existence led by these men who went to war in small boats.

In the hope of persuading the general commanding the French forces in the Algiers district to co-operate in the landings it was decided to put Major-General Mark Clark ashore in great secrecy on a beach west of Algiers. The General, with a number of other American officers, sailed from Gibraltar on 20 October 1942 in HM Submarine *Seraph*. The submarine was skilfully navigated to surface within a half a mile of a lonely pre-selected rendezvous, where the Americans were put in the charge of the small SBS party under Captain G.B. Courtney – Roger's brother Godfrey, known as 'Gruff' – who landed them safely in their canoes.

The meeting with the French duly took place and was carried over to the following night, which necessitated the visitors spending some anxious moments while the French police paid their house a call. Nor was the return journey as smooth a passage as the outward one had been. Launching the canoes was a perilous performance in the turbulent surf, and by the time the party eventually reached the waiting submarine everyone had had a ducking, but personnel and equipment were all intact. The next morning a Catalina flying boat was able to make a perfect landing, and the American generals were ferried to her by the canoeists.

On 25 October, only a few days after her return to Gibraltar, *Seraph* was needed for another similar venture. Two of the SBS party – Lieutenants Livingstone and Foot – who had been with General Clark were now to assist in bringing General Giraud out of France. The General had escaped from a German POW camp and, with his family, was now anxiously watching events from Lyons, in the heart of Vichy France. The Allies needed him, for he was a good general and politically acceptable to most of the French in Algiers; and he was prepared to escape on certain conditions, one of which was that the rescuing submarine should be American. This was not practicable, and so a little chicanery was practised in that *Seraph* sailed nominally under the command of an American naval officer.

After some worrying hours, caused by rough seas and the unwelcome presence of an enemy E-boat, the rendezvous with the fishing boat bringing the General, his son and some of his staff was made on the night of 5 November. *Seraph* then set course for Gibraltar on a line to be overflown at night by a Catalina. But her transmitter broke down, and with surfaced submarines being bombed on sight it was only by good fortune that on the morning of 7 November the aircraft found her and was able to land close by. The General and his party were then transferred – not without difficulty, for Giraud was a tall man who either could not or would not sit properly in the tiny Folbot, which was nearly swamped – and were eventually joined in Algiers by seven more of his staff, who had been retrieved off the French coast by *Seraph*'s sister ship *Sibyl*.

The main assault at Oran was made by the United States 'Center Task Force' supported by the Royal Navy in the Bay of Atzeu. Men from No. 2 SBS (and some COPP personnel – see Chapter 8) were to act as markers to guide the assault craft on to the beach. In September these men had arrived at Gibraltar for intensive training for the operation, and on 1 November Sub-

Lieutenant Peter Harris RNVR (COPPs) and Sergeant S. Weatherall (SBS) sailed in HM Submarine *Ursula* to carry out periscope reconnaissance by day and panorama sketches by night.

On Saturday 7 November the submarine surfaced 6 miles from the appointed place on Z beach and they launched one of the two canoes that had been brought in *Ursula*. The combination of a very choppy sea and the pestering presence of many dolphins caused the canoe to ship a lot of water, and personal kit had to be jettisoned to save swamping, but they reached Z beach at 9.15 p.m. and dropped the kedges, which anchored them some 200 yards from the beach edge. Here they sat, wet and cold, until 12.15 a.m. when they commenced flashing with their RG gear, and the United States Rangers' first landing craft beached exactly an hour later. They continued to guide in the second and third waves, and by 4.15 a.m. their job was done.

However, Sergeant Weatherall was kept busy for the next three days rounding up French crews and pressing them into unloading stores from various ships. He then boarded HMS *Ettrick*, where he met other members of 2 SBS who had been operating, under Captain Colin Pagnum, in Oran harbour with explosives and 2 ft torpedoes launched from canoes. Their Sergeant-Major had been killed, and some others taken prisoner but soon released. The *Ettrick* arrived back at Gibraltar on 14 November.

From the latter part of 1942 until early in 1944 No. 2 SBS was based at Hillhead near Lee on Solent, conveniently close to the submarine base at Gosport and MTB base at Newhaven. During this period there was much journeying between the United Kingdom and the Mediterranean, and operations were carried out in both theatres. However, Courtney became increasingly convinced that European waters were not suitable. The weather was usually unpredictable; Norway was too light in the summer and the sea too rough in the winter; the French cliffs were often unassailable; and likely targets in the Low Countries were heavily guarded and the beaches mined.

Therefore, from 1942 onwards the Special Boat Section's broadening tale of glory is mostly told through their work in the Mediterranean, Indian Ocean islands and the Burma coast. Their principal activities were now to be sabotage, guerrilla work, and reconnaissance on land and above high-water mark, for by this time COPPs had become operational and better able to take care of beach reconnaissance, while the newly formed Royal Marine Boom Patrol Detachment could deal with ship sabotage and harbour work. SBS operations were successfully carried out by various lettered detachments from bases as widely separated as Gibraltar, Malta, Alexandria, Colombo and Chittagong.

In March 1943 Z Special Boat Section, which was a sub-division of No. 2 SBS, left Hillhead for Algiers, where it was attached to the 8th Submarine Flotilla in HMS *Maidstone*. Z SBS was commanded by Godfrey Courtney – now a major – and there were five canoe pairs. Among their duties was the landing and taking off of agents on enemy coasts, and sabotage work independently and in conjunction with Nos. 1 and 2 SAS. In early September of that year, owing to the heavy casualties suffered by COPPs during the Sicily landings, Z SBS carried out beach reconnaissance, and provided guiding beacons for the American 5th Army's landing at Salerno. Again, in November and December, a few men – for most of Z SBS had by this time returned to England to prepare for a move to the Far East – helped COPPists reconnoitre beaches for the Anzio landings.

A typical piece of SBS sabotage in Italy was carried out on 30 November 1942 by Captain R.P. Livingstone and Sergeant S. Weatherall from a submarine. The object was to block the coastal railway at Leigneglia by derailing a train in the tunnel, and to obtain information about local conditions for future operations. The two men left the submarine some 600 yards from the shore and made land on the western outskirts of the town, concealing their boat in the garden of a villa.

A short but exciting march brought them across a main road to the railway line, where a sentry was spotted on top of the tunnel. There was insufficient time to stalk and kill him, for activity in the neighbourhood of the line demanded caution and the rendezvous with the submarine must be kept strictly on time. But eventually charges under the rail and on the steel posts carrying the electric cables were put down, connected in a ring circuit to be detonated by a pressure switch placed under the rail on the outside curve of the track, with some delayed charges. The party then withdrew, but owing to the presence of many obstacles were forced on to the main road. Escaping the notice of an Italian soldier and several civilians, they recovered their boat and rejoined the submarine exactly three hours after they had left her. About midnight they had the satisfaction of watching the first of their explosions wreck a train, and later the delayed charges completely blocked the line.

Another successful Mediterranean operation was a raid on airstrips in Crete. On the night of 6/7 June three parties landed near Cape Trikala to destroy aircraft at Kastelli, Timbaki and Maleme. Lieutenant Sutherland and Corporal Riley found

Timbaki airstrip empty of machines, and Major Kealy with Captain Allott and Sergeant Feeberry found Maleme too heavily guarded to warrant an attack, but Captain Duncan, CSM Barnes and Corporal Barr, together with two Greek guides, had excellent results at the Kastelli field.

Marching by night and lying up by day, these three men were ready for action by 8.30 p.m. on 9 June. Slipping past two dozy German sentries they reached the north-east dispersal area, and after placing a number of bombs on parked aircraft they made a safe getaway to a hideout, despite feverish patrol activity when the first of their bombs went off. The Germans admitted to 70 casualties, and the loss of 7 aircraft, 210 drums of petrol, 6 transports destroyed and 3 bomb dumps. Captain Duncan and his two other ranks (who over a period of time totalled five weeks on Crete) reached the beach three days later. But those in charge of Kastelli airfield were not so fortunate, for the Germans shot the guards and seventeen Greek night watchmen.

At the end of 1943 several members of the SBS were trained as parachutists at Ringway, and about a dozen were sent to HMS *Bonaventure* at Gairloch to be trained in the use of the Welman,* but in 1944 and 1945 the principal SBS operations were carried out in the Far East by A, B, and C Groups. These Groups tended to vary slightly in strength, but the war establishment was for a major commanding, a captain, two subalterns, four sergeants and eleven corporals – of the latter two were storemen and one a clerk, but all were operational.

Z SBS, which had carried out eighteen mostly successful operations in the Mediterranean, preceded the above three Groups to the Far East, arriving in Ceylon at the beginning of 1944 to work under Force 136 of the Special Operations Executive (SOE). They had scarcely arrived before a part of the Section was hastily returned to the Middle East to carry out strategic deception off the Greek coast, and they did not return to Ceylon until June. The work done by Z SBS with Force 136 consisted in the main of ferrying agents and stores into Malaya from submarines. During 1944 the Section was split, and some men were to see service in Australia and Borneo with the Services Reconnaissance Department, which was the Australian counterpart of SOE.

In the spring of 1944, as an adumbration of what was to come, men of the Special Boat Section both in England and the Far East

---

* A one-man submarine designed at Welwyn (hence the name) for attaching limpet mines from the craft's nose to enemy ships.

were invited to transfer to the Royal Marines, for it had been decided earlier at Combined Operations Headquarters that it would be sensible to amalgamate all small boat parties into one unit. Needless to say the proposal did not meet with enthusiasm from the men, who although seconded, were intensely loyal to their parent regiments, and for the time the matter was dropped and SBS Groups continued their activities, mainly in the Far East. But it was only a couple of months later, when decisions for the future were being taken, that Roger Courtney left the unit he had founded on being posted to the British Military Administration in what had been Italian Somaliland.

When A and B Groups, under Majors Kealy and Sidders respectively, arrived in Bombay in May 1944 (C Group under Major Livingstone reached the Far East a little later) they were faced with the all too familiar reception from a staff which had not been properly briefed as to their function. They were shuttled around for a short while before finally coming to rest in Ceylon. In the months that lay ahead there were to be many bases, some hard training and numerous exploits.

In September A Group were back in India at Rawalpindi for parachute training, and in early October they moved to Chittagong for operations on the Arakan front. Meanwhile, in the same month, B and C Groups were detailed to destroy road and rail bridges over rivers on the north coast of Sumatra, before going to Burma at the end of the year, where B carried out operations on the Chindwin, and C relieved A at Teknaf on the Arakan coast. It was during operations on the large Burmese rivers (Chindwin and Irrawady) in early 1945 that the motorized Mk VI rigid canoe catamarans replaced the hitherto universally-used Mk I** paddled craft.

Before describing operations typical of the important and hazardous work that SBS was called upon to do on the Burmese coast, a short digression is necessary to mention the Small Operations Group (SOG) and two formations that were a part of SOG, and which worked in close liaison with SBS Groups. SOG was formed on 12 June 1944 under Colonel H.T. (later Major-General Sir Humphry) Tollemache, RM, who had Lt-Colonel H.G. Hasler (also of the Royal Marines, and whose exploits are described in Chapter 15) as his second-in-command. Its purpose was to co-ordinate raids by a number of special service units, mainly in support of General Christison's XVth Corps' sternly-contested advance in the Arakan. Besides the SBS Groups, SOG consisted of COPP parties, Royal Marine Commando assault troops – known as Detachment 385 – and four Sea Reconnaissance Units (SRU).

Detachment 385, which consisted of a headquarters and three troops, each of six officers and twenty-five men, divided into three sections, was formed at about the same time as SOG came into existence, and became operational early in 1945. Their role was largely in deception raids, and the landing and bringing off of agents and stores; they operated from a specially-designed 20-ft surfboat with a 5 hp engine, or on occasions were launched from Catalina flying boats, making land in canoes or inflatables. From their formation to the end of hostilities in the Far East they carried out some fifteen independent operations, most of which were successful, although early on they lost two troop commanders and four Marines when attempting to create a diversion on Bilugyun Island in Burma.

The idea of the SRU originated with Lt-Commander Bruce Wright, RCNVR, and in June 1943 a unit of eight officers and thirty-two other ranks (to operate in four sections) from all three services was sent to California to train in the use of such exotic equipment as paddleboards, swim fins, sea masks, and 9 mm Welguns. They also trained as parachutists, and in the use of a new type of limpet and other underwater demolitions. Training was a matter of many months before these forty men had become familiar with their various impedimenta and their bodies had become immune to climate, hardship and fatigue through swimming many miles on paddleboards and landing through high surf.

The SRU became operational in Burma in February 1945 and proved of great value in carrying out beach reconnaissance for amphibious operations, and acting as markers and guides for assault boats in the crossing of large rivers. Their four sections were soon operating along the Irrawaddy from above Mandalay to Pagan and at Ramree Island off the Arakan coast. They also worked closely with COPPs in clearing underwater barriers placed in the many chaungs. In all of their many dangerous and difficult tasks the four sections suffered no casualties.

The work of the above two specialized forces was complementary to that performed by the SBS, and in the case of the SRU fulfilled a need which the SBS was not equipped to carry out. Four operations in outline are sufficient to illustrate the constant harassment that a tiny handful of SBS men were capable of inflicting on the Japanese, and which besides gaining useful information kept the enemy constantly looking over their shoulder, and helped to impress upon them that they were not the only masters of offensive warfare.

On the night of 15/16 November 1944, two canoe parties from B Group (No. 1 canoe with Major Sidders and Sergeant Williams, and No. 2 with Lieutenant Wesley and Corporal Hickman) were required to attack an enemy motor boat that had been working the lower reaches of the River Chindwin south of a small place called Paluzawa. One Folbot had a Bren gun mounted in the bows and held in position by two lengths of bamboo secured to cleats, but Major Sidders' and Sergeant Williams' craft was armed only with tommy guns and grenades.

The night was dark with visibility down to a few yards, and at 9.15 p.m. the two canoes anchored in midstream within hearing distance of both banks. They had not been in position five minutes before the Japanese motor boat approached from the west bank of the river. The canoe parties waited until the enemy boat was within 30 yards, and then opened up with all weapons. The Japanese were taken entirely by surprise and made for the east bank, but when their craft was headed off by No. 2 canoe they turned about for the west bank only to be headed off by No.1. Soon the boat was out of control and going round in circles. After two or three abortive attempts to get alongside and capture the motor boat – which was doing some 5 knots – it was eventually boarded; the canoes were then secured and the party returned upstream through their own lines.

The enemy boat was 15 to 20 ft long, and for this trip was carrying an officer and eight men with a quantity of rice, presumably for troops on the east bank. Eight of the Japanese had been killed and the ninth was brought back wounded for later interrogation. The patrol suffered no casualties. In isolation an operation such as this would appear to have little value, but as one of many it induced Japanese jitters, which put them at some disadvantage before the XIVth Army's major offensive.

Only a few nights after this a party of two officers and five other ranks from A Group, under Captain Barnes, carried out a perilous reconnaissance from the sea on enemy positions around Donbaik, which is situated on the west coast of the Mayu peninsula. The Group was at the time based on Teknaf, and the party were conveyed by ML 437 to a beach immediately south of Donbaik. Here they slipped their canoes in very high surf, with the result that all three canoes overturned and the party had to swim ashore partly dragging and partly carried by their canoes – one man lost his tommy gun but dived for it and with incredible luck found it.

Having got ashore and concealed their canoes the reconnaissance, which had started so inauspiciously, was carried out with great success. A Japanese bunker manned by at least two men and armed with an anti-tank gun was approached to within 20 yards, and information on terrain and other enemy positions was gathered before the party regained their canoes without being spotted, and made a hazardous journey through the surf to the safety of the motor launch.

Three days later, on 25 November, the other half of A Group embarked in an LCP from Teknaf to carry out an even more successful reconnaissance. The party consisted of Major Holden-White (who now commanded the Group), Lieutenant Rodney, five other ranks and Captain Knight of the Burma Intelligence Corps. Their task was to discover whether the enemy were occupying an area round Alethangyaw, and if so to obtain unit identification. The party slipped their canoes at the southern entrance to the Naf River, about 8 miles behind the Japanese forward elements in the plain. The interesting part of this raid is the use the Group made of the two V Forces.

V Force has already been described in Chapter 4; its opposite number, the Japanese V Force, was a picaresque collection of Burmese double agents theoretically working under the enemy, but reckoning that by now it was best to back the British so that they were perfectly prepared to double-cross the Japs by supplying useful information. Information thus received had to be acted upon with caution, for a double-double-cross could not be ruled out. Nevertheless members of the British V Force usually knew villages where these Japanese agents were reliable.

And so it proved on this particular patrol. Five Japanese V Force agents were used whose reliability had been vouched for by the patrol's British V Force guide, Bhadur Mia. Two of these agents had knowledge of the area and were able to give the patrol the names of the local enemy commanders, the position of a large supply dump and the strength of and routes taken by Japanese patrols working in that vicinity. Two others were sent into Alethangyaw to discover whether the town was still occupied. They reported it to be free of Japanese. But with the incoming tide the chaungs would soon become dangerous torrents, and there was thought to be insufficient time for the party to ambush an enemy patrol. However, they got safely back with much valuable information concerning the position and identification of Japanese troops facing the 7th Indian Division.

Not long after C Group had arrived at Teknaf (20 December) to take over from A, they obtained, through the enterprising employment of a local Burmese, detailed information of a kind that neither a normal patrol nor air reconnaissance could possibly supply. The Group, commanded by Major Livingstone, left their base at Teknaf in MLs and launched their canoes in Combermere Bay a couple of miles from the tiny Laws Island, which lies a mile to the north of Kyaukpyu, capital of Ramree Island. Having established the fact that the island was free of enemy the Group split up, and Sergeant Weatherall was left in charge of those men remaining on Laws. When a Burmese family landed from a dugout canoe the Group's interpreter proved unnecessary, for the head of the family could speak good English, and explained that he had become fed up with working for the Japanese on Ramree, and had decided to escape to his home on Laws Island.

Sergeant Weatherall saw at once that, if willing, the man could go with impunity to places from which no British soldier could hope to return alive. After considerable persuasion the Burmese agreed to paddle back to Ramree armed with a large-scale map on which to pinpoint the Japanese gun emplacements and fortifications on the west side of this important island. There was, of course, a risk of betrayal, but the prize at stake justified the taking of it. Meanwhile, an ML had been called up and when the new recruit had returned he was sent (again only after considerable persuasion) to Akyab, and from there flown to Chittagong to give Intelligence the intimate details that his carefully marked map could not disclose. As part of his reward this diligent Burmese was permitted to sail in the battleship *Queen Elizabeth* to witness the bombardment of the positions he had located, and the subsequent capture of the Japanese commander.

Thus the pattern continued in the Mediterranean and the Indian Ocean until the two great enemies, Germany and Japan, had been humbled. Men with nerves of steel, seemingly unaffected by imminent peril and prolonged strain, carried out numerous sorties (more than eighty on the west coast of Burma alone) over choppy waters and up treacherous chaungs, gliding silently through the night to bring back vital information or destroy some key installation.

Men of the Special Boat Section did not ask to be recognized; they declared themselves by their deeds, and when they were disbanded at the end of the war they knew how much they had contributed to victory.

For Roger Courtney, who sadly died young in 1949, there was the added satisfaction that the SBS was one of the three special forces to be retained, or reconstituted, in the post-war years. It is true that the present Special Boat Squadron is directly descended not from its predecessor but from the Royal Marine Boom Patrol Detachment (see Chapter 15); nevertheless, the whole conception of swift and silent sabotage on enemy shipping and lines of communication from small boats, and much of the work that went into developing this kind of warfare, belongs to Courtney.

8

Combined Operations Pilotage Parties

After his exploits off Rhodes with Roger Courtney, Lt-Commander Clogstoun-Willmott spent a very active year in the Middle East, working partly in Cairo and Alexandria, partly from the CTC at Kabrit, and also with an RAF intelligence unit attached to the Long Range Desert Group. During this time the urgent need to train men for assault pilotage and beach information was never far from his mind. In the spring of 1942 he was recalled to the United Kingdom for work in connection with navigational equipment – he had specialized as a navigator – but soon found himself organizing a Beach Pilotage School for junior RNVR officers at the CTC in the West Kyle of Bute under Admiral Hughes-Hallett. Then quite suddenly in September he was summoned to collect, train, organize and equip a team of navigators and others for reconnaissance and pilotage work prior to Operation Torch, the landing in North Africa.

Operation Torch was planned to take place in November, which left Clogstoun-Willmott remarkable little time to fit his team for Party Inhuman, as the preliminary reconnaissance was code named. Clogstoun-Willmott, it has been already said, was a man of wisdom and of valour, but he was more than that: he was a man of great determination and a strict disciplinarian who would constantly drive his subordinates to achieve the high standard of perfection he demanded and obtained of himself. At times these subordinates would think he drove too hard but they would never forsake him, for he was one of those people who possessed the capacity to inspire absolute trust.

What had always been clear to Clogstoun-Willmott, now – at almost too late an hour – also became clear to those responsible for conducting Torch. To achieve success with an invasion of this magnitude, requiring landings at many places, night markers in canoes as well as careful beach reconnaissance were essential to success. Clogstoun-Willmott therefore met with few obstructions on this occasion in obtaining his fairly exacting demands for submarines, men and equipment.

Nevertheless, it was a very worrying time and there was a tremendous rush to obtain approval for no fewer than five submarines, and to assemble at Fort Blockhouse, Portsmouth, some twenty-four officers and a similar number of ratings and other ranks – of whom five officers and five corporals together with ten canoes had been lent to Clogstoun-Willmott by Roger Courtney from the SBS. Among the naval personnel who joined Party Inhuman at Portsmouth were three specialist navigators – Lt-Commander Teacher, and Lieutenants McHarg and Amer – and three young officers, Geoffrey Lyne, George Sinclair and Nick Hastings, who were to form the permanent nucleus of Clogstoun-Willmott's later organization.

The time for training, both at Fort Blockhouse and Gibraltar, was far too short, but Clogstoun-Willmott made what use he could of it and drove his team relentlessly. Every night they would be at sea perfecting their night drills and every day was spent in weapon training, rock climbing and swimming. A day or two before the recces were to be made someone at the Admiralty lost his nerve and the order went out that on account of security no landings were to be made, and only submarine and canoe offshore reconnaissance of the beaches was allowed. This was to have serious consequences, for although one beach was eliminated as unsuitable, troops were to be landed on other beaches where, due to the limited reconnaissance allowed, it had not been possible to spot the adverse conditions.

For the actual landings Clogstoun-Willmott's navigators would lead the markers to where their canoes would be positioned close offshore, and from where at zero hour they would flash their torches and infra-red beacons, while the submarines stationed themselves some 8 miles out, and around their beacons the invasion fleet would assemble. The navigators would be tranferred to the assault landing craft and lead the troops towards the markers' lights, behind which lay the landing beaches.

In theory it seemed quite simple; in practice it was very different, for the weather worsened as the fleet drew nearer making it almost impossible for some of the canoe teams to keep their proper station, and Lyne and his paddler were blown adrift on reconnaissance, swamped and temporarily imprisoned. Also, last-minute changes in the landing plans were made which threw out the whole schedule. At Algiers there was absolute chaos in the early hours of 8 November. The surf was so high at some of the beaches that many landing craft and some soldiers were lost; some beaches were found to be suitable only for tracked vehicles, and were soon a shambles of sand-bogged trucks and jeeps; and one important beach 2,000 yards long was found to be usable only for a tenth of that distance. At Oran everything went much better, although at one beach there was considerable confusion when a number of landing craft hit a submerged sandbar.

Despite these calamities the troops eventually got ashore, though many in the wrong places. However, Operation Torch narrowly avoided disaster through the complete lack of proper beach reconnaissance, and the short time available in which to train the pilots for their dangerous and exacting duties. All Clogstoun-Willmott's arguments had been vindicated, and it was now realized that for future landings of any sizeable formation it was vital to have accurate information on the condition of the beaches, and to have it at the planning stage. No one realized this more than Lord Louis Mountbatten, and the CCO was to be a tower of strength to Clogstoun-Willmott in the raising of his Beach Reconnaissance and Assault Pilotage Parties – which descriptive name was for reasons of brevity and security to become Combined Operations Pilotage Parties.

Clogstoun-Willmott had no sooner been given authority to raise, train, equip and command a new unit for beach reconnaissance and pilotage than Force Commanders were clamouring for fifty teams. He at once realized that this would sacrifice quality for quantity, and felt that ten would be the limit; and this number was eventually achieved.

As a result of many conferences the following basic team was eventually agreed upon in December 1942: a lieutenant-commander or lieutenant (navigator or hydrographic specialist) RN or RNR to be officer in charge, a Royal Engineer major or captain to be the military recce officer; two lieutenants RNVR (one to be assistant to officer commanding, the other to be maintenance officer); four seamen ratings AB and above (three paddlers and one maintenance officer's assistant); one electrical mechanic; one Commando corporal to be paddler and guard to the RE officer; and, late in 1943, one RE draughtsman. Later a further midshipman or sublieutenant RNVR came on the establishment as assistant to the maintenance officer. The military personnel were to be found from the SBS, something which did not at first appeal to Brigadier Laycock – then commanding the Special Service Brigade – for SBS teams were also much in demand. However, Clogstoun-Willmott managed to persuade the War Office to add to the SBS establishment enough 'establishment slots' to cover the COPP commitment, and these men he had put onto the SBS roll though they were often trained by COPP and Commando Depot. Thus everyone was satisfied. COPP personnel, when in service dress, wore their respective (RN or SBS) Commando flashes.

Almost Clogstoun-Willmott's first task was to find a base from where he could build up and train his teams. One of his officers recommended the small Hayling Island Sailing Club, situated on a sandspit called Sandy Point. The place was ideal in many respects, such as security and training facilities, but had to be enlarged. Here Clogstoun-Willmott got down to fighting the inevitable administrative battle, which was not made easier by the fact that he was unable to breach security by describing his work – and therefore the urgency for equipment – at the lower levels of supply. Furthermore, a great deal of the equipment required was of a highly specialized, indeed unheard of, type: luminous compasses, underwater writing tablets, watches and torches, RG infra-red homing gear, augers for beach samples at every stratum, beach gradient reels, special swimsuits and indeed waterproof kit of almost every kind. Neither was there, at this time, an adequate type of canoe for the work, and it was not until May 1943 that the COPP teams received the Mk I** type canoe specially designed for them, and which were to remain in use for thirty years after the war.

In the early days makeshift equipment – such as the cumbersome rubber swimsuits known as 'charioteers' – and what canoes could be obtained had to suffice but Clogstoun-Willmott, very ably supported by his maintenance officer and considerably helped by the staff of COHQ, battled away, for he knew time was pressing. New recruits continued to arrive at the Hayling Island Depot and were at once plunged into an almost round-the-clock training programme, for they needed to be both superbly fit and completely familiar with their many pieces of equipment before they could be considered ready to undertake a successful operation. It therefore came as a real blow to Clogstoun-Willmott to be ordered in January 1943 to send two COPP teams to carry out operations in the Mediterranean.

A look at some of the functions that COPPs were required to perform and the methods they used shows clearly how dangerous it was to send them on an operation after scarcely a month's training. Taken to within 3 or 4 miles of the enemy coastline by submarine – or when impracticable to use submarines, by motor launch or motor torpedo boat or native craft – the two-man canoes were slipped and paddled to about 200 yards offshore, or less. From there the COPP officer swam, leaving his mate to remain anchored or to carry out an offshore reconnaissance checking soundings and the bearings of any obstructions. When those ashore had carried out their various tasks the most vital part of the operation – returning to the canoe and then to the submarine without being seen by any enemy – was accomplished by adhering to a strictly-detailed, memorized timetable and the use of the RG or other homing device. When piloting an assault landing, as opposed to a beach reconnaissance, the drill was the same as that attempted in the case of Operation Torch.

The naval and military personnel of a COPP had their own special functions, although whenever possible both were trained to do each other's work. The naval element would be concerned with matters relating to pilotage directions, such as coastal silhouettes for fixing recommended release positions, recommendations for submarine and canoe markers, navigational dangers, sheltered anchorages, conditions of surf, presence of shoals and rocks, beach gradients close inshore, sea minefields and a report on the strengths of tidal streams or currents. While the military members of the team would be chiefly concerned with a detailed description of the beach – type, bearing capacity, obstructions to vehicles, exits and the need for any equipment to develop these – as well as reporting on the presence of minefields, wire, pillboxes, landmarks for troops advancing inland, existing cover from the air and, especially for operations in eastern theatres, the location of fresh water supplies.

By early in 1942 Clogstoun-Willmott had six teams* busily training at Hayling Island, and when the call came for two to proceed to the Mediterranean he sent those who were the most forward in their training: Nos. 3 under Lt-Commander Teacher and 4 under Lieutenant McHarg, under the general control of Teacher. They were the best he had, but neither Clogstoun-Willmott nor Teacher were under any illusion that they were sufficiently trained or properly equipped. On arrival in Algiers the two teams were to find that through a complete lack of com-

---

* Of which No. 2 was a specialized hydrographers' all-naval team with a different establishment and role to the others, trained at Portsmouth.

munication – not entirely unusual where any special service force was concerned – the authorities had little idea of their purpose or why they had come. Fortunately the CCO was visiting Algiers at the time and on receiving a first-hand report from Teacher, Lord Louis was able to put things in a better perspective and a degree of urgency was resumed.

COPP 3 was transferred to Malta, where it was joined by a party of seven naval officers and some ratings who had been sent from Cairo under Lieutenant P.R. Smith. These men had done only a little elementary COPP training, based on information from Clogstoun-Willmott's 1941 Rhodes reports, and were therefore even less prepared for action than the English teams. Nevertheless, they had to be used, for shortly after their arrival in Malta Commander Teacher was told that in the next dark period – which coincided with the last days of February and early March 1943 – teams were required to reconnoitre beaches along the north-east corner of Sicily and the western half of the south coast, for which they had been allotted three submarines, while a fourth was to bring COPP 4 from Algiers for the operation.

During the few nights of the dark period these gallant Coppists, loyally and skilfully supported by the submarine crews, were to make something like ten sorties, and nearly all of them ended in disaster. Of the fifteen canoeists in the operation five were lost and five captured; one canoe party (Lieutenant Smith's) failed to make the rendezvous with the submarine and the two men paddled some 65 miles to Malta, suffering appalling hardships in heavy seas. Commander Teacher was lost in the very first reconnaissance: after leaving Lieutenant Cooper in charge of the canoe he took to the sea and was never seen again. Three nights later Cooper and the military member of the team, Captain Burbridge of the Royal Canadian Engineers, slipped their canoe from the submarine and vanished into the darkness, never to return. And so it went on. Those few who did manage to reach these well-guarded shores were mostly captured.

These extremely serious losses were caused largely by the foul weather the canoeists encountered, and certainly in one case by the inadequacy of the swimsuit. Miraculously security was maintained; at least one canoe was sunk before the canoeist was captured, and the well-rehearsed cover story apparently satisfied the enemy interrogators in every case. There is also reason to believe that two of the men deliberately swam out to sea to avoid the risk of disclosure. Clogstoun-Willmott remained convinced, and future operations were to bear him out, that with properly-trained and well-equipped men losses would be small and amply compensated for by the amount of valuable information acquired.

The weather would remain the greatest and most unpredictable hazard, but even when the sea was smiling there still remained the many mishaps that could occur in homing. With accurate night navigation being so difficult, canoeists risked getting farther out than the submarine and signalling to the open ocean; or the submarine commander might fail to return to the correct waiting position, either through faulty navigation or because of the presence of enemy surface patrols. The margin of acceptable error in this part of the operation was very small, but after Sicily it was unusual for European enemy sentries to cause disaster.

The loss of his Mediterranean teams was a severe shock to Clogstoun-Willmott, but it acted as a further spur to his determination that his men would not in future operate until they had been properly trained and equipped. Once again the CCO took up the cudgels on behalf of COPPs to impress upon the service ministries that the nature of their specialized and secret work demanded that their requirements should be given top priority. It was not popular, but it had the desired effect and gradually Clogstoun-Willmott and his men at their Sandy Point Depot received canoes, swimsuits and underwater gear that could really be relied upon.

Meanwhile, the officers and men found that their commanding officer was driving them harder than ever before in their gruelling training programme. Clogstoun-Willmott reckoned that a COPP team could be properly trained in four to five months, and as he did not have to despatch his next two teams (Nos. 5 and 6) to the Mediterranean until April and May 1943 they fulfilled his training requirement; they were also much better equipped than their predecessors had been.

These two COPPs remained in the Mediterranean until the autumn, when they returned to the Depot. This time the reconnaissances of the Sicilian beaches were entirely successful, and on the night of the Allied assault COPP personnel succeeded in marking the beaches with close-offshore human markers. They then continued their survey work on the coasts of southern Italy: in September COPP 5 carried out a faultless reconnaissance from HM Submarine *Shakespeare* of three beaches in the Gulf of Gioia, bringing back among other information full details of surface gradients above and below water and suitable exit points, and observations on enemy sentries ashore and E-boats afloat.

Largely as a result of these successful operations in the

Mediterranean, the demand for COPPs increased dramatically. Those who had hitherto been somewhat sceptical now clamoured for their services; it was generally recognized that their hallmark was quality, and they bore the unmistakable stamp of a team of experts. COPP 7 had started training at Sandy Point in late January 1943 and was therefore ready to answer a call from the Far East that autumn; COPP 8, which started training in May, went to India shortly afterwards; but COPPs 9 and 10 were not ready to begin training until August of that year.

The policy at the Depot was to have two COPP teams based there, and the one that had been the longest at home should be kept fully operational. COPPs at this time were an independent unit under the direct administration of the CCO, but Clogstoun-Willmott at the Depot had considerable autonomy in respect of training, administration and operational capabilities. Trials of new equipment and necessary technical developments were carried out at Sandy Point, as of course was the initial, and some later, training of new officers and men. The rest was done on the west coast of Scotland. The aim to have ten teams operational was achieved, although there were never ten fit for active service at any one time. It is estimated that in the three-year lifetime of the COPP organization probably 250 men served in all, some of whom were administrative personnel at the Depot. Recruits had to be of a high standard initially, and some had to be trained navigators. Even for so small a force such men were not easily obtained. For many prospective Coppists seafaring, adventure and endurance would be in their blood, while others might need to acquire these characteristics; but all would need a high degree of courage in the face of constant danger.

During the summer of 1943 much of the considerable activity always taking place at Sandy Point centred on preparations for Operation Overlord, the invasion of North-West Europe. Reconnaissance was needed six months in advance, and because of the risk of detection it was thought that X-craft (midget submarines) should be used. Two teams were to be trained for these before the end of the year. X-craft measured 51 ft, had a range of 800 miles and a speed of 6½ knots on the surface and 2 knots submerged. They were usually manned by three men, but when used by COPPs for recce work they carried five; and very unpleasant it was for those men cooped up for days in these exceedingly cramped conditions, inhaling fetid air. Clogstoun-Willmott, and his veterans of COPP 1, became well acquainted with these horrors during a period of intensive training in the autumn at the

X-craft base on Loch Striven* on the Cowal mainland opposite Rothesay.

At the end of the year, about the time COPP 9 went to Loch Striven to train, Layforce II was carrying out deception and information raids on the French coast; but the vital information required by the planners of 21st Army Group could not be obtained from any surface raid – nor were these to be encouraged in the sensitive areas of proposed invasion. Air photographs of the Cotentin-Seine bay clearly showed a fairly wide ridge of dark strips which it was feared could indicate a peat bog formation capable of making the whole invasion plan at that point unworkable. It was imperative to find the true substance of these sinister shadows before the plan could proceed any further.

The first of January 1944 was the last dark night for that period, and so Clogstoun-Willmott decided to carry out the recce between 30 December and 1 January. After all their training it was a slight anticlimax to learn that because of the Calvados Reef, a dangerous rock plateau that stretched for some distance off the Normandy coast and on which an X-craft could become stranded at low tide, part of COPP 1 was to travel in two LCNs borrowed from COPP 2 and towed by Motor Gun Boats.

Clogstoun-Willmott headed a team of six, of which the two army members, Major Scott-Bowden and Sergeant Ogden Smith, were to do the swimming. As the first shadows of night crept across the sea the little LCNs parted company from the MGBs, and with some three hours 'steaming' to the swimmers' release position there was much to worry about when the wind got up and the sea began to heave and break. The nearer to the shore the worse the weather became; steep waves impelled by the ever-strengthening wind reared over gunwale height, and several of the party including both soldiers succumbed to the paralysing effects of violent seasickness. Nothing was going right: rain poured down, visibility was poor, incompetent seamanship by raw borrowed crews resulted in one anchor and sounding pole being lost overboard, the two swimmers were in no shape for their ordeal, and Clogstoun-Willmott seriously thought of heading back to the MGBs; only the great importance of the mission kept him going.

The seaway had lost the boats time, and then the new electronic navigator failed. The swimmers, when they eventually made land,

*It was on this loch, at the same time, that the bouncing bomb trials were carried out by the RAF for the famous Ruhr dam raids.

found that the tide had carried them a little way beyond their intended landing point. 'The shore lighthouse at Pointe de Ver Arromanches was suddenly switched on,' recalls Clogstoun-Willmott, 'which was an advantage and a danger. The latter since it probably indicated that German coastal convoys with their escorts would be slowly passing, cutting off the COPPs' line of retreat, while the light intermittently illuminated the area.'

It was about midnight when Scott-Bowden and Ogden Smith, weak from the effects of the journey, started quartering the beach with their bead line and augers.* When they had acquired a number of samples Scott-Bowden decided there was time to go inland for an inspection. It was nearly their undoing, for they were pinned to the ground by sentries and were in danger of missing the rendezvous. As it was they had an appalling swim back to the LCN in a steep sea, weighed down by their heavy equipment and sample bags of sand and shale.

The journey home was even more ghastly than the one out, for the wind was contrary, the sea was in its most ugly mood, the standby LCN through a series of mishaps twice disappeared in the murk and could not be found, and the MGBs had to be reached before a rapidly approaching dawn. But often in peril and always in stress, Clogstoun-Willmott's craft found the MTBs 20 miles off the coast a little ahead of the missing LCN. The reconnaissance had been a complete success, and the scientists were able to assure the planners that the samples showed there was no peat bog in which Army vehicles might founder. But now another reconnaissance was required to examine the St Laurent sector of the coast.

This second reconnaissance, which took place between 17 and 21 January with much the same team, was undertaken in an X-craft. An initial periscope examination was interrupted by small-arms fire, probably target practice,† which caused a hasty retreat into deeper water; but by nightfall there had been no air or sea follow-up and the same two swimmers as before went overboard – after spending two hours in the cramped conditions of the midget submarine endeavouring to climb into their cumbersome swimsuits. There were sentries on the beach, but they got their samples and regained the submarine. The next day

---

* A thin fishing line beaded at every 50 yards (sometimes less) was attached to the swimmer's waist and each time a bead slipped through the fingers the auger was driven some 2 ft into the sand, filling the tube with every stratum in its correct place and thickness.
† Mistaking the tiny periscopes for lobster-pot buoy sticks adrift.

the coastline was carefully scanned and sketched from the periscope, and that night Scott-Bowden and Ogden Smith went ashore again, obtaining further sand and rock samples, while the X-craft tested outer depths and currents. Another day was spent successfully quartering the coast with the periscope, but that night the weather worsened considerably. The strain of their two sorties and, more particularly, the deleterious effects of being bottled up and overcrowded for so long in the tiny submarine, were showing plainly, especially on the swimmers. No unnecessary risk could be taken to compromise security, and in the circumstances Clogstoun-Willmott wisely called off the last landing.

The plan for Overlord, as far as COPPs were concerned, was for two teams to go ahead of the invasion in X-craft and lie up ready to mark the beaches with their flashing beacons as the armada approached, while a further team was to pilot the leading armoured troops right up to the beach. There were three COPPs (Nos. 1, 6 and 9) operational in the UK at this time, and 1 and 9 were to do the submarine work while COPP 6, whose commander had an utter aversion to midget submarines, piloted the armour from two assault boats. The United States force commanders spurned the British offer of markers for fear of compromising security, but they accepted that of pilots to guide them in – although at this late stage it was difficult for the British to spare any who knew the coast. One of the two beaches (Omaha) lay within the area so carefully reconnoitred in January, so that their naval force commander was in possession of very full information. It was a combination of heavy seas in that area and the lack of any markers which was to make the Omaha landings such a shambles, with some landing craft and almost half the amphibious DD (Duplex Drive) tanks foundering, and many troops being landed wide of their objectives.

In the months preceding Overlord a great deal of thought had been given by Coppist teams as to how their midget submarines and some of their gear might be improved to meet the demands of D-Day, for should postponement be necessary they might have to spend long and uncertain hours submerged. They could not do much to lessen the claustrophobia but at least they devised a fairly satisfactory wireless and a code to be transmitted by the BBC. This was fortunate, for the two submarines left Portsmouth on the evening of 2 June and – as is well known – D-Day did have to be postponed by twenty-four hours until dawn on 6 June.

On the great day everything went according to plan for all three teams, who carried out their marking and piloting duties efficiently and successfully. The job done, they returned to base, where they were to stand by in case they should be needed for further operations during the Allied advance. The call was to come in March, and at very short notice, for members of a COPP team to make a reconnaissance of the far bank of the River Rhine to answer some specific questions for the corps commander prior to the Allied crossing. This job and a similar one across the Elbe were carried out successfully by a combination of special service troops which included men from COPPs 5 and 7 (second commission). The latter task marked the last COPP operation in Europe.

While COPPs 1, 6 and 9 were preparing for and taking part in the momentous invasion of North-West Europe, there were two other COPP teams training at the Depot: Nos. 7 and 8 (and later 4) were in the Far East and Nos. 10 and 4 were busy in the Mediterranean. Here reconnaissance of beaches in conjunction with Allied strategy (such as a recce of the Anzio beaches); assistance to Yugoslav partisans on the Adriatic coast, and later to partisans in the Aegean; and providing useful data for the landing of raiding parties kept their teams fully occupied up to the end of 1944. But once the Allied advance into North-West Europe and up Italy was properly under way it became obvious that the principal work for COPPs lay in the Far East, where the men of South-East Asia Command (SEAC) were about to take the initiative against the Japanese in Burma, Malaya and Sumatra.

Before final victory in August 1945 there was to be some coming and going of COPP teams between the Far East and the United Kingdom. As already mentioned, Nos. 7 and 8 were the first to reach India in the autumn of 1943. They set themselves up at a placed called Cocanada on the beautifully-named Coromandel coast. There were very few senior officers who knew much about them, for the paper entitled *The Uses of COPP* had not yet been circulated and their rightly-secret reputation had not reached India. The early weeks proved a frustrating time, for they needed action to keep themselves up to the mark, and although training and learning the ways of the jungle helped, it was not enough in the opinion of their commanders, Lieutenants Hall and Ponsonby.

However, once the message spread – no doubt helped by the new Supreme Commander, Lord Louis Mountbatten – and the build-up for the offensive in the Arakan had started, there were to be more calls for their services than could be coped with. Many sorties off the Burma coast, and as far as Sumatra, had been undertaken by COPP 7 and at least two by COPP 8 before their commanders found a much pleasanter base in Ceylon. It was from here, at the beginning of November 1944, that No. 8 undertook a reconnaissance of Elizabeth Island, at the mouth of the Naf river, sharing their forward base – Teknaf – with the SBS.

The object was to discover whether the island would make a suitable base during the forthcoming offensive, but reconnaissance of the beaches was somewhat hampered by the presence on the island of a very active Japanese platoon. The swimmers did get ashore on the second night of their attempt (on the first the surf had been too heavy), but the second-in-command of the COPP, Lieutenant Michael Peacock, was captured. He had dysentery, and should never have been on the raid, let alone one of the swimmers. For five months he languished in Rangoon jail before being rescued, more dead than alive, from a column of sick and grossly undernourished prisoners whom the Japanese were unsuccessfully attempting to march from Rangoon into Siam.

Early in 1945 there were two COPP teams still working in the Mediterranean, but the future clearly lay in the Far East, and subsequent to a visit by the CCO (now Major-General Laycock) to Lord Louis certain important decisions relating to COPPs were made. It was agreed that there should be four teams permanently in SEAC, and Clogstoun-Willmott's insistence that COPP service should be strictly limited, if a man were to continue fit for normal duties, was reinforced when both the Admiralty and War Office laid it down that their respective highly-trained specialists serving as senior officers in COPPs could not be spared for more than eighteen months at a time.

This ruling created something of a problem, for it was undesirable to deprive a team of its two senior officers in the middle of an operational tour. It was therefore decided to have only six COPPs: four on operations in SEAC, one in transit and one training at the Depot. It was also agreed that an experienced COPP officer should be attached to the staff of the Small Operations Group who were – as in the case of SBS – responsible for COPP teams in SEAC, so that, among other things, he could make recommendations on the use of COPPs at the preliminary planning stage. Some, but not all, of these decisions were put into practice before the Japanese surrender.

COPPs 7 and 8 had returned to the United Kingdom not long after the Elizabeth Island reconnaissance, and now in late 1944 those in the Far East were Nos. 1, 3, 4 and 9, all on their second commission. The distances in this theatre from base to operation point were often vast, and it was felt that time and other factors would not always permit the use of submarines; consequently trials were undertaken at Oban in September 1944 with Catalina and Sunderland flying boats. It was found that after modifications had been made both of these aircraft could take two Mk VI canoes and a full complement of COPP gear. The idea was to fly parties to a rendezvous out of range of the enemy warning system and then transfer to a submarine, after which normal COPP drill would be carried out with the flying boat returning the following night; alternatively the aircraft might unload the new canoes (which were powered) some 10 to 15 miles offshore and they would move in to within 400 yards of the shore to release their swimmers. The trials were satisfactory but in the event flying boats were never used operationally, for it always proved possible to lift teams by the safer means of submarine, motor launch, or even motor sampan.

Missions for COPP teams came thick and fast until the end of hostilities, for the Army – especially XV Corps slogging its way down the coast through jungle, swamp, chaung and river – placed enormous reliance on the accurate reports delivered. There were many deeds of heroism, and in spite of the great risks involved casualties were pleasantly few. By December 1944 the Japanese defence in Burma was crumbling, and towards the end of that month they abandoned Akyab; the 3rd Commando Brigade entered it from landing craft on 3 January 1945. Japanese troops in the coastal sector were streaming south to pass through the Arakan Yoma before they were cut off, for in the centre of Burma their main armies were being driven back. XV Corps was leapfrogging troops by sea to cut off their escape.

However, before this could be accomplished pockets of resistance remained that had to be cleared up. One such was on the Myebon Penninsula which is off Hunter's Bay just south-east of Akyab. COPPs 3 and 4 had a part to play in this. While COPP 4 was occupied gathering tidal data in the bay, COPP 3 had the task of destroying a number of stakes which a previous recce had spotted stuck in the sand just above the low-water line some 300 yards from the proposed landing point.

Three officers, two leading seamen and an RE sergeant working in three canoes were to do the job on the night of 11/12 January. The canoes were launched from the ML 3 miles from the beach, and with the strong ebb flowing it took nearly two hours to reach the stakes. These were found to be teak, 15 ft high and of between 7 and 11 in. diameter, spaced at 10 to 14 ft. Delay pencils (fuses) were set at midnight. In the area of the stakes the mud was very soft and about 9 in. deep; the canoes grounded and had to be dragged for 150 yards – a noisy operation which luckily was not heard by the nearby enemy posts. Just over six hours later the charges detonated destroying twenty-three stakes, and shortly afterwards the COPP commander piloted the leading assault force ML of 3 Commando Brigade to the beach.

Before Rangoon fell there were to be many reconnaissances for coastal river or chaung crossings by COPP teams operating either direct from Ceylon or from forward bases on the Burmese coast, and there was one occasion when a team exceeded the Coppist charter and let fly at the enemy with a Sten gun, even taking a prisoner. Detailed plans had been laid for a large-scale combined operation assault on Rangoon for 2 May, but before it could be put into practice the Japanese evacuated the city, and when the Gurkhas spearheaded the invasion by parachute they killed just thirty-six Japanese – the only opposition encountered. Long before this the planners had been busy on the assault on Malaya, which Mountbatten hoped would be possible by June or July 1945, and COPP teams were required to perform their usual task of providing valuable beach information.

From Rangoon to Singapore is about 2,000 miles. The island of Phuket, situated just south of the Isthmus of Kra, where the tail end of Burma meets Siam, seemed to be an excellent halfway base complete with good monsoon anchorages, and it was understood to be fairly lightly held by Thais and a few Japanese. In March components of SOG comprising men from COPP 3, Detachment 385 (see Chapter 7) and two RAF officers, all under Major Ian Mackenzie, RE – then senior COPP military officer in SEAC – paid the island a visit from their canoes to survey the beaches and report on the possibilities for airstrips. The party arrived off the island after a 1,200-mile journey from Ceylon in two submarines, and men of COPP 3 went ashore in three canoes. The occupants of two of these succeeded in collecting useful data and rejoined the submarine, but the third canoe – converted to carry an extra man, one of the RAF officers – capsized and the party were discovered. Two of the three were shot in the ensuing firefight, and the RAF officer was later captured.

The larger group from Detachment 385 under Major Mackenzie met a similar fate. Intending to stay on shore for three nights, they had scarcely carried out their first recce when they bumped into a party of Thai police. Escaping from these they engaged in a desparate game of hide and seek with Japanese patrols for the next seventeen days, trying vainly to reach one of many appointed rendezvous with the submarines. Two were killed and the remainder caught; three of those captured – Mackenzie, the second RAF officer and a corporal – were fortunate in being taken by the Thais and survived the war. Two officers and a colour-sergeant who fell into Japanese hands were later executed in Singapore. The tragedy was the greater in that the atom bomb was to make an opposed landing on Phuket unnecessary.

An operation equally dangerous, but with a happier ending, was that undertaken in June 1945 by COPP 3 to survey the Morib beaches near Port Dickson, which is more than halfway down the west coast of Malaya. A party of eight men under Lieutenant Hughes set out in four canoes. Two canoes returned to the submarine having obtained much valuable surface and underwater information, tide heights and particularly the poor quality of the beach chosen for the projected landing. The other two, each carrying an officer and Leading Seaman as paddler, failed to make the rendezvous with the submarine, and were forced to put back to the shore, where the men took their chance on land. After two months of incredible adventuring, and being shepherded around Negri Sembilan by a strange, brutish band of well-armed Malay-Chinese known as the Anti-Japanese Force,* they were eventually conducted to a British force then operating in the Seremban area. By this time they were racked with malaria, but at least they were alive and the war was over.

After the war the Royal Marines SBS carried on the reconnaissance work which had formerly been a part of COPP activities, but there was no longer a strong pilotage requirement, largely because of the perfecting of short-wave coastal radar, and so COPPs were disbanded. Theirs had been a short but very successful and satisfactory life; a small, close-knit family bonded by discipline and danger, and sharing a common brotherhood.

---

* No doubt these gentlemen were among those who later caused many soldiers (including the author) a great deal of inconvenience in the jungles of Malaya between 1948 and 1952.

9

The Long Range Desert Group: The Formative Months

For two and a half years between September 1940 and March 1943 men of the Long Range Desert Group became masters of the vast Libyan Desert, an area the size of India. The desert has great character. It is not, as is sometimes supposed, one huge expanse of flat sand, for there are a variety of natural obstacles, and it is a place of many moods.

At certain times of the year great dust storms sweep like a curtain across the landscape, blotting out the sun and smothering all in their path. By day, in the summer months, the wavering bars of searing heat and the weight of emptiness hanging over the burning sand can drive a man crazy. By night the desert can be cruelly cold. But in the evening and the early morning there are the ever-changing colours and patterns, which produce an indescribable, iridescent beauty. All through the ages men have been attracted by the desert's unending horizons, and the deep hush of its elemental solitude.

Immediately south of the coastal strip in the area which became known (incorrectly) as the Western Desert, the ground – for the most part – is ideal for armoured warfare and motorized reconnaissance, but farther south very different conditions are met with. Here there are great expanses of sand sea, with north-south running dunes rising to several hundred feet, and often without a gap. At the beginning of the war these great stretches of nature's imposing architecture were considered to be virtually impassable to vehicles of any kind. But for some years previous to 1939 a small band of energetic enthusiasts had, mostly at their own expense, done a considerable amount of exploration in the Libyan Desert. More by good luck than good management the combined experience of these desert pioneers – the crucible from which future triumphs would emerge – became available to GHQ Middle East almost as soon as (it should have been well before) Italy entered the war.

Foremost among them was Major R.A. Bagnold of the Royal Corps of Signals. By a fortunate chance the ship taking him from Britain to East Africa in October 1939 put into Alexandria for repairs, and Bagnold's name came to the attention of General Wavell. Tribute to this great commander's perspicacity has already been paid, and as with Fox-Davies 'the Chief' was quick to see Bagnold's potential value, and had his posting to Kenya cancelled. But it was not until shortly after the Italian declaration of war on 10 June 1940 that Bagnold got his chance to put into practice the ideas he had previously tried to impress upon an incredulous GHQ staff.

Wars are the perfect medium for the development of new ideas, many of them hare-brained and quite impracticable, but Ralph Bagnold was a highly intelligent man with sufficient conviction and determination to back the original idea his fertile mind was developing. He was not unmindful of the part played by the Light Car Patrols in this same Libyan Desert during the first year of the 1914 war. Their scope was necessarily limited, but they had done much pioneer work – including the invention of the sun compass, and the first condensers for boiling radiators – and in 1940 Bagnold realized that the need for something similar was more urgent than in 1915. As already mentioned in Chapter 5, the Italian forces in East Africa greatly outnumbered the British, and the Nile Valley as a line of communication was of considerable strategic importance. Italian troops based on the large oasis of Kufra, and with a useful air and land staging post at Uweinat on the Egyptian-Sudan border, could pose a very grave threat to this lifeline.

Bagnold had plans for a watching brief in this area, and for disrupting the Italian lines of communication to Kufra. The principal role of the force he hoped to raise would be reconnaissance – the collection of useful information along the enemy lines of communication – but he realized that the desires of the men he recruited, and the situations they might find themselves in, would demand some offensive action, and he planned to arm them accordingly. In a long interview he convinced the Commander-in-Chief of his ability to negotiate the Great Sand Sea, an area the size of Ireland, and to carry out this type of work. On 23 June his plans were approved, and he was given virtually *carte blanche* in regard to his every requirement – without which, given the prevailing caution and suspicion at GHQ, he could never have succeeded. Even so, the task that he had set himself was a formidable one.

Some of Bagnold's closest cronies in his pre-war explorations were serving in one capacity or another in the Middle East. W.B. Kennedy Shaw, in the service of the Colonial Office, was censoring newspapers in Palestine; P.A. Clayton, who had spent eighteen years in the Egyptian Desert Survey Department, was in Tanganyika; and Rupert Harding-Newman was with the Military Mission in Cairo. In due course these three invaluable assistants were gathered in, and upon them, and Bagnold, fell the task of recruiting, equipping and training the initial intake. Another man, Guy Prendergast, who had been closely associated with Bagnold, was to join them from London some six months later.

The type of volunteer that Bagnold was looking for was the man most sought after by all the special services: the possessor of every virile quality, of courage, intelligence and of such powers of endurance as to bear with patience long periods of hardship during heat-sizzling days and freezing nights on little food and less water. Nor was this all, for the work demanded a variety of highly-skilled craftsmen: wireless opearators, navigators, fitters, drivers and gunners.

It seemed to Bagnold and his small team of experts that men from the recently-arrived New Zealand Expeditionary Force would best fill these requirements. He sought permission from the New Zealand government, through General Freyberg commanding the New Zealand Division, for the release of two officers and about a hundred other ranks to man the three patrols he intended forming. Permission was granted, and men were selected from the large numbers who had volunteered for an undisclosed but dangerous assignment.

A more difficult problem was the finding of vehicles and equipment that would answer the particular requirements and strenuous demands to be made upon them. In the peacetime explorations various types of Ford had been used, but a vehicle with a greater load-carrying capacity (up to 2 tons) was needed in war, and Bagnold felt sure (correctly as it turned out) that a 30 cwt two-wheel-drive truck would negotiate the sand seas. But the army had none to spare, so he and Harding-Newman had to go to the Chevrolet Company in Alexandria for fourteen, and beg the remaining nineteen of his requirement from the Egyptian army. However, if the British Army could not supply the trucks the

RAOC – perhaps inspired by a directive from on high – pulled out all the stops to complete the necessary alterations and modifications in time for the first Long Range Patrols* to start their desert training on 5 August.

But before this happy date was reached there was a mass of detail still to be completed. Bagnold had perfected the original Light Car Patrol's design for a sun compass, but the British Army preferred another type, and once again recourse had to be made to the Egyptian army, which was able to supply a few. These, together with Lewis guns, wireless sets, sand channels, condensers and other refinements for desert work, had somehow to be fitted to the Chevrolets. Reliable maps of the inner Libyan Desert did not exist (the LRDG was later to carry out its own surveys which formed the basis for future maps of the area), and only three theodolites could be found in the whole of the Middle East. Later such esoteric pieces of equipment as azimuth cards and chronometers were added to the navigator's gear. Clothing varied from just shorts to sheepskin coats according to the time of day and year, but two special items had to be drawn: sandals and Arab headdresses. Both were cool to wear, and the latter gave admirable protection from the sun.

As soon as the troops had assembled at Abbassia barracks in Cairo, and the equipment started to arrive, Bagnold and his team – now augmented by Captain E.C. Mitford of the Royal Tank Corps, who was one of the few Englishmen to have visited Kufra – commenced intensive training, which continued throughout August in the desert. The New Zealanders were quick to learn, for many of them were farmers accustomed to a hard open-air life, and being owners of cars (unusual with the pre-war British private soldier), which of necessity they treated with respect, they had acquired some mechanical knowledge. But for the work ahead very high standards of driving under new and difficult conditions, and of navigation and wireless operating, were necessary.

The Libyan Desert in many ways resembled a vast uncharted sea. There were very few landmarks, and navigation had to be by compass and astro-fix observations; nor was the magnetic compass of much value, for vehicular interference necessitated frequent halts to enable the compass to be used dismounted. But the sun compass was ideal. Kennedy Shaw, whose job it was in the

---

* The official designation of the unit before it became Long Range Desert Group some six months later.

early days to instruct navigators, gives the following concise description: 'The sun-compass consists of a horizontal circle, divided into 360 degrees, with a central needle casting a shadow across the graduations. By rotating the circle, which is fixed to the dashboard of the car, throughout the day to correspond to the sun's movement through the sky, the shadow is made to indicate the true bearing on which the car is travelling.'*

The compass was mounted so that the driver could see to steer the vehicle on the bearing laid down, and by a simple method of dead reckoning an experienced navigator was able to work out his position at any moment of the day. The task did, however, call for a very high degree of concentration in order to correct any major diversions in the plotted bearing. Furthermore, when he had brought the Patrol safely to the night's leaguer the navigator's work was not done, for he then had to ascertain his exact position using the theodolite for an astro-fix observation.

Similarly, the wireless operators were kept busy at halts, and often well into the night, taking and making calls and enciphering and deciphering messages. The high-powered sets the LRDG used were capable of transmitting over distances in excess of 1,000 miles, and to keep them constantly in working order required considerable technical ability. The success of every patrol depended upon the skill of these two craftsmen, the navigator and the wireless operator, and in more than two years of desert warfare navigation or communication failure was very rare indeed.

It says much for the thrust and organizational ability of Ralph Bagnold that within six weeks of commencing work he had the first Patrols ready for action. From that time (end of August 1940) until March 1943 there was to be at least one Patrol always at work in the desert. Inevitably there would be changes in the composition, armament and vehicles of the Long Range Desert Group according to experience, but the first Patrols to cross the Libyan frontier consisted of two officers and thirty men, mounted in one 15 cwt and ten 30 cwt Chevrolet trucks, and armed with eleven Lewis guns, four Boys anti-tank rifles, and one 37 mm Bofors gun. Each man carried a rifle or a pistol. The trucks were unarmoured and the lighter one was for the Patrol commander, to give him greater scope for manoeuvre. One 30 cwt carried the navigator and wireless operator; the others each held three men including the driver.

* *Long Range Desert Group*, p.90.

Bagnold envisaged Patrols operating away from base for up to three weeks, and during that time covering distances of around 2,000 miles. This involved each vehicle carrying a considerable quantity of petrol (miles to the gallon averaged only about 6), water and food. The experience of pre-war explorations enabled Kennedy Shaw to devise a well-balanced ration that gained official approval, and in due course was adopted by other units such as the SAS. The water ration at this time was 6 pints a day, which Kennedy Shaw says was ample in winter and good enough in ordinary summer weather, but when the bone-searing hot *gibli* winds blew 'it seemed nothing'.

The first major activity took place at the beginning of September, when the full force (then three Patrols) left their base in Cairo. But much useful preliminary work had been done in August. Clayton was the first to cross the Libyan frontier on a reconnaissance of the Jalo-Kufra track, which it was thought the Italians were using. In the course of this patrol he gained much useful information, including the discovery of a series of sand dunes hitherto unknown to him. On his second reconnaissance, to investigate Italian activity in the area of Uweinat, Clayton covered nearly 1,000 miles, and much of it with a camel that he somehow persuaded to ride in the back of his truck, unshipping it for close-quarters reconnaissance. Meanwhile, Kennedy Shaw was establishing dumps of supplies on the eastern edge of the Great Sand Sea, for until a base could be established west of Cairo distances would prove too great.

The importance of the first full-scale patrols, which lasted throughout September, lay principally in the confidence gained by all who took part, and the very favourable impression they created with those in Cairo – some of whom had been sceptical. In the course of their 1,300-mile journey the Patrols had proved themselves and their vehicles, had made their first small capture, had shown that the much vaunted Sand Sea with its succession of long, parallel, high dunes was not impassable, and had opened up great possibilities for future operations on the enemy's southern flank. The Commander-in-Chief, in a letter to Bagnold, paid tribute to his skill and the success of this early venture. The way was now open for expansion and greater things.

Almost every special force in the last war was raised initially amid a good deal of mistrust and suspicion on the part of the senior staff, but no sooner had it proved itself through its deeds than an immediate, and usually immoderate, expansion was demanded. This was particularly so with the Special Boat Section and the Combined Operation Pilotage Parties. In the case of the Long Range Desert Group the suggested increase was more sensible, but it came at a time when General Freyberg was requesting the return of his New Zealanders. GHQ Middle East had received permission from the War Office to make the LRDG a lieutenant-colonel's command with a Group Headquarters and two Squadrons each of three Patrols. Most fortunately, in the event the New Zealanders were not withdrawn, but before the threat was lifted – and afterwards – there was an urgent need to recruit from other sources, and volunteers were sought from the Yeomanry, Southern Rhodesians and the two battalions of Foot Guards then serving in Egypt. These three, together with the New Zealanders, were to form the basis of the LRDG throughout the desert campaign.

On 7 December 1940 two officers and thirty-six men from the 3rd Coldstream and 2nd Scots Guards, under the command of Captain Michael Crichton-Stuart, formed G Patrol, and they were to be the first of the newcomers to go into action after less than a month together, and a mere two days of desert training. Together with T Patrol of New Zealanders, they formed a force of seventy-six men and twenty-four vehicles destined to join hands with a party of Free French from northern Chad in a raid, conceived by Bagnold, into the Fezzan region of south-western Libya, with the particular aim of attacking the garrison in Murzuk.

The two Patrols, under the overall command of Captain Clayton, left Cairo on Boxing Day and after some 340 miles they entered the Great Sand Sea at Ain Dalla on 30 December. For the next three days they struggled over wave upon wave of the high dunes. In places the going was fairly firm, while in others the trucks ran into soft patches and had to be manhandled. A constant sharp lookout had to be kept to avoid the dangerous razorbacks over which a truck could plunge to disaster. Then there was 90 miles of the Kalansho Sand Sea, and the northern edge of the Ribiana Sand Sea to traverse before, on 4 January and now more than 1,000 miles from Cairo, they were into the Fezzan and near the Chad border. Here G Patrol rested for three days, while Clayton and the New Zealanders crossed into Chad to rendezvous with Colonel d'Ornano and nine French soldiers. On 8 January 1941 the two Patrols, with the French party spread between them, headed for Murzuk.

At a position north of the town, which they had reached apparently without being spotted, it was decided to split the force for the forthcoming battle. T Patrol, under the New Zealand officer, Lieutenant L.B. Ballantyne, leaving three of its trucks, was to make for the airfield, while G Patrol with the remaining New Zealanders took on the main garrison in the fort. This proved to be too hard a nut to crack without heavy weapons, and so Crichton-Stuart took up a position some way back and engaged it with what weapons he had. A mortar bomb set the tower on fire, and his Bofors gun caused some casualties, but enemy machine guns were eventually brought to bear on his party, killing the New Zealand patrol sergeant and wounding three men.

Meanwhile, the aerodrome party met with considerable success. In a short, spirited fight with the Italian garrison they knocked out one post and took a few prisoners from another, and then destroyed three light bombers and their hangar, together with a fuel and bomb store. But sadly this achievement was offset by the loss of the debonair and dashing Colonel d'Ornano. Clayton's car had run into a machine-gun post, and his own gun jammed; the Frenchman, riding in the back, was shot through the throat and died at once.

Clayton decided that nothing further could be done against the fort, and ordered the party to withdraw. This, the first important LRDG action, had so far been a definite success. Ten to fifteen of the enemy lay dead, the airfield was in a shambles, and the fort had been badly damaged; Italian morale was severely shaken amid considerable speculation as to where the attack had originated. On the way back Clayton cleaned up a small Italian post at Traghen, capturing two machine guns and some rifles.

However, after that the return journey became hazardous in the extreme, for Bagnold had flown down to Fort Lamy to confer with Colonel d'Ornano's successor on the possibility of capturing Kufra. Colonel Leclerc (soon to gain great renown, but then totally unknown*) had welcomed the addition of the two Patrols to operate with his own column, and so on 26 January the force struck north from the Chad border travelling via Sarra (where G Patrol was left in reserve) and Bishara. But by now the Italian air force had at last come into action, and besides strafing the vehicles, they directed the well-armed Auto-Saharen Company on to T Patrol. In this combined land and air attack, at a place called Gebel Sherif, the New Zealanders lost a number of vehicles, and worse still Clayton was wounded and captured. Ballantyne then brought them back to Sarra, where he and Crichton-Stuart conferred with

---

* The Vicomte de Haute Cloque, who had adopted a false name on escaping from France in order to safeguard his family.

Leclerc, who clearly saw that any attempt to capture Kufra had to be delayed. He therefore released the Patrols which returned to Cairo on 9 February, after an absence in the desert of forty-five days during which they had covered some 4,500 miles.

But Colonel Leclerc was not a man to be diverted from a design, and by 1 March he had taken Kufra from the Italians. It was to become a great blessing to the men of the Long Range Desert Group. Well situated as a forward supply point for future operations, it had suitable areas where aircraft could land, an abundant supply of excellent water and some very desirable salt lakes. Here, shaded by venerable palm trees, returning Patrols would find a respite from the constant glare of the flaming desert sky – a place of peace, where for brief spells the heroic and the arcadian could merge with each other.

At the beginning of 1941 the LRDG was brought up to establishment (less one Patrol) in accordance with the recent reorganization. Now A Squadron was commanded by Major E.C. Mitford; besides the Guards, it included the two recently-formed Patrols – S formed from the Southern Rhodesians, and Y from the Yeomanry – while Major D.G. Steele (2 NZEF) commanded B Squadron comprising the two original New Zealand patrols. There was also at this time a change of vehicles, for the Chevrolets were beginning to display obvious signs of wear. It was not possible to replace them in kind and Patrols had to make do with four-wheel-drive Fords, which had the same weight-carrying capacity but were not as manoeuvrable as the Chevrolets.

During the first half of 1941 the fortunes of Western Desert Force fluctuated sharply. Wavell's triumphant thrust into Cyrenaica and beyond brought a swift reaction from the Germans, who realized that if they were not to see their allies rolled out of North Africa they must act. Field-Marshal Rommel arrived in April, and before long his Afrika Corps had pushed the British and Dominion troops back to the Egyptian frontier. Only Tobruk remained unconquered, but that was sufficient to keep Rommel looking over his shoulder.

It became clear to Bagnold that with a shifting battle front Cairo was too far back to be a satisfactory base. He therefore decided to move forward, using Kufra and Siwa. The Guards and Yeomanry Patrols of A Squadron, under Mitford, spent most of the summer at Siwa, a smaller oasis than Kufra, but equally pleasant with warm pellucid pools of bubbly, light aquamarine water. The rest of the Group went to Kufra, where Bagnold had command of a mixed French and British force. His primary duty was to safeguard the oasis, and as there were no garrison troops until units of the Sudan Defence Force could be released in mid-July from the fighting in East Africa, men of the LRDG could not be spared for their proper role. However from Siwa G and Y Patrols were engaged in active reconnaissance and some skirmishing.

It is not possible to describe a typical LRDG patrol, for no such thing ever took place. Every sortie differed in one way or another. The object of most patrols was reconnaissance, but a subsidiary role might be to bring in a prisoner and/or to 'do what damage you can'. The War Diaries and Patrol reports are alive with exciting adventures, not least the incredible tales told by survivors who had become 'missing' when their trucks had been destroyed by enemy air action, and who had had to find their way back to safety on foot for distances sometimes of over 100 miles. This called for enormous courage and powers of endurance, and a temperament that was never overwhelmed by the tides of misfortune. It also quite often needed the active assistance of friendly Arabs. These could usually be found among the proud Senussi sect, who over the years had resisted Italian domination with spirit; but in Tripolitania the natives were occasionally untrustworthy, and later in Tunisia nearly always so.

H Patrol, a composite Guards and Yeomanry one of eighteen men and three trucks under Captain J.R. Easonsmith, set out from Siwa in June 1941, and their experiences followed a fairly familiar pattern for a short-distance patrol at this time. Their task was to drop two Arab agents near Gambut airfield without taking undue risks, and to report upon the state of the main tracks in that area. They spent the first night at a place called El Weshka on the Wire,* and the next day in rough going over bushes and hummocks they disturbed two cheetahs, not such a familiar occurrence.

The Arabs were duly dropped at 2 p.m. on 11 June at a point 5 miles south-west of Gambut, and the Patrol then went north to find an observation point from which to survey the traffic on the main Tobruk-Bardia road. In the course of this work a vehicle park was sighted with sixteen heavy vehicles widely dispersed. The Patrol commander decided that to attack this park in the evening would not constitute 'an undue risk'. The W/T truck was detached to block the escape route, but no attempt was made by the enemy to get their vehicles away – chiefly because Easonsmith

---

* A 6 ft high barbed-wire entanglement running southwards along the Libyan-Egyptian border for some 200 miles. It was erected by order of Marshal Graziani to control the native population, but by this time it had a number of gaps in it.

had gained complete surprise – and after a sharp firefight twelve of the sixteen trucks were destroyed and two prisoners taken. During the return journey the Patrol Sergeant's truck broke down, and after working on it all night in vain it had to be lashed back-to-back and towed the 245 miles to Siwa. Such breakdowns were a fairly frequent occurrence, especially on long-distance patrols over the very rough going.

When Guy Prendergast, an experienced pilot, arrived from England in January 1941 to become Bagnold's second-in-command he was quick to appreciate the many advantages that a private air fleet would have for the Long Range Desert Group, which was now operating over great distances: contact with GHQ, emergency supplies, recovery of wounded and so on. At first such a move was strongly resisted by the Royal Air Force, which even forbade the use of their roundels on any private plane, but after a certain amount of pressure had been brought to bear their objections were overruled, and thereafter they gave every possible assistance. Prendergast negotiated a private purchase from Egyptian owners of two single-engined cabin biplanes. These had been made by Western Aircraft Corporation of Ohio, and were therefore known as Wacos. One had a cruising speed of 145 mph, and the other, slightly less powerful, of 115 mph. Prendergast's co-pilot was Trooper Barker, who had many hours' flying experience. Both machines were to serve the Group faithfully for the rest of the war, and proved quite invaluable.

It has been mentioned before that it always took time for the true role of any special service force to be properly understood, and during that time they were very often misused, or left to moulder in frustration. To a certain extent the summer of 1941 was such a period for the LRDG. There were occasions when they were sent on short-range patrols carrying out work for which they were not suited, and which could have led to disaster.

But in these formative months a wealth of experience had been gained and many lessons learnt, which were passed on to higher command. Gradually it was recognized that the Group's forte lay in performing the many vital jobs encompassed by a long-range reconnaissance role, rather than in hit-and-run raids for which other forces were better equipped. Michael Crichton-Stuart has written:* 'I think much of the ultimate success of the LRDG could be traced, in retrospect, to the lessons of that "wasted" summer of 1941.' He was right, and an exciting future now lay ahead.

* *G Patrol*, p.93.

10

The Long Range Desert Group: Freedom of the Desert

On 1 August 1941 Ralph Bagnold, the founding father of the Long Range Desert Group and the man whose genius had made it all possible, was promoted to Colonel and ordered to Cairo to take up a staff job. Command of the Group passed to Guy Prendergast, who was to hold it throughout the remainder of the desert campaign.

The original war establishment had allowed for a Headquarters of twenty-three all ranks with a lieutenant-colonel, and a major as second-in-command; two Squadrons each commanded by a captain, with six subalterns for the fighting Patrols, one navigator and two gunners, or gun numbers, per Patrol. The full total was 230 all ranks with 30 attached personnel. In the forthcoming reorganization these numbers were not greatly altered, although the Signal Section was strengthened. The Section was now commanded by Captain G.B. Heywood, who (except for one short break) served with the LRDG for the rest of the war and always demanded, and received, a very high standard of excellence among his signallers.

But the major change in organization was in the size of Patrols. With the emphasis on long-range reconnaissance it was decided that Patrols of thirty men and eleven trucks were far too unwieldy; in particular there was a concealment problem. The desert does not offer much natural cover from the air although, aided by the excellent random-patterned camouflage nets and making skilful use of the wadis and dunes, surprisingly good results were obtained. Nevertheless concealment and surprise – two essential ingredients for success – would be better obtained with a small number of vehicles. Therefore each of the five existing Patrols was split into two. The New Zealanders became R1, R2, T1 and T2, the Guards G1 and G2, the Yeomanry Y1 and Y2 and the Rhodesians S1 and S2. Each Patrol was, as before, self-contained with navigator, fitter, signallers and medical orderly. In the autumn an RAOC Light Repair Section was a new, and much valued, addition to the Group.

While these important decisions were being implemented the Patrols were somewhat scattered. The Guards, Yeomanry and one of the New Zealand Patrols had returned to Cairo, where – like other desert warriors bronzed of face and lean of body – they enjoyed for a brief spell some of the pleasures of civilization. The other New Zealanders, and Headquarters, were at Siwa and the Rhodesian Patrol was at Kufra. But changes of location were frequent according to the swing of the main battle, and it was intended that the new organization should be ready when the Eighth Army (the successor to Western Desert Force) mounted its projected autumn offensive.

The administrative hub of the whole Group was, of course, Headquarters, where the Signals, Survey, Light Repair and Heavy Sections were located together with the doctor, other attached personnel and the Wacos. The Heavy Section was the Group's B echelon, bringing supplies forward in their 3-tonners from the Eighth Army, Cairo or, when Kufra was the main base, occasionally from Wadi Halfa. The quartermaster, as in the case of a regular battalion, was the link between the supply columns and the fighting troops. Later, when distances became great, forward dumps were made in various parts of the desert, which also helped men forced to return to base on foot.

As already mentioned, the disbandment of Layforce in July 1941 put a considerable number of Commando-type soldiers on the market. One of these was that charismatic and redoubtable figure, David Stirling, whose languid air concealed an active mind and combative spirit. The story of how he formed the Special Air Service belongs to another chapter, but his first unsuccessful venture was the beginning of a great partnership in which the tremendous desert skill of the LRDG and the fighting valour of the SAS were to prove an irresistible combination.

When Stirling had an idea he pursued it with enormous energy and enthusiasm, and in due course he caught the ear successively of Generals Ritchie and Auchinleck (commander of the Eighth Army and C-in-C respectively), and obtained permission to recruit and train some sixty ex-Layforce men for strategic sabotage work many miles behind the enemy's front line. The first operation was a parachute descent by fifty-five men on 16 November 1941 to destroy enemy aircraft on the Gazala-Tmimi airfields in support of the Eighth Army's offensive, which was to begin on the 18th. The weather was particularly foul and the parachutists were dropped a considerable distance from their objectives. A bold idea ended in disaster with no aircraft destroyed, and only twenty-one of the fifty-five men reaching the pick-up point with the LRDG.

However, Stirling looked upon this first failure as a challenge. On his way to the rendezvous with Captain Easonsmith's Patrol he walked into the hideout of a Yeomanry Patrol commanded by Captain Lloyd Owen, and in the course of a lengthy discussion the latter sowed the seeds of co-operation. These fell on fertile ground, and it was not long before Stirling realized that the 'taxi' service that the LRDG could provide was likely to be a much surer (and more comfortable) means of reaching his objectives than parachute drops. If Stirling was at this time unaware of the expertise of the LRDG, Loyd Owen on the other hand must have appreciated that his suggestion would entail an additional risk to the Group's reconnaissance role, for the SAS had a habit of stirring up a hornet's nest every time it went into action. But if any qualms existed they were quickly stilled, for both parties shared a common interest in the discomfiture of Germans.

Meanwhile, six LRDG Patrols had an important role in the Eighth Army's* autumn offensive, of which picking up the SAS was only one small part. They were to be in position by the evening of 17 November along the inland tracks of Cyrenaica with a watching brief on enemy troop movements. Patrols were to report by wireless three times a day, and keep out of sight. But towards the end of November there was a serious setback in the Eighth Army's advance, when Rommel put in a strong counter-attack to retake Sidi Rezegh and forestall the relief of Tobruk. Although he was soon to be pushed back again as far as Agedabia, where he stabilized his line, these were very anxious times, and the LRDG's role was reversed from passive reconnaissance to one of offensive action against enemy transport and other targets.

To carry out this directive the six Patrols were allotted different sectors. The New Zealand and Rhodesian Patrols were to cover the road through the Jebel Akhdar, the two Yeomanry Patrols had the area Gazala-Derna-Mechili and the two Guards Patrols the

* LRDG was now under the command of the Eighth Army until reverting to GHQ troops on 30 September 1942.

Benghazi-Agedabia road. All six had some exciting times and successful actions, and the fortunes of G1 Patrol are fairly representative of what was achieved in the closing days of 1941.

The Patrol was commanded by Captain A.M. Hay, for Michael Crichton-Stuart had fallen ill and on his recovery had returned to the Scots Guards. As the Patrol was approaching the main road near Beda Fomm it was attacked from the air, first fairly half-heartedly by an Italian bomber, but shortly afterwards much more determinedly by a JU87, whose crew systematically bombed and machine-gunned the trucks; however, through a combination of good fortune and skill, these survived untouched.

Throughout the whole of the desert campaign these air attacks were the greatest source of anxiety and danger that the LRDG Patrols had to face. They adopted a drill of rapid dispersion of vehicles and individual 'jinking'. Inevitably there were occasions when these evasive tactics were not successful, but it says a great deal for the skill of the drivers that on the whole the casualties from the many air attacks encountered were comparatively light.

But to return to the story of G1: after surviving the attentions of the Junkers they holed up for the night near Beda Fomm, and on the next day continued their search for a target. This presented itself in the form of a vehicle park near a roadhouse on the main road, which the Patrol commander had spotted through glasses while on a foot reconnaissance. Orders were given for an attack that evening. This involved an approach drive down the main road amid enemy vehicles moving both ways. Here again it was incredible how many times Patrols were left undisturbed while mingling with enemy traffic; this was due partly to a clever use of headlights in the dusk and dark and partly to the fact that the enemy frequently used captured British vehicles.

In due course the Patrol reached the roadhouse, turned off the road and opened up with all they had on the enemy vehicles and the soldiers standing around them. Great was the pandemonium as tracer and armour-piercing bullets ripped into the vehicles, and for good measure to heighten the pyrotechnics grenades were liberally distributed. In the confusion the Patrol slipped away, and lay up that night and much of the next day while enemy aircraft quartered the ground, but failed to find them. Late that afternoon (for these offensive operations were best done in the gloaming) Hay found a suitable piece of ground where he could dismount his machine guns and blast the leading tanker of a south-bound convoy, destroying it and its crew.

The following day the Patrol was recalled to Siwa. Here it was joined by the remainder of the Group (less three Patrols under Captain Steele, which were at Jalo) to prepare for further operations both independently and with the SAS.

Jalo had been taken on 27 November by a mixed force under Brigadier Reid, and from it the next major SAS raid was launched. The essence of David Stirling's operations was that they should be undertaken by small numbers – a party of four or five was considered ideal. On the night of 14 December Captain C.A. Holliman (commanding S1 Patrol) transported sufficient men for three separate raids on enemy airfields west of Benghazi. The men were to be dropped as close to their targets as possible, and then Holliman was to find what cover he could and pick them up after the raid was over.

On this occasion the airfields visited by Stirling and Captain Jock Lewis were empty of aircraft, but Captain Paddy Mayne (one of the great paladins of the SAS and SRS) had better fortune at Tamet, when with five others he killed the aircrew while they slept in their huts, and then proceeded to destroy no fewer than twenty-four aeroplanes and a fuel dump. This sort of performance was to be constantly repeated in the months ahead, and there is no doubt that the lightning-swift SAS swoops which the skills of the LRDG made possible, together with their own independent raids, were immensely damaging to enemy material and morale. They tied up large numbers of men who were constantly encompassed with fear and foreboding.

Around February 1942 a decision was taken to replace the Fords, which had given yeoman service for many months, and Colonel Prendergast arranged for as many Patrols as possible to return to Cairo for refitting. Once again it was to be Chevrolets, this time specially fitted and with a lower petrol consumption, but this advantage was somewhat offset by the fact that these trucks lacked four-wheel drive. Four-wheel drive gave the Ford such a good grip on the sand that it had proved the superior desert vehicle, despite the Chevrolet's greater manoevrability. The armament was improved to include one 22 mm Breda dual-purpose gun for each Patrol, and the Lewis gun (never a great favourite with pre-war infantry soldiers) was replaced by a .303 Vickers 'K' machine gun.

Two Patrols (G2 under Captain J.A.L. Timpson, and Y2 under Captain David Lloyd Owen) were held back from this refit in order to carry out the first of the Road Watches – tedious and monotonous duties that were to last continuously for four and a half months, but which were highly valued by GHQ. In the early days of 1942 Rommel had launched out from his Agheila position and swept across Cyrenaica until the Eighth Army managed to hold him on the Gazala–Bir Hakeim line, and the Army Commander was anxious to learn what was being brought against him. In order to discover this the Guards Patrol was ordered to carry out a traffic census on the Jebel Akhdar roads, and the Yeomanry were to watch roads farther south in the Msus, Solluch and Agedabia areas.

Lloyd Owen's Patrol had a difficult and frustrating time, for it was operating in very open country. The useful information it was able to send back was gained mostly through milling about in a cloud of dust amid convoys of enemy vehicles. But Timpson's was more typical of what was to become the regular Road Watch procedure, and was full of interest and excitement. He had with him that remarkable man John Haselden (see Chapter 5), whose intimate knowledge of the area and special relationship with the Senussi was invaluable on this fact-finding mission.

At a Bedouin tea party engineered by Haselden on their way to the rendezvous it was learnt that 200 enemy vehicles with tanks and guns had passed through their allotted area two days previously, going east. The tribesmen said that two roads were being used, and it was obvious that to avoid undue risk the trucks would have to be left some distance from the southern road. Haselden took the Patrol Sergeant and two guardsmen to the northern road – a trek of some 30 miles from the trucks – while Timpson and the remainder observed the traffic using the southern road. The cover in his area was good, but as so often happened on these occasions the selected hideout suddenly became the focus for a party of enemy setting up a temporary camp. This not only prevented all movement but made it extremely difficult for the recorder to note the traffic, and at dusk necessitated a cautious retreat to another place.

For four days Timpson, his guardsmen and native guides, alternating their watching, made a careful and detailed record of the various types of vehicle that passed along the southern road, and Haselden did the same on the northern one. On reaching the trucks for the homeward journey – Haselden's party covering the 30 miles with their equipment in fourteen hours – they found that the sergeant in charge had attracted a mélange of would-be passengers. Some of these, such as the five British soldiers who had escaped from Benghazi, were very welcome; others like the Mudir of Slonta, his wives, children, chickens and goats rather less so.

These two watches had taken place in country to the east of where, for the next few months, the regular Road Watch was to be kept. This was close to what the British soldier came to call 'Marble Arch', and which was in fact a huge triumphal arch erected astride the Via Balbia by Mussolini to commemorate the grandeur and the glory of Il Duce. The actual spot, so well chosen by Kennedy Shaw that it survived undetected throughout the whole summer of 1942, was some 5 miles to the east of the Arch and south across a gravel plain to the mouth of a wadi at the foot of a low escarpment. The cover for vehicles here was nothing very special, but sufficient if supplemented by the cunning use of camouflage nets, and obliteration of tell-tale tracks.

Lloyd Owen has written:* 'I think in retrospect that the Road Watch, as carried out during those anxious months of 1942, was enough to justify the existence of the LRDG, without even taking into consideration any of the other work that it did.' And so a brief look at the procedure is not without interest.

The normal routine was for a Patrol to spend a fortnight on Road Watch duty, and this entailed tying up three Patrols – one on watch, one returning and one going out – for the distance from Siwa to 'Marble Arch' was about 600 miles and a week's travelling. The actual hideout was an improvised hollow in low scrub some 300 yards from the road; it was just adequate, but to be certain of escaping detection the two men had to lie almost motionless throughout the day. Not only was there a danger of visiting Germans and Italians, but more particularly wandering Arabs, some of whom could not be trusted in Tripolitania.

Before dawn the sentry on guard at the wadi, which was about 2½ miles from the road, would wake the two men whose turn it was for the watch, and they would go forward armed with field glasses and recognition tables to crawl into the hideout and there remain for the whole of the hot day; at night they would come out and get closer to the road for better observation. One of the men would write and the other observe – if the traffic was heavy moving east and west both men might have to write, splitting the direction – and GHQ needed every conceivable detail. Classification of vehicles, even vehicle markings, type of tank, calibre of gun, tonnage of stores, number of troops, were all to be carefully recorded. Shortly before dawn on the next day the pair would be relieved, and then back at the wadi their information would be classified and transmitted to GHQ.

* *Providence Their Guide*, p.87.

Nor were those off duty in a much happier position; they had to while away the time as best they could, listening to the wireless, playing cards, or just lying under mosquito nets trying to dodge the clouds of tormenting flies that always swarmed around a well-used camp site. It was a tedious task, although no less dangerous than any other, and with those who undertook it – as also with the ever increasing numbers of hit-men who relied on the LRDG to take them to their targets – it was very unpopular. But although some of the information was confirmatory, much was unobtainable from any other source, and for the Eighth Army it was a vital duty.

At this time the Road Watch had priority over raids. The latter could not be undertaken in sensitive areas, where the effects might have adverse repercussions on the watch. However, this was not too inhibiting a factor, and despite the demands made upon Patrols by the Road Watch and the porterage of SAS detachments a certain amount of fun was had by those not engaged in these two duties. Captain Nick Wilder took two Patrols of New Zealanders on a very successful sortie against enemy transport on the Benghazi-Agedabia road, where he ambushed a convoy, destroyed the vehicles and killed many of the men before repeating the performance a little farther down the road against vehicles hastily abandoned by their drivers. Other Patrols ordered to interrupt enemy road movement west of Agheila used a variety of artifices and stratagems, which included ambushes, roadblocks and even joining convoys and lobbing time bombs into the truck in front. Some of these were successful, all were exciting.

In May the swing of the pendulum of battle once more went against the Eighth Army. On the 27th Rommel launched a heavy attack on the Gazala line. The French fought valiantly at Bir Hakeim, and 'Knightsbridge' and 'the Cauldron' were to become household words; but little could prevail against this latest German flail of steel, and on 17 June the Army Commander ordered a withdrawal to the Egyptian frontier, once again leaving Tobruk an isolated garrison. But their hopes of survival in this darkling scene were clearly doubtful, and on 21 June disaster struck: Tobruk was taken together with 25,000 Allied troops, of whom a few made a successful breakout.

Even before General Auchinleck halted this tidal bore of victory at El Alamein, it was obvious that Siwa, the LRDG's most useful and pleasant base which they had occupied since the spring of 1941, was no longer tenable. Indeed, when the last trucks left on 28 June it was a near-run thing before the Mersa Matruh-Siwa track was closed, and soon after the escape route through Qara and across the Qattara Depression was lost. Nor was it easy for Prendergast to carry out such a hasty withdrawal with his Patrols scattered over many hundreds of miles. But with good staff and communications work, the employment of Wacos for wounded and sick, and the use of Kufra as a safe fallback base for Patrols operating at a distance it was somehow accomplished.

Shortly after the Eighth Army got itself sorted out at Alamein it was decided that the LRDG should now use the Fayoum (an oasis not far from Cairo) as their main base. Kufra was still available for a forward jumping-off point, and although the Road Watch was called off in the third week of July the oasis was in constant use as a valuable staging post. At about this time the SAS gained recognition as a regiment with its own establishment, which included transport – American jeeps, on which Stirling mounted Vickers 'K' machine guns. This semi-independence was a help, but Lloyd Owen felt that the administrative worries this imposed upon Stirling ill suited his flamboyant character, and that while he retained his charm, courtesy and courage he lost something of his brio.

The SAS jeeps did not herald the end of close co-operation with the LRDG, and there were to be many occasions when the latter acted as guides and escort, which could easily involve them in some exciting brushes with the enemy. On one such occasion G2 Patrol with four trucks under Captain R.B. Gurdon* was acting as escort to a lorryload of SAS on their way to destroy aircraft on airfields between Fuka and Daba, when they were caught in the open by three Italian fighters. Gurdon tried the often successful ruse of waving cheerily to the pilots, but these men were not fooled and in the subsequent strafe he was hit by two cannon shells and a bullet, and his driver was also severely wounded. Gurdon ordered his men in the remaining trucks to go forward and attack the airfields but, getting their priorities right, they disobeyed him and travelled as best they could all through the night to the medical officer. Gurdon died only 4 miles from the rendezvous. He was an officer whom the LRDG could ill afford to lose.

Ever since the proliferation of special service troops subsequent to the disbandment of Layforce there had been many attempts at appointing a coordinating individual or committee. At one time

* Robin Gurdon, a Coldstreamer, had replaced Tony Hay when the latter inadvertently walked into a party of enemy and was captured. He was a man of much courage, always unruffled and possessing the confidence and love of his soldiers.

this task fell to Guy Prendergast, but he was not temperamentally suited, nor was he keen to lose control of his first love, the LRDG; but now the right man had been found in Colonel (later General Sir John) Hackett, who became the head of what was called 'G Raiding Force'. A dynamic, far-seeing, forceful personality with brilliant mental equipment, he had in addition to these virtues the strength of character to control David Stirling's exuberance, for some of David's ideas were as wild as others were masterly.

It is true that one of the first major operations that Hackett was partly responsible for ended in almost total tactical failure. But its strategic object, that of disrupting Rommel's main supply ports during the critical weeks before the breakout from Alamein, was very sound; failure was due to serious laxity in security, and it is almost certain that at least two of the four raids would have had better results if fewer men had been employed.

The LRDG had a part to play in all four, and the raid against the airfield at Barce was purely their affair. Of the other three, the raid on Tobruk has already been mentioned in Chapter 5, and the one on Benghazi, which was an SAS operation, will be described in Chapter 13. The third was the intended capture of Jalo by the Sudan Defence Force, so that it could be used as a base for further SAS raids.* Y2 Patrol, under Captain A.D.N. Hunter, was in support of the SDF, and the party left Kufra on 11 September. The attack by three columns, which went in on foot, was a failure; it seems that the Italians were prepared, and although the SDF got a foothold in the fort it was driven out. After four days of being shelled and bombed on the edge of the oasis (the party had no air support) orders were given to break off the action.

The attack on Barce was led by Jake Easonsmith, who had G1 Patrol under Timpson and T2 under Wilder, together with Major Peniakoff ('Popski' – see Chapter 12) and two of his Arabs, and fortunately Captain Lawson the medical officer. Fortunate because on the way to their target through the Sand Sea Timpson's vehicle plunged over a razorback ridge, cracking his skull and fracturing his driver's spine. The expert attentions of the medical officer probably saved the driver's life, and later during the withdrawal six wounded were greatly indebted to his skilful ministrations and his courage. This accident slightly delayed the party, but they were within 15 miles of Barce on 13 September, the day scheduled for the attack, and in time to allow Easonsmith to go forward on foot with Peniakoff, whose Arabs were to enter Barce and gain

---

* Jalo had been retaken during Rommel's advance to El Alamein.

what information they could. Easonsmith was back with the Patrols that afternoon to give his orders, and at dusk they set off.

It was a dark, moonless night and it seems that the raiders were not expected – perhaps because the target had been changed from Derna to Barce at a fairly late hour. Anyway, the occupants of two Italian light tanks on either side of the road allowed themselves to be quickly put out of action, and then at the crossroads close to Barce the Patrols went their separate ways. The New Zealanders turned right for the airfield, which was to be their playground; the Guards went straight on for the barracks; and Easonsmith with two jeeps set off to beat up the town. Both Patrols left their W/T trucks (vehicles that must always be risked as little as possible) as links and rallying points.

The adventures of the two Patrols have been written about in detail elsewhere (see Bibliography). Suffice it to say here that the thoroughgoing New Zealanders left the airfield in a shambles with twenty-four aircraft totally destroyed and twelve others damaged, while the Guards Patrol, under Sergeant Dennis since Timpson had been evacuated, played havoc with the barracks and prevented any men from going to the assistance of their comrades on the airfield. The Italians seemed incapable of efficient intervention, but both Patrols found that the enemy's main effort was to block their exit with tanks. It needed some dangerous and damaging ramming to burst their way through to safety. Easonsmith had also had tank trouble in the town, but managed to bounce off them comparatively unscathed, and scuppered twelve vehicles he found in an MT park.

The worst part of the operation was the withdrawal, for the enemy were thirsting for revenge and preparing ambushes and air strikes. The latter proved very costly, for the Patrols were travelling in rough, scrub country where dodging was impossible; six men (including Wilder) were wounded and a number of vehicles were damaged beyond repair. Eventually Easonsmith was down to two jeeps and one Chevrolet; he sent the Chevrolet and one jeep back with the wounded, setting out on foot with the others – the remaining jeep carried their rations and water. There followed an anxious trek, but the calm courage and cheerfulness of Easonsmith kept them going until they were rescued by a Rhodesian Patrol. Meanwhile Lloyd Owen had been sent out to Landing Ground 125, where he found Lawson and the wounded. Here he contacted GHQ, and a Bombay was despatched to bring the wounded to Cairo.

Barce had been the one tactical success of the four-pronged

venture. The LRDG Patrols had destroyed or damaged thirty-six aircraft and killed perhaps as many men for the loss of ten of their own captured and fourteen vehicles. The six wounded all recovered to fight another day. Easonsmith and Wilder received the Distinguished Service Order, Lawson the Military Cross and Sergeant Dennis the Military Medal for their skill and bravery in this raid.

The losses elsewhere, particularly in Tobruk, had been far more serious and, although there had been some strategic gain in that Rommel diverted troops and aircraft from the front that could have been used to forestall certain Eighth Army operations, the overall result was a costly failure. Lloyd Owen, while wondering why, if there had been misgivings over size and security, the raids were allowed to go ahead, feels sure that without Colonel Hackett 'they would have been an even bigger fiasco than they unhappily turned out to be'.*

At the end of August Rommel made one more tremendous effort. But wave upon wave of German armour was held. By 5 September the battle of Alam Halfa was over, and despite all Rommel's hopes the Nile Delta remained an elusive mirage. Thereafter General Montgomery, now with a superiority of two to one in manpower, and more than half again as much armour as the Germans, prepared to roll up the Afrika Korps once and for all. There was little time to lose, for possession of the airfields of Cyrenaica was vital if Malta was not to be lost and with it control of the Mediterranean. On the night of 23 October 1942 he struck, and three months later his army entered Tripoli.

During this spectacular advance there was much work of a varied nature for the LRDG. To begin with the Road Watch was reinstated, and continued to provide vital information until the end of December, when it was finally discontinued. This second term was even more tricky than the first, for not only did the rapid withdrawal of the enemy make it necessary to be constantly on the lookout for new positions, but the Germans had learnt the approach routes used, and had taken steps to mine and patrol certain areas such as the Marada–Zella gap.

Timpson, with a strong Patrol of twenty men in five trucks, was worsted in a fight with superior enemy vehicles, and lost all save a jeep, two trucks, himself, Bernard Bruce (also Scots Guards), Sergeant Ollerenshaw (Grenadier Guards) and seven other ranks. Fortunately one of his surviving trucks contained the

---

* *Providence Their Guide*, p.105.

wireless, from which he learned that the New Zealand Patrol T2, which was working in harness with his Patrol, had suffered casualties in a minefield and had had to return to Kufra. And so Timpson was ordered to maintain the Road Watch for two weeks with his party of only ten – moreover, his trucks had to be parked no less than 20 miles from the road. That he accomplished it was a fine feat.

Other duties at this time included 'going' reports, guiding formations over difficult ground, and the collecting and depositing of agents. But almost the last, and certainly the last most important, task was to reconnoitre a way round the western flank of the enemy's formidable Mareth Line in order to let the New Zealand Division break in behind the Matmata massif. Group Headquarters was now at Hon, but this was more than 400 miles from the hills that formed the enemy's position, and so forward dumps were laid out by the Heavy Section to facilitate these reconnaissances.

Throughout January and much of February Patrols were active across the Tunisian border, covering thousands of miles – some had even swept round within a few miles of Gabes – and suffering some men and vehicle casualties. But it was Nick Wilder's New Zealanders who eventually discovered the gap in the hills through which, appropriately enough, the New Zealand Division was to be led on its famous left hook by another New Zealand Patrol under Captain R.A. Tinker. In this great pursuit to victory 27,000 men and 200 tanks were to pour through the gap that was to bring Wilder eponymous fame.

Although the Indian Long Range Squadron was not, of course, a British special force, no account of the Long Range Desert Group would be complete without a brief mention of these gallant Indians. Formed in Syria, Squadron Headquarters and four Patrols, under Major S.V. McCoy, came to Egypt at the beginning of July 1942 and were put under the command of British Troops Egypt. Each Patrol had one British officer and sixteen Indian other ranks, and was mounted in five trucks. They were anxious to be placed under the command of the LRDG, from whom they knew they would learn much about desert warfare. But this did not occur until 1 October, and meanwhile Patrols were used to reinforce the Egyptian army's watch at Bahariya, and to carry out standing patrols with the Polish Carpathian Lancers. Later they proved most useful during General Leclerc's march north from Chad, and in the closing three months of the desert war, by which time they had become highly skilled, the Indians were of great value to the fully-extended LRDG. They shared with them the long spells of little sleep, hard rations and mighty few comforts.

Once the Mareth Line had been breached, and the German army found itself crushed between the upper and nether millstones of the two Allied armies, there was no more work for the LRDG to do, for the country beyond Gabes was quite unsuitable for their vehicles. And so Prendergast led his men back along the road they had watched so patiently for so many months, to the comparative delights of a tented camp near Alexandria, where they could enjoy a well-deserved rest and prepare themselves for the totally new role that soon awaited them.

For two and a half years men of the Long Range Desert Group had performed their duties with great success, reliably and without ostentation. They had carried out their allotted tasks not only with a profound and unflinching courage, but with a degree of skill and professionalism rapidly acquired in a new and exciting type of warfare.

11

The Long Range Desert Group:
A Different Kind of War

The conclusion of the LRDG's desert campaign in April 1943 found the Group at the moment of its fullest efflorescence. Now it was to be called upon to fight a less romantic kind of war; still with the emphasis on reconnaissance, but more akin to that waged over the past three years by the Commandos and Courtney's SBS, extended on occasions by the use of the parachute. Colonel Prendergast remained in command, and had Jake Easonsmith as his second-in-command.

No precise role was immediately forthcoming, but everything pointed towards work in the Aegean islands, and to this end it was considered that some knowledge of Greek and German was desirable. Basic training was aimed at getting men, previously accustomed to travel in trucks, fit to carry out long marches over mountainous country humping full equipment and rations for up to ten days – an average load of 60 lb per man. It was thought expedient to have more men proficient as W/T operators, for it was expected that Patrols (which were to be small) would have a greater use for wireless than in the past. Some jeeps were to be retained, and indents went in to GHQ for weapons, equipment and clothing suitable for the new work. These inevitably took time to materialize, for at first there was no fixed establishment, but as each item arrived it was pressed into immediate use in a rigorous training programme.

Not long after Mareth, 201 Guards Brigade suffered heavy casualties, and when the LRDG work in the desert was completed a request went out for the men of G Patrols to return to their regiments; only a few specialists, whom Prendergast sought leave to retain, continued with the Group. This left A Squadron of New

Zealanders under Major A.I. Guild, and B Squadron of Yeomanry, other United Kingdom troops and Rhodesians under Major D.L. Lloyd Owen.

When the revised war establishment was received it did not differ very much from its desert predecessor. The Headquarters personnel remained virtually the same and there were to be two Squadrons, each commanded by a major and having six Patrols under a captain. The Patrols were ten strong, and the overall strength of the Group with attached personnel was 249 all ranks. In the desert B Squadron had been administered by Group HQ; now it was to have its own headquarters manned mainly by men from the disbanded Heavy Section. A fairly formidable array of transport was laid down including twenty-four pack mules, but when the time came for the Squadrons to leave for the Aegean only jeeps were taken.

In May Lloyd Owen, preferring the crisp, invigorating mountain air and pastoral peace of the Lebanon to the sticky heat and scent of warm dust that pervades the flat Alexandrian landscape, took his Squadron to a place called the Cedars. Here, surrounded by towering snow peaks in an hotel set among the age-old yet timeless cedars of Lebanon, they learned from expert instructors at the Mountain Warfare School some of the crafts and skills of rock climbing and skiing. Less exhilarating, and even more arduous, were the long marches over the mountains, weapon training and battling with recalcitrant mules. The A Squadron remained in Alexandria until 28 June when it took over the Cedars hotel from B, which moved into a tented camp. Both Squadrons then carried out mountain training.

As the summer of 1943 wore on, and the Aegean islands became an increasingly more likely operation area, the Commanding Officer and Squadron commanders felt that to obtain flexibility, and be able to reach targets well inland, parachuting should be added to the Group's other skills. Prendergast therefore arranged for B Squadron to make a start on this at Ramat David in Palestine; but on the evening before a party from the Squadron were to make their first jump, orders were received for the whole Squadron to embark the next day from Haifa.

Lloyd Owen received these orders at Ramat David and had part of his Squadron there, part many miles away in the Lebanon and some Signal personnel in Cairo. This order meant considerable disappointment for the would-be parachutists and an all-night working session for the commanders. However, their lucubrations brought results and the Squadron with its transport and equipment embarked the next evening, 12 September, bound for the island of Castelorizzo.

The strategic importance of the Aegean islands has already been stressed, and with the Italian surrender came a chance not to be missed for taking possession of some of the most important ones: Rhodes, Cos and Leros. The Italians had given gages that if British troops could forestall the Germans they would co-operate. The latter were not in great strength, but for some time past they had been half suspecting that their caitiff allies might withdraw from the conflict, and plans had been formulated to prevent the loss of the islands.

The Aegean story at this time makes sorry reading. Plans for the capture of Rhodes had been made in the summer months, and the 8th Indian Division was to have assaulted the island at the beginning of September; but the necessary shipping had to be sent to the Far East. Immediately after the Italian surrender Lord Jellicoe and Major Dalby were dropped on Rhodes but, not being supported with follow-up troops, failed to persuade the Italians to turn against the small number of Germans on the island (see Chapter 14). However, Cos (second only to Rhodes in importance, for it had an airfield), Samos and Leros were occupied by what troops could be spared and transported. The Prime Minister made urgent and protracted representations to General Eisenhower, and even to the President, for the release of only a small number of ships and aircraft operating, or preparing for operations, farther west to enable the islands to be permanently secured. But the Americans obdurately resisted these pleas. And once again, as will be seen, valuable lives were lost with nugatory results.

B Squadron had not been on Castelorizzo for more than a few days when orders came to proceed to Leros. This was easier said than done, for there was virtually no shipping available, but Lloyd Owen and twenty men got there quite quickly in an Italian motor launch, and the remainder of the Squadron followed a day or so later in caiques. The Italian garrison on Leros was some 5,000 strong, but their senior officers (who wined and dined Lloyd Owen from the finest porcelain and gold goblets!) had paid little attention to the proper defence of the island, and were somewhat surprised to be told to take off their smart tunics and get down to work with the men in improving the situation.

On the arrival of a complete brigade (battalions of the Royal Irish Fusiliers, Buffs and King's Own) whose men had experienced the siege of Malta, there was little more for the LRDG to do,* and together with Lord Jellicoe's Special Boat Squadron they went to the island of Kalimnos, just south of Leros and between that island and Cos. Here they witnessed the German attack on and capture of Cos, with its valuable airfield, and narrowly avoided being sent to counter-attack – which would have been a suicidal and pointless mission. Instead they were ordered back to Leros, and embarked in a fleet of caiques on the night of 4/5 October. The Germans were already beginning to soften up the island with repeated JU88 and Stuka strafing and dive bombing. There was little to be done except await the inevitable attack, and send out Patrols to some of the neighbouring islands (Simi, Kithnos, Mykonos and Stampalia) to report on enemy sea and air movement.

On 15 October a signal was received to say that Colonel D.J.T. Turnbull had been appointed Brigadier commanding Raiding Forces, and on the 18th he arrived in Leros. Some form of co-ordinating headquarters had long been desirable, for there were now seven special forces of one sort or another operating in the Aegean (see Chapter 14). But unfortunately Turnbull was not a particularly sound choice of commander, for he knew nothing about any form of special service work, and the first thing he did was to claim Guy Prendergast as his second-in-command. This was a great blow to the LRDG (and also to Prendergast), but in Jake Easonsmith they found a commander of equal excellence, and he appointed Lloyd Owen as his second-in-command. B Squadron was now to be commanded by Major Alan Redfern, who a month later was killed in the fighting on the island.

The first operation for the LRDG after the inception of Raiding Forces was ill-considered, and unsuitable to their tactics. A Royal Navy caique manned by eight men had sailed, at the beginning of October, from Stampalia with forty German prisoners aboard. The caique had engine trouble and put into Levita (about 30 miles south-west of Leros), where the prisoners managed to overcome their captors and seized control of the island. Nothing more was known, although it might be presumed that in the intervening weeks the forty had been reinforced. The LRDG, with a force of some fifty men, was to retake Levita, which for some reason the GOC Aegean judged to be an easy operation, and in consequence refused Easonsmith's request for a postponement in order to gain more information.

On 23 October four officers (which included the doctor) and

* Both Squadrons were now together on Leros.

forty-five other ranks left Leros for Levita in two Motor Launches. Olforce, as it was called after its commander, Captain J.R. Olivey, a Rhodesian, was organized into three sections each of three detachments, and two landings were made. Lieutenant J. Sutherland with a party of New Zealanders was to land on the north-east coast, and the other half of the Force landed on the south-west end of the island; both parties were to sweep towards the centre. No news reached Leros during that day save for one signal to say that opposition was pretty stiff, and Easonsmith and Lloyd Owen could see heavy Stuka and JU88 attacks in progress.

That evening Easonsmith went himself in a Motor Launch to the agreed rendezvous to pick up the men whose task by then should have been accomplished, but he found only Olivey, the doctor and six other ranks, one of whom was wounded. They had managed to break out from a tight ring of steel that had all but surrounded them, but of the others Olivey knew nothing. A further search the next night was equally fruitless. In fact Olforce had been heavily outnumbered, constantly pinned to the ground by unopposed air attacks, and at one time faced with having to assault an enemy in prepared positions, for which of course they were not properly armed. As a result of this débâcle the LRDG lost forty well-trained men.

As early as 10 October, in view of the fact that there were insufficient troops available to carry out successful operations, the Prime Minister suggested to General (later Field-Marshal Earl) Alexander that it might be as well to evacuate Leros and the other islands, cutting our losses as best we could from this unhappy situation. It would seem to have been the wisest course, for the Germans were known to be massing troops and aircraft for retaking Leros, and the Turks had already become disillusioned and inclined to be uncooperative. But commanders on the spot are usually more able to judge the best course of action, and General (later Field-Marshal Lord) Wilson had hopes of success.

On 12 November 1943, the long-awaited assault commenced. The Germans landed on the north-east coast of Leros and at Pandeli Bay, south-east of Leros village. Later that day parachutists were dropped on the neck of land that divides the island north and south. Fighting was very severe: at first the Germans were held to the beaches, but reinforcements continually reached them, and the British troops were devoid of any air protection. On the third day the Samos garrison (a battalion of the Royal West Kents) landed on the south of the island, but the odds were too great, and on the 17th Leros surrendered.

Throughout the war the British certainly learned the hard way, and sometimes they did not learn at all. This was a repetition of Crete, on a slightly smaller scale: troops, hopelessly outnumbered, sternly embattled on the ground and strafed unmercifully from the air, with virtually no air support of their own; the Royal Navy snatching almost a thousand men from the doomed island and losing six destroyers and two submarines, with a further four destroyers and four cruisers damaged, in the process. Thus was closed in disaster yet another amphibious venture, which at the time seemed hard to justify, although General Wilson in his report said: 'It was a near thing between success and failure.'

Men of the LRDG were in action continuously throughout the five days, and John Olivey and his Rhodesians particularly distinguished themselves in the north of the island. The Italian crew of the heavy coastal guns did not – save for one officer of sterner mettle – stay to fight, and so the Rhodesians turned their guns on the advancing Germans, firing over open sights, until they were overrun. But the next day they retook the position, and fought on in the north until overwhelmed by fatigue they were captured asleep many hours after the surrender.*

At the time of the surrender the LRDG had 123 men on the island,† and of these about 70 managed to escape, mostly via Turkey. One officer, Lieutenant Ashley Greenwood, having got to Turkey bravely returned to Leros disguised as a Greek and managed to rescue a number of his comrades. However, the loss of some fifty good, battle-experienced men was a sad blow, and an even sadder one was the loss of the Commanding Officer, Jake Easonsmith. He had personally led a Patrol into Leros village on what he knew would be a dangerous mission, and fell to a sniper's bullet. Easonsmith was an officer of outstanding ability with self-reliant insight and instinct for battle, a man of great courage who was able to win the hearts of men, and who led by example and never by precept.

He had, with characteristic prescience, sent Lloyd Owen on a mission to Cairo shortly before the German attack on Leros; the latter now found himself temporarily in command of the LRDG. After much heart searching, and a visit for advice to Brigadier Bagnold, Lloyd Owen became increasingly certain that there was a great future for the unit, and he was determined to make good

---

* Olivey was eventually rescued from Athens at the beginning of 1944, and after a spell of leave in Rhodesia rejoined the LRDG in Italy. For his exploits on Leros he was awarded a bar to his Military Cross.
† Lloyd Owen, *Providence Their Guide*, p.144.

the gaps and keep it in being. Very soon he was confirmed in command, for Prendergast – who had stood in when Easonsmith had been killed, and was one of those who had made his way back via Turkey – felt that he was of more use to the LRDG in his present appointment.

It was not an easy time for the new commanding officer, for he was scarcely in the saddle when the New Zealand government finally decided they must withdraw their Patrols. Everything possible was done to persuade them to the contrary, but they were adamant, for their troops in Italy had suffered severe casualties. It was a bitter blow, for the New Zealanders were undoubtedly the richest marrow in the LRDG's bones.* Fortunately, Lloyd Owen was able to procure a good intake of excellent Rhodesians as replacements.

By the middle of December the unit was assuming its new shape with two Squadrons each of eight Patrols. Major K.H. Lazarus, who had joined the LRDG in 1941, was given command of A Squadron – the Rhodesians – and Major Moir Stormonth-Darling, a regular soldier in the Cameronians, took over B Squadron. Both these men had had exciting Aegean adventures. Stormonth-Darling and his Patrol had been rescued from the island of Mykonos, and Lazarus had been stranded on Stampalia for more than a month before finding a rowing boat in which he and four of his men got to Turkey.

At the beginning of 1944 the unit was in a tented camp near Haifa. Here, and once again at the Mountain Warfare School, both old hands and the new intake underwent a varied, intensive and rigorous training programme, which included small-boat handling and a return to Ramat David, where this time the parachute course was uninterrupted. Ever since Leros Lloyd Owen's thoughts had been towards operating in the Balkans in aid of the partisans, and the training was mainly geared to that end.

At the end of February 1944 it was decided that the LRDG should sever its connection with Raiding Forces and sail for Italy. Lloyd Owen flew to Bari at the beginning of March to arrange details, and a week later an advance party of two officers found a good site for a permanent base at Rodi on the Gargano peninsula, north-east of Foggia. There followed the usual period of frustration for, although Commandos had been operating successfully in and from Italy for some months, there were those on the staff at

* A few officers managed to persuade General Freyberg to release them, and they rejoined the LRDG in Italy during 1944.

Army Headquarters who were still a trifle suspicious of special forces, unsure about their purpose and inclined to be indifferent. Eventually Lloyd Owen decided he would palter with them no more and applied to have one Squadron lent to Force 266 (see Chapter 4). This was readily agreed, and in early May A Squadron Headquarters moved to Bari, which became an operational base for sorties into the Balkans.

The first of these was made by a reconnaissance party of four men under Captain Eastwood to investigate a suspected enemy radar station on the north coast of Corfu, which was to be the target for a larger raiding force. They were taken to a neighbouring island in a Royal Navy Motor Launch, where they picked up a Greek agent and rowed to Corfu. They soon located the radar station and in the course of two days, with one of the party disguised as a vendor of fish, they obtained full particulars of the enemy dispositions.

Shortly after this successful beginning another reconnaissance patrol, this time arriving by parachute (the unit's first operational drop), was undertaken by Lieutenant C.J.D. Jackson and eight men from S2 Patrol of A Squadron. Their task was to obtain information about an enemy garrison said to be under siege by partisans near Himara, in Albania, with a view to sending a large force to assist in their destruction. The drop, the reconnaissance and the rescue operation all went according to plan, but the actual attack had to be postponed until a later date.

A good start had been made to Balkan operations, but in Italy things were not so satisfactory. Information about roads ahead of the Allied armies' rapid advance was needed by Eighth Army Headquarters, and B Squadron organized seven Patrols each of four jeeps, mounted with an LMG and carrying food for fourteen days and petrol for 500 miles. However, the advance to Rome and beyond outpaced reconnaissance planning, and the jeeps were discarded in favour of parachute drops farther north to report on the going for all types of vehicles. Four Patrols were required to be dropped on the nights of 11 and 12 June.

The drops had to be postponed twenty-four hours on account of bad weather, but on the night of 12 June M2 Patrol under Lieutenant S.D. Fleming and W2 Patrol under Lieutenant J. Bramley were dropped to the south-east of Siena, and the following night M1 and W1 Patrols with Captain A. Greenwood and Lieutenant Rowbottom came down – some way from their planned dropping zones – south-west of Arezzo. Sadly, Simon Fleming's parachute failed to open and the LRDG lost another competent and courageous officer. Another man of his Patrol was killed in the drop, and the remainder gradually got back to the Allied lines without having achieved anything. The second Patrol of the first drop was the only one that succeeded in the given task. Bramley was able to wireless back a series of very useful reports until on 17 June his batteries failed: thereafter the Patrol made notes, and regained the lines on 28 June with valuable information.

The Patrols of the second drop were not able to send back information, because Greenwood's dropped right into a village held by the Germans, and Rowbottom's bumped into a German post on the evening of the first day. All of Greenwood's Patrol, save himself and one man, were captured, but they soon escaped and got back in the course of two weeks. Gordon Rowbottom and two or three of his men had amazing adventures. Rowbottom himself was captured, but escaped when the German truck in which he was travelling overturned, and he then met two men of his Patrol and joined forces with a band of Italian patriots.* Rowbottom led them for the next few weeks in a series of successful sabotage raids until he and his two men regained the Allied line on 26 July. For his exploits he was awarded the Military Cross, and Sergeant Morley of his Patrol, who had fought a private war of his own and gained valuable information while behind the enemy lines, received the Military Medal.

This colourful, but on the whole unsuccessful, operation was the only one the LRDG carried out in Italy until nearly the end of the war, when places such as Trieste and Monfalcone were in the battle front. After a further period of uncertainty, with operations arranged and then cancelled, Lloyd Owen made a successful representation at Alexander's headquarters for the transfer of B Squadron for work in the Balkans, and it was decided that the LRDG should now come under Brigadier George Davy's Land Forces Adriatic. LFA was the military component of the Balkan Air Force, which was responsible for aid to and co-operation with all partisan forces. There was plenty of work for special service troops in this field both in Yugoslavia and in Albania, as has been seen in Chapter 4, and the transfer had the additional merit for Lloyd Owen in that his two Squadrons were now to operate on one front only.

But some weeks before this happened, A Squadron had become

---

* They were in fact a mixed lot of about sixty, which included, besides Italians, Germans, French and Russians, under an Italian called Captain Raoul.

involved in operations amid the northern Dalmatian islands. The idea was for five Patrols to provide shipping watches on the principal routes, and to carry out a series of swift, bold and unexpected raids on enemy shipping and garrisons in the islands. At the end of May Lloyd Owen flew to Vis to discuss this proposal, and a few weeks later he set up an advanced base on the long, narrow island of Dugi Otok some 60 miles north of Vis. Vis was now an important partisan centre and Marshal Tito's temporary headquarters.

Lloyd Owen had the original and enterprising idea of providing the LRDG with its own supply ship. He would then have acquired a degree of mobility in the air, on land and on sea. The Royal Navy were doing excellent work in and around the Adriatic and Dalmatian islands, but many and conflicting demands were constantly made upon them. From somewhere a fishing schooner complete with motor, MFV *La Palma*, was conjured, and after some modifications had been made for crew accommodation and gun mounting, she was put in charge of Captain A.S. Denniff, a desert veteran, and a small military crew.

La Palma sailed on her maiden voyage in her new ownership for Vis on 18 June carrying a crew of nine, twelve passengers, 11,000 lb of stores, a jeep and other equipment, which gives a good idea of her capacity. She continued in service for the rest of the war, proving invaluable for the transporting of supplies, and on occasions being used to take Patrols in and out of occupied territory. Early in 1945 the LRDG fleet was doubled with the acquisition of an 80-ton schooner aptly named MFV *Kufra*.

The first shipping watch from the Yugoslav mainland was undertaken by Captain Arthur Stokes and four men. It proved to be an even more formidable task than the Road Watch of desert days, for they maintained their vigil for almost five months continually wirelessing back (and great credit for this must go to Signalman Hansell) important information for the RAF to act upon, and constantly being harassed by the Germans, who were determined to eradicate this elusive source of their heavy shipping losses. The party was kept supplied by air drops, but this was a tricky business on account of weather, and the fact that the watchers were frequently on the move dodging Germans. When a small party operating deep behind the enemy lines is constantly short of sleep and food, high–class leadership is at a premium, and Captain Stokes well deserved the Military Cross he was awarded for this job.

By August 1944 both Squadrons were operating in the Balkans, and B Squadron's first emprise was to despatch a Patrol under Captain Gibson to keep a close daylight watch on Mostar aerodrome for seven or more days. Mostar is in mainland Yugoslavia, north of Dubrovnik and some 30 miles inland. It was perhaps not surprising therefore, with Germans thick on the ground and paying particular attention to the partisan band Gibson was operating with, that the party could not reach Mostar. The original idea of wirelessing back enemy aircraft movement in time to allow our fighters to intercept had to be abandoned, and the Patrol was ordered to remain short of Mostar and to report on all enemy movement in the area. This they did for two and a half months, sending back valuable information and frequently harassing the enemy. This Patrol was also supplied by air, and they were often extremely short of food.

Later in the same month two other Patrols of B Squadron left Italy for an operation on the Yugoslav mainland in conjunction with Lord Jellicoe's Special Boat Squadron, which had recently joined LRDG headquarters in Italy to help with the weight of work in the Balkans. Captain David Skipwith and four men landed in the early hours of 19 August, and after a week they had found a suitable target in the form of a large and important railway bridge at Karasovici near Dubrovnik. To help deal with this, SBS men under Captain Anders Lassen* with Lieutenant Henshaw as his second-in-command sailed on the night of 27 August, and were guided ashore by lights from Skipwith's party. There was a big sea running, which did not make it easy to off-load 400 lb of explosives and other equipment, and then there was a face of sheer rock to be scaled. But eventually, wet and weary, they accomplished the climb, and on the third night (29 August) Skipwith's and Lassen's parties duly blew up the bridge, completely destroying its centre. They had with them fifteen partisans who now guided them to a secret partisan hideout in the mountains, where they were well cared for. However, in the early hours of 2 September the hideout was surrounded by about 400 *ustachi*,† and a fierce fight developed which lasted for much of the morning. In the disengagement Skipwith, his sergeant and the Sapper member of Lassen's party got cut off while covering the others and were made prisoner.

---

* Anders Lassen was a Dane who enlisted in the British Army in May 1942. In the course of almost continuous fighting he was awarded three Military Crosses, and in April 1945, as a result of the fighting in and around Lake Comacchio (see Chapter 14), he gained a posthumous Victoria Cross.

†Pro-German Yugoslavs, who were trained and controlled by German officers.

The second of these two B Squadron Patrols was commanded by Captain John Shute and this party, like most of these Balkan buccaneers, had an adventurous time. They started by being swamped in an overloaded assault boat some 400 yards from the shore, and became separated. However, two days later they were together again, and Shute found a suitable target for demolition in the shape of a railway tunnel. His wireless operator had managed to salvage the set from the wreckage, and with the use of a car battery was able to transmit, although not to receive. A second SBS party was landed on 28 August, but with an insufficient amount of explosives to do more than destroy the telephone system and railway points in the target area. The party stayed on the mainland throughout September, existing haphazardly on supply drops, and on 7 October were brought out by air from a partisan airstrip.

From soon after their arrival in Italy until the end of the war the LRDG had Patrols operating almost continuously in Italy, Albania, Yugoslavia, the Dalmatian islands, and Greece or Istria. Sometimes Patrols were operating in two or more countries simultaneously. No description of the various actions is complete without some mention of the enormous amount of work involved in the planning, co-ordination, timing, synchronization and similar matters that took place from Bari. This was done for the main part by the two Squadron commanders, and particularly in so far as the planning was concerned by Major Lazarus.

In contemplating the size of the problem it has to be remembered that Patrols covered a front of some 850 miles, operated in many different types of country and reached their target area by two very different methods, sea and air. Whenever possible Lloyd Owen preferred to send the Patrols in by sea, for the Royal Navy had vessels that crossed the Adriatic speedily and efficiently, and equipment was less likely to get damaged; but when the target area was some way inland the troops were dropped. This, much more than a sea passage, was at the mercy of the weather, which could easily mess up a well-laid plan that might depend upon complicated communication with a reception party at the dropping zone. Getting a Patrol in was perhaps the easiest of the planning stages. Once there the Patrol had to be maintained, and finally it had to be evacuated. Except for one operation, which in the event did not come off, Lloyd Owen was never prepared to send a Patrol in unless he was reasonably certain he could get it out.

Another difficulty which could upset the planners – although it upset the Patrol commanders a great deal more – was the uncertain behaviour of their Yugoslav and Albanian allies. Generally speaking until right towards the end of the war, when Yugoslav tergiversation deteriorated into downright bloody-mindedness, the partisans were co-operative and helpful. But even in the early days one could never be certain they would not, for no apparent reason, suddenly become obstinately difficult. Often it seemed that the Albanians – unlike the Greeks – were more concerned with making importunate demands for gold than with killing Germans. Brigadier Fitzroy Maclean and Lt-Colonel Alan Palmer, in Yugoslavia and Albania respectively, were always active and emollient behind the scenes. Their moral and physical courage, tact and patience did much to maintain a spirit of concord, which for the most part triumphed over the passions and artifices that were never far from the surface.

In Albania, which they first entered at the request of Colonel Palmer whose mission had done sterling work and prepared the ground for them, LRDG Patrols were very active and had a good measure of success. Their fights and adventures are too numerous to be detailed, but Stan Eastwood deserves another mention, for he above others was to become thoroughly familiar with the Albanian hinterland. On 9 August he was dropped in friendly country south of Durazzo and, although he did not know it at the time, he was to endure four months of the hardships, dangers and disappointments that are a guerrilla fighter's lot before being brought back to the comforts of a home base. His was a remarkable achievement of fortitude and perseverance.

After an initial meeting with the partisan leader, Enver Hoxha (later Albanian President) and Colonel Palmer, Eastwood was to make his way north to reconnoitre the area round Durazzo. But before he could accomplish much he was laid low with a very bad bout of malaria, and shortly afterwards changed circumstances were to alter his original role. In the autumn of 1944 the German armies began to suffer serious setbacks on all fronts, and it was no longer possible for them to keep large numbers of troops tied up in the Balkans. Colonel Lloyd Owen felt that such a moment was the time to strike; long columns would be withdrawing from Greece through Albania, and he feared that the Albanians might be content to let them go unmolested. He therefore suggested to Brigadier Davy, who agreed, that more Patrols should be sent at once to Albania to stiffen partisan morale.

Lloyd Owen's fears were justified. The Albanians began to resent the British presence, and opportunities to destroy Germans were in danger of being missed. He therefore decided to go himself to Albania to investigate on the spot. After a hair-raising first attempt he dropped safely, but landed on the edge of a ravine over which he toppled in the dark and fractured his spine. The RAMC orderlies and men of the Patrols did what they could for him, and soon Captain Michael Parsons, the unit's medical officer, parachuted in to give expert attention. In due course Lloyd Owen was able to do a little marching and to direct operations, but on return to Italy he was to spend many weeks in plaster before full recovery.

While Lloyd Owen was still *hors de combat* Eastwood and Lieutenant Simpson, with Patrols S1 and S3, carried out a successful operation – in conjunction with some men of the 1st Battalion of the 4th Partisan Brigade – on the Tirana-Elbasan road between two enemy posts at Misgeta and Cafa Krabs. They completely closed the road for three days, destroyed three trucks, damaged a light tank, successfully beat off two attacks, blew the road in two places and killed eighty Germans. They followed this up on the fourth day with an attack on the Cafa Krabs post in which they inflicted many casualties. In these actions, as in most in Albania, the partisans were not prepared to take prisoners. Besides weapons and equipment they were lamentably short of boots and clothing, and they reckoned that dead Germans supplied these more willingly than live ones.

The first LRDG – and indeed the first British – troops to re-enter Greek soil, Lieutenant Michael Barker and seven men, landed on Kithera at the beginning of September. The Germans had left a few days before and No.9 Commando (see Chapter 4) was to arrrive a few days later. About a month afterwards Major Stormonth-Darling, together with his second-in-command, Captain W.L. Armstrong, and two Patrols of B Squadron parachuted into the Florina area of northern Greece to harass the German withdrawal.

One of their most notable successes was the destruction of a German convoy. Armstrong, with some fellow Sappers of the party, mined two road culverts, and while they lay up in some scrub ready to detonate the charges others took up positions to form a good ambush. Judging an opportune moment to occur when four enemy vehicles were in vulnerable positions on or close to the culverts, Armstrong duly fired the fuse with unbelievably satisfactory results. The vehicles were completely destroyed and, trapped by the resulting road block, fifty Germans were slain before the party faded into the hills. The RAF, answering a radio call, were soon on the spot to complete the good work. It was the sort of total success which those who had such work to do seldom, for one reason or another, achieved in full measure.

John Olivey and his Rhodesian Patrol were also in Greece at this time, but operating in the south. They had a spirited engagement in forcing a passage across the Corinth Canal. Their principal task was to provide the reconnaissance for a strong SBS force which had been sent into harass the German withdrawal. This they did, using jeeps that had been landed with them. They were among the first troops to enter Athens, and then went north, hitting Germans whenever opportunity arose, until joining hands with Stormonth-Darling's Patrols. On their return to Athens Olivey and his men were involved in that unpleasant eirenic role when Greek fought Greek and British troops tried to hold the ring. The city was full of lead from the weapons of the two opposing factions, and Olivey, who was badly wounded on a journey in his jeep (his driver was killed), had to be evacuated to Italy.

Major Stormonth-Darling, with his B Squadron Patrols, had returned to Italy towards the end of 1944, and in January 1945 Lloyd Owen decided that until the Allied armies had reached the northern parts of Italy there was little for his Patrols to do in Yugoslavia. The A Squadron was deeply committed in the Dalmatian islands, and so B was withdrawn from operations and sent to train at a Mountain Warfare School in Terminillo, north-east of Rome, to prepare the men for operations in the mountains of northern Italy and southern Austria. Naturally they were disappointed to be temporarily withdrawn from the fray, and in the event expectations of further action never materialized.

By the end of January an advance base for fighter aircraft of the Balkan Air Force had been established at Prkos, 20 miles inland from Zara on the Yugoslav mainland, and it was decided to set up a small combined operations headquarters – to be known as COZA – at Zara. This comprised A Squadron LRDG, one squadron of the SBS and 11 Troop Raiding Support Regiment, under the command in the first instance of Lt-Colonel David Sutherland, and later (in March) Lt-Colonel David Lloyd Owen. Major Lazarus made his headquarters aboard the schooner *Kufra*, and the rest of COZA were accommodated in a landing craft moored nearby.

At this time the Germans still retained the Yugoslav coastal belt northwards from Karlobag, and the islands immediately north of Zara: Pag, Rab, Cherso and Krk. They had effectively mined the head of the Adriatic, and their shipping in these waters was moving at night with impunity. COZA's principal task was aimed at this sea traffic, and to this end an LRDG Patrol under Lieutenant Reynolds was sent by sea to the south-east of Istria, to establish a watch near the mouth of the Arsa Channel, and to observe and report on the enemy shipping using the channel plying between Trieste, Pola and Fiume. Very useful information was sent back locating the small coves in which these enemy vessels lay up – heavily camouflaged – by day, and the Balkan Air Force was able to take heavy toll of this traffic.

Throughout February and early March there was much patrol activity prior to an offensive by the 4th Yugoslav Army, supported by COZA troops, along the Gospic valley. Captain Olivey's Z1 Patrol was sent to Istria in the Fianona area to watch shipping in the Quarnero Gulf; R1 Patrol, under Lieutenant Pitt, landed on the mainland south of Karlobag to pinpoint gun positions, and later they were sent to the island of Rab. Here they managed to dodge the attentions of the German garrison, despite the lack of cover, and sent back valuable details of enemy positions, which were attended to by the Balkan Air Force.

All these operations by the LRDG and the SBS were most rewarding. The various engagements, and particularly the reconnaissance reports, were immensely valuable to the 4th Yugoslav Army, and enabled them to keep driving the enemy back and to retake one island after another. The subsequent action of these Partisan allies seemed, therefore, to be as ungrateful as it was galling. In the middle of April there were four LRDG Patrols and L Squadron SBS operating in Istria, and starting on the 13th of that month with Reynolds's T1 Patrol they suddenly found themselves put under arrest by the local partisan troops, and ordered back to Zara. On 15 April L Squadron and Eastwood's Patrol suffered this same shameful treatment, and two days later it was the turn of Olivey and his Patrol to be arrested.

The matter was, of course, taken up at a high level, and there was a good deal of shiftiness and equivocation on the part of the partisan corps and divisional commanders, while General Drapsin, commanding the 4th Army, disclaimed all knowledge. The real trouble was that the influence of Moscow now counted for more than alliances; Trieste was the goal ordained, and none but the Yugoslavs should be too close at the finish. Matters drifted on in a very unsatisfactory way, severely taxing the British genius for tolerance; most Patrols had to be withdrawn, and by the end of the war only Olivey (who had successfully played the idiot boy) and his men remained in Istria. It was a great tragedy that a happy and successful alliance, forged over many months on the anvil of sustained endeavour and sacrifice, should be shattered on the altar of Communism.

When the war in Europe ended all eyes were turned towards the Far East, and a great majority of the LRDG personnel were willing to postpone their demobilization to serve in South-East Asia Command, provided they could do so as a unit. As far back as November 1944 Lord Louis Mountbatten had asked for their services, but then they could not be spared; in July 1944 and again in January 1945 Lloyd Owen made out a powerful case for future employment when Europe was won. But it was not to be: a short period of indecision was terminated towards the end of June by a War Office ruling that the Long Range Desert Group should be disbanded.

And so another fine chapter in the story of the British special forces ended officially in August 1945, when the LRDG ceased to exist after five years of magnificent service through endless toils and hazards. Captains Browne, Tinker, Landon Lane and Croucher, and Private Hawkins were among the original volunteers in that summer of 1940 who were still serving when the unit was disbanded. A remarkable record, which surely entitles them to rare distinction.

But much of the credit for success should go to Lloyd Owen, who commanded throughout the last two years of the war. When the Patrols were widely scattered and often faced with appalling difficulties, they knew that the Commanding Officer was always busy on their behalf. As an old desert fighter Lloyd Owen was, quite rightly, most commissariat-minded, but it was not easy for a man of his temperament to be held back encumbered with administrative details. However, together with his dedicated Squadron commanders, he handled this side of the job supremely well, and always he looked forward to being in the battle with exuberant delight.

12

Popski's Private Army

Of all the many British special forces that burgeoned in the Second World War few have caught the popular imagination so much as Popski's Private Army. This is almost entirely due to its creator and leader, and the book he wrote about it.* This is a good, well-written tale based on fact, and in parts deeply reflective with many forceful and moving passages. But there are some exaggerations and the occasional falsehood, so that although it makes an admirable legend, it is somewhat misleading as a history.

As the story of PPA is largely the story of Popski himself – for he created, controlled, directed and inspired the force – a brief outline must be given of his origins and the more important facets of his colourful and very complex character.

Vladimir Peniakoff† was born to Russian parents who emigrated to Belgium at the end of the last century. At the age of fifteen Popski went to Brussels University, and quickly stamped himself as a highly intelligent, precocious young man well ahead of his contemporaries in his chosen subjects of engineering, physics and mathematics. The invasion of Belgium in 1914 dispersed his family (his mother and father made their way to Holland) and Popski came to England where, in 1915, with the help of some English friends, he got into Cambridge University. He enjoyed the life and made a number of friends, but he was a pacifist, if not a conscientious objector, at a time when life was

---

* Vladimir Peniakoff, *Private Army*.
† The LRDG found 'Peniakoff' too much of a mouthful for transmission purposes and nicknamed him 'Popski'. The pseudonym stuck until the day of his death, and is used throughout this book.

hard for such people in England. He came down from Cambridge without a degree, and not long afterwards – possibly to avoid arrest – he left for France, where he certainly worked in a factory for some time, and may have done a stint in the French army.

After the war he took charge of his father's chemical factory in Selzaete in Belgium, but he was never entirely happy in that country, and when in 1924 he obtained the chance of an engineering job in the large French-owned Egyptian sugar company he was glad to make a fresh start. For the next fifteen years he worked in and around Cairo and at Nag Hamadi in Upper Egypt, filling various posts in the mills and refinery of the vast sugar monopoly. He quickly took a lasting dislike to his colleagues, and although he enjoyed the good life of cosmopolitan Cairo he disdained the social graces that usually accompanied it. He learned to fly, did some sailing, read discursively, but widely in the classics, and became fascinated by the desert although his brief explorations were limited to its fringes. After several love affairs he married, in 1928, an Austrian girl many years his junior who gave him two daughters and, surprisingly – for it was a somewhat ill-assorted match – a happy home until, in 1942, they were divorced.

When war broke out Popski was 42 years old, and although only 5 ft 9 in. tall he was thickly built – a powerful man physically, who left the imprint of an equally powerful personality on all who came in contact with him. His character was not only extremely complex, but full of contrasts. His moods were mercurial: you could never be quite sure whether he would hug or bash you; and his men, when summoned to the presence, were never certain what to expect. Action was the leitmotif of his picaresque military career, and in battle he set, and demanded, a high standard. He could be intolerant of those who fell below this standard, but to those who satisfied his exacting requirements he offered strong and unfailing loyalty. 'Feared rather than loved, respected by all' was the verdict of his second-in-command, Bob Park-Yunnie.

Men not directly under Popski's command, but who had cause to deal with him during the war, often found that he rebelled against set patterns and orthodoxy, was sometimes deceitful and untrustworthy, and that he could lie with artistic fervour. But above all everyone recognized that he was quite outstandingly brave.

By 1939 all pacifist ideas had long since evaporated, and Popski was anxious to get into the fight. John Willett in his admirable and most sensitively written biography* says: 'Love of England was his main motive for entering the war.' Certainly he had enjoyed his short spell at Cambridge, and had been back to Britain for holidays in the twenties and thirties; he had also met a number of Englishmen in Egypt, and seems to have admired many traits of the British character. In his book Popski writes: ' . . . the simple fact was that, to my knowledge, England was in danger of falling under the control of the Germans and my simple duty was to assist those who strove to prevent such a misfortune.'† To such an admirable sentiment must be added a love of adventure, which he felt the war would supply.

Inevitably there were difficulties: the sugar company was loath to let him go; and there were his nationality – for Popski was still a Belgian citizen – and his age. However, in October 1940 he obtained a commission as a second lieutenant on the General List, and by persistence, and a little lying, got himself taken on as a company commander in the Libyan Arab Force. This force had been raised by Colonel Bromilow and comprised some 3,000 Senussi Arabs, mainly refugees from Italian atrocities in Cyrenaica in the early thirties. Popski remained with them for fifteen months, obtained command of a battalion, and saw some action around Tobruk. But their principal role as garrison and lines of communication troops he found frustrating, and he was never a happy soldier until in March 1942 he was appointed, as a major, to command a detachment from the LAF to be known as the Libyan Arab Force Commando.

Here was a chance to develop his ideas of guerrilla warfare, and collect and collate intelligence on enemy activity in the Jebel Akhdar. For this purpose he selected twenty-two Senussi from the LAF, a British sergeant to be in charge of them and one Arab officer. It was to be an independent command but, like the SAS at this time, Popski relied heavily on the LRDG for conveyance into action. He was very familiar with the mountain ranges and the inland desert plain of the Jebel Akhdar, and was accepted almost as a brother by the Senussi tribesmen, which gave him many advantages. On the other hand some of his LRDG colleagues were inclined to find his almost completely Arab mentality with its total disregard for time, and its unhurried, cautious and indecisive approach to problems, quite infuriating.

For the next five months Popski and his Arabs operated in the

* *Popski: A Life of Vladimir Peniakoff.*
† *Private Army*, p.31.

Jebel behind the enemy lines carrying out, with the help of the LRDG – whose members he came to admire enormously – a number of operations similar to those performed by other irregular troops in the desert. These included a road watch, the destruction of a large petrol dump (450,000 gallons), and the rescue of some British airmen. He also devised a bold plan for the release of Allied prisoners from a POW camp, which involved him in a daylight reconnaissance of occupied Derna. All of his operations were imaginatively conceived; some were successful, but many failed through lack of sound administration and through 'being planned in a carefree Boy Scout manner', to quote an LRDG colleague.

With Rommel poised to march on Alexandria, and Siwa uninhabitable as a forward base, the LRDG pulled back, and Popski accompanied them in Captain Hunter's Patrol. In Cairo he found his command had been disbanded, and by most officers in GHQ he was unwanted. But Colonel Shan Hackett, recently appointed to control all Middle East special forces, had read a report on irregular warfare that Popski had submitted from the Jebel, and suggested that he should accompany the LRDG on their Barce raid, with a view to something more definite later on. He was therefore with Easonsmith at Barce, where he was wounded in the leg and left hand, which necessitated a spell in hospital. On his discharge he suggested forming an extra LRDG squadron, but their war establishment would not allow for this, and so once again – but only for a short time – he found himself in a vacuum.

It was now that his success in destroying the large petrol dump, together with his Jebel report, bore fruit. Shan Hackett – a most perceptive officer – felt that Popski's talents could be put to good use in command of a small motorized force. He was therefore given command of the smallest independent unit in the British Army, with a war establishment of five officers (one major, one captain and three subalterns), eighteen other ranks and six vehicles. It was at first called No. 1 Demolition Squadron, but Popski did not consider that a sufficiently glamorous title, and on Colonel Hackett's suggestion Popski's Private Army was born;* it was ordered to be ready for action by 15 November.

In fact it was 22 November before Popski and his small band left Cairo for Kufra, for even a tiny unit like PPA requires time to form, and when Popski left Shan Hackett's office he was the sole

---

* Although for the rest of the war it continued to be designated in official documents as 'No. 1 Demolition Squadron. PPA'.

representative of the 'army', nor did he have any equipment. But Popski was nothing if not resourceful, and soon he had wheedled out of the Libyan Arab Force a Scottish captain called Bob Park-Yunnie and the promise of a French lieutenant, Jean Caneri. He even managed to persuade the Colonel of the King's Dragoon Guards (with whom he had served briefly in the desert) to let him have SSM Waterson, who was just out of hospital and awaiting re-employment. The LRDG gave him a one-eyed warrior of ferocious mien named Corporal Locke, who was to prove a great stalwart, and from the various reinforcement depots in the Canal Zone he managed to collect a few more recruits. These were mostly RASC drivers with little or no battle experience, but one of them, Driver W.J. Wilson, was the only man – save the founder – to remain with the unit until its disbandment.

When PPA left Cairo its strength was only two officers and twelve other ranks (plus three Libyan Arabs), but they were the proud possessors of PPA shoulder flashes, and a black Tank Corps beret on which was fitted a small brass badge bearing the design of a sixteenth-century Italian astrolabe. They rode in four jeeps armed with twin Vickers 'K' .303 machine guns, and carried in two 3-ton lorries eleven days' rations, over a ton of explosives (the men had been on a short demolition course at Kabrit), and petrol for 1,500 miles, but very few spares – they were unobtainable.

The long run across the desert (made longer through getting lost) brought the inevitable breakdowns, and consequent delay. Kufra was eventually reached on 4 December, by which time the Eighth Army had pushed Rommel's Afrika Corps beyond the Jebel Akhdar, which Popski regarded as his special preserve. This hasty retreat, and the consequent shortening of the German lines of communication, meant that PPA's principal value had virtually disappeared, for in the Jebel Popski could command the allegiance of almost every Arab and had the right size of force to destroy vital petrol dumps. Now with Tripolitania a rapidly vanishing battleground, and Tunisia a more likely one, the situation had altered greatly – a hostile population and a very different type of target. Logically the force should have been disbanded before it ever went into action.

The open desert flank had gone, and the country was becoming more difficult for vehicles, with enemy dumps and airstrips less vulnerable. But Popski's fertile mind was always casting forward for opportunities, and meanwhile at Zella, and later Hon, he hitched his wagon to the LRDG, whose men he rightly felt could give his people valuable training. At Zella he was joined by Jean

Caneri. Caneri was a French lawyer, conscripted into their Syrian army, who at the time of the surrender had come to Egypt and offered his services. He was to prove a tremendous asset to PPA. Popski's men accomplished little in Tripolitania, and on one patrol in the Jebel Nefusa, with Captain Lazarus of the LRDG, they had an officer captured and a jeep destroyed. Popski was quite glad to see the officer go, but lamented the loss of the jeep. However, together with men of Captain Tinker's LRDG Patrol, PPA did play a valuable part in reconnoitring suitable ground for armour in Montgomery's left hook which outflanked the Mareth Line.

This reconnaissance was not without its darker side. When the party was some 60 miles south of the Mareth Line, at a place called Qaret Ali, it was decided that Tinker and three of his New Zealanders with Popski, Caneri and one of the PPA Arabs would go forward in three jeeps, leaving Captian Yunnie behind with the heavy vehicles and stores. Yunnie was to spend his time making a supply of Lewis bombs,* for it was intended that when the reconnaissance was completed PPA would remain in the area raiding enemy airfields and landing grounds. The base camp was betrayed by unfriendly Bedouin, and within the space of ten minutes three Messerschmitts had completely demolished vehicles, ammunition, explosives, spare weapns, petrol and rations. Luckily the only casualties were two New Zealanders wounded in the legs.

The reconnaissance party returned a few days later, and their jeeps were used to drive the wounded 180 miles through enemy-held territory to Tozeur, where they would receive attention, and from where the valuable information that Popski and the others had gathered could be transmitted to Eighth Army Headquarters. Popski was justifiably upset by what had happened to Yunnie (and blamed him, perhaps a little unfairly, for incompetence), for not only were his men now faced with a long and dangerous walk, but the high hopes he had placed on making a name for his unit – whose future was still slightly in the balance – raiding behind the Mareth Line had been shattered.

The walking party was eventually rescued by an American jeep patrol of the First Army, and the whole of PPA was united in Tozeur at the beginning of February 1943. After a few days' rest Popski took them to Tebessa in Algeria, where he managed to persuade the quartermaster's department of the American Second

---

* Lewis bombs were the invention of Captain J.S. Lewis of the SAS. They were simple portable time-bombs with incendiary after-effects.

Corps to issue them with a complete outfit of clothes and a very generous quantity of rations. PPA belonged to the Eighth Army and should have flown back to Cairo to refit, but this entailed too much inaction for the impetuous Popski. And as his bold march and drive through the enemy–held gap between the two armies had caught the imagination of the press and First Army Headquarters, no obstacle was placed in the way of his being the first unit to transfer from the Eighth to the First Army.

At this time General Anderson's line was fairly static, reaching from the Mediterranean coast southwards for 180 miles to Gafsa with the British on the left, the French in the centre and the Americans on the right or south flank. Montgomery's Eighth Army was preparing for its attack on the Mareth Line. Popski felt that there was a lot for his men to do in creating alarm through a series of small raids on the lines of communication connecting the principal supply ports (Tunis, Bizerta, Sfax and Gabes) that fed the German armies now tightly trammelled between the Allied First and Eighth.

For this purpose they could travel lightly in armed jeeps and within nine days Popski had begged, borrowed or bartered five of these vehicles, and Second Corps Headquarters had provided belt-fed Brownings, the .50 gun being capable of dealing with armoured cars. The first raid necessitated a long drive to an airfield where only five aircraft were found, and these were destroyed. But before the war in Africa finished there were to be other operations, sometimes lasting up to eight days and covering many miles over appalling going, in which German convoys were successfully ambushed.

PPA's contribution to victory in Africa was insignificant, but for the size of the force highly creditable. In addition to the petrol dump already mentioned 34 aircraft, 6 armoured and 112 other vehicles had been destroyed, and 600 Italians captured. Moreover, the daring exploits of this small force and its determination to overcome numerous difficulties had won the hearts of those whose task it was to plan the invasions of Sicily and Italy. Popski's army was now accepted alongside those other irregular forces operating in this theatre, and that as much as anything else was what he had striven for.

For almost four months between the end of the fighting in Africa and the 1st Airborne Division's landing in Italy, PPA was in limbo. Popski himself had been found a billet with the Allied Force Headquarters' planners just outside Algiers, but he had to plan for a completely new type of warfare, and meanwhile his 'army' still had to live by its wits. At first he got his men attached to Lt-Colonel W.S. Stirling's 2nd SAS at Philippeville, where they trained under Yunnie, while Caneri returned to Cairo to sort out the large number of administrative problems that must inevitably arise with a force answerable to no one and gathering recruits, stores and vehicles as it went along.

Until the end of November, when he was given a revised establishment and authority to enlist volunteers from any unit, Popski's recruiting methods were most unorthodox. While the fighting in North Africa was still in progress he managed to lure Corporal Cameron, a ghillie by profession and a first–class fighting man, from the SAS; at much the same time he rescued a Sapper sergeant called Curtis, a sole survivor in no-man's-land after his party had been ambushed by Arabs, whom he took on the strength and who became one of the pillars of the force. Later he worried someone in 1st Armoured Division of the First Army into letting him take three volunteers from the Derbyshire Yeomanry, and in May he obtained five men from the LRDG. These were not all reinforcements, but to a certain extent replacements, for some men had been found unsatisfactory and weeded out, and there was no further need for the three Arab soldiers.

It is difficult to be certain on what grounds these various volunteers were allowed to leave their units. It has been suggested that if not actual throw-outs they were men who could well be spared. This may have been so in some cases, but if they could not prove themselves in battle Popski had no use for them, and they were promptly returned to their units. In fact almost all fought with great courage and distinction. They were undoubtedly the type of men who fitted more easily into a fraternity where discipline was, not to put too fine a point on it, loose. Officers and men lived as one sharing everything, saluting was optional, and what the men wore could not be described as uniform. Popski was a shrewd judge of character (although he had some unreasonable prejudices, mainly against the officer class), and he took a great pride in the performance of his men in action. This was justified, although there were occasions when their performance out of the line could not be a subject of pride. They were, to use his own name (borrowed from Churchill), a 'Band of Brothers', close-knit by constant danger and tempered by friendship. By the time they left for Italy the 'Band' had increased to four officers and forty other ranks.

On his return to Philippeville from Algiers Popski was still uncertain of the best role for his unit; he had dismissed parachuting and landing by submarine, for he considered the damage that could be done by men limited to carrying a load of 60 lb did not justify the serious risk of losing highly-trained men. Eventually he settled on the use of gliders. He was encouraged in this by General Hopkinson, commanding 1st Airborne Division, and soon PPA was attached to the division at Msaken and training with a view to landing six gliders in Calabria – five of them carrying an armed jeep and two PPA men, and the sixth just the pilot and stores to be distributed on landing. Training on loading and unloading jeeps, together with night exercises to practise jeep parties in target location, went on for several weeks, but in the event PPA was not to carry out glider-borne operations either at this time or later. On 1 September 1st Airborne Division was ordered to stand by for embarkation at Bizerta and PPA was to accompany it with five jeeps and land in the first wave.

The Division sailed on 7 September for Taranto, and landed unopposed on the 9th after the Italian surrender on the previous day. PPA's first task was one of reconnaissance, and liaison with Italian commanders. Information was required on landing grounds between Taranto and Brindisi, and on German activity within this area. Popski took all five jeeps on this mission, and was back in Taranto after twenty-nine hours with a certain amount of information imparted by willing Italians, but having encountered no Germans.

Almost at once the party set off again, this time for Bari. Here they found a very jittery and inexperienced Italian corps commander who had no idea how to deploy his three divisions should the Germans attack. Having put what heart they could into the craven general, the jeeps made for the Altamura and Murge areas. The 1st Airborne Division was out on a limb at Taranto, but like the Eighth Army now moving through Calabria its present task was to relieve the pressure that was building up against the Fifth Army at Salerno. It was important that the Division should know the strength of the enemy before leaving its perimeter, for an airborne division advancing on its own without air or artillery support is fairly vulnerable.

Popski was always looking for gaps through which to get behind the enemy lines. These were comparatively easy to find in the desert, less so in the Tunisian fighting, and considerably less so in Italy even in the early days; later they dried up altogether when the Germans established their famous lineal defences which ran the breadth of Italy. But now he managed to squeeze his jeeps between detached posts on the German flank east of Gioia del

Colle, cross this main supply route (Foggia-Gravina) by night and establish himself in the lonely hill country of the Murge, which had good cover, easy jeep access to roads and friendly inhabitants.

In this sequestered corner of southern Italy the party split up, carrying out a number of road watches and reporting back details to HQ Airborne Division, but the real coup came with a typical piece of Popski bravado. He had made friends with an Italian farmer who provided black market nourishment, through the mess president, for the officers' mess of the German garrison in Gravina. Posing as a loyal Italian quartermaster (and giving references supplied by the farmer) he telephoned to ask the officer if he would like a case of good brandy for the mess. Unable to resist, the officer gave orders to the guards to admit two people that night in a captured American car. Popski and Corporal Cameron duly arrived, lugged a rations box full of stones up to the major's office, slugged him with a rubber truncheon, and on going through his papers found the complete ration strength, dated 12 September 1943, of the 1st Parachute Division and the attached troops supplied by the distributing centre in Gravina, as well as the location of units. When this information was wirelessed to 1st Airborne, not surprisingly they required confirmation.

The sum total of the intelligence gathered during those few days behind the enemy front showed clearly that the Germans had only a small number of fighting troops in the area, which were not being reinforced. It seemed they were holding a watching brief and would withdraw when our troops, now being reinforced, advanced from the Taranto area. This being the case Popski, influenced by the fact that, except for Cameron and himself, the days spent on reconnaissance in the Murge had been rather dull, decided – without obtaining any authority – to sever his connection with 1st Airborne Division, and go north swanning around behind the German lines doing what damage he could.

In fact the damage he did during the next few weeks was not very considerable, although the presence of even a small mobile enemy force appearing suddenly at various points behind their front line tended to confuse the Germans in that area. Mines were laid on two occasions with some effect, although Popski in his book, while asseverating that his men were out for results and to hurt the enemy whenever possible, claims that they got 'little satisfaction from this achievement at second hand'. They never used mines again except as protection. They did, however, occasionally give vent to their boyish enthusiasm by destroying the wheels of enemy vehicles with miniature self-made gadgets constructed in the shape and colour of mule droppings, which they scattered on the roads and designated 'Turds mule, Calabrian'.

A side issue of this road-watching, vehicle-bashing tour in the Foggia-Bovino area, but as it turned out a useful one, was the typically unorthodox enlistment of two more recruits. While the party were lying up in a grove awaiting darkness they were approached by two shabbily-dressed men, whose strong features and soldierly gait seemed to indicate a greater pride and vitality than those of the average Italian peasant. They turned out to be two Russian soldiers who had been captured at Smolensk and put to work with the Todt Organization in northern Italy from where they had escaped. Popski did not require much persuasion to enrol them, and Ivan and Nikolai served with distinction in PPA for the remainder of the war.

By the end of September the situation in southern Italy was well under control. The American Fifth Army was into Naples, patrols of the 1st Airborne Division had reached Bari by 15 September, Foggia airfields were taken by the 25th, and all the time reinforcements were pouring in. With these came the men of PPA, under Caneri, who had not come over initially with 1st Airborne Division. Now, with his unit up to full strength, Popski felt able to give Yunnie command of the Patrol he had trained in Africa, and sent him to reconnoitre the Gargano Peninsula. Bob Yunnie was, second only to Popski, perhaps the most remarkable man who served in PPA. A civilian before the war and now aged over 30, he was a born leader, a skilful and courageous fighter with a keen, incisive mind and resilient spirit. He was more of a disciplinarian than the other officers, but would mix freely with his men who loved him dearly and would follow him anywhere.

His mission, with only ten men and four jeeps, among the steep, tree-covered hills and valleys of the Gargano was an important and difficult one, for it was thought that the Peninsula held a fair number of Germans, and besides reporting on their presence his party was if possible to winkle them out of it.

They drove to Manfredonia and then up the winding pass to the mountain village of Sant' Angelo, where they learnt that the last Germans had only just left the Peninsula. Pausing only to transmit this news to the Fourth Armoured Brigade (recently disembarked at Bari) they hurried on across the mountains, and down to the coast where late in the afternoon they caught up with a party of German sappers laying mines in a ford across the River Fortore.

They joined battle with these at once and drove them back into the hills; then, crossing the ford, they ran into heavy opposition and barely escaped being destroyed by mortar fire as they recrossed the river.

There followed three enchanting nights in the Castle of Ripalto, whose châtelaine was a beautiful London girl married into the Parlato family. During this time the small party kept the ford open and, before continuing on their way, guided the armour across it and into Serracapriola.

While Yunnie and his men were alternately chasing Germans across the River Fortore and enjoying the comfort of the Parlato castle Popski was, according to his own account, engaged in the most incredible long-distance reconnaissance. Having overheard at Army Group Headquarters the suggestion (not a very prescient one) that the Germans might shortly pull back to the Alban Hills, Popski felt it would be useful to take a look at the place. These hills, which were to feature so prominently in the Anzio plan, were something like 125 miles as the crow flies behind the front line. Motoring via Cassino, and then northwards along Route 6, he reached the Alban Hills, found them empty of any enemy, glanced at Rome and then returned. It had been a foolhardy and virtually useless country drive, for apart from being able to give Army Headquarters information about the presence of the 16th Panzer Division (and irritating one of their squadrons with demolition charges) the patrol accomplished nothing, and could well have ended in disaster.

By November the German line was beginning to stabilize across the breadth of Italy, and the weather was deteriorating sharply. Popski and Yunnie attempted a further sortie or two, and had some lively brushes with the enemy. Near the small town of Alberona Popski found the South African General Klopper wandering about; he had been captured at Tobruk and recently escaped. But they were no longer able to find gaps in the line through which they could pass their jeeps.

Popski knew he commanded men who needed always to be in action – although in due course too much of it was to play on the nerves of some of the best, and they had to be transferred. He endeavoured never to let their enthusiasm be soured or their courage grow dim, and now he became worried that there was little future for his force. But at Eighth Army Headquarters*

---

* Although Popski was in the habit of attaching his unit to whichever army was the most convenient, officially PPA belonged to the Eighth Army.

Major-General de Guingand (Chief of Staff) assured him this was not the case, and suggested that he moved his base from Lucera back to Bisceglie and rested his men while a new and larger establishment was worked out. This he did and at the beginning of December he and Caneri flew to Algiers to get official sanction for the establishment he felt necessary for PPA's changed, and slightly more orthodox, role.

The new establishment allowed for six officers (one major, two captains and three subalterns), two warrant officers, four sergeants, five corporals, five lance-corporals, fitters, wireless operators, armourers and mechanics to a total of eighty all ranks, with sufficient armed jeeps to transport them. Moreover, he was given *carte blanche* to call for volunteers throughout all units of the Central Mediterranean Force – although in practice the base depots were his main source of supply. From a loose organization of two scratch Patrols and makeshift repair facilities, he now planned to have three operational Patrols of six jeeps each, a small HQ Patrol commanded by himself and known as 'Blitz', a workshop and wireless section and an administrative section under Caneri. This was recognition at last, and all that remained after recruiting and training the new men was to find worthwhile tasks for them to perform.

Yunnie was put in charge of Patrol organization and training. Each Patrol was to comprise an officer, a sergeant, two corporals, a fitter, wireless operator and six driver-gunners.* Great attention was paid to navigation, and each man besides being a highly-skilled driver had to be a good machine-gunner, mechanic and demolition expert. It is not surprising, therefore, that recruiting proved difficult, and out of every 100 volunteers interviewed usually no more than 15 proved suitable. Finding officers was especially troublesome, for there were vacancies only for sub-alterns and many officers disliked the idea of dropping rank, and most subalterns at the base depots were too inexperienced.

Time was short for training the new intake, which took place by day and night in the snow-covered mountains, for in the middle of January PPA was warned to be prepared to take part in the Anzio landing. On the 17th, just as the loaded jeeps were leaving for Naples, a signal was received cancelling their participation. This was a bitter blow (although probably a lucky one), and

---

* The figures are Yunnie's (*Warriors on Wheels*, p.178) and probably correct, but the War Office files gave the strength of each Patrol as one officer and seventeen other ranks – and incidentally eight, not six, officers as the full establishment.

perhaps to satisfy his eagerness for action Popski was asked to send a foot patrol to destroy a bridge over the River Capa d'Acqua in front of the position held by 201 Guards Brigade on the Garigliano front. It appeared to be a forlorn task and anyway, as Yunnie who was to lead the patrol pointed out, the bridge could be bypassed.

The result was a complete disaster, for the patrol ran into an uncharted minefield in which one man was killed and two seriously wounded. After being subjected to heavy mortar fire during which one other man was slightly wounded, Yunnie managed to get the patrol and the wounded out, but the bridge was never blown. Popski, who had little admiration for the Brigade of Guards, quite wrongly blamed them in his book for not knowing of and informing him about the minefield.

The revamped PPA had got off to a bad start, and their prospects as a jeep unit did not look too bright, for Popski was still thinking of work well behind the enemy lines. He therefore sent men on a parachute course, and moved his base to San Gregorio at the foot of the Matese Mountains, where they trained incessantly. During this time he worked on a plan for a seaborne landing, not in the form of a raid but to deposit his men and their jeeps for at least a month. He would then establish a mountain base from which he would operate, and be supplied by air.

Operation Astrolabe, after three months of intensive preparation, got under way on 12 June when Yunnie, and a small advance party, sailed in a naval motor launch for the mouth of the River Tenna some 60 miles behind the lines. He was to get in touch with A Force agents (see Chaper 3) and three days later, if all was well, to come down to the beach to guide in the main party.

A short time previously No. 9 Commando had been involved in taking off a number of escaped prisoners from this same point, and it was reported that there was just enough water for a loaded LCT to negotiate a sandbar. This was confirmed by two naval officers who went ashore with Yunnie and who, with Sergeant Porter of PPA, returned to give Popski a full report of the beach. It was with some confidence, therefore, that the LCT sailed on the night of 14/15 June carrying twelve jeeps, thirty all ranks of PPA and a detachment from No. 9 Commando of four officers and sixty-nine other ranks, who were to hold the beachhead while Popski and his men landed, and then return with the LCT.

At 11 p.m. on the night of the 15th Bob Yunnie's 'all clear' signal was seen, and the LCT lurched over the sandbar and dropped anchor at 11.30 p.m. The Commando immediately went ashore, followed by Popski who met Yunnie on the beach. The latter painted a gloomy picture of heavy German traffic everywhere, for their army was in full retreat, and he did not think that PPA had any chance of survival. It was a bitter blow for Popski, but after only a little hesitation he decided to cancel the operation. The Commandos were called in and the jeeps remained aboard. But when the LCT started her engines she was found to be fast aground.

No amount of strenuous effort would shift her, and when the escorting ML was asked to come in she too ran aground. Popski therefore made a plan for the LCT and its jeeps to be blown up, and for the troops and crew of both ships to land and in small parties take their chance in this enemy-infested coastline. However, luckily the ML got herself off the bar, and so the landing was cancelled (but not the demolition) and the troops were ferried across to the Motor Launch in a very hazardous fashion. It had been a most unfortunate operation in which an LCT and twelve jeeps were lost.

But Yunnie, and four men with a wireless set, were ordered to remain on shore to retrieve something useful from the shambles. After a hair-raising week around Fermo, during which they sent back information and managed to prevent some German sappers from blowing the river bridge, they found a comfortable billet with an Italian count and countess until being ordered to rejoin Popski at the mountain village of Sarnano, 40 miles south-west of Fermo.

No sooner had Popski arrived at Sarnano than he made for the River Chienti which he intended to cross, and then with the help of some partisans he hoped to be able to drive his remaining ten jeeps northwards, taking advantage of the temporary confusion caused by the withdrawal to get through and behind the German lines. But the Chienti was strongly held, and in their attempt to find fords PPA suffered two serious casualties. The faithful Corporal Cameron was killed while sitting next to Popski in his jeep, and soon afterwards Rickwood, in command of R Patrol, was shot through the stomach and put out of action until the last month of the war. Popski was not insensible to the horrors of war, and greatly revered its sacrifices; he was deeply distressed by the death of Cameron, who had been his friend and driver for more than a year.

An important phase had now been reached in PPA's existence: one of cooperation with Italian partisans. They quickly realized that there were two types, fighters and marauders. The former were mostly derived from the professional classes and were true patriots with whom it was a pleasure to operate, but the marauders, who were the more plentiful, were virtually bandits and caused more trouble than they were worth. It was largely due to the difficulties they had had in trying to cross the Chienti that Popski and his men joined forces with Major Ferri and his brother Giuseppe – a history professor at Pisa University – who together commanded a band of some 300 partisans.

Popski had decided to pull back to Sarnano and try to cross the 4,000-ft mountain range between that town and Bolognola. Eventually a precipitous sheep track was found over which the jeeps crawled and slid down the farther slopes into Bolognola. Here they found the partisans under their two intelligent and dynamic leaders. They had already achieved some success with their captured German weapons, and the Ferri brothers were delighted to combine with PPA. The partisans' knowledge of the country was enormously valuable, and PPA enjoyed teaching them ambush and other guerrilla skills, for as yet they were somewhat inexperienced. Popski was overjoyed to have found at last a mountain base within enemy territory, which overlooked the upper reaches of the Chienti and beyond to the walled town of Camerino, the headquarters of a German mountain division.

At first it was not possible to cross the Chienti, for the bridge was blown and German troops were in strength along the lateral road on the north side. But most nights PPA and the partisans would swoop down to the river to shoot up and ambush German convoys on the far bank. After enduring these attacks for a little while the Germans pulled back from the river area and Popski's men crossed it, and blew the bridge over the next river, the Potenza, some 7 miles behind Camerino. Some very skilful deception tactics accompanied by frequent, strong and well-separated attacks bluffed the German commander into thinking he was all but surrounded by a superior force. The division withdrew across the Potenza, and PPA with the partisans entered Camerino in triumph. Popski, who had virtually assumed overall command of the joint PPA-partisan force, now appointed Giuseppe – the professor – to be civilian governor of the town and his brother to be in charge of the troops.

Popski himself remained in the town he had captured for two days, helping the Ferri brothers to elect councillors and set up an administration until the arrival of the official Allied Military Government of Occupied Territory (AMGOT), and then he and his men moved north across the Potenza in search of further action. For the next few months his Patrols, acting independently, thoroughly enjoyed themselves raiding German outposts, ambushing convoys, destroying dumps and liberating villages. Although they were vaguely in touch with armoured car regiments on either flank, PPA were the only Allied troops operating in the central mountains. In the course of three months, with a strength at any one time of no more than fifty men, they cleared 1,600 square miles of mountains and killed over 300 Germans for the loss of but one man killed and three wounded.

Several weeks without a break behind the enemy lines, constantly raiding and never out of danger, can impose a tremendous strain, but on this occasion no engagement was of unpleasantly long duration, and always the men had the help and hospitality of the peasants. In fact at this time there was no illness nor any nervous breakdowns, except that Popski himself was forced into hospital for ten days with malaria, and again later with bad digestive trouble. In his absence Jean Caneri took over.

The Allies broke the Gothic Line, which stretched across Italy from Pesaro on the Adriatic to Pisa on the Tyrrhenian Sea, in the middle of September 1944, and on the 20th Rimini was taken; but the anticipated rapid German retreat and glorious pursuit did not materialize. Instead the extremely competent Field-Marshal Kesselring extracted the last ounces of strength from his weary divisions, which for the next few months sternly contested every river and canal crossing in the north of Italy.

It was a gloomy time for PPA, for their jeeps seemed useless with so much water to cross, and they had now become expert light armoured mobile fighters. But Popski somehow discovered the presence of DUKWs in the country, newly arrived and apparently not in great demand. He immediately gained possession of some for training back at Ancona, and laid plans for seven DUKWs to a Patrol – six with jeeps and one carrying a chain-lifting crane and supplies.

After some intensive training and much splashing about with the DUKWs, their first use in action was to get some jeeps across the river Savio on 1 November. On the north bank in a pine forest, with the pouring rain sifting through the branches, they met elements of what were probably the best-organized partisans in Italy – the 28th Garibaldini Brigade, commanded by Arrigo Boldrini, popularly known as 'Bulow'. They were Communists, but very ready to co-operate with anyone fighting the Germans, and Bulow, who was himself in the marshes north of Ravenna, sensibly split his force to work with units of the Eighth Army in whatever role they could be most useful. The band that Popski's men had met were commanded by Ateo Minghelli, a thickset ruffian whose forename – meaning 'atheist' – partly conveyed his attitude to life, but like his men (and women) he was a brave and trustworthy fighter.

Popski was quick to appreciate the true value of Ateo and his party, and arranged that they should be attached in groups to each of his Patrols. This arrangement worked very well on both sides. PPA was now officially under command of Porter Force, a mixed armoured and artillery flank force under Lt-Colonel Andrew Horsburgh-Porter commanding the 27th Lancers. He allowed PPA almost complete operational freedom, but was at hand to give support if needed. In this new role, in the closing months of the war, PPA's contribution to the army's overall success was probably greater than on any previous occasion in Africa or Italy.

Despite the cold and wet of an Italian winter they thoroughly enjoyed themselves in their forest hideouts, from the cover of which they harried the Germans and pushed them back whenever opportunity occurred. Although only a very small unit their Patrols had tremendous firepower,* and the DUKWs enabled them to negotiate the frequent and tiresome waterways. If frontal operations proved too difficult Patrols outflanked the enemy by sea, using either their own DUKWs or for longer trips LCTs, but the lesson of the River Tenna had been well learnt and DUKWs were taken aboard the LCTs so that the latter need not come in too close.

Inevitably there were casualties, although considering the risks run surprisingly few, and gradually the old desert hands began to fall away. Corporal Cameron's death has already been mentioned, Sergeant Curtis was killed not long afterwards, and now Sergeant Porter blew himself up while minelaying. Other stalwarts from the early days who had become battle-weary and had had to leave were Sergeants Waterson, Sanders and Beautyman, and the one-eyed Corporal Locke. But worthy successors were found, and a young officer, John Campbell, of the Argyll and Sutherland Highlanders, who had joined twelve months ago, now took command of S Patrol and distinguished himself greatly in one or

---

* The armament of a Patrol included six .50 and six .30 machine guns mounted on the jeeps, two Bren guns with ground mountings, a bazooka, a 3 in. mortar and a smoke generator fixed to the rear of each jeep. Later a 'Wasp' flamethrower was mounted on some of the jeeps. Personal weapons consisted of eight tommy guns, eight rifles, sixteen .45 pistols and hand grenades.

two spectacular and daring raids which earned him a Military Cross and bar.

PPA, with its partisans, was among those who entered Ravenna at the beginning of December 1944, and Popski quickly pushed R Patrol north up the road to make contact with the retreating Germans. On the 9th two dismounted troops of the 27th Lancers were surrounded by the enemy in a position they had taken up along this road, and requested urgent help. B Patrol, under covering fire from a troop of tanks, drove to within 30 yards of the enemy, who were two companies strong and well dug in on a canal bank. In a fierce fifty-minute firefight the Germans lost thirty men killed before they withdrew. Popski, who had accompanied the Patrol, concluded his report on this action with: 'By an extraordinary piece of luck the only casualty of the Patrol was one man slightly wounded.' Such modesty is in pleasing, and characteristic, contrast to his usual rodomontade reserved for the exploits of his men – for the casualty was Popski, who lost his left hand and who was awarded the Distinguished Service Order for his part in the battle.

This was virtually the end of Popski's colourful fighting career, although after two or three months in hospital and convalescing in England he did rejoin PPA – complete with a fearsome hook, which he later abandoned – two weeks before the German surrender. While he was away Jean Caneri commanded the unit with distinction both in the field and, when winter bogged down most activity, on training. He organized a varied training programme, which included parachuting, skiing, and mountain climbing.

The last man to leave PPA was the only officer who had been with it from the very beginning. In the middle of April 1945 that *beau sabreur* Bob Yunnie obtained a compassionate home posting, for his only son had died suddenly. His place in command of B Patrol was taken by a recently-joined young officer from the 27th Lancers called McCallum. Sadly he was killed, together with his gunner, when leading his Patrol into a village around Lake Comacchio in what was almost PPA's last action of the war.

After a fairly long period of training the men were becoming restless, and were delighted when on 21 April Caneri led the whole force into battle, with his own headquarters organized as a fighting Patrol. For seven days, with the partisans of the Garibaldini Brigade and the 27th Lancers, they fought the enemy in the watery maze of Comacchio. Then they crossed the Po and the Adige to confront a formidable force of Germans before Chioggia. Caneri, well tutored by Popski in the art of bluff, persuaded the commander that to continue fighting was hopeless. Seven hundred men surrendered, and two days later Campbell's Patrol charged and captured a battery of 88 mm guns together with 300 men. Two other Patrols, R and B, sailed across the Gulf of Venice and hastened the departing Germans out of Iesolo.

These spectacular triumphs may not have been as hard come by as some of the other prizes that fell to PPA during its twenty-nine months' existence (of which twenty were spent in active operations), for the enemy was by now becoming demoralized. Nevertheless, the capture of 1,335 prisoners, 16 field guns and many smaller weapons in the course of ten days is an imposing enough record on which to close the book – which was officially done on 14 September 1945.

13

The Special Air Service: The Desert, 1941–1943

Shortly after the battle of Crete in May 1941, when Layforce was in limbo and likely to be disbanded, four members of No. 8 Commando (B Battalion) thought that parachuting, if not exactly enjoyable, might certainly be a useful addition to their military repertoire. In this they were encouraged by Colonel Laycock, but the problem was parachutes and, to a lesser degree, suitable aircraft from which to drop. At that time the nearest British instructional centre for parachutists was Ringway in Cheshire.

However, part of a consignment of parachutes destined for India had inadvertently been off-loaded at Alexandria and some of these were mysteriously purloined by Lieutenant J.S. Lewis – a most resourceful, highly intelligent and courageous Welsh Guards and Layforce officer. Furthermore, he managed to get the use of a Valencia aeroplane, which although most unsuitable for the job was the only machine available. One of those interested in this somewhat hazardous drop was Lieutenant A.D. Stirling. In due course the jump took place and all landed safely with the exception of Stirling, whose parachute was in a faulty condition, and he hit the ground far too hard. For several days he was paralysed from the waist down, and for some weeks was confined to hospital.

David Stirling, who has already featured in this book (see Chapter 7), stands 6 ft 6 in. tall and is proportionately well built. Soft spoken, courteous and unassuming, he is the possessor of a lovely sense of humour, and a rock-like strength of character without a scintilla of pomposity. In battle he was brave, daring and adventurous; in pursuit of his objective along the corridors of power ruthless. He started his military career before the war in the Supplementary Reserve of the Scots Guards; his annual attachments were always lively and a source of great joy to his fellow subalterns, not only for his charm and gaiety but also for the effect they were apt to have on the picquet roster. Stirling became one of the truly great men of the last war, and certainly one of the least rewarded. It is not given to many to found a regiment in the British Army, and one which was the paradigm for certain foreign armies. He soon became a legend in the desert akin to the paladins.

While he languished in hospital he pondered upon a type of strategic warfare based on the Commando raids that destroyed targets on the enemy lines of communication, but using about one-twentieth of the number of men. The desert war was essentially one of supply, and Stirling envisaged raids in depth behind the enemy lines by four-man parties with every man trained to a high level of proficiency. Strategic operations aimed at the destruction of supply lines, landing grounds and enemy headquarters could only be successfully achieved, he argued, by the element of surprise and guile. And surprise and guile could be better effected by small groups of four determined men, exercising their own individual perception and judgment, than by larger numbers.

This was the philosophy upon which the SAS was founded, and these first principles governed the development of the Regiment from the day of its inception. Obviously there were to be growing pains, and a large number of difficulties to be overcome or bypassed. Foremost among these was an initial lack of understanding by GHQ Middle East that the new unit's role must be an exclusively strategic one, and that tactical tasks belonged to others. Stirling was also insistent that the SAS should plan their own operations, and at first this led to difficulties with SOE who considered that they should plan all strategic operations behind the enemy lines. However, it was made clear that SAS operations could be put at risk if planned by staff officers unfamiliar with SAS methods.

But Stirling had first to get his ideas off the ground, and this was not very easy for a young subaltern with no credentials. However, armed with an outline paper he hobbled (for he was still lame as a result of his drop) into GHQ without a pass and, in attempting to dodge the wrath of various staff officers he had encountered, he took refuge in a room which happened to be the office of the Deputy Chief of the General Staff. General Ritchie, an officer of considerable perspicacity, although clearly surprised at the intrusion, agreed to read the paper and immediately saw some merit in it.

The outcome was that three days later Stirling was summoned to see the Commander-in-Chief, General Auchinleck. He requested to be allowed to recruit and train sixty-five men from the remnants of Layforce, and the use of five Bombay aircraft from which to drop them two nights before the Eighth Army's planned offensive – some four months ahead – and his request was granted.

The new force, as Stirling had wanted, was to come directly under the Commander-in-Chief, and was to be known as L Detachment of the Special Air Service Brigade. No such brigade existed, except as part of a deception plan instituted by Brigadier Dudley Clarke, of Commando fame, but the letters SAS were in due course to be made famous by this small unit about to be raised. Recruiting did not take long, for Stirling knew the sort of man he required, but first it was necessary to pluck Jock Lewis from Tobruk, where No. 8 Commando was among those under siege. Other notable recruits were Captain R.B. ('Paddy') Mayne, and four non-commissioned officers, Bennett, Cooper, Lilley and Riley.

Mayne, who like Stirling was powerfully built, was an Irish rugger international and a renowned boxer. Normally a quiet man he could be dangerous when roused. He was a shrewd judge of character, a magnificent leader of men, and a dedicated destroyer of all things German. In the course of twelve months in the desert he had personally accounted for over 100 enemy aircraft. Mayne would one day command the 1st SAS, and before the war was over he was to win the DSO and no fewer than three bars. Of the four invaluable non-commissioned officers, Cooper (whom Stirling commissioned on the field – a piece of unorthodoxy which caused quite a stir), Bennett and Lilley were later to serve in the reconstituted post-war regiment.

L Detachment's camp was sited at Kabrit on the edge of the Great Bitter Lake, and it was due to the resourcefulness of its occupants rather than to Q Branch at GHQ that it soon became fairly comfortable. The training programme was intensive and arduous, and Stirling insisted on a high standard of discipline. There were two fatal casualties during the course of parachute training, but by November Stirling had the men ready for action. By now they had acquired, through the ingenuity of Jock Lewis, a completely new bomb. The problem arose when it was discovered that so few men could not carry the number of bombs required, for two types would be needed – an explosive and an incendiary bomb. Official enquiries as to the possibility of a combination met with totally unproductive results, and so Lewis went ahead with his own device. After many failures he eventually came up with a successful small explosive/incendiary bomb (a formula of oil, plastic and thermite) which very properly was to be known as the Lewis bomb, and became the principal weapon of aircraft and vehicle destruction.

The Eighth Army's attack was scheduled for 18 November 1941, and Stirling planned to drop fifty-five men from five Bombay aircraft to destroy aeroplanes on five airfields in the Gazala-Tmimi area the night previous to the attack. This meant that the drop must take place on the night of 16 November, so that men could lie up during the 17th, and go on to the airfields that night. A part of Stirling's original request was that an LRDG patrol should be available to collect his men from a given rendezvous. The complete failure of this operation and the loss of many men has already been described. But out of it came the invaluable and long-lasting association with the LRDG, for David Stirling was not the sort of man to be downcast by one failure; rather, it acted as a spur to greater efforts in his determination to prove conclusively to the vilipenders – and there were quite a few – that his theories were sound.

The first successful raids took place during the following month, and were the outcome of the willingness of the LRDG to act as a 'taxi' service for L Detachment, and a chance introduction Stirling obtained to Brigadier Denys Reid, who was then in command of E Force and under orders to proceed from Jalo (where the LRDG then had their base) to the Agedabia area in connection with the Eighth Army's forthcoming attack on Benghazi. He was anxious that aircraft on Agedabia airfield should be eliminated on the night of 21 December to facilitate his advance on the 22nd.

This was just what Stirling wanted, and he made immediate plans for two initial raids to take place against Sirte and Agheila fields on the night of 14/15 December, and a third in support of Reid against Agedabia on the night of the 21st. There would then be two further raids a week later on these forward airfields to coincide with the actual attack on Benghazi. Stirling and Mayne with ten other ranks would take care of Sirte, and Lewis would lead the raid on Agheila, while Captain Bill Fraser (another of the original recruits) would remain at Jalo until leaving for the Agedabia job. All three parties were carried by LRDG patrols.

The result of these first land-based raids was a triumphant success and entirely vindicated Stirling's theories, even though his own raid was the only one to draw blank. The approach to the target area contained similar hazards to those so often experienced by the LRDG, whose men by now had become masters of desert travel. Some 50 miles south of Sirte Stirling's party was spotted by an enemy plane, and he felt that better results might be obtained by a split. He therefore sent Mayne to the Tamit airfield, while he and a sergeant carried on to the original objective. They decided – as it turned out unwisely – on a night reconnaissance, and in the process disturbed a party of Italians. These men never constituted a danger, but the resulting alarm decided the enemy to evacuate the airfield on the following day. This was a bitter blow for Stirling, who knew full well that the success or failure of these raids would decide the future of his new force.

However, he need not have worried. Mayne's party had gained complete surprise until he blasted his way into a Nissen hut and shot up an officers' mess. Leaving a small party to hold the building he took the rest on to the airfield and managed to plant bombs on twenty-three aircraft and, using his own terrific muscle, destroyed the cockpit of another; before they departed, having suffered no casualties, they also blew up a petrol dump. Lewis had found Agheila airfield empty, but a few miles to the north at Mersa Brega he knew of a roadhouse usually full of officers and men. Joining an enemy convoy on the main road, he paid the place a surprise visit, and while some of his men were engaged in a sharp firefight he and one other planted about forty bombs on parked enemy transport. But Fraser's party, which returned to base a few days later, had had the greatest success of all. They had delighted Brigadier Reid, whom they met shortly after the raid, when they were able to report the destruction of thirty-seven aircraft without loss to themselves.

The follow-up raids which set off from Jalo on Christmas Eve were, except in one instance, less successful. Stirling was again unlucky. This time there were to be no recces, everything was to depend upon surprise; but before he could get to the airfield he found the road blocked solid by enemy armour and transport. He was obliged to retire before ever reaching the Sirte field, and was fortunate to escape with his life when failing to give the password on arrival at the rendezvous. The sentry fired at point-blank range but had omitted to put a round up the spout!

Mayne's party of five were again triumphant at Tamit, where twenty-seven newly-arrived aeroplanes were the recipients of time bombs. But Lewis and Sergeant Lilley had managed to destroy only one aircraft, for they were well dispersed and a half-hour fuse went off just as a bomb was being placed on the second (later it was decided that half-hour fuses were too short), and all hell broke out. On the way back to the rendezvous the party was attacked on open ground by a low-flying Italian Savoia, and Jock Lewis was killed. His was a most serious loss, for apart from being a greatly-loved officer and superb leader, he had done so much for the construction and organization of L Detachment.

Fraser and his four men were also unfortunate. They found the Marble Arch airfield unoccupied, and somehow there had been a muddle over the rendezvous. In consequence there was no one there, and they waited six days before deciding to march. It was one of those nightmare treks not unknown to many of the men who entered upon these hazardous long range patrols. Short of rations, desperate for water and frequently having to avoid (or sometimes clobber) enemy patrols, they never had a proper rest and there was always the sun, the sand and vague, tantalizing outlines in the haze. It took them eight days to regain Jalo, during which they covered 200 miles.

Inevitably there had been setbacks. No one could have expected those daring raids far behind the lines to be carried through without some loss to men and material, but the sum total of this December series was a most impressive one, for ninety enemy aircraft had been destroyed, and probably more if Stirling's habitual caution in estimating is taken into account. The force now returned to Kabrit and Stirling went to Cairo, where he saw the Commander-in-Chief who was well pleased with what had been achieved, and receptive to Stirling's next idea. This was to be a raid on the port of Bouerat, which with the impending fall of Benghazi he felt sure would be full of vital shipping that could be destroyed. Auchinleck agreed the proposal and authorized Stirling to recruit a further six officers and forty men.

Recruiting for any form of special force was a problem, for understandably commanding officers were loath to spare their best men, nor was much help usually forthcoming from A Branch at GHQ. No amount of training (and Stirling always insisted, where it was at all possible, that no man went into action before his training was complete) could fashion a man if he was not the right type. Besides courage and physical fitness, which were fairly obvious requirements, self-discipline, determination, resourcefulness and quickness of perception were some of the attributes Stirling looked for in a recruit – and such men were not usually found hanging about base depots.

But what now proved a useful addition to the unit was a parachute detachment of Free French, under Commandant Bergé.

These men were at the time in Alexandria, but in order to get them under his command Stirling had to go to Beirut to see General de Gaulle. At first the General was adamant that in no circumstances were Frenchmen to serve under British commanders, but Stirling's charm alloyed with a little cunning won the day, and these excellent French paratroopers were virtually the precursors of the French SAS. At about the same time as they joined him, Stirling chanced to meet Fitzroy Maclean and persuaded him to enrol. Not long afterwards the colourful, courageous but unpredictable (some thought unbearable) Randolph Churchill joined L Detachment for a short time.

While the principal targets continued to be airfields and the raids followed much the same pattern as the December ones – until in 1942 the unit received its own jeeps – attacks on harbours to destroy shipping were also undertaken. Although calling for immense coolness and courage, and packed with excitements and occasional moments of pure farce, these were never as successful (so far as actual shipping was concerned) as raids against aircraft, or for that matter operations to mine roads and destroy vehicles. The first of these shipping raids was the one planned against Bouerat, and for it Stirling had borrowed (for as yet they were not under his command) Captain Duncan and Corporal Barr from the Special Boat Section.

The LRDG provided a full patrol, together with wireless truck, commanded by Captain Hunter and navigated by Michael Sadler – probably the best navigator in the desert; he later joined the SAS and, like Cooper, was commissioned in the field by Stirling. They left Jalo on 17 January 1942 and headed for the Wadi Tamit, reaching the edge of it on the evening of the 22nd, but delayed the tricky descent of the escarpment until morning. Wireless silence had to be broken in order to obtain the latest information about the tankers in Bouerat harbour. This was a calculated risk which did not come off, and the party was spotted the next day on the steep slope entering the wadi, but all save the important wireless truck survived the subsequent strafing. Nearing the target area Hunter felt that as Bouerat was sure to be well guarded one vehicle would have to suffice, and the collapsible boat should be taken into the harbour assembled.

The last 30 or so miles to the hard road were very rough going, and the heavily loaded single vehicle met each obstacle with a sickening thud. The vehicle itself survived but the boat did not, which added to the loss of the wireless vehicle was an almost insurmountable blow. But for a man of Stirling's calibre it was just an irritating inconvenience, and certainly no reason for abandoning the venture. He immediately gave orders for a change of targets. Duncan and Barr were to deal with a nearby wireless station, while his party of fourteen would split into two sections on entering the town and engage other targets on and around the waterfront.

There was less than two hours from the time they left their truck in which to do their work, if they were to be back at the desert rendezvous before first light. But in that time a great many bombs were placed on vulnerable targets such as vehicles, machinery installations and, best of all, huge petrol carriers found fully loaded in a car park. And when they got back to the rendezvous Captain Duncan reported the destruction of the wireless station. In the end the result was far better than it might have been with the canoe, for the harbour appeared to contain few, if any, tankers that night.

The destruction of many targets was a satisfactory, exciting and often enjoyable part of these frequent SAS/LRDG raids, but there was a much grimmer side to each operation in the withdrawal to the rendezvous and beyond. By then a vertible hornets' nest had been disturbed and the enemy, animated by their desire for vengeance, pursued the raiders relentlessly in the air and on the ground. So long as they were in the jebel concealment was not too difficult, but in the open desert, where scrub was intermittent and often insufficient, the camouflage nets had to be placed with the greatest cunning. Vehicles would break down and need speedy and expert attention, some had to be abandoned and others might be destroyed by enemy action. The compass and the sun, the stars and even the sandstorm could all be friends, but the desert – as terrible as it was beautiful – could be savage and cruel beyond belief.

The port of Benghazi was visited by Stirling's men on several occasions. The first was in the middle of March 1942 when he again borrowed some men from the SBS, and with a canoe – which, mindful of Hunter's misfortune, was to be inflated *after* crossing the harbour wire – he hoped to place a number of limpets and thereby do considerable damage to shipping in the harbour. But the sea was found to be far too choppy to launch the craft, and the party retired without attempting to alert an unsuspecting enemy by the destruction of lesser targets. However, Mayne and two men, who had accompanied the party to the rendezvous but not gone to Benghazi, succeeded in blowing up fifteen aircraft on the Berca satellite field.

For the next attempt on Benghazi shipping Stirling had Fitzroy Maclean and Randolph Churchill with him. Their hilarious encounters with Italian sentries and drunken soldiers have been well told in many places, notably by Fitzroy Maclean in *Eastern Approaches*; but their adventures were greater than their achievements, for once again there was boat trouble: this time two canoes had punctured and could not be inflated. Perhaps the most important lesson learnt was how useful it was to have on these raids men who were fluent in one or both enemy languages – some knowledge of Arabic was also helpful. The sequel to the raid was very unfortunate; on the way back to civilization Maclean and Churchill were badly damaged in a car smash.

Benghazi was to feature twice more in SAS operations, but neither time was shipping involved. The second occasion was in September 1942 when their operation, code-named 'Snowdrop', was nearly as disastrous as the simultaneous Tobruk raid ('Daffodil') already recounted. Too many troops, too great a distance and total lack of security militated against success. The party approached from the south-east through Berca and were soon heavily engaged by a strong and well-prepared enemy force. Nothing could be done, and at least six 3-tonners and nine jeeps were destroyed by enemy air action,* although casualties were not too heavy. However, the earlier visit in June, which was part of an operation by eight patrols, was a much more satisfactory and rewarding affair.

The summer of 1942 was a desperate time in the desert. In June Rommel was still standing firm on the Gazala line, where he had dug in after his counter-attack in February, but he was poised to renew the offensive. Auchinleck had not felt strong enough to comply with Churchill's persistent promptings to drive the enemy back and thereby regain the important airfields of Cyrenaica, so badly needed for the protection of Malta convoys. But Stirling was asked what he could do to safeguard the passage of a convoy that was to run the gauntlet in the middle of the month. His answer was to organize the despatch of eight five-man patrols to operate on the night of 13/14 June. His desert targets were to be aircraft located on airfields at Barce, Benghazi and the Derna-Martuba area, and in Crete at the Heraklion aerodrome.

The desert raids were to follow much the same pattern as hitherto, except for those in the Derna area, where German troop

---

* Figures from the account in PRO document DEFE 2/7118. Philip Warner in *The Special Air Service* gives 25 trucks and 18 jeeps.

concentrations were particularly heavy. There were to be six French patrols on these raids, and Lieutenant Jordan (Bergé's second-in-command) was to take three of them to Derna. In order to get his patrols to their targets it was decided to make use of Captain Buck's intrepid SIG men.* This was Buck's first mission since he had gathered his band together and put them through a rigorous training course in German methods and behaviour. On its formation, in order to attain the highest possible standard of impersonation, SIG had been allotted two carefully-screened, supposedly anti-Nazi German prisoners of war, and these two men were to come on this raid in addition to Buck's six simulated Germans.

The procedure for getting through the German posts was much the same as that used three months later for the Tobruk raid – Afrika Corps vehicle signs and German uniforms – although on this occasion the raiders were invisible under tarpaulins. In spite of the fact that the password for June was not available (it was obtained later through a piece of chicanery), the patrols passed successfully through every barrier and reached the rendezvous, five miles from Derna, in time for Jordan and a small party to make his reconnaissance. For the raid Jordan split the patrols: one under Corporal Tourneret was to attack the Martuba field, while Jordan himself and Corporal Bourmont would attack two Derna fields.

Jordan and Bourmont started together, with Brückner – one of the two Germans – driving the lorry. It was not until too late, indeed just as the trap was sprung, that the Frenchman realized Brückner had betrayed them. Frenchmen and Palestinians fought valiantly, but the dice were too heavily loaded. Only Jordan managed to break clear of his captors and reach the rendezvous, where Buck was awaiting him. The two officers speedily removed themselves to the LRDG meeting place some 20 miles distant, but although they waited there for several days no others appeared. The rest, from all parties, had been killed or captured, for the betrayal had been absolute.

The fourth French patrol, under Commandant Bergé, went to Crete and with him went Lord Jellicoe, who had recently joined the SAS and who was a fluent French speaker. They travelled to the island in the submarine *Triton*, and after humping their heavy loads over the rough mountainous tracks reached the airfield in time for a daylight reconnaissance. This showed them that there

* See Chapter 6 for more about the Special Identification Group.

were more than sixty JU 88s and a number of Stukas on the field. That night, when they moved in to place their bombs, they were lucky in having the fortuitous assistance of a lone British raider, which dropped a stick of bombs on the runway just as their hole in the perimeter wire was about to be discovered. In the resulting confusion the patrol placed bombs on twenty-one aircraft and a petrol dump; two hours later they had the satisfaction of hearing these explode. But while waiting to be taken off the island their hideout was betrayed, and all the party, save Jellicoe and a Greek guide who had gone to signal the submarine, were killed or captured after being heavily outnumbered in a short, sharp engagement. Jellicoe embarked safely three days later.

Thus four of the six French patrols had met with disaster, although Bergé's had achieved a usefully large bag. But the other two – Zirnheld's, which went to Barce, and Jaquier's, which went with Stirling to the Berca-Benghazi area – destroyed planes and workshops without loss. Nevertheless, the destruction of thirty-seven aeroplanes did not save the Malta convoy from severe losses; only two out of the seventeen ships got through. But these two were sufficient to keep the island going until the next convoy, and but for the destruction of the thirty-seven aircraft they too might have gone to the bottom. The SAS record to date of 143 aeroplanes destroyed was a forceful reminder to the enemy that his lines of communication were constantly at peril from a small but deadly force of dedicated saboteurs.

The grim days of anxiety and disappointment, but never of despair, which followed this series of raids, and saw Rommel's triumphant drive across the Egyptian frontier, marked a new phase in SAS operations. Paddy Mayne had suggested to David Stirling that their own independent transport in the form of the American jeep might prove invaluable, and it did not take Stirling long to get his hands on fifteen of these newly arrived vehicles, and a number of 3-ton lorries for supplies. Possession of their own transport was most beneficial, and from now on they were independent in this respect, and moreover did much of their own navigating. This did not mean that they were to be entirely severed from the LRDG, for there was still the need for the occasional combined operation, but it allowed the SAS to set up their own resupply bases, sometimes as far as 1,000 miles behind the enemy front line. It also enabled the unit, which now numbered some 100 trained men, to adopt new methods of attack against a wider range of targets.

The front line had now been established between Alamein and

the Qattara Depression, and almost at once Auchinleck was thinking in terms of counter-attack to push the enemy back anyway as far as Mersa Matruh. Could Stirling destroy aircraft operating from the forward airfields? Stirling was never one to say no, but the plan gave him precisely four days to get his new jeeps armed with the type of weapon he wanted. Twin Vickers 'K' guns (which had been used in the now obsolete Gloster Gladiators) were mounted in pairs at the front and rear of the jeeps – later they were supplemented by .50 Brownings – and twenty 3 ton lorries were brought from Kabrit. Thus armed and fully mobile, the SAS could stay in the desert for up to three weeks, attacking targets as opportunity arose.

In the event Rommel stood his ground; but, navigated by two LRDG patrols under Robin Gurdon and Alastair Timpson, the jeeps found a hole in the line and got through round the edge of the Qattara Depression. Mayne managed to place bombs on a number of planes on Bagush airfield, but when to his fury some of these proved to be damp and failed to explode Stirling was quick to turn this temporary setback into a permanent advantage. He decided they should drive on to the airfield to see what could be done by the jeeps. The average rate of fire from the Vickers 'K' gun was 1,200 rounds a minute, and so great was their firepower that in one drive round the perimeter of the field they had reduced seven aircraft to matchwood. This new technique had a considerable bearing on future operations, more especially as by now the Germans, seriously worried at their heavy aircraft losses, had ordered men to sleep by their machines.

Further raids with varying success took place in the middle of July, and then Stirling decided it was time to replenish supplies. Leaving some thirty men at the forward base – about 60 miles north of Qara on the west side of the Depression – he and a few others, with three jeeps and eight trucks, returned to Kabrit. It was not an easy journey, for the Germans had blocked the edge of the Qattara Depression. This deep bowl with its vast salt bog bottom, stretching 150 miles in length and 75 across at its widest place, had only a very few hard crossings, and most of these were not suitable for heavy vehicles. It was an ugly prospect. Mile upon mile of cracked salt and wavering heat bars, while above a flaming sun scorched down from the immense dome of blue sky. And not only the sun was there, for enemy aircraft were watchful, and therefore the crossing was made more treacherous through having to be attempted during periods of heat haze. That it was eventually accomplished was due to the pioneering work of the LRDG patrols, and the skill of navigator and driver.

Once back at the rendezvous, with fresh supplies and vehicles, Stirling determined upon an operation of majestic splendour based on jeep firepower and designed to deliver maximum devastation of enemy planes on Landing Ground 12 at Sidi Haneish. The moon was full and so the enemy, hitherto accustomed to destruction by stealth, would not be expecting this new form of attack; with reasonable fortune complete surprise would be achieved.

The rendezvous, where the eighteen jeeps destined for the attack were assembled, was some 40 miles to the south of the airfield, and on the night previous to the attack the proposed battle formation was meticulously rehearsed. For the last half-mile or so Stirling ordered that all eighteen jeeps would advance in extended order, bringing to bear the full weight of their machine guns frontally against the enemy defences. On entering the actual field a green Very light would be the signal for the jeeps to form two lines some yards apart but connected by his and two other jeeps in the front, and proceed in Indian file between two rows of aircraft. Therefore seven jeeps would bring fourteen guns to bear on aircraft situated to the flank of each advancing line, and the leading jeeps would fire frontally at the aerodrome defences. Only the navigator's jeep, which was behind the three leaders, would initially remain silent. Thus something like 80,000 rounds a minute would lash into aircraft and defences like wind-driven rain.

The initial approach over exceptionally rough going was, as always, extremely difficult with the usual vehicle mishaps necessitating speedy and skilful repair or improvisation. Mike Sadler performed a fine feat of navigation to bring the party right on target, and after a brief pause for checking and adjusting arms and ammunition Stirling ordered the advance in line abreast. As they drew close to the field it was suddenly brilliantly illuminated as though they were expected, but there was no going back by then, and in fact surprise was complete, for the lights were only a guide to an incoming machine.

Once on the field the Very light went up and the drill into double line was smoothly executed. No poacher could have wished for roosting pheasants to have been so perfectly outlined against a moonlit sky as were these German aircraft, and in a remarkably short space of time the massive weight of firepower tore them to shreds or turned them into a blazing inferno which almost scorched the raiders. In a frenzy of desperation the enemy brought to bear a mortar and a Breda on the column. The front gunner in one jeep was killed, but little else was achieved before those weapons were silenced, and the SAS proceeded to complete the carnage of the field and then withdrew, dispersing into small parties for the long and dangerous trek to the rendezvous.

The exact number of aircraft destroyed could not be definitely ascertained, but certainly it was more than thirty for the loss of only three jeeps. Besides the gunner killed in the attack the cheerful and much-liked Frenchman, André Zirnheld, died of wounds received from an air strike on the way back. In his debriefing David Stirling was critical of the inordinate amount of ammunition unnecessarily expended, leaving insufficient for the destruction of all aircraft on the field; but by any standards it was a magnificent mounted manoeuvre performed to perfection.

In the middle of August, when those operations with pretty names (Daffodil, Tulip, Snowdrop and Hyacinth) and ugly results were under consideration, Stirling was summoned to the British Embassy, where he met the Prime Minister and General Alexander. The latter had just replaced Auchinleck as Commander-in-Chief. It may well have been due in part to conversations that took place then that, shortly after the conclusion of the disastrous Benghazi raid (Snowdrop) in September, the SAS was given an official place in the roll of regiments of the British Army as the 1st Special Air Service Regiment, with David Stirling in command as a Lieutenant-Colonel.

This honour included authority to expand to more than double the present size, and as raids had to continue Stirling was anxious to obtain recruits with battle experience quickly; but in General Montgomery, who had assumed command of the Eighth Army on 13 August, 'the boy Stirling' (as Monty would later refer to him with grudging admiration) had met his match. No man could be spared from the Eighth Army, and so Stirling was forced to draw on men from the base depots who would need a considerable period of training. He therefore formed a squadron of his most experienced men under Major Mayne to carry out operations, based on Kufra, against the enemy lines of communication. These enjoyed considerable success, although it was disappointing for Stirling that his new regiment could take no major part in the battle of Alamein. There was, however, much activity at Kabrit where the new recruits were joined by the Special Boat Squadron and the Greek Sacred Regiment. Stirling had been negotiating for some time to get the latter under command, for he felt they would be a particular asset for operations in the Balkans. His meeting with the Prime Minister, mentioned above, was the determining factor.

Stirling's ideas for operations in support of Montgomery's advance to Tripoli were submitted in a paper to Colonel Shan Hackett – now controlling all Middle East raiding forces – who was one of the few officers on the staff of GHQ with whom he was in full accord. His plan was to establish two main bases from which sixteen jeep detachments (each of three or four jeeps) would mount up to two raids a week on the coastal stretch between Agheila and Tripoli. The principal object of these raids was to mine the road, attack laagers and all transport using the road; and generally to harass enemy communications by night so that Rommel was forced to use the road during daylight when his columns would be at the mercy of the Royal Air Force.

The plan met with Montgomery's approval, and operations were to coincide with the Eighth Army's advance. It was also necessary to synchronize the raids with patrols of the LRDG, who were still maintaining their Road Watch. Stirling decided to use two squadrons, A and B (although the latter contained many men with little or no experience) under Majors Mayne and Street respectively. B Squadron with ninety men, thirty jeeps and twelve lorries left Kabrit on 20 November and joined A, which had come from Kufra, at Bir Zalten south of Agheila. Stirling had decided to accompany B to their area of operations, which was to be the westernmost sector of the 400-mile stretch of coast to be raided – from Bouerat west to Tripoli.

Allotted the sector Agheila to Bouerat, A Squadron in the event had time to carry out only one or two raids before it became pointless to destroy the road immediately ahead of the Eighth Army's rapid advance. B Squadron had more time in which to operate, but in an area that was comparatively densely populated by Arabs, many of whom were unfriendly.

The squadron was divided into eight patrols each of three jeeps, and the patrols were allotted separate sections of the road. Undoubtedly their initial attacks caused the enemy considerable consternation and inconvenience, for intensive air and ground searches were mounted which kept the patrols constantly on the run. In the end casualties were grievous: Captain Hore-Ruthven was killed, and six out of the remaining nine officers were captured. It was noticeable that the few officers and men who did eventually get back were those with most experience, emphasizing the point so often made by Stirling that experience was a most important ingredient for survival.

At the end of January 1943 the posted strength of the 1st SAS Regiment was 47 officers and 532 other ranks, but at this time they were somewhat short of establishment. Under Major Mayne, A Squadron was operating in the desert from Kufra, until sixty-six officers and men left for the Lebanon on 24 January to start a ski course. B Squadron commanded by Major Street, C led by Major Lea and the French patrols under Captain Jordan were earmarked for important operations in support of the Eighth Army's advance into Tunisia. D Squadron had been formed on 6 January under Lord Jellicoe. The fifteen officers and forty other ranks of No. 1 Special Boat Section, which had been absorbed by the SAS, formed a part of this squadron. Stirling was anxious to have a sea raiding group, and the squadron spent some time training in boatcraft, although the War Diary reports that on 25 January Jellicoe left Kabrit for the desert with 41 officers and men, together with 121 officers and men of the Greek Sacred Regiment.

Four operations were planned for January. One group would disrupt communications to the west of Tripoli to hasten the enemy's departure from the town (which was under attack from the east) in the hope of preventing the destruction of the port installations. Another (the Frenchmen) would raid the lines of communication between Sfax and Gabes; a third would observe and report upon work being carried out to strengthen the Mareth Line, and Stirling himself with about fourteen men would spy out the land in northern Tunisia to report upon going conditions for the link-up of the Eighth Army with the First. His eldest brother, Bill, had recently formed the 2nd SAS Regiment and was with the First Army, and David was secretly thinking in terms of an SAS brigade.

The Tripoli party did not get much time to operate, for Montgomery's advance was very rapid. However, at least one patrol from B Squadron, Captain Galloway's, achieved some success against enemy transport on the road between Zuara and Ben Gardane (about 80 miles west of Tripoli). The section split, and although Galloway did not have much fortune and had to walk 80 miles after losing both his jeeps, his number two, Captain O'Sullivan, got among a number of heavy lorries and Scammels in a German laager, on which he deposited four Lewis bombs, and shot up the other vehicles.

The unexpectedly rapid advance of the Eighth Army was to produce a considerable degree of urgency in those groups whose task it was to reconnoitre the Mareth Line and blast the rail track and coastal road – Rommel's only remaining threads of supply route. But it was not until the patrols were in the vicinity of the forward rendezvous, Bir Soltane, that Stirling became aware of this urgency. They had travelled, independently, west across the desert to Ghadames, and thence north across the eastern edge of the Grand Sea Erg. A very difficult and unpleasant route, and a far worse experience than negotiating the Great Sand Sea of the Western Desert, for in the Sea Erg the sand was formed not into long sweeping rollers, but back-breaking narrow ridges.

As soon as Stirling had joined up with Jordan he ordered him to push on quickly through the Gabes Gap, an enemy-held bottleneck only 5 miles across at its narrowest point. The three French patrols had almost 100 miles to go, but it was necessary for them to get through the Gap that night in order to start operations on the following one. They left the rendezvous with nine jeeps at 4 p.m. on 21 January, and found the going so bad that it was impossible for them to reach the Gap by nightfall, let alone get through it.

By dawn on the 23rd, however, they were through, or at least some of them were, for by then Captain Jordan had only three jeeps left. After several hours of cautious driving they had run straight into a German convoy, which included three armoured cars. The latter quickly accounted for three of their jeeps, and a fourth was put out of action when a little later they encountered three lorries which, as surprise had already been lost, Jordan – perhaps a trifle unwisely – decided to engage. In the schemozzle the remaining jeeps became separated, and before the patrols were clear of this dangerous trap the wireless car broke its sump and the engine of Jordan's own jeep seized up so that it had to be abandoned.

Once through the Gap the small party achieved considerable success in blowing the railway line in several places. But, rather rashly, they decided to return in their jeeps to the scene of an earlier triumph and complete the work by shooting up a transport camp. Here they were fiercely engaged by a very alert enemy, and although all the jeeps managed to disappear into the darkness unscathed they became separated. The occupants of two were betrayed by Arabs while extricating their vehicles from a bog, and Jordan with his two companions ran into a well-sited, heavily-armed Italian ambush. With his machine guns out of action he was forced to surrender.

David Stirling had carried out a quick reconnaissance of the country flanking the Mareth Line before he joined Jordan's patrols at the Bir Soltane rendezvous. Here he left Lieutenants Alston and Thesiger to reconnoitre the fortifications on the Mareth Line, which was only some 30 miles away, while he and his patrol of fourteen drove through the Gabes Gap not more than twelve hours behind the Frenchmen. The enemy were by now very watchful, and the jeeps were spotted from the air, but too late in the day for an air strike to be mounted; the patrol took good care not to hang about, and despite the appalling going were safely through by dawn.

When they had driven some 20 miles north of the Gap they found a wadi which offered excellent lying-up cover for the day, although further investigation showed it to be dangerously close to a road junction busy with enemy traffic. However, it would have been impossible to move before nightfall, and the men were desperately short of sleep. The enemy were quite unaware of their presence and Stirling very rightly decided they should sleep, so as to be properly rested for a raid on the Sousse railway that night. But although man can make his decisions, the hand he is called to play is often dealt him by fate. And so it was for Stirling, upon whom the beams of fortune had for so long shone so brightly.

The Germans had diverted troops with the special task of hunting down the SAS, so concerned were they by their depredations; but it was purely by chance that a strong company of men stumbled across the patrol's well-concealed hideout. Mike Sadler and Sergeants Cooper and Taxis (a Frenchman) were able to make a lucky dash for freedom, but the rest were taken, and conveyed by lorry to a large empty building for the night.

From here Stirling and Lieutenant McDermott succeeded, through a desperately chancy plan, in getting clean away, but in the dark they failed to join up. Stirling, having covered 15 miles that night, sought refuge in an Arab farmhouse, whose occupant proved to be (unusually for Tunisia) most generous in his help and hospitality to a British soldier on the run. But thirty-six hours later Stirling's luck again deserted him when he was betrayed by a young shepherd greedy for reward. This time it was the Italians who had caught him, and by now they knew whom they had got and were taking no chances. McDermott was not at liberty for long, but Sadler, Cooper and Taxis after some nerve-racking adventures got through to the First Army lines.

Reporting Stirling's capture in his journal Field-Marshal Rommel wrote: 'Thus the British lost the very able and adaptable commander of the desert group which had caused us more damage than any other British unit of equal strength.'* And he was right. The British Army in general had lost a most gifted,

* *The Rommel Papers*, edited by B.H. Liddell Hart, Collins, 1953, p.393.

vital and adventurous officer, and the SAS in particular its founder and the mainspring of all its activities, which included, *inter alia*, the destruction of almost 400 enemy aircraft during the desert war.

14

The Special Boat Squadron and Raiding Forces

It is fairly easy to confuse the work of the Special Boat Section in the Mediterranean with that of the Special Boat Squadron in Aegean waters, because the letters SBS are sometimes used in the same documents, or even in the same books, to describe operations by both forces. In fact the two organizations are only connected in that Lord Jellicoe, who was to head the Special Boat Squadron, had under his command a number of men from No. 1 Special Boat Section, which on Roger Courtney's departure from the Middle East had been commanded by Major Kealy, and in the autumn of 1942 came under the wing of David Stirling's SAS.

At the beginning of September 1942 seven men of No. 1 Special Boat Section undertook what was to be the last of the many daring raids carried out by that unit. Captains Allott and Sutherland with five other ranks, two Greek officers and two Greek guides were taken to Rhodes in a Greek submarine, where they were to attempt the destruction of aircraft on two airfields. It was a desperate venture, for the island was swarming with Italian troops, and no sooner had they successfully placed their bombs than the hounds were in full cry after them. Sutherland and Marine Duggan, after many hours of nerve-racking hide and seek, slipped through the cordon and took to the sea. Flashing their torches, they swam for 1½ miles and were lucky to be picked up by the submarine. The remainder of the party were caught. The loss of these irreplaceable men, following on similar recent losses in the Mediterranean, was the deciding factor that brought about the absorption of the Special Boat Section remnants into the SAS.

The SAS at this time had four squadrons and Stirling was quick to see the value to his force of seaborne raiders, and so D Squadron

– which now contained members of the old SBS, together with a troop from the Greek Sacred Regiment – formed this element. Training of the Squadron was done in the Lebanon – under Sutherland as soon as he had recovered from his exertions in Rhodes – and the course, which was later to become standardized, included parachute training and skiing. This last originated from a request made by General Wilson for SAS ski troops should there be a need for them in the Caucasus. Captain Fitzroy Maclean was sent to Baghdad in November to recruit suitable men from Persia and Iraq Command (PAIC), and having done this to take them into the mountains to learn their craft. Some two months earlier Lieutenant Langton and a few men had been detached to take part in the Tobruk raid already recounted.

Thus elements of D Squadron were employed during the winter of 1942–43 in training in various parts of the Middle East, or trying to escape after the unsuccessful raid on Tobruk. The other SAS squadrons were raiding far in advance of the Eighth Army's drive to Tunisia. It was on one of these raids, in Feburary 1943, that the Germans at last caught up with David Stirling – although they did not realize their good fortune until he was recaptured by the Italians after he had eluded his first German captors.

The author once saw a Japanese order which began: 'No one in the Imperial army is indispensable, generals will go forward . . .' David Stirling always went forward, but he was in fact virtually indispensable to the SAS at this time, for the simple reason that he seldom committed anything to paper and kept all the plans for his forces – administrative as well as operational – firmly in his head. When he went there was chaos, for no one knew, least of all his adjutant, where all his men were, what they were meant to be doing and what plans he had for them in the future.

The sensible solution adopted was virtually to start afresh with two new units. One, the Special Raiding Squadron, to which most of Stirling's men were drafted, was led by Major R.B. Mayne; and the other, under Lord Jellicoe and known as the Special Boat Squadron, was in effect the old D Squadron SAS. Both the SRS and SBS retained the beige beret and SAS insignia, and they were placed under the overall command of Lt-Colonel Cator (late of 51 Commando) in a unit which at first styled itself Raiding Forces, but which Cator soon renamed 1 SAS Regiment. (The title 'Raiding Forces' was later to be used again – see below.) Before long the SRS was doing fine work behind the lines in Italy (see Chapter 3), and later they fought with distinction in North-West Europe as the reconstituted 1 SAS Regiment.

Meanwhile, the Special Boat Squadron was divided into three detachments: L, M and S, so designated after their commanders – Langton, Maclean and Sutherland. Each detachment had five patrols commanded by an officer with twelve other ranks, which included two signallers, and the detachment commander had a small headquarters patrol of his own. The Squadron therefore numbered around 230 all ranks, and in addition there were some administrative personnel – storekeepers, cooks and parachute packers. The official date for its formation was 1 April 1943, and the unit was based by the sea at Athlit a little to the south of Haifa.

Not long after the raid in which Major March-Phillips was killed (see Chapter 2), and following further losses in the winter of 1942, it was decided that the Small Scale Raiding Force (No. 62 Commando) should be disbanded. Brigadier Laycock, who was back in England commanding the Special Service Brigade, selected two exceptional officers from that Force to be posted to the Special Boat Squadron. They were Philip Pinckney and the Dane, Anders Lassen. Pinckney was shortly to be posted to 2 SAS in Tunisia; but Lassen was to remain with the SBS until his death in 1945, and probably accounted for more dead Germans than any other man in the whole war.

During the spring and early summer of 1943 Jellicoe kept the new unit training assiduously but never monotonously. They quickly achieved an *esprit de corps* based on professional pride and comradeship, and the enemy garrisons of the Aegean islands, which hitherto had been largely unmolested, were soon to suffer drastically from these masters of the seaborne raid.

The first operation was directed on to a familiar target, airfields in Crete. Almost exactly a year earlier the men of the Special Boat Section had visited Kastelli and other places on the island, as already related. Now Sutherland's S detachment were to make a three-pronged attack on aircraft at Kastelli, Timbaki and Heraklion airfields. Sutherland, with a dump party and two patrols, landed on the south of the island on the night of 22 June; the third patrol was to land four nights later, and re-embarkation for the whole party was planned for the night of 11/12 July.

Lieutenant Lamonby's patrol was to go to Heraklion, Anders Lassen had Kastelli for his objective, and the third patrol under Lieutenant Rowe was to visit the airfield at Timbaki. Many are familiar with the rough going that is often met with on the island of Crete, and it was no picnic humping 70 lb of equipment over this enemy-infested land of soaring hills and sharply-cut valleys. Guides were not always reliable, but the patrols could count on considerable help from the inhabitants, without which their missions could not have been accomplished.

Lamonby received information that Heraklion was now seldom used by aircraft, and that none was there at present. He therefore turned his attention to a large petrol dump near Peza, some 12 miles south of Heraklion. It required skill to infiltrate through sentries and guard dogs, and there were breathtaking moments of excitement and apprehension; but the operation was successful, and after laying bombs, which in the ensuing holocaust of explosion and fire destroyed some 44,000 gallons of petrol, the patrol got safely back to base.

Rowe's patrol had a most disappointing expedition, for after a long and tedious trudge Timbaki was found, as was the case in the previous year, to be void of aircraft. But Lassen, who seemed to possess a built-in radar system constantly beamed onto dangerous enemy targets, gave his patrol plenty of excitement and gained considerable success. The approach march was accomplished without incident; but near the airfield, which contained five JU 88s and eight Stukas, the locals told him that the Stukas – his principal target – were very well guarded. Although he felt that the Cretans had exaggerated the position he decided to divide his party, and while with Gunner Jones he created a diversion he sent Sergeant Nicholson and Corporal Greaves to attack the aircraft at the opposite (eastern) end of the field.

Lassen and Jones, having dealt with a series of sentries in Lassen's own inimitable style of bluff and bloodshed, found themselves confronted with at least twenty of the enemy who had come to their assistance. This called for a liberal use of grenades, and some rapid fire and movement. The 'diversion' had now become a first-class fight, and when troops started arriving from the east end of the airfield Lassen knew his job was accomplished. His withdrawal to Sutherland at the base dump was prolonged by being betrayed in a hideout, and having to spend some time lurking in the mountains. Meanwhile, Greaves and Nicholson had cut their way through the wire and had managed in the confusion caused by the diversion, although not without considerable difficulty and danger, to destroy a JU 88, three Stukas and a petrol dump. By then searchlights illuminated the entire area, but somehow they slipped through the beams, shook off a close pursuit, and three days later regained the base.

This, the Special Boat Squadron's first operation, had been most rewarding, marred only by the death of Lieutenant Lamonby – the one casualty. Shortly before the party was due to re-embark, and therefore when undue noise was to be avoided, some Cretans got over-excited at the prospect of wiping out a four-man German patrol that had appeared. Sutherland sent Lamonby to quieten the Cretans and pursue the Germans, who had not been captured. He attempted to stalk two of the latter, who withdrew skilfully covering each other, and although Lamonby killed one the other got him.

While Sutherland's men were employed in Crete, L detachment were engaged in a bizarre and not very happy mission at the other end of the Mediterranean. The invasion of Sicily was shortly to be launched, and by way of deception a preliminary raid from the sea and the air was directed on Sardinia. Ill health had resulted in Langton returning to England, and Captain John Verney temporarily commanded the detachment. There were to be two parties for this Sardinia venture; one commanded by Verney, with Captain Edward Imbert-Terry, was dropped north of Lake Tiso, and the other under Captain Brinkworth came in by sea.

Both Verney and Brinkworth were German speakers, and they had some delightful adventures ragging large parties of Italian soldiers and *Carabinieri* with outrageous bluff, and generally causing a considerable uproar; but it had to come to an end, and as the arrangements for their evacuation seem to have been entirely lacking they were eventually captured. Some were taken to a prison camp in Italy from which they escaped after the Italian armistice (though Verney, Imbert-Terry and Brinkworth were by then in Germany), but in accordance with the rule at that time escaped prisoners did not serve again in the same theatre.

A small number of L detachment men had not gone to Sardinia, and Jellicoe arranged for them to be dropped into Sicily with 2 SAS. They carried out some sabotage of installations, and after minor adventures joined up with the recently-arrived British forces. But the detachment, after this excursion to the western Mediterranean, had to be virtually reconstituted. Its new commander was to be Major Ian Patterson, who until recently had been second-in-command of the 11th Parachute Battalion. M detachment was also to get a new commander, for in July Fitzroy Maclean had been summoned for work in Yugoslavia and his place was taken by Major J.N. Lapraik, who had been with 51 Commando in Abyssinia.

The Aegean story after the Italian surrender has already been touched upon, and mention made of the need to secure Rhodes through Italian co-operation. To initiate this co-operation Lord Jellicoe, Major Dalby and Sergeant Kesterton made an adventurous parachute drop on to the island with a view to persuading the Governor, Admiral Campioni, to surrender it peacefully. Dalby broke a leg in the jump, but Jellicoe succeeded in meeting the admiral, who proved to be a man of straw much more afraid of his German masters than of the British. Jellicoe repeatedly asked GHQ Middle East to send him some back-up troops, but either they could not or would not do this, and soon the party was hustled out of Rhodes, its mission a failure.

Rhodes was the key to the south Aegean islands, and without its airfields – or participation by Turkey on the side of the Allies – it would have been better to pull out for the time being rather than try to hold some of the other islands, especially when there was no air support available. However, it was considered necessary to forestall the inevitable German attempts to take them over. The work of the Long Range Desert Group towards this end has already been recounted, and that of the Special Boat Squadron was very closely related – indeed both units were soon to come under the umbrella of Brigadier Turnbull's Raiding Forces. The Royal Navy, too, using powered caiques and motor launches, was active in harrying enemy shipping whenever opportunity occurred, and in spite of being outgunned and faced by faster vessels in dangerous uncharted waters did much damage.

The struggle for control of the Aegean islands was unrelentingly pursued during September and October, but possession of the Rhodes airfields gave the Germans an overwhelming advantage. In those islands where there was even a small German garrison the Italians were effectively deterred from any sort of handover. However there were a number garrisoned only by Italians and many of these were quickly occupied by men of the SBS, LRDG and Greek Sacred Regiment. The Italians usually showed little inclination to resist, and the Greek inhabitants were mostly welcoming. Jellicoe, who had collected a small fleet of armed caiques and schooners, deployed his troops with great skill and energy. Castelorizzo was the first island to be taken over, and this was followed in due course by a string of others – Cos, Samos, Stampalia, Leros, Kalimnos, Icaria and Simi.

The last of these came under British influence when Major Lapraik with a composite party from M and S detachments landed on 17 September. Lassen was in the van and had quite a bit to say to those Italians foolish enough to open fire on him with two 20 mm guns. Lapraik improved the island's defensive positions and then used it as a base for offensive operations, which included sending an officer on the dangerous task of discovering what was happening in Rhodes – he was there in all for more than three weeks and collected some very valuable information. In October the Germans methodically set about retaking many of the islands, following up their success on Cos with a powerful punch at Simi.

The attack came at first light on 7 October, but the enemy found Lapraik ready for them. The first caique to attempt a landing was successfully engaged and put out of action, but the Germans succeeded in getting a considerable number of men ashore and occupying the southern ridge of the island. Fighting was stiff both there and in the town, with the enemy calling up air support. The Stukas did not, however, do much damage and Lapraik's Bren guns, combined with a frontal and flank attack, were sufficient to push the Germans back into their waiting boats. He despatched a caique to head off the largest craft of the departing fleet; the caique was not fast enough, but drove the German schooner within range of Lapraik's Bren gunners, who raked the densely packed decks. The SBS had one man killed and two wounded in this very successful action, and the Italians – who after a little forceful persuasion from Lassen had fought with some spirit – had ten men wounded. Sixteen Germans were killed on the island, thirty wounded and six captured, and undoubtedly they suffered heavy casualties on the schooner.

Lapraik's men were not permitted a peaceful enjoyment of their victory, for during the succeeding days the island was subjected to severe dive-bombing, and on 12 October they were ordered to withdraw. But towards the end of November, when the SBS had reverted to their more accustomed role of raiding rather than defending, Lapraik was back again at the head of three patrols to cause consternation and casualties among the enemy.

On 18 October 1943 a new organization commanded by Brigadier Turnbull, who had been concerned with some of the previous operations in the Aegean, came into being. It was given the previously used name of Raiding Forces. Jellicoe had for some time been advocating a co-ordinating headquarters, and now Turnbull was to have under his command the Special Boat Squadron, the Long Range Desert Group, the Greek Sacred Regiment, the Kalpaks (a body of rough and tough saboteurs) and the Holding Unit, Special Forces. Two months after Raiding Forces' inception the Raiding Support Regiment was added to them, and in the summer of 1944 a section of the Royal Marine Boom Patrol Detachment came under command.* There were

---

* See Chapters 4 and 15 for details of the RSR and RMBPD.

also troops nominally attached, but in reality as much a permanent part of the force as the rest. These came from the Sappers, REME, RAMC and, most importantly, included detachments from the Royal Corps of Signals. British, Greeks, Turks, South Africans, New Zealanders and Americans (who served with great gallantry as medical orderlies) mixed happily together in Raiding Forces.

When Leros fell on 16 November 1943 it could be said that the Germans dominated the Aegean, and were in a position to make grave difficulties for Allied operations in Italy and the Adriatic. Raiding Forces therefore had the task of isolating and tying down some six German divisions from being used in vital theatres of war, disrupting communications with their important base in Crete and preventing any outward extension towards the oilfields in Iraq. In fulfilling this mission they paid 381 visits to 70 different islands in the Dodecanese and Cyclades groups; they would slip in quietly by night from the sea to gain information, stalk a few sentries, slit a few throats, blow up vital installations, and then disappear as silently as they had come, leaving the enemy guessing as to where the next blow would fall.

For these tasks a man needed to be fierce, tough, independent, cunning and predatory. But he needed also to be very well trained in a number of special skills. He was therefore a most highly regarded non–expendable article, whose life could not be lightly risked in some pointless or ill-considered operation. In Raiding Forces the attached troops underwent the same rigorous training as the British and Greek regular raiders, and humped the same equipment on a patrol – indeed the signallers, on whose standard of excellence an operation could succeed or fail, usually carried a greater burden. A man had to be self-sufficient on a raid, for only occasionally was there any transport. Besides his arms and ammunition (which included grenades), he had in his pack spare clothing and rations for what could be anything up to a fourteen-day operation.

Obviously the raids varied widely in composition and character. Some had a purely reconnaissance objective, others might be reconnaissances which turned, intentionally or unintentionally, into fighting patrols, and still others – especially towards the end of 1944 when the scale of operations was stepped up – were raids intended to obliterate entire garrisons. Whole books have been written (see Bibliography) recounting in detail many of these numerous raids. Here it is only possible to mention one or two in outline to illustrate the type of work that had to be done.

At the beginning of 1944 Brigadier Turnbull received a directive from GHQ ordering him to concentrate on the destruction of enemy shipping; the enemy was managing to consolidate his position in the Aegean by operating an inter-island caique traffic which sailed by day, and MTBs of the Royal Navy were unable to intercept these craft for lack of air support. Accordingly Jellicoe set about sending his SBS men into various harbours.

At the end of January a patrol under Captain M.E. Anderson visited Stampalia. They landed in the neck of the island, and lay up until the following day. The plan then was for Anderson to sail round the island to the main harbour while another party, under Corporal Asbery, went overland to pay attention to a seaplane and a number of caiques that lay at anchor in Marmari Bay. Asbery's men cut their way through barbed wire, negotiated a minefield and placed Lewis bombs on the wings of the seaplane; their approach had been undetected but on their way to the next target – the caiques – they were heard and fired upon. However, they got clear and reached the beach. Four men then swam out to the caiques and placed bombs in the engine rooms of three of them. The patrol then withdrew and in due course the bombs did their work. Anderson, the following night, discovered two enemy caiques in the bay still afloat. These he disposed of, and the party disappeared leaving Stampalia without any shipping.

Shipping raids were only one part of the overall plan of destruction. For a time a ban had been imposed on Raiding Forces visiting the Cyclades group of islands, as a more esoteric force needed them kept quiet while their agents were operating there; after this was lifted in April, Turnbull evolved a slightly different type of operation. This entailed the elimination, in the course of only forty-eight hours, of a number of small German garrisons which were transmitting important Allied shipping and aircraft movements.

S detachment was detailed for the job; Lieutenant Lodwick was to attack the enemy on Mykonos, Lassen with two patrols (his own and Lieutenant Balsillie's) was given Santorini at the south of the group, and Captain Clarke's patrol was to deal with the two islands of Ios and Amorgos. All three missions were perfectly executed and entirely successful; the Germans were either killed or captured and their transmitting equipment was destroyed. The SBS lost two men killed (one was Lieutenant Stefan Casulli, an Alexandrian Greek who had volunteered for the British special forces) and three others were slightly wounded.

As a result of these and other raids the Germans greatly strengthened their garrisons, but this did not deter Sutherland from sending Lassen to Paros and Clarke to Naxos. Lassen divided his party, and set off himself to attack a gun position, but the plan was foiled when the alarm was given before his party was near enough to attack. The gun position was in an open field guarded by twenty Germans, and even Lassen felt that such odds, with no hope of success, were unacceptable. But his other two patrols met with better fortune and killed a number of the enemy whom they attacked in a house. On Naxos, where Clarke's patrol joined forces with the local *andartes*,* a group of eighteen Germans were surrounded in three houses, and in the destruction of these houses the whole lot became casualties, although a relieving force prevented Clarke from making those who survived prisoners.

When, towards the end of 1944, Raiding Forces adopted a policy of large-scale raids with a view to obliterating whole garrisons and liberating islands, the smaller type of harassing hit-and-run patrols were still continued against those islands unsuitable for the larger operations. It was more than ever necessary to husband the highly trained manpower by declining to take unjustifiable risks, but unless there were exceptional circumstances a superior enemy garrison within a ratio of six to one was considered fair game.

The prototype for these larger raids took place on Simi in July 1944, and was led by Brigadier Turnbull with Lapraik as his deputy. As a preliminary to any landing it was necessary to put two enemy destroyers out of action, and this was accomplished by a patrol of the Royal Marine Boom Patrol Detachment who paddled their canoes into the harbour and placed charges against the sides of the warships. This major obstacle to the operation having been skilfully and courageously removed, the business of contacting and concentrating the many outlying components of Raiding Forces went ahead, and by 13 July 224 officers and men were ready to sail in three parties.

The landing of the main force at 2.10 a.m. on 14 July was not without incident: sadly, two Greek officers slipped from their rubber boat and drowned under the weight of their heavy equipment. Otherwise the three parties disembarked safely, and immediately commenced their marches over very rough ground to take up positions from where at daylight they could observe

* On this occasion these Greek guerrillas were said to have been very helpful, but on others they proved to be most disappointing. They were well armed by the British, and with their local knowledge of the tracks, much (perhaps too much) was expected of them. However, they were often dilatory and inclined to adopt a very insouciant approach to operations.

their objectives prior to assaulting. A mortar barrage on the Castle was the signal for all three parties to attack.

West Force operating against a post at Molo, and South Force against troops holding the Monastery, made good progress and gained their objectives, but the attack on the Castle was most stubbornly resisted. Ammunition was running short, and the long and difficult haul from the beach was exposed to enemy machine-gun fire. The situation seemed to have reached an impasse, so Brigadier Turnbull pinned his hopes on bluff. A German petty officer, captured when five MLs had forced two German EMS craft to surrender, was sent under a flag of truce to inform the garrison commander in the Castle that the island was now completely in British hands and further resistance would be useless. The bluff worked and, after a brief parley, the Germans surrendered at 3 p.m. That night the force, less a party left behind for twenty-four hours to destroy military installations and to distribute food brought in by caiques, withdrew from the island.

This trial run for bigger and better operations had proved highly satisfactory and most rewarding. For the loss of the two Greek officers and six other personnel wounded Raiding Forces had put out of action 185 of the enemy, destroyed two ammunition dumps, a fuel and explosive dump, and nineteen caiques, and captured the two EMS craft, which were still serviceable. But, sadly, some of these early successes could not be permanent, and one has to admire the courage of the Greeks who were so welcoming and helpful, knowing full well that their islands could soon be reoccupied – if only for a short while.

Participation in the Simi raid brought to a close the work of the SBS in Aegean waters. In August they sailed (less Lapraik) from Suez to Italy, and set up their headquarters in Monte Sant' Angelo. But Raiding Forces, with the Greek Sacred Regiment now fully trained and taking the lion's share of the work,* continued to maintain a deadly pressure on the occupied islands. In October Turnbull despatched twenty-four men of the Regiment under Colonel Taigantis to Samos. Some of the Italian garrison surrendered without trouble, but those in the capital, Vathi, stood firm and the Greeks could make no headway. So Taigantis took a leaf out of Turnbull's book and tried bluff by explaining the fate that would befall them when reinforcements (Turnbull with twenty-five men!) arrived. At first the Commandant was unimpressed, but a signal from Turnbull promising immediate extinction from

* The LRDG had left Raiding Forces in February 1944. See Chapter 11.

an air and seaborne attack did the trick, and no fewer than 1,200 prisoners fell to this small band for no Allied losses.

But the affair on Lemnos a few days later was a very different matter. The large German garrison was in the process of evacuating the island, and a strong raiding force supported by a clutch of distinguished senior officers – Turnbull, Lapraik, and Lt-Colonel Roussos, chief-of-staff of the Greek Sacred Regiment – were hoping to sweep them into the sea. Lapraik, with an advance party of seventy-five all ranks, landed at Kastrou two hours before dawn on 16 October, and proceeded to march (the *andartes* had failed to produce the promised mules) 20 miles across devilish country in pouring rain before they came to the outskirts of Mudhros. The main party was delayed at sea by bad weather, and later by the difficulty of getting their jeeps across rivers where the Germans had blown the bridges; but Turnbull managed to get some past these barriers, and joined the advance party soon after noon.

From the high ground overlooking the harbour the raiders could see the Germans jostling each other on the quay for caiques and other craft, and German E-boats that had put to sea being turned back by British MLs lying in wait for them. They could also see a well-armed Siebel ferry loaded with troops, which was just moving away from the wharf. There was no time to wait for the main body to catch up, and so while their Vickers guns poured a devastating fire into the scattering group of caiques the remaining men charged into the mêlée. The fight on the quayside was a sharp affair of close-quarter grapple, and part of one report reads: ' . . . here two Allied colonels, armed only with pistols, shot it out with a party of Germans attempting to escape in caiques.' The Siebel ferry, firing from 2,000 yards out, caused some anxiety – and nearly accounted for Brigadier Turnbull – but when she miscalculated and came within 1,500 yards to take in tow a large fuel lighter lying in the bay, the force's machine guns were able to sweep her decks, killing many Germans.

The whole affair was concluded in not much over twenty-four hours from the time of landing. By then personnel of Raiding Forces had rounded up the last fugitives in the hills behind Mudhros and cleared the island. The force then withdrew, leaving a troop of the Greek Sacred Regiment as garrison, and to clear up the mess in and repair the valuable dock and harbour facilities.

When the Germans were no longer able to mount counter-attacks, and Raiding Forces began the permanent liberation of the islands, Turnbull was faced with a difficult administrative task.

The needs of the islanders, who were pathetically undernourished and distressingly short of such essentials as medical supplies of every kind, soap, disinfectants and clothing, were very great. Although faced with a new type of work his staff, forming what became known as Force 142, coped admirably in the running of two large districts until the Brigadier handed over these civilian relief responsibilities to UNRRA in June 1945.

But before this occurred the last link in the long chain of those spectacular raids was forged on Rhodes. On 2 May 1945 a lightning hit-and-run affair by 180 all ranks, commanded by Colonel Lapraik, was successfully completed in six hours. The work of SBS, LRDG and all others of Raiding Forces had contributed mightily in safeguarding a vital flank. A dangerous threat to the crucial strategic area between the Levant and India had been first held and then lifted by the endeavours of a small number of courageously determined men, unselfishly supported by the professional skill of the Royal Navy and Royal Air Force.

Some of the trials and triumphs that awaited the Special Boat Squadron in the closing months of the war should now be recounted. After they arrived in Monte Sant' Angelo their activities ranged through the Adriatic, Greece and Italy, and they were now once again to work closely with the LRDG, both forces being under Brigadier Davy's Land Forces Adriatic command. And indeed the first SBS operation after their arrival in Italy was a joint one with the LRDG, when Lassen and a newcomer, Lieutenant J.C. Henshaw, joined Captain Skipwith of the LRDG for the raid against the bridge at Karasovici (see Chapter 11).

Like most of those who fought alongside the Yugoslav partisans, men of the SBS found them at times to be extremely trying and untrustworthy allies. Sutherland's patrols, which were infiltrated by air and sea into Yugoslavia and Albania at the end of August, soon found their operations hampered by this unexpected intransigence and occasional treachery. However, Lieutenant Ambrose McGonigal, a recent arrival from England but an experienced raider, whose patrol was landed by sea, achieved a good measure of success. He adopted the wise precaution of keeping his partisan allies in the dark as to his intentions; this had the twin advantages of causing them to accompany the patrol – for they were anxious to learn what was afoot – and of making it less easy for them to practise obstruction or betrayal.

In their first operation, to destroy a railway tunnel and points on the line, the patrol was confronted by a party of fifteen pro-German Chetniks, whom they dealt with swiftly and surely; and during the next fortnight they created a considerable amount of havoc in the area around Bar, just north-west of the Albanian border. The patrol destroyed a number of trucks full of Germans, and ambushed enemy patrols sent to seek them out. In the last engagement of this particular operation a troop train was successfully blown up, and those who survived the explosion were machine-gunned. The patrol had not only accounted for over fifty Germans and a number of *ustachi*, but had thoroughly disorganized the enemy command in that area, and all for the loss of just one man – killed in the fighting round the troop train.

Although S detachment was to continue operations in Yugoslavia and Albania, the main focus of events for the SBS in the autumn of 1944 switched to Greece, where Ian Patterson's L detachment, as a part of a larger force (codenamed Bucketforce), were to be dropped on the airfield at Araxos. The Germans were in the process of evacuating southern Greece at this time, and were anxious to maintain troops in the Peloponnese – even though they were somewhat out on a limb – for as long as possible so as to prevent punishing losses to their troops still in the main part of the country.

Lord Jellicoe, now a lieutenant-colonel, was to command Bucketforce, and besides L detachment SBS, the force comprised an LRDG squadron, one section of No. 40 (RM) Commando, 2908 Squadron RAF Regiment (Squadron-Leader Wynne), two companies (later the whole battalion) of the HLI and a few COPP personnel – in all some 450 all ranks. Men of the Special Boat Squadron, as a part of this force and independently, were in the course of the next few weeks to help clear the enemy not only from the Peloponnese, but from most of southern Greece.

A preliminary drop by Lieutenant Bimrose's patrol just to the south of Araxos reported the airfield as being clear of enemy, and on the morning of 23 September Patterson and fifty-eight men made a successful descent on to the airfield. Patterson immediately sent two patrols forward to investigate the situation in Patras, a town about 20 miles to the east. This was held by 865 Germans and a Greek Security battalion – about 1,500 collaborationists. On 24 September Jellicoe arrived on Araxos airfield in a Dakota laden with stores, and eight Spitfires also landed there, while the RAF Regiment's squadron landed by sea at the nearby port of Katakolon.

Long before British troops returned to Greece, Special Operations Executive's military mission there had been carrying out a whole series of successful sabotage operations against the German lines of communication. Their work had been very considerably hampered by the bitter rivalry between the various Greek politico-military forces. Now the British troops operating in Greece mostly became, at one time or another, unwillingly involved in the complex affairs of that nation. These factions were distinguished by what became familiar acronyms; thus the National Liberation Front (EAM) had a Communist-dominated army (ELAS), while the moderates or royalists were known by the letters EDES. Both these main parties wanted to hold power after the liberation, and were bitterly opposed to each other. EDES felt their best hope lay with the British, which made it necessary to treat ELAS supporters with caution. The result was that commanders often needed to exercise considerable diplomacy to avoid a flare-up, and the troops constantly found themselves confronted with those dismal concomitants of all civil wars – treachery, deceit and bitterness.

And so it was in Patras. It required all of Jellicoe's considerable diplomatic skill, combined with bluff and finally an ultimatum to persuade the Greek Security battalion to surrender, and after they had done so to preserve them from partisan vengeance. The Germans were totally unaware that their 'allies' had defected until two SBS patrols and men of the RAF Regiment entered the town that night. But even the element of surprise was not sufficient for twenty men and two armoured cars to achieve immediate success against 865 determined and well-armed Germans. They inflicted severe casualties on the enemy before withdrawing, and registered a heavy mortar barrage on the town the next day.

When the Germans commenced evacuation of the town Patterson's and Wynne's men with great dash drove outposts from the surrounding heights, and captured a 75 mm gun with which they promptly sank a Siebel ferry packed with troops. Although the superior firepower of the enemy enabled them to hold the port while most embarked, demolition charges left activated under the port installations were discovered in time and defused.

After barely waiting to receive a rapturous acclaim from the inhabitants of Patras, patrols set off for Corinth in the hope of catching the German craft, which were heading down the Gulf. But numerous demolitions along the route so delayed the party that Corinth was not reached until 7 October. Now came the task of trying to cut off the German withdrawal from Athens. L detachment crossed to the north side of the Gulf by improvised ferry, and Bimrose then took three patrols towards Thebes. Moving rapidly on foot he managed to ambush outlying parties of the enemy, and eventually made contact with their main body. Here he found stubborn opposition, for in no theatre of the war were the courage, determination and skill of the German soldier eroded in adversity. Realizing their strength, and having lost men in the ensuing action, he withdrew his patrols.

Meanwhile, Balsillie's patrol had been detached and was entering Piraeus – the first Allied soldiers to do so – and the RAF Regiment had been left in the Peloponnese to accept the surrender of the remaining Security battalions. This left Patterson with insufficient troops to make any real impression upon an enemy who had at last correctly assessed his weakness. He did, however, succeed in mopping up a few men by letting them infiltrate his position and then surrounding them. But it was the arrival on 11 October of a company of the 4th Parachute Battalion, which dropped (not without casualties in the gale-force wind) on Megara airstrip, that decided the Germans to hasten their withdrawal from the Athens–Thebes locality. Lt-Colonel Coxon, commanding the 4th Parachute Battalion, had dropped with the company and he now assumed command. He sent Jellicoe and Milner-Barry* off to Athens to investigate the position there. These two officers landed by caique, and entered the city in triumph on the only transport available – two German bicycles.

After three days of celebration and revelry in liberated Athens, during which SBS men accepted their fair share of adulation and hospitality, Jellicoe decided it was time to move on, and was himself put in charge of a new force called Pompforce – throughout the war impromptu forces would suddenly appear, bearing the name of their commander or one, however inappropriate, that took somebody's fancy. Pompforce consisted of the SBS, the 4th Parachute Battalion, some paratroop engineers, an RAF Regiment contingent and a battery of 75 mm guns – in all about 950 men. Captain Clarke set off by caique through the Euboea Channel with two patrols in the hope of cutting off the German retreat in the area of Lamia, but they were not in time, and it was not until Pompforce had crossed the River Aliakmon that they found the enemy in a defensive position south of Kozani.

It was decided to split the force here and Coxon carried out a left hook with his battalion, bypassing Kozani and making for Florina. Patterson with the remainder put in a frontal attack before his

---

* Walter Milner-Barry joined the SBS at Athlit. He was rather older than the normal run of officers. He had been commissioned into the Trans-Jordan Frontier Force, and had later served in the Western Desert with the Greek army.

artillery had come up, and not surprisingly the troops were soon pinned down. Only a lucky mortar bomb lobbed slap into a machine-gun nest, and the eventual arrival of the guns, enabled them to go forward. By that time the Germans, realizing that the paratroops were in the process of cutting them off from Florina, were pulling out. In a running fight from Kozani to Florina casualties were inflicted on the enemy, but Flying-Officer Dennis of the RAF Regiment was killed while standing in the turret of his armoured car. At Florina, where the Germans did not wait to be attacked, the two elements of Pompforce were reunited, but British troops were forbidden to cross into Yugoslavia. However, Milner-Barry in an uncharted venture into Albania managed to contact David Sutherland in the town of Korce, which is situated some 30 miles south-west of Florina.

In the month of October Anders Lassen was officially confirmed in command of M detachment in the place of Lapraik, who had remained with Raiding Forces. He and his men had not taken part in the Peloponnese and central Greece fighting; but on 22 October he embarked with a party of forty, which included his naval liaison officer, Lieutenant Martin Solomon, and the invaluable Henshaw, to investigate islands in the Sporadhes. The enemy had already departed from most of these, but sadly Lieutenant Robert Bury, one of the best and most experienced officers in the SBS, was killed when his caique approached an island held by royalist partisans, who opened fire thinking it contained their ELAS rivals from whom they were expecting an attack.

Lassen was to be relieved of this uncongenial island-hopping when a schooner arrived bringing him a jeep and orders to proceed to Salonika. This was an assignment much more in keeping with his restless nature and fiery dynamism, and now that he had a jeep there was no holding him. The Germans were in the process of pulling out, unhindered by the ELAS troops in the area who preferred to keep their powder intact for the forthcoming internecine strife. Furthermore, the ELAS Commandant informed Lassen that his men were not to put any pressure on the enemy; he had of course chosen the wrong man for that sort of behaviour and was quickly made to realize it. The jeep was much used and nearly lost when Henshaw (who spoke fluent German) and Solomon, having failed to bluff a German battery commander into surrender, were suddenly faced by two tanks, six self-propelled guns and two lorryloads of troops. Abandoning the priceless jeep they hid all that night, and were lucky enough to find the vehicle the next day completely unharmed.

Shortly afterwards Lassen discovered four fire engines in the western outskirts of Salonika in which he drove his men into the middle of the town, and there they set about a thoroughly disorganized German rearguard. Henshaw notched eleven dead and Lassen eight, while in all the enemy suffered sixty casualties without loss to the patrol – these constantly favourable casualty ratios indicate the professionalism of the patrols.

By rapid movement and constant action Lassen's men had given the enemy an impression of being a powerfully-armed and considerable force. A senior officer later affirmed that without them Salonika would not have been free of Germans as early as 31 October.

During November patrols from L and M detachments gradually assembled in Athens, but early in December Lassen and M detachment were sent to Crete, where the Germans had concentrated their few remaining troops in the north-west corner of the island. They landed at Heraklion on 3 December with a watching and reporting brief. The situation was much like that at Salonika in that ELAS and *andartes* personnel had in half-hearted fashion invested the 13,000 Germans but were putting no pressure on them. Lassen's policy was to attempt to keep the rival Greeks apart, and to encourage either side when they showed willingness to attack the enemy. It was an invidious task which ended in tragedy with nothing much accomplished. In a deliberate attack by ELAS troops Captain Clynes and Private Cornthwaite were killed and Lieutenant Bimrose wounded. This decided Lassen to have nothing more to do with either Greek faction.

The end of 1944 was in some respects a dark period for the Special Boat Squadron. In addition to the losses mentioned above an even more serious one was to occur shortly before Christmas, when the Dakota taking Major Patterson to Monte Sant' Angelo to check up on important administrative matters crashed on a hillside south of Bari, killing all but one crewman. Patterson possessed the pride and force of the warrior, and had become deeply respected and revered by all in SBS. In the month before his death he had been intimately involved in that distressing and dangerous task of trying to prevent Greek killing Greek for a purpose that must have seemed to many of them to have been at the very least obscure.

It could only have been an enormous relief when at the beginning of January some semblance of order returned to Athens, and the SBS detachments were able to leave for Italy. But it was a relief tempered with sadness, for they left without their commander. George Jellicoe was to go to the Staff College; he had commanded the Special Boat Squadron sinces it inception in April 1943 and had brought to the task breadth of view, administrative competence, courage and humanity. The choice of his successor was never in doubt: David Sutherland, a regular soldier in the Black Watch, was the senior in rank and in service with the unit, and his experience of raiding from small boats went back more than three years. A proven leader of the very first rank, he was to command the Squadron with a high degree of competence and courage for the remainder of the war. His place as commander of S detachment went to Captain Clarke.

Besides the difficulties they encountered in working with the Yugoslav partisans, the SBS did not find island-hopping the same jolly business it had been in the Aegean. The approach from their Zara base was often made hazardous by the presence of mines, of a type not met with in the Aegean. Liberally strewn in the past by friend and foe, these mines were laid only a few feet beneath the surface to sink small craft, and quite a few were uncharted. Moreover, the islands were often garrisoned by Aegean veterans who knew exactly what to expect, and prepared their defences accordingly. Surprise – the raiders' most valuable ingredient for success – was therefore impossible, and special forces were seldom properly equipped or supported for set piece frontal attacks.

Two engagements by men under Captain McGonigal (who had taken over Patterson's detachment) illustrate this point. In the first, twenty-one men – which included no fewer than four officers – landed on Lussin unopposed, but a patrol under Lieutenant Jones-Parry was soon challenged, and surprise was immediately lost. The principal target was a strongly-held villa, which now had to be brazenly and openly attacked. In the ensuing room-to-room fighting, although many of the enemy were killed, the SBS lost an officer and a Marine, and eight others of the party were wounded, some severely. It was later discovered that about twenty Germans, hiding in cellars, had survived this operation which had cost the SBS dear.

In the second engagement McGonigal, this time with thirty-eight men, left Zara on 18 March 1945 to destroy the bridge linking the islands of Cherso and Lussin.* Here again the landing was accomplished without trouble, but on the long march to the objective one of the patrols met a party of five Germans, and the

* Presumably the bridge had been repaired since its destruction by No. 9 Commando in the previous August. See Chapter 3.

noise of the ensuing skirmish (in which four of the Germans were killed) alerted the entire garrison of eighty men, so that McGonigal had to launch a frontal attack against an enemy well protected by wire. A fierce fight developed with casualties on both sides, but the odds were too great against a determined defence by troops entrenched behind wire. The Germans, although losing twenty-seven men, held the bridge and the SBS party were forced to withdraw. At the beginning of the battle Henshaw attempted, with total disregard for his own safety, to cut a way through the wire and was killed.

Shortly after this abortive operation the advancing Yugoslav 4th Army reached Senj, which meant that the string of islands north of Zara – delightfully named Pag, Rab and Krk – were isolated and ripe for reclaiming. There was now little to stop Sutherland from turning his attention to Istria for what he hoped would be a more rewarding experience for his men. Most of the peninsula, which contains the towns of Trieste, Fiume and Pola, had been awarded to the Italians after the first war but the inhabitants were mainly Slovene, some of whom had been conscripted into the Italian army and had fought with great courage and distinction. Yugoslav partisans were present in strength, and were determined that they and not the British would liberate this corner of the Adriatic which they coveted so dearly.

Sutherland had already sent his Intelligence Officer, Captain Riddiford, to Istria in early March to contact the partisans, and to liaise with the LRDG who were carrying out their useful shipping watch in the Arsa Channel. Riddiford reported that the partisans seemed very willing to co-operate, and so a patrol of McGonigal's men (which included himself and Lodwick) landed – after some nerve-shattering experiences at sea – just east of Fianona.

But the Istrian story as far as the SBS were concerned is a sorry one. The partisans were willing to co-operate only on their own terms, and these did not include attacking the Germans; moreover they were insistent that the SBS troops would not do so either. Indeed, when the latter set out for their various targets they were apprehended and confined. Great opportunities were missed while tedious negotiations dragged on. Sutherland, who had been in the peninsula since the end of March, was faced with a series of difficult decisions and potentially explosive situations. That he successfully steered a course free from unpleasant incidents was due to his strong personality which radiated unruffled calm.

When the final offensive of the British Eighth and American Fifth Armies was launched at the beginning of April in the north of Italy, Anders Lassen's detachment was to carry out the last of the many operations performed by the Special Boat Squadron. The situation facing Brigadier Tod's No. 2 Commando Brigade at Lake Comacchio, and the manner in which that Brigade attacked the extreme left of the German position, has already been told in Chapter 3. But the part played by the Special Boat Squadron, which was attached to the Brigade, has been left until now.

It will be remembered that the Commandos were to attack the enemy positions on the strip of land at the east side of the lake, and two of them were to do this from assault craft. Lake Comacchio is a shallow sheet of water seldom deeper than 2 ft, except in the middle and along certain channels. It was necessary to locate these channels, for the draught of a Goatley when carrying ten men and their equipment is a full 2 ft. Lassen was given this task, and enjoyed himself immensely sculling around the lake in a Folbot with his devoted housecarl, Guardsman O'Reilly, from whom he was seldom separated. Getting, as was his wont, far too close to the enemy for comfort, he was nearly captured, but he found and plotted channels of sufficient depth.

The attack took place on the night of 8/9 April from the south-east corner of the lake, and Lassen's men led the Commandos along the channels they had reconnoitred. The approach across the water, although it came close to disastrous delay by initial mishaps in the mud, was entirely successful; and the separate landings of the two Commandos (Nos. 2 and 9) took the enemy unawares. Lassen then, in accordance with orders, landed a patrol some 2 miles farther north to create a diversion.

Advancing up the road the patrol, which Lassen himself commanded, soon ran into serious trouble. It was confronted by a series of pillboxes manned by Germans who, unlike their comrades to the south, were not taken by surprise. In the first burst of fire Trooper Crouch was killed and O'Reilly severely wounded; the survivors, understandably, flattened themselves as best they could. That is all but Lassen, who advanced on the pillbox, silenced the occupants with a grenade and then proceeded along the line, followed by others of the patrol who, inspired by his fine example, had now joined him. He personally silenced three more of these strongpoints, miraculously surviving although the air by this time was thick with lead. The enemy in the fifth pillbox deemed it wiser to hang out a white cloth in token of surrender, but as Lassen approached to accept it he was shot at close quarters. The Germans did not survive their treachery by many seconds, but Anders Lassen died from his wounds as his men were taking him back. For these acts of great gallantry and superb leadership he was posthumously awarded the Victoria Cross.

The end of the war in Europe meant, for the time being at least, the end of the Special Boat Squadron, for although there was some regrouping and training for operations in the Far East the Japanese surrendered before the SBS could be sent. In the pursuit of their professional performance they had carried out a wide variety of tasks with courage and skill, and an adaptability that showed genius. It is good to know that the spirit of the men who fought and died in the Special Boat Section and the Special Boat Squadron lives on in the force reconstituted in 1949 under the aegis of the Royal Marines.

15

Royal Marines' Special Forces: Force Viper and the Royal Marine Boom Patrol Detachment

During the Second World War men of the Royal Marines served with great valour and distinction in a number of special forces. Their nine Commandos – some of whose actions have been touched upon in earlier chapters – were the forerunners of those they now have in the permanent order of battle. Formed originally from battalions of the Royal Marine Division, the first (No.40) was raised on 14 February 1942, and the last (No.48) on 2 March 1944. Their first action was at Dieppe, where No. 40 received heavy casualties. Royal Marine Commandos fought in Europe, the Mediterranean, the Adriatic and the Far East, and played a prominent part in every major landing except North Africa, being particularly well represented in the Normandy and Arakan fighting. Five of their senior officers were later to rise to the rank of general.

Their deeds have been recorded in many books, but less is known of two other smaller units: Force Viper and the Royal Marine Boom Patrol Detachment (RMBPD). Another small RM special force – Detachment 385 – was a part of the Small Operations Group in the Far East (see Chapter 7).

Mobile Naval Base Defence Organization was manned by men from the Royal Marines, whose job it was to provide the Fleet with a base in any part of the world, and then to defend it. There were two such formations raised at the beginning of the war, and in February 1942 a call went out for volunteers from MNBDO 1, then in Ceylon, for an undisclosed but hazardous task. From the many who responded three officers, a medical officer and 102 Marines were selected by Major Duncan Johnston, who was to command them.

Opening his sealed orders on leaving Colombo, Johnston learned that their destination was Rangoon. By this time the Japanese were beginning their triumphant thrust in Burma which was to take them – in the face of a gallant but pathetically undermanned and equipped opposition – from Tenasserim to the Indian border in the space of little over four months. The original idea was that Force Viper, as this small party of Marines came to be called, should patrol the Gulf of Martaban in boats to prevent Japanese soldiers, transported by rafts, from infiltrating behind the British, Indian and Burmese troops then fighting in Moulmein. But by the time Force Viper first saw the Shwe Dagon towering in sheets of gold above the crumbling city of Rangoon, Moulmein had been lost, and Major-General Smyth's 17th Indian Division had withdrawn to the Sittang river, where shortly they were to suffer a major disaster. There was no role for the Marines, nor indeed were there any boats for them.

Johnston had formed his force into three platoons under his three subordinate officers, Captain Herbert Alexander and Lieutenants Douglas Fayle and Peter Cave. Colour Sergeant Harry Wonfor, who was about the only pre-war member of the force, acted as Sergeant-Major. There was a formidable armament available of Bren and tommy guns, a Vickers 'K' aircraft gun, 2 in. mortars, rifles and revolvers, but the men had had no training in power boats, which all too soon they would have to man and manoeuvre. Anyone who has taken part in a long withdrawal over difficult country, in the face of strong opposition constantly infiltrating and cutting one off, will have experienced the confusion caused by unavoidable order and counter-order. Force Viper were soon to feel the full effects of this when they were ordered to carry out river patrol work, despite the fact that they lacked both the training and the boats.

But even in the darkest hour something usually turns up for men who refuse to despair, and the first piece of good fortune for the Marines was the arrival of Lieutenant Guthrie Penman, a naval liaison officer now without a job, and a man of considerable ingenuity who had worked in Burma before joining the Burma RNVR. He knew where to lay his hands on four government touring launches complete with Chittagong crews. Johnston and his men were now in business, and could commence training ready for their first assignment, which was the defence of the Burma Oil Company's refineries at Syriam on the east bank of the Irrawaddy.

A full account of the adventures of the men of Force Viper up the Irrawaddy as they guarded, from their launches, motor boats and stern-wheelers, the right flank of General Alexander's hard-pressed soldiers, and later assisted in ferrying those same men safely across both the Irrawaddy and the Chindwin, can be found in Cecil Hampshire's *On Hazardous Service*. Here it is only possible to give a brief description of a few of their tribulations and triumphs.

General Alexander, who had arrived in Rangoon only on 5 March, agreed on its evacuation two days later and Force Viper's small fleet of seven – each boat proudly wearing its White Ensign – started its long haul upriver. Eleven million pounds' worth of oil and equipment were destroyed at Syriam, and the army – with its riverain flank guard – headed for Prome. The flotilla reached the town on 13 March and were given the task of preventing the Japanese from coming upriver and crossing behind the 17th Division's lines. Now, and indeed throughout their journey, vessel changes were made, for as the engines of ageing craft gave out, fresh waterboats or Irrawaddy steamers had to be commandeered, and these were in some cases fitted with armour hammered out in the flotilla's repair ship.

Force Viper's first engagement was fought at Henzada on 17 March. They had been joined by a small party known as 2 Burma Commando, under command of a Sapper major, Mike Calvert (of whom more later), which had found its way from Maymyo when the Bush Warfare School there had been closed. The Commando and a party of Marines attempted a demolition raid on Henzada and met with fierce resistance. The flotilla's launches were repeatedly hit, but returned a heavy and accurate fire, while the land party had been forced to fight their way back to the river. Two men of the Commandos and one Marine were killed, and two Marines in ML *Rita* were wounded. It was later learned that the enemy had suffered heavy casualties.

Enemy interference was not the only hazard to be encountered when sailing up the Irrawaddy. That great waterway has many shallows and sandbanks which can only be avoided by following deep-water channels (themselves subject to the rise and fall of the river), from which marking buoys had frequently been removed by hostile Burmese or dacoits. When the boats went aground, as happened occasionally, troops and stores had to be ferried above the shallows and hours of hard work were required to get the boats afloat again. When occasion permitted all river craft had to be destroyed before they could fall into the hands of the enemy, and again when possible the Marines would land to take on board their craft some of the hard-pressed refugees fleeing before the oncoming Japanese.

At Padaung the Marines and the Commandos (who remained with them for about a fortnight) ran into a trap. They were betrayed by supposedly friendly villagers and found themselves surrounded by Japanese troops. Before regaining the launches they were engaged in a very hot battle, during which parties became separated, and most of Johnston's No. 1 Platoon and half the Commando never regained the boats. It was learned later that this was one of the occasions when the Japanese used their prisoners for live bayonet practice.*

By early April, when Force Viper had the task of preventing Japanese craft from disgorging troops to cut off parts of the newly formed 'Burdiv' (Burma Division), the flotilla was beginning to have mechanical problems. Many of the vessels had been over-worked (as indeed had the troops), diesel oil was becoming difficult to obtain, and the enemy had by now complete air superiority, which meant that the flotilla was being constantly bombed. One of the most serious disasters occurred on 24 April, and it was not caused by enemy action. The *Kohinoor* was anchored in midriver as guardship, when with no warning a gale-force gusting wind blew up, darkening the river and both banks with clouds of dust. The ship capsized, drowning seven of the eight Marines on board.

By the last days of April the Japanese three-pronged advance (up the left bank of the Irrawaddy, up the river itself and through the Shan States to Lashio) was sweeping all before it; a wedge had been driven between Alexander's army and the Chinese armies. The latter were to fall back on China, while Alexander's men had to cross the Irrawaddy and the Chindwin, and then embark on a very long march through dense jungle country, with the many chaungs swollen by flood water and their bridges swept away in the devastating monsoon rains.

Force Viper performed its most signal service to the British, Gurkha, Indian and Burmese soldiers in ferrying so many of them across these great rivers in the face of difficulties that would have defeated many less resourceful men. The rivers were at their lowest just before the monsoon, and only small motor boats could enter the Chindwin at its confluence with the Irrawaddy. This meant that part of the flotilla had to be destroyed and new vessels conjured up from somewhere. Landing stages had to be con-

---

* A friend of the author, serving with him in Burma, suffered a similar fate.

structed – for the army's stores were carried in bullock carts – brushwood roads had to be laid, native boats had to be lashed together for conveyance of the mechanized transport, and the river had to be denied the enemy who were continually pressing and harassing on land, up the Chindwin and in the air.

The 17th Division crossed the Ava Bridge below Mandalay and then destroyed it, but 'Burdiv' had to be ferried across in the Myingyan area. Much of the army was then on a sort of peninsula formed between the two rivers, some 80 miles wide in the Shwebo area. On both banks the troops were making for Monywa, while Force Viper did their best, with their motor boats and one stern-wheeler, to forbid the Chindwin to the enemy. But the task proved impossible and the Japanese captured Monywa on 30 April, imperilling Alexander's plan of withdrawal.

The whole army, less those few troops marching up the west bank, were now to cross the Chindwin at Kalewa – about 100 miles north of Monywa – and at a place called Shwegyin, 6 miles downstream. The operation was controlled by Colonel Biddulph, the army's Director of Inland Waterways, who relied to a very great extent on Force Viper and their few remaining vessels.

The river crossings at Kalewa and Shwegyin, which had to be carried out by night, were chaotic. No proper landing stages had been constructed, no order of priorities prepared, and no shore parties organized to work moorings. A mass of vehicles had been abandoned anywhere, and there were thousands of refugees clamouring to find places on the boats. A boom of sorts had been constructed below the crossing points, and Major Johnston took his three recently-acquired anti-tank guns across to the west bank and set them up under a small party of Marines, while the rest of the force were working the ferry boats as best they could. Somehow by 9 May the bulk of the army had crossed the river, and two days later the armoured brigade (having destroyed their tanks) was also across. It had been a close-run thing, for the Japanese were daily drawing nearer in strength; but it had been accomplished with very little loss.

Force Viper's duties did not end with the river crossings, for on 11 May orders were received to embark the 48th Gurkha Brigade and take them about 100 miles upriver to Sittaung, and there the Force's boats would be destroyed and the Marines would act as a rearguard to the Gurkha Brigade on the march into India. The journey was comparatively uneventful, and Sittaung was reached on 14 May. Here Johnston and three Marines left the remainder to carry out a final mission, the conveyance of money and secret orders to the District Commissioner at Homalin, a further 90 miles up the Chindwin.

The march into India was a nightmare for everyone who took part in it. The monsoon had broken, the chaungs had become raging torrents, the steep and narrow jungle tracks were deep in mud and slime, and all the time cholera – no respecter of class, colour or constitution – was claiming hundreds of victims. The Marines, whose feet had not been hardened by marching but rather softened by constant water work, stumbled on with the rest, carrying out their rearguard duties until, eventually by road and rail, they reached Calcutta on 25 May. On the next day they were joined by their commanding officer whose experiences had been even more harrowing and exhausting.

On 14 June a sergeant and seven Marines, who had been missing and presumed dead or captured since Monywa, arrived in Calcutta with an incredible story of hardship and danger over-come by guts and ingenuity. It concludes the strange, exception-ally useful and courageous saga of this small party of Royal Marines of whom 58 out of the original 107 lived to tell the tale. Sadly their commanding officer, Major Johnston, was later shot in error by one of his own men while engaged in one of those daring raids carried out on the Arakan coast by men of Detachment 385.

Meanwhile, in England – a month before the men of Force Viper set out on their hazardous journey through Burma – another Royal Marine, Major H.G. Hasler, had joined a small, select team which for some time had been working, with considerable expertise, judgement and enthusiasm, on designs for assault landing craft and other types of small boat. The team was led by Captain T.A. Hussey, RN, at the Combined Operations De-velopment Centre (CODC). Hasler had been intensely interested in handling small boats in and out of water ever since he was a boy; in 1940 his Royal Marine Landing Craft Company had been engaged in putting troops ashore in Norway, and a year later he had submitted a paper to Combined Operations Headquarters outlining methods of attacking enemy ships by the use of canoes and underwater swimmers.

At the time this paper was considered too avant-garde, and anyway there was a grave equipment problem; but when the Italians struck a powerful blow in Alexandria harbour with their 'human torpedoes' it was decided to give serious consideration to this new type of warfare. Therefore Hasler's particular task in CODC became the study of ways and means by which enemy shipping could be attacked by stealth while in harbour. The obvious prototype on which developments could be based was a captured Italian explosive motor boat.

The Italians had been well in advance of other countries in their experiments with all types of underwater guerrilla fighting, and their original explosive boat was designed by d'Annunzio in World War I. Hasler inspected one of the captured contraptions, and on it he based the Boom Patrol Boat (BPB), which in fact was never used operationally, but it played a significant part in the formation and training of the Royal Marine Boom Patrol Detachment (RMBPD).

Work commenced on the BPB in April 1942, and throughout that year its development proceeded sometimes smoothly, sometimes anxiously and sometimes in moments near to despair. The Italian prototype had a 500 lb warhead. The motor boat was carried to the target area by surface craft and lowered over the side by derrick. As it neared the target the pilot pulled a lever which enabled him to fall, together with a folding raft, clear of the stern. When the charge exploded the pilot, by that time on his raft, was safe from underwater concussion; he then surrendered. Hasler was determined that in the British counterpart the pilot should be provided with means of escape; he was also dissatisfied with the Italian method of approach, and directed his attention towards producing a craft that could be parachuted, complete with pilot, reasonably close to the target.

The hull and escape gear of the new boat were to be designed by Messrs Vosper (Commander Du Cane, their Managing Director, was a member of the Combined Operations scientific staff), and the explosives and firing gear by a civilian firm under supervision from HMS *Vernon*. Originally ten boats were ordered, and these were to be powered by Lagonda engines, although later delivery was taken of American engines. One of the earliest problems was the difficulty of getting the boat over surface obstacles such as a boom, and Hasler, who had never allowed the BPB to replace completely his work on canoes and underwater swimming techniques, gave consideration to a canoe suitable for this purpose and for rescuing the pilot.

From this there came the very useful Cockle Mk II, designed jointly by Mr Fred Goatley and Hasler. It was a 16-ft collapsible two-man canoe, which could carry 150 lb of equipment through rough water. The canoe was of narrow design and travelled low in the water, which made it an ideal conveyance for a stealthy approach to the target. Its normal propulsion was by each man using a double-bladed paddle which could be converted into a single-bladed one when quietness and concealment were necessary.

At about the same time as Major Hasler was working with BPB another strange craft, an SOE production, known colloquially as the 'Sleeping Beauty', but officially as the Motor Submersible Canoe (MSC), was being constructed. Briefly, it was a 12-ft, metal-constructed, electrically-driven, one-man canoe, capable of submerging to an operational depth of 40 ft. The driver, who wore a light diving suit and oxygen breathing apparatus, could get in or out of the cockpit when submerged. The range of the craft under water was 16 miles, but more than double that could be covered on the surface, and it was very seaworthy. Once launched from its intermediate carrier (a specially designed Mobile Flotation Unit) it could make for the enemy harbour on the surface, then dive if necessary for the final approach to the target to place limpets.

Not long after Major Hasler had started work on designing the BPB he saw the need for a small unit to operate it when it was ready, and to work the canoe which it seemed might be necessary to accompany the boat on operations. Lt-Colonel Langley, then commandant of the CODC, agreed with the proposition Hasler put forward, and suggested that a small team of Royal Marines should be recruited. After the usual objections and difficulties which inevitably accompany any innovative thinking had been duly aired, Lord Louis Mountbatten, then Chief of Combined Operations, officially approved the idea. He suggested, however, that the title of the new unit should be changed from Royal Marine Harbour Patrol Detachment to Royal Marine Boom Patrol Detachment.* The RMBPD was officially born on 6 July 1942, for the purpose of assisting in the destruction of enemy shipping resources.

The establishment decided upon was to be a major in command, a captain as second-in-command and two lieutenants to command the two sections, each of which was to consist of an officer and twelve men. The Royal Navy was to take care of the Maintenance Section with twelve men under a sub-lieutenant (Engineers). It was the original intention that No. 1 Section should become the MSC experts (for it had been decided to allocate some of these boats to the RMBPD), and No. 2 Section was destined for BPBs.

* The cover name Boom Patrol was chosen because they trained at the northern end of the boom guarding the eastern end of the Solent, and pretended to be a defensive patrol against enemy clandestine raiders.

Lord Louis specially asked that Hasler should be appointed to command, and Hasler at once selected Captain J.D. Stewart, whom he knew from personal experience to be in every way fitted for the tough and hazardous work ahead. Volunteers were called for from the Royal Marines, and they were told that the qualities required included eagerness to engage the enemy, an indifference to personal safety, a high standard of physique, sound intelligence, freedom from close family ties, and the ability to swim. Many of the best men had already answered the call of the Royal Marine Commandos, but in spite of this Hasler was able to obtain sufficient who he felt could achieve the necessary high standards. And for the command of the two sections he was given two first class young officers in Lieutenants J.W. Mackinnon and W.H.A. Pritchard-Gordon.

The RMBPD was based initially at Southsea, the men being billeted out and granted the special Commando rate of subsistence. Very soon they became a devoted, dedicated, well-disciplined and athletic band who took particular pride in their parent unit (whose insignia they continued to wear), their turnout on and off parade, and their standard of excellence in training. With the BPB and MSC still in the embryo stage this consisted principally of becoming thoroughly familiar with a variety of small craft – canoes (the Cockle Mk I, until the Mk II was ready for service), assault craft and surfboats – perfecting underwater swimming; learning about explosives, particularly the limpet; and coastal navigation. Later Hasler arranged for the Detachment to do a parachute course, for he envisaged situations where they might have to be dropped close to targets. Attention was also paid to physical training and close-quarters combat.

The RMBPD, like Force Viper, was a perfect example of raising a special force to perform a particular task (and that is the sole *raison d'être* for any special force), but as was so often the case in the last war the time between forming the force and requiring it to be ready for action was lamentably short, and in consequence the men often had to go into battle without being fully trained in specialist skills. And so it was with the RMBPD in the difficult arts of navigation and seamanship. Hasler, an expert in both, did what he could in the time available, but it was impossible to achieve in a matter of months what became instinctive in the course of years. Nevertheless, a high standard in all disciplines was reached in a remarkably short time.

The Cockle Mk II had completed its trials successfully before the first operation, which was scheduled for early December 1942.

The canoe had been designed for loading into a submarine down the forward torpedo hatch, but initially there was a problem as to how to launch it. Hasler felt it essential to be able to launch the canoes from the submarine in rough water, which meant launching them with the crew and stores in place and the cockpit covers done up. And so he designed a special sling that would make it possible to launch the canoe fully loaded, and a clever contraption was thought out as a surrogate hoisting gear, for the submarine had no davits or derricks.

At the time of the first operation, to be codenamed Frankton, no proper underwater swimming equipment was available. Hasler had been working on this, for he felt sure that a close approach to the target by canoe would soon become too dangerous, and that the limpets would have to be placed by a man swimming the last 100 yards. Stewart, Hasler's second-in-command, took over this work while the latter was absent on Frankton, and in due course the special equipment, which was to become such an important factor in the last years of the war, came into use.

Meanwhile, the limpets would have to be positioned by the use of a 6 ft steel placing rod, which had a hook to which the magnetic mine was attached. As the canoe came alongside the enemy ship, one of the crew would make it fast by attaching a magnetic holdfast device held level with his shoulder, while the other man carefully lowered the limpet (which had, of course, been fused before the final approach) to a depth of 6 ft and clamped to the hull. After this he unhooked the rod, and the canoe drifted, or was quietly paddled, to take station for the next emplacement. All this sounds relatively simple, but apart from the obvious requirement of great courage it called for a high degree of skill, stealth and cunning, all of which No. 1 Section spent many hours in trying to acquire before the first operation.

Operation Frankton, in which a party of twelve men in six Cockle Mk IIs were to paddle up the Gironde estuary and place limpet mines on a number of German blockade runners in Bordeaux harbour, has been well told in a book,* and made the subject of a full-length film. Nevertheless, as it was the most famous exploit carried out by the RMBPD, and arguably the most famous of its kind during the whole war, it must be included, at least in outline, in any account of that force.

There were known to be a number of German blockade-running vessels in the Bassens–Bordeaux area, which were used to

* C.E. Lucas Phillips, *Cockleshell Heroes.*

convey important war materials to and from the Japanese. A Commando-type assault would require a large number of men, would be very costly and, lacking surprise, would probably fail. Aerial bombardment was ruled out on account of the number of French civilian casualties it was sure to inflict, and so the job of paddling stealthily up the Gironde seemed tailor-made for the recently-formed RMBPD. Originally Hasler, who with difficulty had managed to persuade Mountbatten to allow him to lead the raid, planned to take only three two-man canoes, but later Mountbatten decided that six canoes must go in order to have a sufficient reserve against accidents. As it turned out this was a very wise decision.

When Frankton was first mooted the RMBPD had been formed for only two and a half months, and the training programme although tough and thorough was incomplete. However, as the sailing date (which was dependent on many factors, in particular the state of the moon and tide) would not be before the end of November there were almost two months for Hasler to concentrate the training of No. 1 Section towards the special needs of the operation, in so far as secrecy allowed. Apart from acquiring a familiarity with the limpets, these included the loading, stowing and launching of the Cockle Mk IIs, rough-water drill and many lessons in navigation.

The outline plan was pleasantly simple, if extremely hazardous. It was essential that the moon should be in its empty quarter, and this restricted the operation to the nights between 3/4 and 12/13 December. No. 1 Section would be conveyed by submarine to the disembarkation point off the French coast, where the canoes would be launched. They would then be paddled up the Gironde estuary for the full period of the flood tide, travelling by night and lying up by day. It was estimated that an advance base, some 10 miles from the target area, would be reached on the third night, and that the attack should go in on the following night. Hasler, when he broke secrecy once the men were at sea, elaborated this plan and decided that in order to minimize detection with a fleet of six canoes, and to facilitate the selection of lying-up places, they should proceed up the estuary in two divisions.

There was nothing new in hit-and-run raids from submarines, but what was new in Operation Frankton was the deep penetration that the canoeists were to make – some 75 miles upriver – and the fact that it was considered impossible to arrange any means of picking the men up after they had completed the task. Their orders were to make their way back overland via Spain, and certainly Lord Louis Mountbatten, and the few officers in the secret, were under no illusions as to the men's chances of survival, although it was greatly hoped that some might get through while others would eventually return via a prisoner-of-war camp. The party, travelling two men to a canoe, consisted of two officers (Hasler and Mackinnon), Sergeant Wallace, Corporals Laver and Sheard, and Marines Sparks, Conway, Mills, Ellery, Ewart, Fisher and Moffat.

The Section left the Clyde in HM Submarine *Tuna* on 30 November, and during the week's voyage spent many hours in launching rehearsals and familiarizing themselves with every detail of the plan. After a 24-hour postponement due to the difficulty in obtaining a good astro-fix in misty conditions, and the presence of inconveniently laid mines, they disembarked about 8 p.m. on 7 December. All too soon the party was in trouble.

Ellery's and Fisher's canoe fouled the torpedo hatch of the submarine and could not be launched, but the remaining five, all heavily loaded, set forth on the flood tide for the long paddle to the mouth of the estuary, a good many miles to the north. Everything went smoothly until the canoes were confronted with the first of three tide-races – terrifying phenomena in the blackness of the night, with swirling, angry waters pounding over rock or sandbank. These treacherous obstacles came as an unpleasant surprise, not having been shown on the charts. The men knew their rough-water drill, and that they had a fair chance if the cockpit covers were tightly secured and they kept the Mk II's head into the waves. But Sergeant Wallace's and Marine Ewart's craft disappeared while attempting to negotiate the first tide-race, and Corporal Sheard's and Marine Moffat's capsized in the second. The two men were towed to near the bank, and had to be left to escape as best they could. Of the remaining three canoes, another (Lieutenant Mackinnon and Marine Conway) went astray while the party was negotiating a dangerous defile between the Le Verdon jetty and three enemy warships anchored in line ahead just off the jetty.

After the turmoil and tragedy of the dark hours just two canoes were left to be beached at the first selected lying-up place (Pointe aux Oiseaux on the left bank of the Gironde), although it was possible that Mackinnon and Conway might still be afloat and operating independently. Alternatively, had they been captured or their canoe found the game might be up. In fact only Wallace and Ewart were captured early on, and their courage under interrogation ensured that secrecy held.

239

As the four men made their way stealthily up the river, lying up by day and paddling for the six hours or so of the flood tide by night, it is not difficult to imagine the labyrinthine miseries of nervous fatigue, allied to anxiety over the fate of their missing comrades, that must have afflicted them. Each day was one of tension lest their hideout be discovered by a German patrol, or betrayed by one of the civilians with whom it was impossible to avoid contact. But both now and later during the escape the majority of French men and women, once they had satisfied themselves as to the bona fides of the canoeists, were extremely helpful.

Originally it had been planned to place the mines on the selected targets on the night of 10/11 December, but the time lost on the traumatic first night meant that the two canoes were not far enough upriver to do this and still have a good getaway chance. It was therefore decided to have an intermediate lying-up place within close range of the harbour. They were now on the river Garonne, and a suitable place of concealment was found for the canoes inside a clump of reeds within sight of two enemy ships. Here the four men rested in their canoes during 11 December.

Hasler decided that he and Sparks would make for the main docks at Bordeaux that night, while Corporal Laver and Mills would reconnoitre the east docks, and if no suitable target was to be found they were to return to Bassens South and attack the two ships they had sighted from their hideout. Both parties would withdraw on the ebb tide and make their escape separately from the eastern bank, having first scuttled their canoes.

The weather was against them, for it was a calm, clear night and the young moon did not set until 9.30 p.m., which meant a half-hour delay that was undesirable from the time point of view. But as they launched their canoes from the muddy bottom of their hideout, gone were the hours of tension, when doubts and fears come unbidden to the brain, and in their place the exhilaration of the hunter as he views his quarry.

The placing of the limpets in the main harbour and in Bassens South was accomplished with skill and valour under the very noses – indeed at one time under the torch – of enemy sentries, but their excellent camouflage, their watercraft and their luck triumphed over the many hazards. Hasler and Sparks placed three limpets on a cargo ship of about 7,000 tons, two on the engine room of a *Sperrbrecher* (a small naval vessel), two on the stern of another cargo ship also of about 7,000 tons, and one on the stern of a small tanker. Laver and Mills had found the east docks empty, but they put five limpets on one of the two ships in Bassens South and two on the other. The limpets had a nine-hour setting on the time delays, but the timing mechanism was faulty and the mines exploded at intervals, thereby causing even greater consternation and mystification to the Germans, who were appalled by the damage done to their valuable ships.

On the withdrawal the two canoes chanced to join up, but Hasler insisted on their separating before they landed. Hasler and Sparks made land just to the north of Blaye, and there they scuttled the canoe in which they had paddled a total of 91 miles. Their eventual escape through France into Spain, and from there back to England, with its moments of danger, tension, humour, kindness and, above all, the will to endure and overcome the exhaustion of body, mind and nerve makes a proud and thrilling story of its own. Laver and Mills covered some 20 miles before being picked up, still in uniform, by the French police and handed over to the Germans.

Not until after the war did their fate, and that of the four other canoeists who had been captured, become known. Mackinnon and Conway had got most of the way up the river independently before being wrecked on an underwater obstruction. Eventually all six men, although known to be soldiers and prisoners of war, were shot; their burial certificates simply stated 'Found drowned in Bordeaux Harbour'. Every civilized person will mark such an action with repugnance and an abiding stigma.

Hasler and Sparks got back to England in April 1943, but of course No. 1 Section no longer existed, and had been replaced by a fresh intake of volunteers under Lieutenant Hurst. Work on the BPB had been in progress for exactly a year and still had some way to go, and so it was fortunate to have Hasler back to resume interest and advice, especially as the Germans had salvaged three of the canoes from the Gironde, and therefore had full knowledge of this method of attack. A fresh approach was required, and although the Navy were busy developing the midget X–craft submarine and the 'chariot',* much was expected from the 16 ft hydroplane BPB with its 500 lb charge. However, 1943 was an anxious year for the designers.

It had been decided early on that the craft should be dropped near the target area, and the necessary alterations had been made to a Lancaster bomber. In November 1942 trial drops were made

---

*A torpedo-shaped underwater craft manned by two 'charioteers' who clamped the explosive part of the 'chariot' to the enemy ship, escaping on the other.

with 4,000 lb bombs – equivalent to the full weight of the BPB – and on 5 April 1943 the actual boat made its first descent. This was not a success, for first one parachute collapsed and then another, and finally the boat capsized on landing and could not be salvaged. Later that month Vospers reported finding difficulties with a new design, but by June developments were proceeding satisfactorily.

At the turn of the year four successful trial drops were made and on 10 June Lieutenant David Cox, who by then led the BPB team, very gallantly took his place in the boat and was despatched from a bomber off Harwich. After one or two extremely anxious moments, when the BPB was snatched out of a vertical descent by opening parachutes, it floated down on an even keel and Cox landed safely without too much splash. Eventually sixteen boats were produced, but none was used operationally, although there were several occasions – particularly for projected operations in Norwegian waters – when the Section, together with six Lancaster bombers, was stood to for immediate action only to be stood down for one reason or another. What might be termed 'on-off operations' cannot always be avoided, but, as already mentioned, they can have a most demoralizing effect on troops keyed up for action after months of hard training.

In the autumn of 1944 the MSC Section of the RMBPD was involved, like the BPB Section, in the plan to attack enemy shipping lurking in the Norwegian fjords, but continual bad weather caused the operations to be cancelled. Shortly afterwards the Germans became aware of the MSC's potential when they captured the boats being used operationally in Norway by two Norwegian officers attached to SOE.

That summer the RMBPD had undergone two important changes. In May Hasler, now a Lieutenant-Colonel, was posted to the Far East to set up SOG (see Chapter 7), his place in command being taken by Major Stewart, and in June of that year approval was given for control of RMBPD to be transferred to the Admiralty. Hitherto the Detachment had come under the Chief of Combined Operations, but General Laycock, then CCO, felt that with its work of demolition against seaborne targets and harbour installations it was more appropriate for the Admiralty to assume full control. After much argument and heart-searching this was agreed, although the Commandant General Royal Marines retained responsibility for the welfare and discipline of the unit.

At this time the paper strength of the Unit was ten officers and sixty-four other ranks, of whom five officers and thirty other ranks were operational, divided into five sections of an officer and six other ranks; but in actual fact there were never more than two operational sections. In February 1944 No. 2 Section under Captain Pritchard-Gordon, with Lieutenant J.F. Richards as his second-in-command and sixteen other ranks (one of whom was Marine Sparks), left for the Middle East, taking with them some of the new Cockle Mk II**s. These were stronger versions of the Mk II, collapsible so that three stowed in a submarine took up scarcely more space than a single assembled Folbot. Pritchard-Gordon's men in the Middle East, known for security purposes by the curious name of Earthworm Detachment, were based near Raiding Forces' hutted camp at Athlit in Palestine. Here they carried out intensive training with their new Mk II**s.

The monotony of training was relieved by a call to Alexandria to assist in quelling a mutiny that had broken out aboard the Greek warships in the harbour, but fortunately the trouble was resolved without the Section becoming too involved. Soon after this they were moved from their camp in Palestine for operations in the Aegean. Castelorizzo, almost the only island in the Dodecanese group from which the Germans had not ejected the Allies when they gained virtual control of the Aegean in November 1943 (see Chapter 7), was used as a transhipment post to operational areas. It lay conveniently close to the Turkish coast, where suitable hideouts for craft were available.*

Pritchard-Gordon had divided his men into two sections, or groups, and his one was shortly flown to Malta to take part in Operation Portcullis, which was to be an attack on German ammunition ships in the Cretan harbour of Suda Bay. The Marines left Malta, tightly packed with their canoes and equipment in HM Submarine *Unruly*, on 15 May. But sadly when they arrived off Crete no suitable targets presented themselves; they remained at sea for seventeen days before it was decided that the operation must be called off.

However, in the moonless period of mid-June Richards's group was to carry out a most successful operation. Orders were received at the beginning of the month from Flag Officer Levant and Eastern Mediterranean (FOLEM) to sink enemy ships (destroyers, escort vessels and merchant ships in that order of priority) which were known to stage at Portolago, a harbour on Leros. Richards, together with Sergeant King, Corporal Horner, three Marines and a liaison officer from Raiding Forces, with whom

---

* In Aegean waters Turkish neutrality was apt to be disregarded by both sides at this time.

they now worked, were to proceed to a hideout up the Turkish coast until aerial reconnaissance reported the arrival of the convoy at Portolago.

On 16 June air reconnaissance reported the presence, and photographed the exact location, of three destroyers, three escort craft and two merchantmen at anchor in Portolago Bay, and FOLEM signalled Richards to attack. Having studied the relative positions of the ships, Richards allotted targets to each of his three canoe parties. On completion of their tasks the canoes were to make for the small island of Kalimnos, south-west of Leros, which could provide adequate daylight concealment before they made for the pick-up point the following night.

During the waiting period off the Turkish coast the Marines had carefully checked and prepared their equipment. Items included limpets, radios, compasses, Stens, grenades, fighting knives, camouflage nets for canoes, spare paddles, food packs and bird calls – these latter being the RMBPD's favourite method of keeping contact in the silence of the night. For this operation the limpets were armed with four-and-a-half-hour delay charges. All this gear and the Cockles were somehow stacked in ML 360, which was to take the six men to the point of disembarkation about 1½ miles from the bay, and which they reached just before midnight.

Richards had allocated for himself a destroyer and three escort ships. He and his mate, Marine Stevens, crossed the defensive boom successfully, but as they were paddling quietly into the harbour they were challenged by a sentry from the shore. The canoeists froze, and the challenge was repeated accompanied by a flashing torch, but eventually, undetected, they paddled on and before 2.30 a.m. – by when it was high time to get clear of the harbour – they had placed limpets on the three escort ships and the destroyer which were their particular targets.

Corporal Horner and Marine Fisher were not so successful, for when they came alongside to place their limpets on one of the big merchantmen they were spotted by men on board, and were extremely fortunate in being able to make their escape to the open sea. But Sergeant King and Marine Ruff probably had the most nerve-racking time of all, for they had scarcely left the ML when they discovered their Cockle was leaking, which meant that the number two was almost continually baling. However, they crossed the boom, and in spite of being challenged on two separate occasions they slid through to their first target, a destroyer, to which they affixed no fewer than six limpets, before deciding that the state of their craft and the time did not permit of any further venture. They cleared the harbour all right, but it was daylight before they reached Kalimnos, where they ran the gauntlet of a fishing fleet and were later befriended by a Greek fisherman before setting out that night for the rendezvous.

The operation had been a tremendous achievement: the two destroyers were severely damaged and the three escort vessels sunk. A great reception from men of Raiding Forces awaited the section's return – via Castelorizzo – to Athlit, for the destruction of the enemy warships had cleared the way for the large-scale raid on Simi led by Brigadier Turnbull and described in Chapter 14.

Another operation from Malta in mid-July was aborted when HM Submarine *Unsparing* was at sea, through a combination of impossibly heavy seas, an outbreak of sandfly fever and the fact that the enemy had been well alerted when *Unsparing* fired two torpedoes which missed their target. But the Earthworm Detachment undertook other operations of a Commando nature in the Aegean with Raiding Forces, and Pritchard-Gordon with Sergeant King made a successful recovery of an underwater mine in Khios. However, by the late summer of 1944 the tenuous command of the Aegean Sea, which the Germans had enjoyed briefly, was passing insensibly but irresistibly to the Royal Navy. And as there did not seem to be any further worthwhile targets Pritchard-Gordon flew to England in October and obtained permission for the Detachment to return. In England they were absorbed for training in one or other of the two specialized sections.

At the end of 1944 and the beginning of 1945 plans were in hand to send two sections of the RMBPD to join SOG in the Far East; but this did not materialize, for by that time operations were being planned for the assault on Japanese-occupied Malaya, and there did not appear to be any requirement for attacking enemy shipping. The Royal Marines did, however, have Detachment 385, a general-purpose raiding force, doing duty in the Far East from 1944 to 1945.

When the war ended much thought had to be given to future needs for amphibious operations. Operations from canoes and by swimmers were an important constituent in this type of warfare. In 1946 there were in existence a number of serving personnel from SRU, SBS, COPP, RMBPD and RM Detachment 385 – officers, petty officers, NCOs and men who had had considerable experience in both surface and underwater operations from small boats. The largest group of these, who returned home from the Far East, were stationed at Fremington (the School of Combined

Operations) and became known as School of Combined Operations Beach and Boat Section (SCOBBS). RMBPD had moved from HMS *Mount Stewart* at Teignmouth to HMS *Appledore* in North Devon. The majority of ranks in both these units were Royal Marines and so it was naturally and sensibly decided that the Royal Marines should assume responsibility for all special boat operations.

Towards the end of 1947 the Royal Marines moved both these units to the RM Barracks Eastney at Portsmouth, where they became absorbed as the Small Raids Wing of the newly formed Amphibious School RM. By the beginning of 1950 operational units were formed, and a specialist trade of 'swimmer-canoeist' found its place among Royal Marine qualifications. The units were called Special Boat Sections – after their illustrious predecessors – and the parent organization was called Special Boat Company (instead of Small Raids Wing). It was here that swimmer-canoeists were trained and policy for training and employment of the SBS was evolved. From 1950 the SBS served in Germany, the Mediterranean, Aden, Malaya, Borneo and Northern Ireland, and their needs in craft, equipment, weapons and communications were answered by the improvements and developments that came with time.

In 1975 the Special Boat Company was redesignated Special Boat Squadron. It numbers about 120 men who operate mostly in four-man teams, and is commanded by a Royal Marines Major. The men, who have to undergo a series of suitability tests and swimmer-canoeist qualification courses, are all chosen from volunteers who usually have already had three or four years' Commando service behind them. Although the SAS – who have a close, but at times love-hate, relationship with the SBS – have Boat Troops which do excellent work, there are certain specialist skills beyond the SAS range in which men of the SBS have to be highly proficient.

The special skills of the SBS include a variety of underwater work, small boat and canoe handling, demolitions and placing of limpet charges, and beach reconnaissance. The nature of their isolated operations requires them to be expert in other special service skills which include radio and communication devices, astral navigation, parachuting, marksmanship, operations from submarines and first aid.

The raiders of the Second World War were not only highly courageous but sufficiently well trained technically to enable them to get ashore and carry out successful operations against enemy targets. The task of their successors, forty years later, has been magnified many times through the introduction of a large range of highly sophisticated and deadly defence devices. To master these demands an exceptionally high standard of technical knowledge and training.

The SBS, like the SAS, took part in the Dhofar operations and, also like them, play a part in Northern Ireland, but it may be many years before the full scope of their activities can be told. Their principal task is geared to participation in a European war, and to this end they take part in exercises from the north of Norway to the Mediterranean. They are involved alongside the SAS in national defence plans, and they also have a responsible commitment in the security of the North Sea oil rigs and the protection and recovery of merchant ships at sea.

But as the eyes and ears of amphibious operations, undoubtedly the Special Boat Squadron's greatest opportunity to date came with the South Atlantic Campaign, where its patrol work generally and its official task of beach reconnaissance prior to amphibious landings played a vital part – as will be seen in Chapter 19.

The Royal Marines Amphibious School also had under its wing a cadre of the Royal Navy Beach Control Party. This was the name given in 1948 to what had been the RN Beach Commandos, which had been formed in early 1942. These men achieved little glamour but performed a most important, difficult and dangerous task with considerable skill and courage.

An RN Beach Commando consisted of sufficient officers and men to handle the craft required to land a brigade, their attached troops, vehicles and stores. It was made up of a principal beach master, three beach masters, six assistant beach masters, three petty officers, six leading seamen, eighteen able seamen and thirty-nine ordinary seamen. The Commandos were designated by letters A to W (the last of these was an all-Canadian unit), and they were often split into three parties each capable of handling the craft required to land a battalion.

They arrived on the beach usually just behind the first waves of assault troops, and therefore often found themselves pinned down by mortar or machine-gun fire, which did not make any easier their work of marking the positions for larger craft and calling them into the shore by radio, Aldis lamp or even loudhailer, and endeavouring to ensure that the various types of vehicle could be disembarked with the right priorities. Other duties included organization of salvage parties to clear stranded minor craft from the shore; and firefighting, for which they had DUKWs containing trailers with pumps. On occasions beach parties were called upon to help the military clear pillboxes and other obstacles, and therefore they had to be fully trained in the handling of various small arms. The principal beach master was in constant communication with his beach masters, and from a patrolling craft – usually an LCA or amphibious vehicle – he would assess the situation on all the beaches in the sector.

RN Beach Commandos were employed in all major assaults and large raids. They were in action at Dieppe, Lofoten, Vaagso, North Africa, Madagascar, Sicily, Salerno, Anzio, Normandy, the Scheldt, Lake Comacchio and the Arakan, among other places. Working constantly under the hazards of a hostile beach called for courage, cool judgement and a high standard of technical knowledge.

16

The Special Air Service: Europe, 1943–1945

The confusion and uncertainty that reigned in the 1st SAS after the capture of David Stirling have already been remarked upon (see Chapter 14), for almost everything relating to operations – present and future – was carried in Stirling's head. The immediate command (at 15 February) devolved on Major Street, but on 9 March Lt-Colonel Cator assumed control, and ten days later the Regiment was organized into two parts. The activities of one part, the Special Boat Squadron, have been related; the second part was designated the Special Raiding Squadron, and it was commanded by Major Mayne. The SRS was organized into a Squadron headquarters, and three troops each of three sections. An officer commanded each section.

Training, of a very strenuous and thorough kind, took place from a tented camp at Azzib, a Palestinian village just south of the Syrian border. In April, after about six weeks of this training, General Dempsey, commanding 13 Corps, paid the troops a visit and told them that they were to be under his command for the forthcoming assault on Europe, and that their first task would be to silence a battery that commanded the approaches to the invasion coast. Thereafter, although without knowledge of the country, let alone the location of the battery, the SRS concentrated on perfecting their assault tactics through the medium of diagrams and sand-table models. On 4 July 1943 they sailed from Suez bound for Sicily; at that time they were 287 strong.

Meanwhile, the 2nd Special Air Service, under Lt-Colonel W.S. Stirling (David's brother), was undergoing equally arduous training with the First Army based on Philippeville. They had been recently formed, but (like 1 SAS earlier, whose initial recruits came mainly from Layforce) were fortunate in obtaining a nucleus of experienced men from the recently-disbanded No. 62 Commando, although (also like 1 SAS) on expansion they had to rely on base depots.

Their earlier operations in Tunisia had not been particularly fruitful, owing to the unsuitability of the terrain for jeeps and the fact that the line was static, making penetration difficult. They had also carried out some seaborne raids on Lampedusa, Pantellaria and Sardinia. Now, along with the SRS, they were destined for Sicily. Some men would be dropped on the north of the island, and a small party of thirteen (reduced from forty-five through malaria) were to land at the tip of Cape Passero ahead of the 51st Highland Division to seize a lighthouse thought to contain a nest of machine guns, and which commanded the landing beaches. In the event the lighthouse was found to be unoccupied.

The SRS operations on Cape Murro di Porco were very tidy and highly successful. They landed in LCAs from the *Ulster Monarch* on the night of 9 July, and in the course of only one – very long – day they had taken three batteries from the Italians, whose losses amounted to 700 men killed, wounded or captured. The SRS had only one man killed and two wounded. After this they re-embarked and were to have returned to the Middle East, but General Dempsey suddenly required them to clear the Germans from Augusta. There was no time to plan the operation, but they performed it – admittedly against only light opposition – with speed and skill before being taken off in two destroyers. Their next brush with the Germans was to be behind the lines at Bagnara on the toe of Italy, where they first disrupted communications and then seized the town.

Immediately after the landings in Italy operations by 2 SAS and the SRS took the form of long-range penetration patrols in jeeps, of the type carried out by Popski's Private Army, and the SRS was involved with Brigadier Durnford-Slater's brigade in the taking of Termoli (see Chapter 3). The fighting at Termoli, in which the SRS lost sixty-eight men, was not of a kind for which the force had been designed, but it showed – and this was to be reinforced later – how adaptable these troops were to every type of offensive operation. Shortly after this successful action the line became stabilized, and the SAS were employed in the entirely satisfactory role of seaborne raids against the lines of communication.

An operation performed by 2 SAS in November 1943 was typical. A party of 16 was sent by MTB from Termoli to land from rubber boats at the mouth of the River Tronto, some 35 miles north of Pescara. They were to be ashore for six days, during which time they were to pay special attention to the railway line and do what other damage they could. The weather was appalling, bitterly cold with torrential raid that had turned the countryside into a quagmire; but the railway was blown in several places on the second night, and other damage done.

The withdrawal to the pick-up point some 20 miles down the coast was fraught with difficulty and danger. More than 20 miles had to be covered to avoid enemy-held villages and strongpoints, and the parties were working to a strict deadline. All save two men, who had been captured when their party of four was caught in a German-occupied village, were taken off safely at the appointed time.

The SRS sailed from Algiers for the United Kingdom on Christmas Day, but the 2nd SAS spent the early months of 1944 in North Africa, and were not home until March. It was now decided to form an SAS brigade, which would be under command of 1st British Airborne Corps. There were to be three internal changes. The beige beret, which had hitherto formed the official SAS headdress, was replaced by the red one worn by airborne troops,* though the badge was retained. The Special Raiding Squadron was to revert to its original title of 1st Special Air Service Regiment, and remained under the command of Paddy Mayne; it was considerably enlarged, each troop becoming a squadron and each section a troop. The third change involved the command of 2 SAS.

Bill Stirling had been in disagreement with higher authority during the Italian campaign, for he was not permitted to use 2 SAS in what was its proper strategic role. He had advocated dropping small parties of men well behind the lines to disrupt the supply system in the rear areas. There was ample opportunity, especially in the early stages, for a great deal of damage of a strategic nature to be carried out, but in the event only one party of twenty men was dropped. These, however, proved the point by doing an immense amount of destruction.

The argument for proper use of SAS personnel came up again when planning their D-Day role. It was then proposed that they should be dropped immediately behind the landing area, interposing themselves between the enemy's front line and his reserves. It was a hopeless proposition, which might have resulted in heavy losses out of all proportion to any damage they could do. Instead

* It was restored in 1956.

251

Stirling called for the setting-up of a number of small bases many miles behind the fighting line, which would be resupplied and over long periods could, in conjunction with local resistance forces, play havoc with the enemy's rear echelons. Stirling stood firm on this principle and resigned, although in fact his philosophy was in the end adopted.

His place in command of 2 SAS went to Lt-Colonel B.M.F. Franks, who had been in the special forces almost from the beginning. He had served with No. 8 Commando, and become Signals Officer of Layforce, after which he was the first squadron commander of Phantom (see below) in the Middle East before becoming Brigade Major to Durnford-Slater's composite brigade in Italy. A tall, athletic man with a constantly cheerful disposition, plenty of courage and initiative, he was admirably suited for his new command.

The SAS Brigade, which was commanded by Brigadier R.W. McLeod, consisted of 1 and 2 Special Air Service Regiments, two French Parachute battalions (3rd and 4th SAS, but in fact the 2nd and 3rd Régiment de Chasseurs Parachutistes), and a Belgian Independent Parachute Squadron;* in addition, F Squadron, GHQ Liaison Regiment (Phantom), was attached as signal section. There was also a Royal Signals Squadron, which carried out the base signals requirements from Tactical Headquarters, Moorpark, working to the Phantom Squadron with operational information, and in direct contact with an RAF Mosquito Group at Northolt. The total strength of the brigade was 2,500 all ranks. In order to co-ordinate the activities of the brigade with other agents, special forces and resistance movements, Lt-Colonel I.G. Collins, who had considerable experience in the planning of irregular forces' operations, was in charge of a special branch of the staff at Airborne Corps.

Phantom's job of obtaining first-hand information from the forward positions and passing it back by wireless to GHQ made it, in the words of the Regiment's historian,† 'something between a Commando and a Signals Unit'. Its founder was Lt-Colonel (later Major-General) G.F. Hopkinson, and it started life as the Hopkinson Mission alongside No. 3 Air Mission, with the task of transmitting information from the forward areas to Air Officer

---

* Later increased to a regiment consisting of an RHQ with a Defence, Administration and 3 in. mortar troops, and two squadrons each with an HQ, a jeep and assault troop.
†R.J.T. Hills, *Phantom Was There.*

Commanding-in-Chief and GHQ BEF during the German advance through Belgium in 1940. The personnel of No. 3 Air Mission were all lost when their ship was torpedoed on the way back from France, but so successful had the combined mission been with its rapid communication and air-to-land link that official recognition was quickly achieved, and Phantom was born.

From the summer of 1940 the Regiment grew continually in strength and renown. Re-formed after Dunkirk as No. 1 GHQ Reconnaissance Unit, it received its final official title of GHQ Liaison Regiment on 31 January 1941, and its groups became squadrons, which were to operate with great distinction in Greece, the Middle East, Sicily, Italy and North-West Europe. Squadrons were subdivided into patrols, each of which was commanded by a captain, who had a corporal and four men (one of whom was a driver-wireless-operator) under him. Personnel wore their regimental badges, but were distinguished by a white 'P' shoulder flash on a black background.

At the beginning of 1944 the future of F Squadron was in doubt owing to alterations in the invasion plan, and to save the squadron Lt-Colonel Mackintosh, then commanding Phantom, called for volunteers to serve with the SAS Brigade. The response was more than sufficient to form a headquarters and four patrols under the command of Major J.J. Astor. Two patrols (under Captains Moore and Sadoine) were attached to 1 SAS and two (under Captains Hislop and Johnsen) to 2 SAS. The French and Belgians had their own signals, but F Squadron had the difficult task (linguistically) of training them in the use of the new wireless sets. Phantom's work with the SAS was quite invaluable; operating from the bases established behind the lines, they had some of the most vital and harassing jobs of anyone. They were the squadrons' lifeline, and on their expertise might hang the success of an operation and the survival of a patrol. Besides their almost round-the-clock monitoring service, they played their part with SAS patrols in such dangerous chores as clearing a dropping zone after a resupply.

For some three months before D-Day the whole brigade and F Squadron underwent exhaustive training over the Ayrshire countryside, covering long distances with heavy loads in all weathers by day and night. There were a large number of new recruits who had much to learn on the ground and in the air. Parachuting was done from Prestwick aerodrome, and included jumping with the legbag. This was a piece of equipment similar to the army kitbag, and was secured to the right leg with two straps, from which it was freed by a quick-release cord so that it swung from the belt on a length of cord, hitting the ground just in advance of the parachutist.

SAS operations during 1944 were concentrated on France and Belgium, but for some time after D-Day almost half the brigade was held in reserve in England. Shortage of air transport restricted SAS parties initially to a few reconnaissance drops in connection with early operations: selection of suitable bases 50 miles and more behind the front line. It was not until 21 June that the first whole squadron (A Squadron, 1 SAS) went to France.

From that time onwards operations of one sort or another, and in various places, were virtually continuous until the end of 1944 – and from some bases went on right through the winter. These operations took place mainly from carefully selected, codenamed bases. They were scattered well behind the front in areas of strategic importance. Houndsworth was the codename for one of the earliest from a base south of Dijon; Kipling – another 1 SAS operation – was situated between the Seine and the Loire near Auxerre; to the north of the River Lek the Belgian squadron conducted a six-month-long operation, Fabian; and on Loyton, which was based in the Vosges, ninety men of 2 SAS successfully harried the Germans for ten weeks, but lost a third of their men in the process. The French parachute battalions had bases stretching from St Brieuc south-east to Limoges, and virtually drove the Germans out of Brittany single-handed. This is to mention only a few of the forty-three important and widely scattered operational bases in France.

The initial selection of an area was made from the map. A small advance party with wireless would then be dropped to reconnoitre, and confirm or reject the suitability of the site for a base from which patrols could operate for a fairly long period of time. These reconnaissance parties were either dropped 'blind', or came in under the guidance of the French Resistance. Three essentials for a base were ample cover, a convenient supply of water, and the availability – either ready-made or able to be made – of a dropping zone. Once the site was confirmed it would be reinforced by troops and, if the terrain was suitable, by jeeps which were dropped with the aid of four parachutes.

Squadrons were often many miles apart – for example B Squadron, 1 SAS, was south of the Loire while D Squadron was in the Forest of Fontainebleau – and in the campsites themselves sections were apt to be well dispersed. On at least one occasion this saved lives when a base was surprised by the enemy. It was often necessary, when a campsite became too warm for comfort, for a hasty move to be made to a safer spot, but it was very seldom that a base was surprised. This was to a large extent due to the friendliness of the local population, and the co-operation and co-ordination patrols had with the Maquis.

The combined work of the SAS and the French maquisards was on a much happier note than operations by other special forces with Yugoslav partisans. The Maquis were well organized, and usually well commanded – sometimes by ex-regular officers – although their military efficiency varied considerably. Campsites were always cleverly and usually comfortably laid out. Often SAS patrols would share the hospitality of these Maquis camps, when the atmosphere might become one of reckless gaiety, for these were men who never so keenly enjoyed life as when they were in danger of losing it – and, after all, merriment is the crown on the head of friendship.

The maquisards performed prodigies of daring, and the constant liaison with the couriers they employed, together with their local knowledge, were of the greatest value to SAS patrols carrying out operations of long or short duration. But they were temperamental, and at times mistrustful and not easy to work with. They also contained Communist and non-Communist elements, who were bitterly opposed to each other. On the whole squadron commanders preferred to work independently, although there were several occasions when a common danger demanded joint action, or a successful combined operation was planned. An example of the former occurred at the Houndsworth base in August 1944, when the Germans launched an attack on the maquisard camp and the men of 1 SAS – who possessed a 6-pounder gun – helped defend the site and cover the evacuation. During the same month at the Wallace base the Maquis co-operated (although with considerably fewer men than promised) in a successful attack by a squadron of 2 SAS on the Germans holding Chatillon.

What type of work was carried out from these bases in France, and how was that work achieved? The SAS was organized into small parties; a camp was seldom occupied by more than fifty men. The principal task was to disrupt enemy communications in every way possible; this involved the mining of roads, bridges and railways, ambushes on convoys, and where feasible the annihilation of camps, and parties of the enemy. Important, and extremely damaging, as these undertakings were, perhaps even more so was the collation of information and its rapid communication, through

Phantom, back to headquarters. In this way many important targets in the rear areas, such as armoured columns and enemy command posts, were pinpointed and subsequently attacked by RAF Bomber Command.

That these small SAS patrols, or sections, were able to accomplish so much for comparatively little loss was due principally to two factors: the excellent use they made of surprise, and the very high firepower and the manoeuvrability of their jeeps. There was one occasion in Les Ormes when information was received that the SS were present in force and about to execute a number of the inhabitants. A jeep patrol swooped upon the village and caught the SS men before they could perform their dark deed. Once they had rallied a sharp fight ensued in which the patrol lost a man, but the concentrated fire from the jeeps was responsible for the death of many Germans, and swept the rest from the village.

Action acted as a tonic to these men, and they took pride in the professional skill they exercised in the successful ambush of a convoy, a raid on an enemy encampment, the destruction of large sections of road and rail, and the rapid reporting back of vulnerable targets too big for them to tackle. SAS men were not often surprised, for the French and the forest were their friends; with warning of a large-scale German search it was usually possible to slide deeper into the forest. But long periods of lying-up in enemy–occupied territory inevitably posed a strain, for all soldiers in close contact with danger are apt to become emotionally, if not physically, exhausted.

After several months of this hazardous life whole squadrons, or lesser parties, had to be got out, which usually meant going through the German lines. This was, of course, fraught with fearful danger, and yet there were some who did it almost regularly either on foot or in jeeps, with remarkable skill and cunning. Occasionally there would be an air evacuation after an RAF officer had first been dropped to make the necessary arrangements.

Naturally, these almost continuous operations were not achieved without casualties. Fortunately, these were not too heavy, save on one or two occasions such as when a camp occupied by men of B Squadron, 1 SAS, was surprised and overrun. One officer was killed and thirty-three men captured. Hitler had issued an order that captured SAS men were to be exterminated; Rommel in the desert had ignored it, but now most prisoners – along with maquisards and French civilians suspected of helping them – were shot, many of them having first been subjected to appalling torture. Field-Marshal Smuts in conversation with Field-Marshal Lord Harding on the cruelty of the German people once said it was not so much their cruelty he disliked, for in his opinion cruelty was not far beneath the surface of most men, but what he could not abide was their moral turpitude.* This indictment may perhaps be too sweeping, but it has some measure of truth.

A regular and vital feature of all these operations was resupply. This was almost invariably done by parachute.† The camp would be notified of the estimated time of arrival for a drop, then jeeps would be carefully concealed round the field, and the men would settle down to what could be a long, cold wait – for timings had to be flexible. When the sound of the engines was picked up flares would be lit on the dropping zone – a procedure which could have unpleasant consequences if aircraft recognition, which was made by engine noise, was at fault. As soon as identity was definitely established the code letter would be flashed by torch, after which the aircraft circled to make its run-in and the first stick of containers would float to the ground.

It was not as simple as it sounds, for if the release was made at too great a height or a strong wind blew, personnel, containers and jeeps – for which a larger DZ was required – might land some way off the field. This made the task of collection more difficult and hazardous, for the field had to be clear well before daylight. Even more trying was when containers – and sometimes soldiers – got lodged in trees. But things seldom went very wrong, and for this high praise must go to the RAF Groups who flew hundreds of missions as a matter of routine, often in difficult conditions and always low over enemy territory.

There was one drop that did go very wrong for a reinforcement of twelve men of 1 SAS on the night of 4/5 July 1944. The Germans had gained details of the drop including the code letter for that night. When the reception party arrived on the field they were fired on and, realizing that all was not well, but unaware that the enemy had the recognition letter, they withdrew. As the men touched down they made easy targets. Three dropped wide of the field and managed to escape, the other nine were captured (four of them wounded) and all save two corporals, who successfully ducked out of the way of the firing squad and were rescued by the Maquis, were later shot.

* Related to the author by Lord Harding.
† But as mentioned above, there were one or two occasions when a specially-trained RAF officer was dropped to prepare a landing ground.

During the early part of 1945 there was a comparative lull in the fighting in North-West Europe, and the call on the SAS was commensurately reduced. But their record up to the end of 1944 had been most impressive. British, French and Belgian squadrons had performed with outstanding success. Large numbers of the enemy had been killed (the 1st SAS alone accounted for over 1,000 Germans in the course of four months), many military vehicles and some armoured cars had been destroyed, and numerous targets had been pinpointed for the RAF to bomb. Allied airmen had been rescued, while on the other hand many prisoners had been taken – according to Philip Warner* the French in their Operations Haggard and Moses were responsible for the surrender of no less than 18,000 Germans. Obviously there had been casualties and good men had been lost, but achievement far outstripped expenditure.

In December 1944 it was decided to send an SAS squadron to Italy, where despite the appalling winter conditions there were many opportunities of a strategic nature, and large bands of partisans who needed to be organized and galvanized. Major Roy Farran, a squadron commander in 2 SAS who had been in Italy earlier with that regiment, was given a new squadron and left by air on 15 December, with the heavy equipment to follow by sea – these Italian operations were notable for the use of heavier weapons. The squadron was composed mainly of volunteers from the airborne regiments. Many of these were regular soldiers; they were often excellent men and had trained hard, but they mostly lacked battle experience – however, they were very keen to get it. To bring the numbers up to requirement Farran recruited two officers and ten men from the Infantry Depot in Italy.

The squadron remained in Italy for the rest of the war, and during that time there were three or four major operations, and some smaller ones. The first, very successful, venture was code-named Galia. Major Walker-Brown and thirty-three men were dropped in an area north of La Spezia on 27 December, and for nearly three months in Arctic weather he and his men fought a series of guerrilla actions. These included taking the town of Borghetto on 1 January, a rewarding ambush near Valeriano on the 4th, another on the Aulla-La Spezia road at the beginning of February, and the destruction of many vehicles. Some 6,000 German troops were deployed trying to catch them. In the various engagements of this operation the 3 in. mortars and medium

---

* *The Special Air Service*, p.151.

machine guns, which were humped by mules, more than justified their inclusion; their greater range made them a most successful innovation. On 15 February the party made its way back through the German lines.

A later operation in the same area, which included an unsuccessful attack on the Fascist HQ at Pontremoli, was somewhat disappointing and met with fairly heavy casualties. A very gallant failure was the operation codenamed Cold Comfort, when Major Ross Littlejohn and three other ranks were dropped north-east of Verona on the night of 17/18 February (reinforced by a further drop a week later) with the principal task of blocking the Brenner Pass by causing a landslide. It was a near-impossible mission on account of the ghastly weather conditions which prevented re-supply. In consequence the men went hungry, while the cold air pierced their lungs, and their hands stiffened on the carbines. Before they could achieve their main object they were worsted in an encounter with the enemy on 7 March, and Littlejohn and Corporal Crowley were captured. Later they were both executed.*

There were, however, other operations with happier results. A number of aircraft were destroyed on the ground by one party; others carried out successful raids along the Adriatic coast, coming ashore from canoes to blow up railway lines and bridges, and a Canadian officer, Captain Macdonald, in a joint operation with partisans, captured the town of Alba, 36 miles south-east of Turin. But by far the largest and longest operation of this the second SAS campaign in Italy was that codenamed Tombola, which was led in person by the Squadron Commander, Roy Farran. He has given an excellent and entertaining account of it in his book *Operation Tombola*.

The general plan was to join forces with partisans from one of the local partisan headquarters, or *Commando unico* as they were called, and form a base from which to harass German supply lines over a period of some weeks in an area just south of the Milan–Modena highway. Each *Commando unico* had a British or American officer attached to it, and Major Michael Lees, in Reggio (Emilia) province, showed the most enthusiasm for Farran's ideas. And so, having received the necessary authority from 15 Army Group, Farran planned to set up a base in the valley south of the River Secchia near Villa Minozzo.

* Captain Philip Pinckney of 2 SAS had also been dropped near the Brenner Pass in the autumn of 1943 to blow one of the tunnels, and he too had been captured and shot.

With a small, select advance party he dropped on 4 March. He had been specifically banned by 15 Army Group from taking an active part in the operation, but not for the first time nor for the last Farran disobeyed an order and 'accidentally' fell out of the aeroplane. It was just as well, for not only did his outstanding qualities of leadership make him a natural selection to direct and organize this type of operation, but his second-in-command, Captain Eyston, badly dislocated his shoulder in the jump and was not immediately available to plan the battle order with Lees and the partisan leaders.

Each *Commando unico* consisted of a number of brigades (of approximately British battalion strength), and the men were a very mixed lot. There were Communists, right-wing Christian Democrats, simple Italian peasants who preferred plunder to politics, and a sprinkling of escaped Russian prisoners. Farran raised and led the fifth brigade of the Reggio *Commando unico*, and besides his British troop, which numbered forty, he had a Russian and Italian one to each of which was attached one British officer and four other ranks.

It was agreed between him and the military commander of all the partisans in Reggio Province that the *Battaglione alleato* (as the new brigade was to be called) would operate under orders from Allied Headquarters in Florence, but would be under the partisans for administration, and would of course co-operate with them in the case of an emergency. Supply drops were masterminded by Walker-Brown from Florence, and contributed very considerably to the success of the operation. Despatches to Florence were sent by the hand of partisan girls, for whom the term was *staffetta*, and they had little difficulty in passing through the lines. These girls had an important role in the partisan organization, and some of them formed the Intelligence Squad.

The first two weeks or so were spent in training and equipping the *mélange*, who received instruction from the British soldiers attached to each troop. Most of the weapons were new to the partisans, but the British private soldier was to prove both an intelligent instructor and a competent detachment commander, and the partisans – especially the Russians – extremely apt pupils.

Active operations lasted for about a month until towards the end of April, when the Allies had reached Modena, and the SAS men were ordered back to Florence. In the course of this month there were two major actions. The first was an attack on the headquarters of the German 51 Corps at Albinea – a few miles south of Reggio – and the second a series of raids on Highway 12, running from Modena to Lucca. By the time this took place the *Battaglione alleato* had moved to the Modena Province.

The German corps headquarters was manned by about 300 men and in the compound were two main buildings, the Villa Calvi and the Villa Rossi; one was the Chief of Staff's villa and offices, and the other was the Corps Commander's billet. Farran decided to concentrate on these two villas; in each case ten British soldiers would force an entry to be quickly followed by twenty Italians. The Russian troop was to form the cut-off screen.

The attack on Calvi had the advantage of surprise but went in a shade too soon, which meant that the enemy in Rossi were on full alert. The German posts throughout the compound opened up with everything they had, and the darkness was quickly lit by lurid bursts of flame. Meanwhile inside both villas it was close-quarters fighting of the very fiercest kind, for the enemy, although suffering heavy casualties, resisted with spirit. Before Farran's Very light gave the signal for withdrawal both villas were burning merrily.

It is estimated that some sixty Germans were killed including the Chief of Staff, and this important focal point for all operations in that area had been virtually obliterated along with maps, plans, records and orders. The loss to the attackers was three British killed, eight wounded (including Michael Lees, very seriously), all of whom were brought safely out of the fray, and six Russians captured – and no doubt later executed. Apart from the damage done, the psychological effect on all other headquarters was bound to be considerable, causing more troops to be withdrawn for garrison duties.

The Germans reacted predictably with a large-scale roundup in the valley where Tombola was based, but in a series of defensive engagements they were kept at bay. Nor were they able to disrupt a number of resupply drops bringing in stores, ammunition and – most importantly – jeeps. On 13 April orders were received from 15 Army Group for the 'battalion' (now established in Modena Province) to operate offensively along Highway 12. Farran allotted the northern section of the road to the British, the Italians took care of the centre, and the Russians had the south. Enemy columns were attacked with such aggressive vigour that, apart from casualties inflicted, the German withdrawal along this route was thrown into disarray.

Meanwhile in North-West Europe there were a number of bases that were active throughout the dark months, such as two of the three – mainly reconnaissance – Belgian parties, Fabian, Gobbo and Regent. The first two were dropped in September 1944 and not withdrawn until the middle of March 1945. Regent was a somewhat larger operation in the eastern Ardennes from 27 December to the middle of January. It comprised a number of small jeep and foot patrols under command of 29 Armoured Brigade, which worked closely with 61 Reconnaissance Regiment reporting upon enemy dispositions, blown bridges and mined roads. The patrols also provided interpreters, and gave covering fire to the assault section of the Recce Regiment.

The small Gobbo party (Lieutenant Deberfe, a sergeant and five other ranks) operated from 26 September to 17 March in the flat countryside of north-east Holland, which provided little cover. During this time they sent back a large amount of invaluable information, including photographs of fortifications, V1 and V2 emplacements, and news of troop movements and of railway and canal traffic. They had to go to ground for periods of varying length to avoid the attentions of the German and Dutch SS troops. In the report of their operations the latter, who wore a black uniform with red cap band and red collars, were labelled as 'very dangerous', although the vast majority of the Dutch were exceedingly brave and helpful.

In early January the 4th SAS (French battalion) was also active in Operation Franklin in the Ardennes, carrying out road patrols and ambushes behind the enemy lines in the St Hubert area. They were under the command first of 87 US Infantry Division and then of 17 US Armoured Division, but by the end of the month the line had stabilized in their area and infiltration became so difficult that they were withdrawn.

On 14 March Brigadier J.M. Calvert took over command of the SAS Brigade from McLeod, who had done a tremendous job in the difficult formative months and was now posted to India. Calvert had already achieved great renown in Burma, where he had command of a brigade of Orde Wingate's force. He was an ideal choice to lead the SAS in the final weeks of the war. With the coming of better weather activity along the whole front was stepped up and SAS work became increasingly important and arduous, although sometimes – especially in the final stages – the regiments were not used in their proper role. Out of a very large number of operations it is only possible to mention one or two quite briefly.

Operations Amherst (both French battalions), Larkswood (the Belgian regiment) and Keystone (two small parties from 2 SAS) were all designed to assist the advance of the 1st and 2nd Canadian

Divisions, in western and northern Holland respectively, by disrupting enemy communications through sabotage and ambuscade. In Amherst the French battalions dropped 694 men on the night of 5/6 April and they were supported by 268 Belgians. The French had the additional tasks of arming and encouraging local resistance in the area, and of preserving Steenwijk airfield. In the course of considerable fighting they killed over 200 Germans and wounded and captured a further 400 for the loss of 29 killed, 96 missing and 35 wounded. Their operations undoubtedly paved the way for the rapid occupation of north Holland. The Belgians took 250 prisoners, and by seizing a number of bridges intact greatly facilitated the Polish advance to the North Sea.

Keystone was a much smaller affair, and lasted for less than a fortnight. The party of three sections each of nine men, and ten jeeps, under Major Druce, accounted for a number of Germans while working ahead of 1 Canadian Division, although deep penetration was found to be impossible without heavier armoured vehicles. Captain Holland with the other patrol, whose signal for jeeps to be dropped was never received, operated in the area south of Ijsselmeer, and in seven days they blew the railway line in several places, killed or captured twenty Germans and destroyed a few vehicles.

Two squadrons (B and C) of 1 SAS, under Colonel Mayne, sailed from Tilbury (they had been brought back to England in the first week of March 1945) on the night of 6/7 April to carry out Operation Howard in support of the 4th Canadian Armoured Division in the area north-east of Meppen. The squadrons were organized into patrols of three jeeps, and their initial role was to operate on the Armoured Division's left flank in the advance to Oldenburg. In this spearhead action of forcing a gap through which the Division would pass they had taken the place of armoured cars, and apart from this not being a proper role for SAS troops, jeeps were a poor substitute for armoured cars.

Mayne ordered the squadrons to advance in two columns, and they were very soon into a good deal of trouble – Major Bond, commanding B Squadron, and Trooper Lewis being killed during the attack on a strongpoint near Borgerwald, and the leading patrols held up. The situation was quickly resolved by Mayne in person, whose single jeep charged straight into the *point d'appui* not once but three times, with guns blazing. Thereafter some fairly rapid progress was made in which the squadrons took a number of prisoners, and destroyed ammunition and explosive dumps.

Their second day in Germany brought more trouble, for they had outstripped the armoured division, who were fighting hard over to their right. Having cleared a few villages and taken more prisoners C Squadron went to the assistance of B, who were held up in a village, and soon came under intense mortar fire. That night both squadrons formed a laager in a big wood. They had covered some 30 miles from Meppen, their petrol was getting low and a number of the jeeps had been damaged and were on tow. At first light a patrol was despatched to try to make contact with the Canadians, and soon afterwards the remainder were attacked by a strong German force sweeping the forest for them. The fighting was confused, with the Germans firing blind in the dense cover. Five Bren gunners went forward to seek out the enemy, amid a storm of lead, and with them walked Paddy Mayne – armed only with a camera. The situation was restored by the opportune arrival of the Canadians' Sherman tanks.

The two squadrons then pulled out to reorganize and refit, for they had suffered casualties to both men and jeeps. The increasingly difficult country with cratered roads and blown bridges inhibited any deep penetration on the left, and for the next ten days the squadrons patrolled the right of the armoured division with the armoured reconnaissance regiment. On 23 April they came under command of an independent armoured brigade operating towards Oldenburg, and were with them until the end of hostilities. During their various engagements in suppport of the Canadians, B and C Squadrons had killed approximately 100 Germans and taken over 300 prisoners, besides destroying a considerable amount of equipment.

Operation Archway is related in rather more detail, for it was one of the largest and most diverse of all those carried out by SAS personnel in North-West Europe – although, again, much of the action was not of their genre. Squadrons from both regiments took part, and the composite force was commanded by Lt-Colonel Franks, and became known (inevitably!) as Frankforce. The 1st SAS squadron was led by Major H. Poat and had three troops, each consisting of three sections with three jeeps. They had a 3 in. mortar section at Squadron Headquarters and a reserve of twelve jeeps. Their total was 155 all ranks. The 2nd SAS squadron was under the command of Major P.L.J. Le Poer Power and was slightly smaller with two troops (129 all ranks), and twenty-two jeeps. In addition there were heavier vehicles for B echelon transport, and jeeps for Phantom personnel.

Frankforce came by sea from England and arrived at Ostend on

20 March. It was initially under command of the 18th US Corps, and it was to carry out short-range reconnaissance with the airborne units in their bridgehead over the Rhine north of Wesel; when the bridgehead period was over the force was to attempt deeper penetration and attack lines of communication. On 25 March they crossed the Rhine in amphibious Buffaloes at Bislich, and on the following day Power's squadron was in action during the advance from Hamminkelm. In the course of some skirmishing they killed several Germans and captured forty-two without loss, although three jeeps were damaged.

On the 27th they were relieved by Major Poat's squadron, which was required to assist 6th Guards Armoured Brigade in their task of seizing crossings over the Dortmund-Ems Canal in the advance from Wesel. Major Fraser's troop was soon in action against a force of Germans endeavouring to hold up the advance from well-sited positions in a wood. An attempt to achieve surprise by a flank attack failed and Fraser was wounded and his jeep ditched, but the troop immediately deployed for what became a very successful set-piece battle. Lieutenant Riley's section destroyed the machine-gun post which had blasted Fraser, Lieutenant Jenson's silenced bazooka and Spandau positions on the German left, while Lieutenant McLellan's section cleared the enemy from a group of houses on the right. The outlying positions liquidated, the troop then dismounted and, covered by the jeeps, proceeded to clear the entire wood.

Major Tonkin's troop (1st SAS) was the next to see action and, while reconnoitring ahead of 6th Airborne's advance to Ostrich, to give another fine demonstration of jeep firepower. Meeting, just short of Ostrich, three British tanks and a scout car the joint force continued down the road until the scout car was knocked out, and the enemy poured a withering fusillade on the column from both sides of the road. A long fire battle developed until the enemy was eventually silenced. Infantry were then called up and, covered by the jeeps, cleared the area. Eighty Germans were killed and seventy captured, and an 88 mm gun was taken before it could open fire. The SAS casualties were surprisingly light – two seriously and two slightly wounded.

On the same day, 29 March, a section from the 2nd SAS squadron had an unpleasant contretemps with some German tanks. The squadron was employed covering the left flank of the Guards Armoured Brigade, and patrols had to move down tracks and side roads. Lieutenant Glynn-Evans's section encountered three German tanks in a woodland ride; two of his jeeps were completely crushed, and the other two were captured after their crews had abandoned them.

The many reconnaissance and protection tasks carried out by patrols of both squadrons clearly demonstrated what these powerfully-armed jeeps could achieve when boldly handled, but the need for constant mobility in close country was very apparent, as was the fact that jeeps were dangerously vulnerable against snipers operating from woods on both flanks.

At the end of March there were a number of administrative and some operational changes. Frankforce came under 8 Corps which had taken over from 18 US Corps, and 1 SAS were to work with the 11th Hussars (7th Armoured Division). The Hussars operated with one squadron up and two in reserve, and 1 SAS worked its troops (one with each Hussar squadron) in the same way. The 2 SAS squadron was to continue with the Guards Armoured Brigade until the capture of Munster, and then would revert to 8 Corps reserve. This occurred on 1 April. A week later Second Army changed 1 SAS squadron from the 7th to the 11th Armoured Division, which having better ground after crossing the Weser was likely to operate faster. The whole of Frankforce was now concentrated north of Minden, and 1 SAS carried out a number of operations under command of the Inns of Court Regiment (the recce unit of 11 Armoured Division) until they reached the Elbe.

Numerous engagements of a type similar to those described took place during the advance to the Elbe. For a period from 9 April the 2nd SAS squadron was put at the disposal of the Military Government and was responsible for the capture of a number of political prisoners. From 14 to 19 April they worked with the 15th Division's Reconnaissance Unit, which proved to be a very fruitful partnership, for their mobility counteracted the comparative slowness of the Recce Unit, whereas the latter's heavier firepower and armour dealt with opposition too big for the jeeps.

The Elbe was reached on 19 April. After a period of rest the river was crossed on the 29th and 30th, and there was more fighting in the Lübeck area before on 3 May (the day before the German Command's agreement to unconditional surrender) Major Poat's 1 SAS squadron, together with 30th Assault Unit, reached Kiel. Frankforce sailed for home on 10 May.

Operation Archway had been a great success. For the loss of only seven killed and twenty-two wounded Frankforce had accounted for a great many dead Germans, and even more captured. The fighting had never been against demoralized troops;

the Hitler Jugend resisted with fanatical determination, and within the Wehrmacht the last bonds of discipline did not snap until almost the end.

In the course of operations in France, Belgium, Holland and Germany the SAS Brigade had suffered 330 casualties out of some 2,000 engaged. In their turn they had killed or seriously wounded 7,733 of the enemy and made 4,784 men prisoners. Approximately 700 motor vehicles had been destroyed together with a number of trains, engines and trucks.* They had also been responsible for locating many important targets for the RAF.

On 12 May an advance party from Brigade Headquarters and 1 and 2 SAS left Britain for Norway, and the main body flew into Stavanger airfield a week later. Stationed first at Kristiansund, they moved on 27 May to Bergen. Their occupation duties in connection with the surrender included the task of helping to disarm about 300,000 Germans. The period of readjustment to conditions of peace by men who for several years had not lived outside the vortex of total war was made easier by the fact that their former enemy in Norway had clearly enjoyed *la douceur de vivre*. Champagne, smoked salmon, caviar and fresh Danish butter had formed a significant part of the German officer's ration.

No sooner was David Stirling out of prison than he was bursting with plans and ideas for the use of SAS personnel in the Far East. Doubtless the regiments would have played as vital a part against the Japanese as they had done against the western enemies, but like other special forces they were deprived of this fresh venture by the atom bomb. The SAS Brigade returned from Norway in August; in September the Belgian regiment became a part of the Belgian army, and a few weeks later the French battalions were handed back to the French and incorporated into their army. On 8 October Brigade Headquarters and the two British SAS regiments were disbanded. For four years their quality and their deeds had sparkled in the military galaxy. Their star would rise again.

---

* Figures from Philip Warner, *The Special Air Service*, p.172.

17

The Special Air Service:
Malaya and Borneo, 1950–1966

Less than a year after the SAS had been officially disbanded in October 1945, the War Office instigated an enquiry into the future role, if any, of the special forces. As a result it was decided that no matter to what extent methods of conducting war might change, there would always be a need for small parties of well-trained and well-handled men operating behind the enemy lines. Inevitably the Special Air Service filled this requirement; however, the times were not judged propitious for the introduction of another regiment into the Regular Army, and so a compromise was reached in the form of an SAS Territorial regiment.

It was to be designated 21 SAS. The figure 21 was arrived at by a somewhat typically convoluted army method, which need not be elaborated, and the new regiment was formed under Lt-Colonel Franks, who had commanded 2 SAS in North-West Europe. He had as his second-in-command Major L.E.O.T. Hart who had been DA and QMG to the SAS Brigade, and he was followed in command by such stalwarts as Lapraik and Sutherland, who have already appeared in these pages. When recruiting commenced in September 1947 a number of ex-SAS personnel volunteered, and these provided the Regiment with a wealth of experience from the start.

A wise decision was taken to merge with the Artists' Rifles. The Artists had been raised as far back as 1859, and since 1928 had been affiliated to the Rifle Brigade. In the 1914 war the Regiment had fought with great distinction from 1917 onwards, but in the last war it had been employed as an Officer Cadet Training Unit. The merger resulted in the new unit's official title of 21 SAS (Artists) TA, and until 1950 (when the SAS became a Corps of the Army) it was a part of the Army Air Corps.

Two further SAS regiments were formed in the next few years. The first of these, 22 SAS, had a typically *ad hoc* origin which will be described shortly. In 1959 another Territorial SAS regiment – 23 – was launched under Lt-Colonel H.S. Gillies, and its Headquarters are now in Birmingham. Both the Territorial regiments have squadrons in various parts of Britain (23 SAS, for example, has a squadron in Newcastle, Glasgow and Dundee). Their commanding officers, adjutants, training majors and squadron sergeant-majors are all regular SAS personnel, but the remainder are volunteers. There is also 63 (SAS) Signal Squadron manned by men of the Royal Signals, which provides basic signal back-up for the Territorial regiments, and a reserve squadron, R, as a means of recruiting men for 22 SAS in times of emergency.

The genesis of 22 SAS was in the Malayan emergency. The year 1948, like its counterpart in the previous century, was deeply disturbed by the dark clouds of revolt – only this time they hung mostly over the Far East. In China, Indo-China, Indonesia, Burma and Malaya – among other places – it seemed that malign figures symbolizing cruelty and turbulence were emerging everywhere to preach, convert and lead their many followers into acts of rebellion, sabotage and terrorism. In Malaya, where alone of those countries rebellion was eventually crushed, well over a thousand Communists (mostly Chinese), many of whom had once formed part of the British-led Force 136, returned to the jungle under their leader Chin Peng,* where they uncovered and quickly put into commission long-hidden caches of weapons.

Their technique, comparatively new in 1948, was soon to become all too familiar. The aborigines were terrified into submission; raids would take place on European rubber plantations, where foremen and managers were murdered, roads were ambushed, and machines destroyed; and then there would be a return to safety in the embosoming jungle. It was exceedingly difficult for orthodox infantry battalions to catch up with them, for the terrorists (or bandits as they were officially called) were kept well informed, supplied and often financed by the secret support of non-combatant Chinese sympathizers known as the Min Yuen.

General Sir John (later Field-Marshal Lord) Harding was Commander-in-Chief of Far East Land Forces, and in 1950 he sent for Brigadier Calvert, then on the staff in Hong Kong. Calvert,

---

* Chin Peng had been awarded the OBE for his work in the war! Those who were with him in Force 136 speak of his great charm and ability.

with his great experience of jungle fighting together with his former leadership of the wartime SAS Brigade, was uniquely qualified to advise the Commander-in-Chief on a possible solution to what appeared to be an insoluble problem. After a long discussion Harding told Calvert to go off and consider the matter deeply, and then to produce a detailed report on how it might be resolved. Calvert thereupon disappeared for six months, most of which time he spent in the jungle trekking, often unescorted, along bandit-infested tracks. He also interviewed as many people as possible who were conducting or participating in the campaign.

His report at the end of this time clearly showed the need for small parties of specially-trained men to infiltrate into the jungle, to live there for long periods of time, to win the 'hearts and minds'* of the Sakai inhabitants and to isolate them from the guerrillas. In due course these ideas were built into the 'Briggs Plan' by which General Sir Harold Briggs, the Director of Operations, aimed to remove villagers from their isolated and vulnerable shacks and establish them in fortified 'kampongs'. This formed part of later, and most successful, draconian measures to deny food to the terrorists.

Two months after submitting his report Calvert was authorized by Harding to set about raising his special force, which he called Malayan Scouts (SAS). It was the progenitor of 22 SAS, which received its official title in May 1952. Recruiting for the new force was hard work, and before it was completed Calvert had travelled many thousands of miles, which included a visit to Rhodesia from where he selected volunteers to form what became C Squadron. The A Squadron comprised local volunteers, some of whom were to prove unsatisfactory. There could be no method of selection; many were excellent material and some had already served in SOE or Force 136, but inevitably there were others whose regiments were delighted to see them go. Though unfortunate, at least it emphasised the need for careful selection in the future.

B Squadron was made up of volunteers from 21 SAS (Artists) and reservists from other wartime special forces, and they were a well disciplined, close-knit body of men. Originally a composite squadron, known as M Squadron, and commanded by Major A. Greville-Bell, it had been formed to go to Korea, but while it was training at Aldershot news came of General MacArthur's successful push to the Chinese border. Its presence in Korea, therefore,

---

* This telling phrase was coined by General (later Field-Marshal) Sir Gerald Templer, when he was High Commissioner in Malaya in 1952.

no longer seemed necessary, and so it was agreed that the Squadron should be sent to join the Malayan Scouts, where it acquired its own designation. Before Calvert left Malaya in 1951 (a very sick and grossly overworked man) he had formed a fourth squadron, D, which had been locally recruited.

Calvert's training, from the base camp at Johore Bahru, was most realistic – live ammunition was invariably used, and individual stalks were arranged with the men armed with air guns and protected (partially!) by fencing masks. As squadrons became ready (and naturally A Squadron being locally raised was the first) they went to the operational base at Ipoh from where small groups were despatched into selected jungle areas known to be used by terrorists. There they lived for long periods (one patrol was operating for 103 days, but that was exceptional) laying ambushes and directing RAF strikes. Resupply was almost entirely by parachute from RAF Dakotas and Valettas; it was never easy, for the jungle presented a dense, opaque panorama from the air, and the sky above it was turbulent, thundery and treacherous. Calvert, with very limited resources at his disposal, was a pioneer of 'hearts and minds' among the aborigines, whose maladies he attempted to treat in improvised clinics.

These early operations by the Malayan Scouts had had some success against the bandits for only a handful of casualties. But the force had made a very bad impression on a number of influential people through the indiscipline and wild behaviour of a fair proportion of the local volunteers. Calvert was succeeded by Lt-Colonel John Sloane, an Argyll and Sutherland Highlander, who had had no special force or jungle experience, but was a man who knew the value of discipline, and he did a very fine job pulling the unit, with its somewhat disparate parts, together and shaping it into a cohesive and proper SAS-type formation.

One of Calvert's original officers, who gave him and his successors invaluable assistance in the training programme, was Major J.M. Woodhouse. He had joined the army in 1941 from school and seen a great deal of active service; he also spoke Russian, and remarkably had been sent to work as an interpreter with the Russians and not with, say, the Chinese or French as tended to happen in days gone by. In 1952 he was sent to England to organize a training and selection programme for the Regiment. Tony Geraghty in his excellent book *Who Dares Wins* has given a full account of the selection and training course an SAS volunteer has to undergo before he is accepted. Here it is only possible to give a brief outline.

The first course that Woodhouse organized took place from the Airborne Forces Depot at Aldershot, but soon much more exacting and longer courses were arranged making use of some of the wildest and most rugged parts of Wales. When, in 1960, the Regiment made Hereford the permanent headquarters for 22 SAS the soaring crags of the nearby Brecon Beacons offered ideal conditions for fitness training, and for map and compass work in country where mists of grey vapour often masked even the lower slopes of the mountains.

The full selection course now lasts almost four months, and although it is undoubtedly very tough, calling for the utmost endeavour of mind and body, the degree of toughness has sometimes been exaggerated and has led to misunderstandings. The course is not designed to break a man but to make him. Apart from the special characteristics and qualities of excellence required of an SAS soldier, which have already been mentioned, these long courses seek to discover the man who is an individualist with self-discipline enabling him to work, often in a detached situation, either on his own or as a member of a small group. A successful candidate needs to have plenty of stamina, to show himself ready and able to respond quickly to the need of the moment, and to face difficulty and danger with optimism.

The weeding-out process is continuous throughout the various phases of the course. Some men quickly realize that it is not for them, others may chuck it, or be chucked, at the time of the long and lonely endurance marches with heavy packs (known as 'bergens'); still others at the time of parachuting, and even a few when it comes to the final phase of combat survival training. Only a very small percentage of the original volunteers survive to receive the coveted beige beret and badge. These highly talented men are then ready for specialist training – languages, navigation, medical skills, signalling and free-fall parachuting, to mention just a few – which quite likely will not be completed until the man has done two years out of his initial three with the regiment. The average age of a fully-trained SAS man is twenty-six.

An officer who passes the selection course joins the SAS for three years. He then reverts to a period of regimental duty and/or the Staff College course (for which, if he is recommended to the Selection Board for attendance, he may be exempted from the entrance examination) before being eligible to return to the SAS, if he so requires and is wanted, for a further three years – and so on. The interim periods of more orthodox and less exciting regimental duty can be irksome, but they are very necessary if the officer hopes for higher command. It is probably true to say that until the late sixties secondment to the SAS was a disadvantage for promotion within the parent regiment; for those who remained constant in their service to the regiment were inclined to resent the comings and goings of those whom they erroneously considered to be at best specialist prodigies and at worst professional assassins.

However, a broader outlook is now taken; the SAS is recognized as an essential and highly-specialized service, and service in it is regarded with favour certainly in the Army generally, if not always in the narrower confines of the regiment. Officers who have served in the SAS now hold, or have held, high rank in the Army. The other ranks (many of whom have been NCOs in their regiment, but have had to revert to trooper on joining the SAS) tend to stay on a more permanent basis. They can have an immediate extension of three years, and then after six can be taken on as part of the permanent cadre.

Before Woodhouse returned to England in the summer of 1952 to organize the early training and selection courses outlined above, he had been involved in the first big operation that the Malayan Scouts had undertaken since their return to the jungle. By February 1952 the 'Briggs Plan' was beginning to have some effect and the bandits, no longer finding supplies of food from the villages so plentiful, were being driven deeper into the jungle, where they made clearings in which to grow their own food. One such area was in the Belum Valley near the Thai border, where they were not only growing food but had control of two villages at either end of the valley. The Malay Scouts formed part of a combined operation with the Royal Marine Commandos, Gurkhas and Malayan Police to drive the enemy away from this food-producing site.

The valley was cleared, but the operation was only a partial success, for the extremely difficult – and at times noisy – approach to the target had given the Communist terrorists (CTs was another semi-official name) plenty of time to evacuate their camp-sites. Catching up with the enemy was one of the problems in Malaya; they had the advantage of terrain as well as the eyes and ears of the many Chinese squatters, or the more organized Min Yuen. The SAS task in this operation was for two squadrons to march over a difficult and steep mountain track into the valley, while a third squadron of fifty-four men dropped into a very confined space. It set the pattern for the work 22 SAS were to do during much of their time in Malaya.

On these patrols the marching men – especially when there was to be no resupply – had to carry a great weight over slippery mountain tracks and treacherous valley quagmires. Apart from personal weapons (submachine guns or shotguns, and until 1957 Brens), grenades, spare clothing, water bottle and field dressings, there was the seven- or fourteen-day ration pack, and for some the heavy wireless set. The torrid heat and thundery depressions brought out clouds of pestiferous insects; snakes and leeches were ever present and the occasional wild animal could prove dangerous if unduly provoked.* At night 'bashas' (shelters) would be erected from branches and leaves, which if skilfully constructed could keep out much of the persistent rain. Such were the conditions a fighting patrol would have to endure, and always be ready for instant action.

Those who arrived on or near the scene of operations by parachute might have a less arduous initial lot of shorter duration, but it was a good deal more dangerous. The Malayan jungle with its lofty trees and squelching ooze appears from the air to be a solid mass of near impenetrable foliage. Even where there were natural or artificial clearings it was inevitable that some men would land in trees, and so they were provided with a 100-ft rope in the hope that they would not be too damaged as they crashed through the canopy, and could let themselves down. In the Belum Valley operation there were in fact no casualties, but that happy state of affairs did not persist, and although 'tree jumping' became an SAS speciality, after a while the dangers of the jump and the makeshift abseiling technique caused it to be abandoned.

Among the earliest 'tree jumping' casualties was Lt-Colonel Oliver Brooke, who had succeeded Sloane in 1953. He damaged a leg so badly that it needed long treatment in England, but before he was forced to give up command he had made a considerable contribution in the development of Calvert's original ideas for gaining the confidence and co-operation of the aborigines. This required a lot of patience, and an ability and willingness to tune into their thought process almost as closely as two lobes of the same brain. It paid rich dividends in Malaya and later in Borneo, and on a different level, but to an equally great extent, in South Arabia. In Malaya the winning of minds significantly reduced

---

* Some patrols both in Malaya and Borneo shot and ate monkeys, which they claimed to like. Lord Harding told the author that he thought the dish he was given when he visited one of Calvert's patrols was the nastiest thing he had ever tasted!

British casualties and shortened the conflict, while in Borneo it gained the SAS patrols invaluable information.

Oliver Brooke was succeeded in command for a short spell by Michael Osborne, who was followed by George Lea. Lea, an exceptionally fine officer who was to become a general, found a certain amount to displease him. He, perhaps more than any other officer, put 22 SAS into proper shape. There were officers who he considered were not up to standard, and several were smartly returned to their regiments. Moreover, the discipline was not what he considered it should be. That is not to say that Lea tried to enforce normal Army procedures: on operations SAS officers and men lived on equal terms – the word 'boss' was more often used than 'sir'. There was a great comradeship, and the touchstone of that comradeship was unselfishness and the willingness to share risks; at its best such discipline was never lax, it was merely transferred from being one based on authority, and even fear, to that less easily–defined type which gives to a man a deep desire to obey. Soon Colonel Lea had built up a strong team of officers, which included Woodhouse, now back from England as a squadron commander; Harry Thompson; John Cooper, one of David Stirling's old desert hands; and Peter de la Billière, who like Woodhouse would one day command the regiment.

At this time (1955/56) there were some squadron changes and additions. C Squadron, whose men had not always found it easy to adapt themselves to the 'hearts and minds' part of the work, and who were susceptible to jungle diseases, returned to Rhodesia. They were replaced by the Kiwi Squadron, a splendid body of handpicked men who had been well trained in their native New Zealand before they flew to Malaya in December for further jungle training. They included a number of Maoris who quickly became expert trackers. An additional squadron (making five in all, and bringing the regiment's total to 560) was one from the Parachute Regiment under Major Dudley Coventry. And also at this time the first batch of Fijians transferred to the SAS. These excellent men, whose numbers were to increase, remained with the regiment for many years, taking part in the Borneo and South Arabia campaigns.

It took ten years to clear the terrorists out of Malaya or into surrender, and for most of that time SAS squadrons were, like the many other troops in the country, at full stretch deep into the jungle or taking part in large-scale operations. One such was Operation Termite in 1954, which lasted five months, and opened with a heavy bombing raid* to clear areas into which two SAS squadrons parachuted. At the end of it all only fifteen bandits were accounted for, and it became obvious that SAS troops were more usefully employed living for long periods in the jungle, gaining intelligence and the confidence of the aborigines. Good results could be expected against guerrillas by employing guerrilla tactics: tracking, hunting, ambushing and killing the enemy by accurate snap shooting.

One of the last great hunts was carried out in the spring of 1958 by D Squadron under Major Harry Thompson. The object was to eliminate two groups of bandits which, under their notorious leader Ah Hoi, were terrorizing the neighbourhood from their base in a large (18 miles by 10) coastal swamp north of Telok Anson in Selangor. Thirty-seven men of the squadron were parachuted into the edge of the swamp, and for three weeks they waded through filthy, leech-infested, brackish water sometimes up to their necks, slinging their hammocks in trees by night, trying to catch a glimpse of their elusive enemy, who were operating on home ground with its many advantages to them.

Surprise was probably lost through the need to evacuate an initial parachute casualty by helicopter, and thereafter helicopters were used for resupply. In consequence de la Billière's troop, which spearheaded the operation, only found recently-abandoned camps in their long pursuit. It was not until the whole swamp had been cordoned off by a large force of police, and the two troops of D Squadron had trapped the terrorists in a rapidly-closing pincer movement, that Ah Hoi, through the medium of a lady emissary, agreed to surrender.

A notable feature of this, and many other operations in Malaya, and later in Borneo, was the skill shown by the patrols in tracking. At the very beginning of the emergency a number of Dyaks from the Iban tribe in Sarawak had been brought to Malaya, and much use was made of their superb fieldcraft. In return for being taught some rudimentary military principles the Sarawak Rangers, as they were called, imparted much of their tracking knowledge to SAS and other troops.

By 1958 the end was in sight, but it had been a huge and costly business in which thousands of troops had been deployed, and thousands of civilians and soldiers killed. Eventually, starved of

---

* Air strikes of any kind in the jungle were generally considered counterproductive, for the risk of killing innocent natives outweighed any damage that the enemy might suffer.

provisions and outfought in the jungle, the bandits became fed up with the hard, unrewarding life and surrendered in droves, or melted quietly away. The SAS had formed only a small part of the vast force committed, and indeed their contribution in number of kills – 108 in eight years – was well below that of many other units, particularly the Gurkhas. But following the precepts laid down by Calvert they had achieved much through their long-range penetration patrols deep into the jungle, where they lived among and encouraged the aborigines, and acquired a great deal of valuable information.

For most of their time in Malaya the SAS had been only a part of the force specifically raised for the emergency. But following the 1957 Army cuts, and the reorganization of regiments that took place the next year, it was decided to include 22 SAS in the permanent Order of Battle, albeit reduced to two squadrons. This was a great milestone in the Regiment's history; but the battle for independence was to continue into the sixties until a determined attempt to incorporate SAS troops into the Parachute Brigade was firmly and finally resisted. Ever since the war the SAS had strongly objected to being regarded as airborne troops forming part of the Army Air Corps in the Corps Warrant.

On its return from Malaya the two remaining squadrons of the regiment (A and D, each of about seventy men and forming four troops) spent much time retraining in the United Kingdom and the United States, for there was no opportunity for active service until, towards the end of 1962, what was euphemistically called the 'confrontation' between Britain and Indonesia broke out.

When in 1949 the Dutch, after much trouble and intermittent fighting, withdrew from their Indonesian empire the charismatic but sinister and rapacious President Sukarno, although unable to govern properly his 100 million subjects who were spread over a thousand islands, quickly developed designs for expansion. His first piece of naked aggression was against the last remaining Dutch foothold in West New Guinea, which he obtained in 1962 together with a large number of well-trained, very willing guerrilla fighters (some being Malays). He next set his sights at attempting to prevent the imminent formation of Malaysia – the Federation of Malaya, Singapore, Sarawak and British North Borneo, which despite Sukarno was formed in 1963, although Singapore seceded two years later. His subversive cells in Malaya and Singapore made only small headway, and it was the revolt in Brunei (which he did not instigate, but may well have encouraged) that decided him to concentrate on Borneo.

Brunei was the original name for the whole, very large island later called Borneo, but at this time applied only to a tiny hereditary sultanate sandwiched between Sarawak and North Borneo (Sabah), both of which, like Brunei, were British dependencies. Two-thirds of the whole island had been Dutch, and was now Indonesian and called Kalimantan. The Brunei revolt, in December 1962, had been the work of an overambitious sheik who had ideas of carving out a territory for himself from the three British protectorates. Guerrilla attacks launched against government offices and strategic buildings were soon crushed by troops rushed across from Singapore, but large numbers of the rebels went to ground in the jungle, and would obviously join forces with another group of potential saboteurs, mostly from Sarawak, known as the Clandestine Communist Organization (CCO). There was obviously going to be trouble from Indonesia in this area, and so the British troops were to remain and Major-General Walter Walker was appointed Director of Operations.

When A Squadron arrived in Brunei in January 1963 the revolt was over, but General Walker was pleased to have them, for their special skills would be invaluable in his almost impossible task of guarding against trouble an area slightly larger than England and Scotland with an open, and in many places unmarked, frontier of 970 miles. For this he had five battalions, one of which was a Royal Marine Commando. The type of country varied from majestic mountains, whose rugged peaks disappeared from sight in lowering clouds, to fertile plateaux and valleys with broad and fast-flowing rivers lapped by swamps, which in the north-east were lined with rivulets giving access to the sea. And most of the land was covered by primary or secondary jungle – the latter supporting dense undergrowth – criss-crossed by numerous jungle tracks leading to hill or riverside villages with their rows of wooden longhouses. People of many different ethnic groups inhabited these wild but beautiful parts of North Borneo, and apart from the CCO most of them were disposed to be friendly.

The frontier with Kalimantan was often ill-defined, but in many places easily crossed either by river, or more usually by tracks across mountain passes or through swampland. It would therefore be no problem for any Indonesian patrol to infiltrate into Sarawak or Sabah, for it was impossible to guard so long a frontier, and cover from air was absolute. The SAS role was very much what it had been in Malaya: small patrols would be spaced at very wide intervals – seldom less than 20 miles – covering the most obvious approaches from Kalimantan, and there they would remain for upwards of three months integrating with the local people, mapping their large area and collating a vast amount of information. The only effective way of establishing a wide intelligence network was to use the natives, for four or five men on their own could do little. To acquire this co-operation, therefore, was of paramount importance and it required much tact, patience and practical demonstrations of goodwill through medical attention and other individual skills a patrol might possess.

Patrols from A Squadron on their first tour were placed along the east coast of Sabah west from Tawau, on the Brunei border and as far distant as the First and Second Divisions of Sarawak* – areas considered to be the most vulnerable. After he had dispatched his patrols Major John Edwardes, the squadron commander, proceeded to visit them, covering the vast distances alone and on foot; a remarkable feat testifying to his high standard of fieldcraft, endurance and good fortune. It had been decided that squadrons should be relieved after a maximum of four months, and A Squadron's first tour, which began in January 1963, was pleasantly peaceful until almost the end of their time. Then on 12 April a platoon of Indonesians carried out a hit-and-run raid on the police station at Tebedu in the First Division. Tebedu was only a mile or two from the border, and had a road leading to it by which armoured cars of the Queen's Royal Irish Hussars could be quickly on the spot, and so A Squadron's 1 Troop, whose area it was, had rightly given it a low priority.

This raid, although insignificant in size and damage done, showed clearly what was to be expected, and General Walker was given more troops and helicopters. The troops were positioned in improvised forts near the border at various vulnerable points, and a number of attempted incursions were speedily broken up; meanwhile the police were busy among the CCO, who were found to have large and active cells in many Sarawak towns. General Walker, a resolute, clear-sighted commander with a keen mind, had taken prompt action with the forces at his disposal; but the long frontier could never be made secure without a much wider intelligence net than could be provided by one SAS squadron. He therefore decided to raise and train a local force to be called Border Scouts.

D Squadron, whose tour lasted from April to August 1963, was taken off patrol work for a time, to share with the Gurkha

* Sarawak was divided into five divisions from the south-west (First) to the north-east (Fifth).

Independent Parachute Company the duty of training the locally-raised levies. Obviously basic weapon handling and tactics were necessary; but the proper role for these excellent tribesmen was the gathering of information, for which their jungle skills and knowledge admirably equipped them, and not as a paramilitary force which was how they were at first used. Given shotguns for protection, and out of uniform, they moved about the jungle in their accustomed style, following close upon the spoor of any Indonesian patrol that ventured into their territory. Before the end of D Squadron's tour Border Scouts were working with their patrols. A year later about forty of them were selected for cross-border operations under Major Muir Walker, and they were to prove themselves bonny fighters.*

When not employed in training the Border Souts, men of D Squadron resumed their long-range patrols, border surveillance and intelligence work. Usually these patrols were of only three or four men, but occasionally they were enlarged to include Ibans and/or members of the local tribes such as the Muruts, part of whose territory embraced the virtually-unexplored strip of the southern border of Sabah, known as The Gap. One such patrol with Captain Dennison and Sergeant Lillico spent six weeks taking a close look at this wild piece of country, with its towering mountains forming a backdrop to the many unmapped streams and gullies. Navigation through the dense jungle had to be by compass, and the constant encountering of impenetrable barriers meant that bearings needed to be frequently checked and adjusted. A degree of accuracy was very necessary if only to assist the resupply aircraft, for there were no villages nor human beings – only the eldritch cries from the denizens of the jungle and the frequent profanities from the patrol disturbed the Arcadian peace.

In the late summer of 1963 the Federation of Malaysia came into existence; only the Sultan of Brunei of the Northern Borneo states chose to retain his as a British Protectorate, but he was wholeheartedly co-operative against any form of subversion. He put at General Walker's disposal two houses near his palace, one of which (known as the Haunted House through its association with the spirit of a European lady murdered by the Japanese) became the SAS headquarters, and was a useful communications and rest centre for patrols out of the jungle. Sukarno was enraged by the

* Their return from ambush duty with the occasional head no doubt pleasantly revived atavistic memories, but was a trifle embarrassing to their British instructors.

formation of the Federation, and put Indonesia on a war footing. This meant more troops for Walker, who was thus able to cover the ground more adequately and, since despite Sukarno's repeated gasconades nothing serious occurred, there was talk of withdrawing the SAS. But then, shortly before the end of D Squadron's tour in August, the Indonesians launched their first large-scale offensive against Song, some 40 miles into the Third Division of Sarawak.

This raid was quickly broken up by the Gurkhas, who killed or captured many of the enemy before they reached their objective; but it was not long before others were mounted. In September at Long Jawi, also in the Third Division, and which had recently been abandoned by an SAS patrol, 150 Indonesians had some success when they surprised six men of the Goorkha Rifles and 21 Border Scouts. This was followed three months later by an attack on the Royal Malay Regiment's base at Kalabakan in east Sabah. The Malays suffered grievously, but the enemy were eventually accounted for by men of the 1/10 Gurkhas, and some of them were identified as Indonesian Marines. There was no longer any thought of the SAS being released; indeed General Walker would have liked a second squadron, for he badly needed information about the enemy's crossing points, river patrols and assembly areas.

Soon after D Squadron returned for its second tour in December, what had been a somewhat insensate economy was put to rights when the Ministry of Defence approved in principle the restoration of the two SAS squadrons that had been disbanded after Malaya. The new B Squadron had to be raised and trained to readiness for operations in less than a year. The pursuit of excellence is never easy, but neither Colonel Woodhouse nor Major Watts, who had been selected to command the squadron, was prepared to accept anything less. Volunteers were plentiful, but as usual the majority failed to survive the selection and training courses. And those that did had a lamentably short time in which to be crammed in the many crafts and skills that go to make up a fully qualified SAS man. However, helped by a stiffening of experienced NCOs from A and D Squadrons, and constantly encouraged by his commanding officer, Watts had the Squadron ready for departure for Brunei by early October 1964, where by day and night they perfected their jungle training.

There was, of course, no hope of raising a fourth squadron at that time, and the Guards Independent Parachute Company, under Major L.G.S. Head, was sent to Borneo to perform duties similar to those of the SAS. They proved themselves so adept at this type of work that in 1966 a Guards squadron – G Squadron, 22 SAS – was formed.

By the time B Squadron commenced their first tour in November 1964 General Walker had received permission from London to extend operations across the border. These were codenamed Claret, and they needed to be regulated with extreme caution, for despite public announcements and gages given by Sukarno that he would crush Malaysia by the beginning of 1965, Britain was not officially at war with Indonesia.

Cross-border patrols were intended to halt 'confrontation' before it became war by making Indonesian penetration too costly in lives for any purposeful gain. Parties of the enemy would be ambushed along jungle tracks, or on the rivers, and their forward bases destroyed – initial penetration was to be only 3,000 yards, although it was later extended to 10,000. These operations of inroad and foray were to be carefully planned and rehearsed, and only troops well versed in jungle warfare were to take part. Before withdrawal all traces of British presence were to be painstakingly removed; if the Indonesians suffered reverses – and they did fairly consistently – Sukarno was unlikely to publicize the raids.

In these cross-border operations SAS personnel were used to spring ambushes along jungle tracks – often using the Claymore mine, a devilish device that exploded 900 steel balls up and down the track – to intercept enemy craft on the rivers, and to act as guides to larger formations entering enemy territory. They were particularly well suited for this latter role because, some months previous to the commencement of Claret, Woodhouse had advocated the use of four-man patrols in cross-border reconnaissance work. When a little later his suggestion was acted upon a great deal of useful information was gained on the location and extent of enemy bases, the river routes used, the type of boats and number of men in them; and maps were made indicating suitable ambush points.

On these hazardous deep-penetration patrols into enemy country the men had to travel light. Their only weapon was the Armalite 5.56 mm light automatic rifle (not a standard issue in the British Army, but powerful, portable and well suited to the jungle); and the weight of their bergen rucksacks was reduced to 30 lb. Once the helicopter had dropped them at the jungle entry point they were on their own, for there was no chance of resupply and not much scope for evacuating wounded – although this was accomplished occasionally by helicopter.

If a man was killed he had to be stripped of identification and hastily buried; if he was wounded, or went down with one of the many jungle diseases, he usually had to march or crawl – as in the case of Trooper Thomson with a shattered thigh and Sergeant Lillico with both legs out of action – for long distances before being rescued. It was not often that these highly-skilled SAS patrols were ambushed, but in the jungle the mobile hunter is always at a disadvantage. It was even less often that a man got killed by a wild animal, but an elephant did account for an Australian SAS trooper.*

Squadrons succeeded each other – although after the formation of B at slightly longer intervals – until in the summer of 1966 a peace mission headed by Colonel Moerdani of the Indonesian Parachute Regiment, who had narrowly escaped being killed in an SAS ambush when on river patrol, visited Kuala Lumpur. Shortly afterwards, in August, peace was declared with the egregious Sukarno being replaced by General Suharto.

During their latter tours when the number of Indonesian incursions had reached a high level the squadrons, whose men had by now become superb jungle craftsmen, sent out constant patrols to survey, seek out and slay Indonesians and their Communist allies bent on bringing down the Federation. In between tours there would be periods of rest in England, and desert training in South Arabia – indeed in April 1964 A Squadron was involved in a brief Radfan operation, which will be touched upon in the next chapter.

The 'confrontation' had lasted three and a half years. The British and Commonwealth casualties were just under 300, as opposed to known Indonesian ones of 800. The SAS, whose squadrons did a total of nine four-month tours, and whose men were constantly exposed to the perils of the jungle and the proximity of the foe, had only three men killed and two wounded.

Before the end of the campaign – indeed only a little more than halfway through it – there occurred two changes in command both of significance to the SAS. In January 1965 Colonel Woodhouse left the Army, and his place in command of 22 SAS was taken by Lt-Colonel Michael Wingate-Gray. Woodhouse had been pre-eminent in getting the SAS into the action, and his deep understanding of guerrilla warfare coupled with his immense personal force made him an outstanding commanding officer.

* New Zealand and Australian SAS squadrons were operating in Borneo from April and May 1965 respectively.

In March of the same year Major-General George Lea, a former SAS commander from Malaya days, succeeded General Walker. The latter, whose concern for his beloved Gurkhas had possibly hastened his departure, was a great admirer of the SAS and in particular of their professional performance in Borneo. They in their turn lamented his going, the more especially that he should go unhonoured and – until much later – unrewarded for his magnificent work. He has the distinction of being the only general who is an honorary member of the SAS.

18

The Special Air Service: South Arabia, 1958–1976

In the course of SAS operations in Malaya, and later in Borneo, there were two brief interruptions during which a squadron was engaged in fighting – as opposed to training – in South Arabia. The first occurred in 1958, and the second in 1964.

The area of these operations was the Sultanate of Muscat and Oman – an independent state ruled by the Sultan and having long-standing treaties of friendship and co-operation with Britain – and the Aden Protectorate. Oman, the largest state in the Persian Gulf, is approximately the size of England and Scotland with a population then of not much over half a million. It is of great stategic importance to the West because, situated on the south-east corner of the Arabian peninsula, with its northern point commanding the Hormuz Strait, it controls the corridor through which flows much of the non–Communist oil.

The topography of the Sultanate varies considerably. In the north, where the boundary was then with the Trucial Oman States (now the United Arab Emirates), there is a formidable mountain range running north-east to south-west, with the 10,000-ft Jebel Akhdar (Green Mountain) the highest point; in the west the desert of Oman borders that of the Rub al Khali (the Empty Quarter); the coastline of almost 1,000 miles has a flat plain up to 10 miles wide in places; in the south-west is the province of Dhofar, separated from northern Oman by 400 miles of desert, whose people have a different cultural and social background from the Arabs and Baluchis of the north. The climate is one of extremes: on the coastal plain the temperature at night can be well over 100 degrees Fahrenheit, while in the mountains it can drop so quickly as to freeze the water in a soldier's water-bottle – and always in the mountains there is a wind. Predominantly Oman is a harsh land, but there are fertile areas.

The origin of the trouble which brought D Squadron of the SAS hurrying from Malaya in November 1958 went back a long way, but more immediately to 1952. In that year the Saudis occupied the Buraimi oasis, a fruitful and strategically-valuable tract of land on the Abu Dhabi border, and partly owned by the Sultan of Oman. It was three years before they were evicted, and by then they had spent a lot of time and money undermining the Sultan's authority.

Oman is fruitful ground for subversion; it has had a blood-thirsty and turbulent history with piracy and land grabbing from without, and tribal rebellion from within. Murders and acts of treachery have left their curse and vendetta behind – and many of these have been connected with the Imams. These spiritual heads of the country have not always been good and pious men; the Sultan's authority has frequently been challenged by the Imam of the day, as it was in the mid-fifties.

By the time the Saudis had been expelled from Buraimi the old Imam, a friend of the Sultan's, had died and the new one, Ghalib bin Ali, was very much influenced by the Saudis. He himself was a weak man, but he had an extremely strong, intelligent and ambitious brother, Talib, and the two of them lost no time in engaging in active opposition to the Sultan. Moreover, they enlisted two important allies in Suleiman bin Himyar, Lord of the Jebel Akhdar, and the powerful Sheikh Salih bin Isa. In 1955 the Imam, backed by the Saudis, was in dispute with the Sultan over oil rights, and the Sultan settled the matter in December with his British-officered Muscat and Oman Field Force. Ghalib abdicated, Talib escaped to Saudi Arabia, and the Lord of the Green Mountain gave insincere gages of loyalty and retired to the top of his mountain.

But in little over a year the principals were together again; and Talib was now at the head of a strong band of guerrillas whom he had trained with Saudi instructors while in exile. The brothers raised the standard of revolt, and aided by Sheikh Suleiman completely destroyed the Muscat and Oman Field Force. At this juncture the Sultan requested British aid, which was immediately forthcoming, and a company of the Cameronians and the Trucial Oman Scouts, aided by the RAF, recaptured the Imam's base at Nizwa and drove the rebels up the Jebel Akhdar, which was the best such a small force could achieve.

In 1958 the British government agreed to provide assistance

towards the reorganization of the Sultan's army, and in the early summer Colonel D. de C. Smiley, who had commanded the Blues, arrived in Muscat as Chief of Staff to the Sultan and in command of the Sultan's Armed Forces (SAF). He did not have many troops at his disposal: the Northern Frontier Regiment with 450 men was the backbone of the army, and the British component amounted to a troop of the 13/18th Hussars, with a brigade major and detachment of Royal Signals at headquarters. Periodically squadrons of the Trucial Oman Scouts were available.

It did not take Smiley long to appreciate that this small force was totally inadequate to dislodge the powerful band of rebels from their seemingly-impregnable mountain refuge, unconquered since remote antiquity. Moreover, they were not sitting placidly on the mountain plateau, but were causing serious vehicle and personnel casualties by the mining of roads and tracks. The Royal Air Force from Aden gave assistance with Shackleton bombers and Venom fighters (for at that time the Sultan's air force had just two single-engined machines), but bombing and strafing alone would not be sufficient. More British troops were needed. Smiley asked for two battalions, of which one should be a Royal Marine Commando, a Parachute battalion, or an SAS squadron. He was eventually given D Squadron of the Life Guards and D Squadron SAS.

In October 1958 Lt-Colonel Anthony Deane-Drummond was in command of 22 SAS and, having confirmed from a quick reconnaissance in Oman that this was SAS work, he had been given fifteen days in which to extract D Squadron from the jungles of the Malaya/Thailand border and transport them to Oman. Somehow, by helicopter, marches, and rafts, the Squadron covered the 250 miles back to Kuala Lumpur in forty-eight hours. There then followed an intensive programme of training and reorganizing. In the jungle snap shooting at fleeting targets with sawn-off shotguns or FN (Fabrique Nationale) rifles was the formula, and a fight lasted only minutes. In desert conditions, with target visibility often up to 2,000 yards, it could last hours or days, and 3 in. mortars, rocket launchers, energa grenades* and Brens would be needed.

The highest peaks of the Jebel Akhdar rise to over 8,000 ft, and at 6,000 ft there is a broad and fertile plateau 20 miles by 10, on which there are villages whose houses and crops then accommo-

---

* These were ballistic grenades fired from a rifle, *à la* mortar, to damage tanks. They were not very effective.

dated and fed the 600 or so rebels. There are also caves where they could shelter during air strikes. The steep approaches through narrow ravines were easily guarded, although some were considered by the rebels to be impassable. Daylight movement on the side of the mountain was impossible, for the enemy were alert, well armed with modern weapons and extremely good shots.

D Squadron, under Major Watts, arrived on 18 November, and four days later they commenced their first patrolling and probing. It was to be seven weeks before they could rest from their labours. Shortly before their arrival a patrol of the Muscat Regiment, led by Major Tony Hart, had discovered an unguarded route to the plateau, and while two SAS troops led by Captain Walker carried out fighting patrols on the southern side of the mountain – during which they lost a good corporal from a sniper's bullet – the other two accompanied Hart for a lodgement on the plateau. Walker and his men gained the plateau undiscovered, but came under attack from rebel strongpoints near a feature known as the Aqbat al Dhafar. The enemy although mauled could not be defeated, and the troops occupied sangar positions on the plateau, from which they operated patrols during December.

Meanwhile, on the south side of the Jebel in the Tanuf area the Life Guards (fighting stoutly in an unaccustomed infantry role) together with the Northern Frontier Regiment had a fierce battle, and the SAS troops, supported by Venoms, attacked a cave and killed a number of rebels. Life on the Jebel was extremely tough, with freezing temperatures and a bitterly cold wind by night, and the men pinned down by snipers in the hot daylight hours. Supply was by parachute, and not always reliable. On 27 December Walker's two troops carried out a strong night attack on the Aqbat position, with covering fire provided by the Life Guards. Having scaled the steep cliffs with ropes they engaged the rebels in hand-to-hand grapple inflicting casualties, but failing to break the fortitude and furious resolve of the embattled tribesmen.

Smiley, who was in overall command of all the troops, clearly saw the need for another SAS squadron, with which Deane-Drummond readily agreed. On 12 January Major Cooper's A Squadron arrived from Malaya, and it was not long before they were sent to relieve D Squadron, whose men were in need of a short rest – and incidentally of new boots, for the sharp rocks of the Jebel had played havoc with their special SAS ones.

Colonels Smiley and Deane-Drummond made many low flights over the Jebel, and from what they saw prepared their plan for the final eviction of the rebels. Like all good plans it was a simple one, based mainly on surprise through diversion and deception. In broad outline there was to be a feint against the Aqbat al Dhafar which the enemy, expecting the attack to be made there, had reinforced. The main attack would go in from the Wadi Kamah, in the south, against the rebel strongholds in the Habib–Sharaijah area. Deane-Drummond had selected a likely-looking slope leading out of the wadi, which the pack animals could ascend even though there was no track.

This latter was important, for if the weather in the morning prevented flying the recently-imported Somaliland donkeys were the only means of resupply. On the night before the assault the head donkey wallahs were told in strictest confidence, with dire penalties for disclosure, that they were to lead their donkeys the next night up the Tanuf track – some 6 or 7 miles from the selected approach. It was learnt later that within twelve hours the rebels had this information. The poor little desert donkeys were to find the unaccustomed steep slope altogether too much for them, but their part in the deception, and the need to replace their loads by a parachute drop, contributed greatly to the success of the operation.

The feint against the Aqbat position was successful after two hours' close-quarters fighting, and A Squadron, less one troop, then made a forced march over very difficult country to join D ready for the attack on the night of 26 January. The march started at 8.30 p.m. with the SAS squadrons leading a troop of the Life Guards. The deception had been complete: only one picket remained to guard the chosen route, and this post was easily winkled out. The climb was extremely stiff, and to ensure that the plateau was reached before first light the leading troops dropped their bergens and scrambled up with only their rifles. But there was no resistance; the enemy had been outwitted. When they saw the resupply parachutes descending they mistook the canisters for men, and made the best haste they could to disappear. The arsenal they left to be captured was well stocked with most forms of modern weapons. The SAS lost two men when unluckily a sniper's bullet hit an energa grenade in one of the men's packs.

The next time that SAS troops were operational in South Arabia was in April 1964, following the declaration of an emergency by the Federal government (in 1963 Aden had joined the Federation of South Arabia, which included several of the British-protected tribal states in the hinterland of Aden) in December 1963. The long and turbulent story which ended the British connection with Aden in 1967 cannot be told here. Many books have been written on the subject, and for SAS readers it has been neatly summed up by Tony Geraghty.*

Briefly, one of the immediate causes of trouble was the Egyptian-inspired revolt in the Yemen in September 1962, which overthrew the hereditary Imam and replaced him with a Republican regime that Britain did not recognize. There had for a long time been Yemeni claims to the Aden Protectorate and to Aden itself, and there was a strong pro-Yemeni faction in Aden led by the head of the trade unions. A year later, in December 1963, there was a bomb attack against the High Commissioner and Federal ministers at Aden airport, whereupon the Federal government closed the frontier with Yemen and declared a state of emergency. The insurgency pot was well stirred by Nasser with his venomous and tendentious radio propaganda, and Russia wasted no time in backing Egypt, which sent a formidable army into the Yemen.

The situation developed into a colonial-type war, fought vicariously by Egypt and Russia on the one side and Britain and the Arab monarchies on the other. A number of retired British soldiers, including Colonel Smiley and some ex-SAS men, took service as mercenaries with the Royalist Yemeni army under the Imam (who had escaped assassination), and fought with distinction over a period of almost eight years until at last, in 1969, a compromise peace was arranged by Saudi Arabia's King Faisal. But that was in the future; in 1964 the British and the Federation found themselves engaged in two very different types of campaign – a tribal uprising in the Radfan mountains of the Aden Protectorate, and urban guerrilla acts of terrorism in Aden State.

The five principal Radfan tribes could probably muster about 6,000 fighting men, all of them fine shots and good guerrilla potential. They were people who had lived very backward lives in great poverty, and they were therefore extremely susceptible to Egyptian promises of gold, weapons and ammunition in return for causing the maximum inconvenience to the Federation, and through it to the British. They started to cause trouble on the flimsy pretext that their lucrative customs trade – levied on caravans passing through their territory – had been stopped, and the Federation decided to take military action to uphold law and order.

Accordingly an operation was launched at the beginning of January 1964 using three battalions of the Federal Regular Army, a troop of the 16/5th Lancers and some Gunners and Sappers. The

* *Who Dares Wins*, pp.63–85.

operation was merely a demonstration in force to drive out a number of dissidents and show the tribesmen that the Federal government had the ability to enter the Radfan. It was entirely successful, but it merely sparked off more trouble with the Egyptian-backed Yemeni Republic, which stepped up its propaganda and actively encouraged rebellion. It was therefore decided to launch another, larger operation; and the Federation, under the terms of the Defence Treaty, requested the help of British troops.

A strong force of brigade strength, called Radforce, supported by the RAF, was to operate against the Radfan tribes to reassert authority and to stop various aggressive incidents. An intended short, sharp lesson that was to last about three weeks in fact stretched to three months before it was successfully concluded. The SAS was only concerned in a small part of it. Its A Squadron was due to carry out training in the Aden area – between Borneo tours – during May and June 1964, and the commander, Major de la Billière, who was there making preparations, suggested bringing the Squadron over early in order to take part in the operation.

This was agreed, and the Squadron – together with elements of Headquarters to make it self-supporting – flew from England in time for the planned brigade operation against some three to four thousand dissident tribesmen. By the time the Squadron arrived at Thumier in the Radfan mountains preliminary positions round the valley had already been taken up by infantry and Commando battalions, and the Squadron's pre-attack acclimatization took the form of long-distance patrols by night on the flanks of the infantry positions.

The plan was for Radforce to seize certain areas and tactical features so as to break up rebel strongholds. This was to be done through the capture of the prominent feature codenamed Cap Badge, and another known as Rice Bowl in the western half of the valley. There were to be four phases, and in phase three 22 SAS was to mark out a dropping zone for the 3rd Parachute Battalion on the night of 30 April/1 May. The task was given to a patrol of nine men under Captain Robin Edwards, and as they had a very long approach march up a wadi before reaching the forward defence lines they set off in armoured cars. However, the terrain did not permit the vehicles to get very far, and the patrol dismounted early in the evening of 29 April with about 8 miles of very steep going still to cover on foot. It was hoped they would reach their objective before first light and lie concealed until nightfall. However, the pace was slowed by one man who was unwell, and the party was short of its objective at dawn; but they were fortunate in finding two caves, or cracks in the rock, with sangars piled in front, which as part of the scenery should not attract unwelcome attention. Edwards reckoned that the comparatively easy remaining 3 miles to the projected DZ could be covered quite quickly at dusk.

Lying up in enemy territory is a most unrelaxing pastime, especially when there is little or no protection from the scorching sun, and movement of any kind is fraught with danger. It was therefore particularly galling that having obeyed all the rules, and endured several hours of suspense in sweltering heat, the patrol should have been discovered by the unlucky chance of a passing herdsman, who raised the alarm. In next to no time tribesmen were in action, and soon the patrol was surrounded at pretty close quarters. Edwards requested air support, and a close wireless link, via Squadron Headquarters, with the Brigade Air Support Officer ensured almost continuous strafing by Hunter aircraft throughout the day. This kept enemy heads down to a great extent; nevertheless in the constant sniping exchanges two men were hit, and towards the end of the day when the enemy attempted to close in the troop signaller was killed.

Towards evening a heat haze put an end to air support, and Edwards had an urgent wireless conversation with the commander of 22 SAS (Lt-Colonel Michael Wingate-Gray) who was at Squadron Headquarters. With two men wounded and a shortage of ammunition and water there was now no chance of completing the mission, and Wingate-Gray ordered Edwards to break out. It was a near-hopeless situation in the face of tremendous odds, but it was achieved with considerable skill, the tribesmen being kept at bay by accurate covering fire – the patrol had one Bren – but soon after leaving the sangars Edwards was killed. Throughout the night the party, obviously tired and dispirited, wound their way over extremely rough and difficult going – a great ordeal for one man, badly wounded in the leg. An artillery stonk had discouraged pursuit, but three or four tribesmen caught up with the party, only to be expertly dealt with through a hastily-improvised ambush. An hour or two after first light on 1 May the seven survivors eventually reached safety.

A second attempt was made by another troop to mark out the DZ. But the enemy in that area were now fully alert, and the helicopters carrying the troop were badly shot up and forced to return. The parachute drop was then cancelled, and the Radforce plan adjusted accordingly. There was a bizarre and unhappy sequel to this affair, when a propaganda broadcast from the

Yemen announced that the heads of Captain Edwards and Trooper Warburton had been displayed on the walls of Sana – which was later confirmed through discovery of the decapitated bodies.

Not long afterwards A Squadron returned to England as planned, but it and other squadrons would soon be back in the Federation carrying out very realistic training. The exemplary chastisement meted out in the Radfan campaign kept the rebel tribesmen from venturing anything on a large scale – until the British departure three years later, when they partook in the general upheaval to bring the Federation down – but they took every opportunity to carry out guerrilla warfare. Clashes were frequent and casualties quite high.

SAS patrols had a variety of tasks, laid down by Headquarters, Middle East, in both the Radfan and the Aden hinterland. These included the establishment of cleverly-concealed forward observation posts from which they could direct artillery fire and air strikes on parties of the enemy, and the interception of arms and supplies being sent to the Aden city revolutionaries. This latter involved long-distance patrolling, and ambushing routes from the North Yemen border. The extreme heat and shortage of water in the barren, ridge-backed Radfan mountains made this gruelling work, and some may have envied their colleagues the more arcane, although equally dangerous, duties in Aden State.

Terrorism had begun there in late 1963, shortly after the British government had announced their intention of pulling out not later than 1968. There was no longer much reason for the local Arabs to show any great loyalty to people who would soon be unable to protect them, and Egypt was not slow to point out the wisdom of hastening the departure of the 'oppressors'. The Egyptian-sponsored National Liberation Front proved a very successful terrorist organization, infiltrating its members into many influential posts from where they carried out acts of intimidation, assassination and some indiscriminate grenade throwing.

The SAS role was mainly an undercover one in the rat-ridden, adulterated alleys of Aden. From a central headquarters about twenty specially picked men, whose features most lent themselves to the impersonation of natives, would split into parties of two or three and infiltrate into districts of the Crater and Sheikh Othman, where the hard-core terrorists were most active. Military intelligence was important and very scarce, so even the occasional arrest and subsequent successful interrogation was of great value. SAS men occasionally brought off an important arrest, or outgunned some evilly-disposed thugs, but on the whole not very much was accomplished in this their first attempt at undercover operations; although lessons learnt in training and in action were to prove useful in the future.

The longest, most important and most fruitful work that the SAS was to do in South Arabia resulted from their presence throughout the Dhofar war, which lasted (as far as the SAS were concerned) from 1970 until 1976. The province of Dhofar lies at the south end of Oman, and is about the size of Wales. Its inhabitants are of different stock from the northern Arabs, and for the most part live a hard life on the jebel massif, which runs parallel to the sea, forming a backdrop to the coastal plain which in some places, such as Salalah, is very narrow. The jebel rises steeply behind the plain to form a plateau at some 3,000 ft. From June to September it is washed by the south-west monsoon (*khareef*), and the plateau is pleasantly lush. But as water becomes scarce in the dry months the *jebelis* abandon their dwellings for the caves of the deep wadis that scar the mountain side. Water is the key to life on the jebel, and the jebel was at that time the key to life in Dhofar.

The regime of Sultan Said bin Taimur was medieval in concept and totally lacking in any form of progress. There was great poverty and much disease, no hospitals and no education – many sought this elsewhere, sometimes in Russia – and inhuman punishments were meted out for any transgression of the Sultan's word, which was law. And yet Said was not entirely bad; he was a well-educated, courteous but misguided man who thought to solve his country's problems by isolation and autocratic policies. Instead he sowed the seeds of rebellion, which first broke out, in a minor way, in 1962. The repressive punitive measures that followed only made matters worse, and the rebels formed a political party – the Dhofar Liberation Front, which later became the People's Front for the Liberation of the Arabian Gulf – which was quickly backed by the recently formed People's Democratic Republic of the Yemen (PDRY), by the Russians and, until 1972, by the Chinese.

From these and other sources the rebels received arms and financial support, and Oman was rapidly clattering into anarchy. Something had to be done to lift the Sultan's affairs out of the catalepsy by which they were afflicted, and the Sultan's son did just that by lifting the Sultan out of his palace in an almost bloodless *coup d'état* on 23 July 1970. The new Sultan, Qaboos, was then twenty-nine years of age, he had been educated at Sandhurst and had very different ideas from his father. He at once declared an amnesty, and launched plans for development in every department. The amnesty brought a number of the rebels, who had become fed up with Communist atrocities and ideology, back to their allegiance, but it had little effect on the many hard-liners, and the PDRY doubled its efforts at coercion.

Sultan Qaboos realized, and so did the British commander of the Sultan's Armed Forces, that his troops were not sufficiently well equipped nor trained to drive the rebels from the jebel and to occupy it permanently themselves. He therefore sought help from Britain and later from Iran, Jordan, India and Pakistan. The response was good, for it was in everyone's interest to ensure that Oman did not fall into the hands of an unfriendly power – but it was always understood that the war was the Sultan's and foreign troops acted only under his overall command while in Dhofar. Military hardware of every kind was one requirement, but equally important was the need to win the 'hearts and minds' of the *jebelis*, and to improve the lot – medically, educationally and nutritionally – of the entire population. Lt-Colonel Watts, then commanding 22 SAS, was sent to Oman to make a report. The subsequent fulfilment of his recommendations has been brilliantly described by Colonel A.S. Jeaps in his book *SAS: Operation Oman*.

Civil and military aid could be only on a temporary basis with a view to bringing immediate relief while the Omanis themselves were being trained to take over. With this in mind Watts stressed the need for five immediate requirements, all of which the SAS with their varied skills were well able to give. They were medical assistance, intelligence gathering, information dissemination (not mindless propaganda, but the simple truth and only the truth), veterinary aid – for the Dhofaris placed great store on their live-stock – and the training of tribesmen willing to fight the rebels.

At first all that the SAS were permitted to send was a totally inadequate party of nineteen men, but in February 1971 the first full squadron arrived; thereafter throughout the war squadrons did, as in Borneo, four-monthly tours, and on one occasion Colonel Watts had two squadrons in Dhofar. The initial party, under Captain Shaw, which came into Dhofar under the official designation British Army Training Team (BATT), although small, rapidly made its presence felt. It included a medical and veterinary officer, and Shaw soon arranged for two four-man Civil Action Teams to set up clinics in Taqa and Mirbat, two towns on the coast east of Salalah.*

---

* Because of Sultan Said's almost permanent residence in Salalah it had become in recent years more the capital of Oman than the official capital, Muscat.

These small Civil Action Teams were an extremely important feature of the SAS work in Dhofar. They always included a medic and at least one Arabic speaker; they travelled by Land-Rover* and at each village they visited they immediately established a clinic, and did what they could for the large number of people suffering from every form of medical neglect. Their reports on the food and water conditions in the areas where the fighting had receded were of value to the government's Civil Aid Department (CAD), which would arrange food distribution, drill wells and improve educational facilities. There was a lot to be done (and even more in the early days before the CAD was set up), and the veterinary officer had an equally stern task, for the tribesmen's animals were, if anything, in a worse state than the tribesmen themselves.

But the greatest contribution of the SAS to the Sultan's ultimate victory was their work with those fierce bands of paramilitary men which were known as the *firqats*. They were mostly made up from surrendered enemy who were carefully screened, given a short period to think things over and then invited to join their tribal *firqat*. They were a hard, wild, unpredictable lot wrought by a lifetime of fighting, but their knowledge of the ground, and the snowballing effect their successes had, made them an invaluable part of the SAF – even if they did not always see eye to eye with the Omani soldiers. Starting in a fairly humble way, their numbers grew almost weekly and by 1975 there were twenty-one *firqats* widely dispersed and totalling about 1,600 men. There was a headquarters for Firqat Forces, commanded by Lt-Colonel McLean, which had the difficult task of undertaking overall administration.

The *Firqat Salahadin* was the first to be raised by the SAS/BATT, under its bold, charismatic fugleman, Salim Mubarak. Discipline was always something of a problem and Salim Mubarak thought that it would be easier to enforce in a multi-tribal *firqat*, which would avoid the tribal passion for equality. But it did not prove a success and the system was not continued, all subsequent *firqats* being tribal. No virtue was more necessary than patience in trying to organize, train and equip these enthusiastic, temperamental tribesmen, and the small SAS teams in the difficult role of advisers, not commanders, did a magnificent job.

Often, in the first instance, tribal problems would have to be

---

* Land-Rovers were essential, for travel on the few Dhofari roads was made virtually impossible by rebel mines.

sorted out, and then there would be arguments over weapons. The general idea was to replace the .303 rifles with the more modern FN which was an SAF issue, but the tribesmen wanted the lighter, fully automatic, Russian-made Kalashnikov (AK 47). They were told that the only way they could get one of those was off the enemy. Once the training phase was over the intention was to establish the *firqat*, with the aid of SAF personnel, in their tribal area, and BATT would accompany them on operations to clear that area. Then the Civil Action Teams would take over to organize the social services before the area was handed over to Firqat Forces. BATT was then free to start work raising another *firqat*.

Training and administration of the *firqats* was the primary role – hence the official BATT title – but the SAS are fighting troops and were not to be kept out of the battle. There was plenty of fighting for everyone, either with the *firqats* or occasionally when the enemy would take on, or be taken on by, small parties of SAS operating on their own. It must not be thought that in this war the SAF were fighting badly-trained, poorly-armed bands of tribesmen. The enemy in fact had an arsenal superior to that of the Sultan's troops in the early days of the war. The hard-core fighting men of the Front all carried the AK 47 fully automatic rifle, which they handled with considerable skill and accuracy. Also from Russia came the anti-tank weapon (RPG 7), and various other types of rocket launchers (75 and 82 mm, and the large 122 mm Katyushka which had a range of 7 miles), while the Chinese contributed the 60 and 82 mm mortars. Besides the mortars there were light and heavy machine guns, and so the enemy firepower was very considerable.

A seaborne venture to clear the town of Sudh with the *Firqat Salahadin* and two troops of SAS met no opposition, but some valuable lessons were learnt before the next and more serious operation on the jebel, which is where the war would be won or lost. The highest ground in the Eastern Area was the Eagle's Nest, from where the enemy could overlook the town of Mirbat. A small SAS patrol with six *firqat* men carried out a reconnaissance; it was an exceptionally steep climb to the summit, and the patrol could not achieve it in one night, but concealing themselves by day they were on the top the next night to find it unoccupied. Not long afterwards two SAS troops and sixty men of the *Firqat Salahadin* made the ascent, and prepared to stay there for several days with resupply by helicopter.

When after three days the enemy had not attacked, and water

was short, the force threw out pickets and moved down off the high ground in column to lusher country, where enemy posts were known to be situated. Before long the rebels engaged with desultory small-arms fire, and the SAS commander felt it safe to call for mortars and ammunition to be flown in. But the helicopter had no sooner gone than the position was subjected to intense and accurate mortar fire. After a few days of this the enemy closed in, and thirty-five *firqat* trainees from Mirbat were hastily despatched as reinforcements. Helicopter supply was now impossible and it was too dangerous to attempt more than one parachute drop.

Water was, as always scarce. The hillside had been burnt black by the mortar bombing, and both SAS and *firqat* were desperately short of sleep and sustenance. The force was therefore withdrawn, after what had been a most satisfactory initiation for the *firqat*. They had killed at least nine of the enemy without loss to themselves, and the fact that they had successfully engaged the foe on their own ground soon became common knowledge and greatly encouraged would-be dissidents.

This was the pattern for many SAS-*firqat* operations, but they very often had to end, however satisfactory the result of the action, in withdrawal, and this inevitably had an adverse effect on the *jebeli* civilians. But larger operations were mounted with a more permanent object; and one such to seize and occupy a firm base on the jebel brought out the difficulties SAS and SAF commanders could have with some of the more froward *firqat* men.

In October 1971 a comparatively large force of some 800 men which included two SAS squadrons, two strong SAF companies and 300 men from five *firqats*, all under command of Colonel Watts, were to seize a former SAF airstrip near Jibjat in that piece of land between the jebel and the desert called the *negd*. Ramadan was about to begin when Muslim troops, in a flaccid state, are never at their best, but dispensation was granted by the religious leaders and the Sultan.

There was no hope of secrecy with the assembly of so large a body of men, and so a careful deception plan was mounted in the south to keep the enemy guessing, while one part of the main body carried out a most arduous march over the jebel, and the other – with the heavy guns – was airlifted. The airstrip was taken but found to be breaking up under the weight of traffic, and so Watts decided on a move westwards to Jibjat. One *firqat* flatly refused to move, although later the men did consent to join in the battle, which succeeded in clearing the enemy off the plateau and into the wadis. However the important position thus won had to be abandoned when no less than three *firqats* decided they would, despite the dispensation, observe Ramadan.

They returned to their duty after the end of the fast, and in the meantime their more reasonable colleagues continued to engage the enemy, who had counter-attacked with spirit. In the end, after a lot of hard fighting, the operation was entirely successful, but not before the *firqats* had again proved contumacious and issued a threat to the government – some individuals even disbanded – that unless the latter took immediate steps to bring their animals off the jebel and provide a market they could see no reason to continue the battle. A spectacular rodeo resulted with the cattle being shepherded off the hill by the Sultan of Oman's Air Force (SOAF). This accomplishment was in fact a psychological blow to the enemy, but the whole affair serves to show that operations with the *firqats* could be vitiated by calculated contrariness.

Probably the fiercest fight a BATT team was engaged in during the six-year war occurred at Mirbat on 19 July 1972. On that morning eight men of B Squadron, under Captain M.J.A. Kealy, some 30 poorly-armed askaris (African soldiers), and 25 Dhofari Gendarmerie were surprised in a carefully-planned dawn attack by about 250 proven warriors, armed with automatic rifles, festooned with grenades, and supported by mortars, machine guns and rocket launchers. Against them there was one rather ancient 25-pounder, a .50 Browning and an 81 mm mortar in the BATT compound.

A wire perimeter surrounded the three inland sides of Mirbat town, and inside the north-east end of it stood the Gendarmerie fort with the gun pit close by; about 800 yards north of the wire there was a small and very exposed Gendarmerie picket. The BATT Headquarters house was some 400 yards south-west of the fort. The rebels made short work of the outpost, and then proceeded to launch a well-disciplined fire-and-movement attack against the fort. They were confident of a numerical advantage, for they had previously decoyed a strong *firqat* patrol into the jebel.

As the first shell thundered into the compound Kealy awoke from sleep. The trial of a young commander had begun, when everything depended upon his ability to keep his head. From the top of the BATT house it was difficult at first to assess the size and nature of the attack. But soon it was all too clear, as tiny white spots of rifle fire began to snap like firecrackers from an extended line of oncoming rebels, and an intense and destructive fire crashed upon the fort. In the gun pit the Omani gunner was struggling to find a target; at the outbreak of the battle two SAS Fijians – cool, determined men – dashed to his assistance, and the SAS mortar team went into action.

Kealy desperately tried to maintain wireless communication with the gun pit, but the area of the fort was under heavy bombardment, casualties were suffered and wireless communication spasmodic. Moreover, the enemy were at the perimeter wire, and some would soon be through. Kealy wirelessed for a helicopter to evacuate the wounded (it was unable to land), and an air strike. He then decided to cross, accompanied by the medic – Trooper Tobin – the 400 yards between the BATT house and the fort. It was a courageous decision, for the intervening ground was torn with great explosions and racked with rifle and machine gun fire, but somehow they made it to find a scene of desolation and chaos.

It was now about 7 a.m. and some of the enemy were across the wire and closing on the gun pit in seemingly irresistible strength. A close, intense firefight developed, but the small party were temporarily saved by a daring and very telling air strike from the Sultan's air force, flying through the hazards of the monsoon. There was a brief lull before the rattle of small-arms fire and the thud of cannon resumed. A second air strike, carefully directed by the defenders' wireless, produced another lull, but the tide was turned and the enemy finally defeated by the arrival of reinforcements. It was a lucky chance that some men of the relieving G Squadron were in Salalah; they were landed by helicopter outside the battle area and, together with those men of the *firqat* not on patrol in the jebel, bore down upon the enemy.

Kealy, who was awarded a well-deserved DSO for his conduct on this day, then insisted on taking out a patrol to aid the *firqat* still on the jebel, who might be caught by the retreating rebels – which indeed they were. He never found them, but later they returned with three wounded, and bringing with them four of their dead. The SAS had lost the medic, Trooper Tobin, and one of the Fijians, Trooper Labalaba, and two Omanis were killed; the enemy lost thirty dead for certain and a number of wounded were taken. They also lost a great deal of face, for this had been a well-organized, set-piece attack on a large scale designed to capture Mirbat, and it had been completely routed through the courage of a few men, the skill of the Sultan's air force and the fortuitous presence of a relieving squadron.

Gradually the enemy were driven along, and sometimes off, the jebel in a westerly direction by the Sultan's formidable force – some 15,000 troops by 1974. The SAS continued their important role with the *firqats* and with their civil aid. Small teams would be attached to *firqats* and SAF troops occupying strong sangar positions, from which they would sally forth to set ambushes and carry out searches in the many wadi caves, where the enemy would fight savagely in protection of their large caches of arms. These operations, besides harrying the enemy from place to place and capturing much valuable booty, destroyed their credibility and encouraged further desertions.

As the Sultan's armed forces, as well as those of his allies, brilliantly supported by the SOAF, gained in strength and experience and more and more *firqats* were raised, so the enemy found it increasingly difficult to maintain his position on the jebel, despite the fact that Russian arms – including a SAM 7 missile – continued to arrive across the PDRY border. But the problem of relating strategy to what was tactically possible remained; this was partly solved by the construction of a number of formidable lines of defence. There were eventually five in number, proceeding westward as areas were cleared and the enemy thrust back. British and Jordanian engineers were largely responsible for patiently and painstakingly erecting these impressive wired, mined and booby-trapped lineal defences, which stretched from the top of the jebel to the sea – a distance in one instance of 35 miles over appallingly rugged country. They were manned by SAF troops, while the *firqats* with their SAS teams used them as a firm base from which to operate offensively in their tribal areas, dealing with dissidents and extending government influence.

As the war neared the PDRY border in the closing months of 1975, the SAF came increasingly under heavy bombardment from Yemeni-based weapons, and the Sultan ordered retaliatory strikes. These may have had some effect on Yemeni thinking; but it was probably pressure from the Saudis, coupled with the growing lack of empathy with the dissidents amongst the civilian population, that led eventually to a rather messy and inconclusive end to the ceaseless bloodletting of more than six years. The Sultan announced that the war was over on 11 December 1975; but spasmodic eruptions from across the border lingered on until March, and there were still well over 100 rebels active on the jebel who had not joined their brothers in the bitter, despairing march to the comparative safety of the PDRY. Small BATT teams were therefore active on all parts of the jebel for many months after the official end to hostilities.

It had been a long war, and the brunt of the fighting had fallen upon the Sultan's forces, which for the most part had performed splendidly on the ground and in the air. The SAS contribution was the smallest in numbers, but by no means the least in importance. The *firqats*, which they largely raised and trained, were the eyes and ears of the army; the Civil Action Teams were the means of winning untold numbers of 'hearts and minds', and this had been another of those semi-colonial wars in which the winning of the local people was ultimately responsible for the winning of the war. The last SAS squadron left Dhofar in September 1976. The Regiment had contributed mightily in bringing peace to a people who had found their destiny on stony paths.

19

The Special Air Service: Recent Years

Between the ending of the Dhofar campaign in 1976 and the Falklands battle in 1982 there was no war in which the SAS took part. But over the years as their fame spread there was, and still is, an increasing demand for their services in many parts of the world, and in various roles. Men have been loaned to heads of state for such purposes as training of bodyguards, and in at least one case – Oman – raising and training whole SAS-type units. Small parties are sent unobtrusively to survey possible trouble spots, where military action might be required; instructors are provided for the Long Range Patrol School in Germany, which is connected to NATO; at home there is the need for constant readiness in the very important anti-terrorist role, and since 1976 there has been the Irish commitment on a regular basis.

The SAS understandably shun publicity and, until some eye-catching event such as the Iranian Embassy siege hits the headlines, little is heard of their present-day activities – and that is how they like it. But where the dictates of secrecy do not intrude there is a natural desire to know something about Britain's foremost special service, what they have done and what they are training to do. And this mostly concerns 22 SAS based on Sterling Lines, Hereford.

22 SAS has four 'Sabre' squadrons, A, B, D and G. The missing C was the Rhodesian squadron formed at the time of the Malay Scouts, and which remained in being until that country became Zimbabwe. G Squadron was formed shortly after Borneo, as a Guards squadron, but now guardsmen usually comprise less than 50 per cent of the strength. Each squadron has a boat, mountain, free-fall and mobility troop – the latter are motorcycle experts

and skilled in the mechanics of every type of potential enemy vehicle. A troop is commanded by a captain and there are fifteen other ranks.

Basically the four squadrons rotate between Northern Ireland, Special Project Teams, overseas training, standby, skills training and leave. The standby squadron, which is available to fly anywhere for a military job, can be on training in this country or abroad as long as it has with it the necessary kit for an emergency deployment elsewhere. The Special Project Teams (formerly known as Pagoda) can vary in strength, but are found from one squadron, and one team will always be on immediate call and a second at three hours' notice. There is also a team permanently in Ireland with reinforcements on call from Hereford.

In order to achieve the very highest standard of excellence in quick shooting and close-quarters combat, so essential for survival and success in any anti-terrorist operation, a Counter-Revolutionary Wing (CRW) was set up some years ago, whose importance has been increasingly recognized with a consequent considerable improvement in its training facilities and weaponry. The CRW has a staff of some twenty men (usually a three-year job) fulfilling a wide variety of training tasks, of which the principal one is the running of the Body Guard (BG) and Close Quarter Battle (CQB) courses. These involve hard work in the indoor CQB building – colloquially known as 'the House', an abbreviation from 'the Killing House'. On these courses every man is provided with a minimum of 1,500 rounds of ammunition and taught, among other things, to handle a wide assortment of weapons with a deadly familiarity, and to deal most expeditiously with magazine changes and possible stoppages.

'The House' is realistically furnished to resemble an ordinary (but bullet-proof) sitting-room with terrorists and hostages represented by dummies. Training is carried out with the many sophisticated weapons now used, such as the Heckler and Koch MP5 9 mm sub-machine gun; the American-made Ingram machine pistol; the Browning automatic 13-round pistol; stun grenades; and tear gas. On first bursting into the room the man must be able to distinguish hostage from terrorist, and then carry out fire and movement of exceptional accuracy and velocity, not to spray the room but to thump a couple of bullets into an enemy before he can even bring his weapon to the ready. Obviously surprise is an essential ingredient in this type of fighting – as in most types – and is often obtained by gas and grenades. But the reflex action required for this quick, close-quarters killing business against alert, well-armed thugs holed up in a small space has to be even more strongly developed than that needed for the equally dangerous street fighting.

The CRW staff, as well as running the BG and CQB courses, are closely concerned with the training of the Special Project Teams. When, for example, a squadron returns from training abroad and is due to take up the SP role, the handing-over squadron may run a refresher course for the newcomers, but the CRW are on hand to co-ordinate the training and teach the various specialist skills, such as observation-post work. It is understandable, therefore, that the CRW and the Special Project Teams need to spend very many hours in 'the House'; but the building can be booked by any troop at Hereford which wishes to brush up its close-combat skills. Every man in 22 SAS has to be fully trained for this work.

There are numerous civil and political threads to be unravelled before a Special Project Team of the SAS goes into action. The police, at any rate initially, will handle acts of criminal intimidation and violence, and when political terrorism is involved the committee known as COBRA (Cabinet Office Briefing Room), which is chaired by the Deputy Prime Minister, directs the operation. The SAS are represented by advisers on this body and are therefore in direct touch. Negotiations and persuasion are tried exhaustively by the police, sometimes with success. But on other occasions impossible demands are relayed back to COBRA and are dealt with patiently and diplomatically, while preparations for a possible break-in proceed quietly on the spot. Then, perhaps, the terrorists' patience runs out and a hostage is murdered. Such deeds sow their crop of dragons' teeth, and when this happens terrorists can expect no mercy, for then a Special Project Team will surely be unleashed.

The classic example of this is, of course, the Iranian Embassy siege, when on the morning of 30 April 1980 six Arab nationalists forced their way into that embassy – taking with them in the process the police constable on guard – and for five-and-a-half days held some twenty-one hostages (including four women) captive, until on the evening of 5 May they brutally murdered the Iranian press attaché and threatened, unless their demands were met, to perpetrate similar acts of violence every half hour.

The SAS team were on site a few hours after the trouble had started. They travelled from Hereford in plain clothes, and took up temporary quarters in a truck at Hyde Park Corner. During the long days of tedious and futile negotiation they assisted, from the neighbouring house, in making tiny peepholes through the adjoining walls by which a fish-eye television camera could record the exact layout and position of hostages and terrorists. Then, on the evening of the fifth day, when the head of the Metropolitan Police on the spot reported the assassination to COBRA, the decision was made by the Prime Minister, Mrs Thatcher, to send in the SAS.

The thrilling and extremely successful twelve-minute attack that followed has been often and fully described; within less than forty-five minutes the building had been cleared of terrorists, all but one of whom had been killed, the hostages – save the assistant press attaché, who was of course already dead – had been rescued unharmed, and the SAS had handed the building back to the police.

The five principal ingredients for the success of this operation were first and foremost the high standard of professionalism of those taking part, born of many months' careful preparation and training in 'the House'. Secondly, there was the use made of the time allowed for reconnaissance; the photographs of the gunmen, armed with their formidable Uzi sub-machine guns, and of the occupied rooms, indicating the type of opposition to be encountered and the probable location of hostages. Thirdly, men had been able to spend time on the roof making preparations for the difficult abseiling manoeuvres to blast their way into the back and front of the building. Fourthly, the choice of weapons proved exactly right for the task – framed charges of plastic explosive, stun grenades, CS gas, personal intercommunication wireless, and the deadly machine pistols so expertly handled. And fifthly, among the twenty-five SAS men engaged there was at least one with knowledege of Arabic and Farsi.

There have been other less spectacular but fairly similar operations carried out by small SAS teams, and no doubt more that have never been disclosed, for the Regiment has worldwide anti-terrorist interests in an advisory, exploratory, protective and reconnaissance capacity. In January 1975 the hijacking of an aeroplane from Manchester ended in farce when the hijacker, an Iranian with a dummy pistol, found an SAS reception party awaiting him at Stansted airport, where he was landed – much to his surprise – instead of the hoped-for Paris. And later that year in London four members of the IRA, trapped by the police in a Balcombe Street flat, decided to give themselves up when they learned that the SAS were preparing to come in and get them.

But the Lufthansa hijack from Malta in October 1977, in which two SAS men (Major Morrison and Sergeant Davies) played a prominent part, was a much more serious business. The hijack was carried out by four Palestinian terrorists, who were demanding the return by the West German government of certain members of the Baader-Meinhof gang – and there were no dummy pistols in their armoury. After the Munich massacre in 1972 the Germans had raised their own anti-terrorist squad (GSG-9), and when the hijacked aircraft was known to be heading for Dubai – a state which had close British affiliations – a senior member of GSG-9 flew to London to seek help.

As SAS men had trained the Dubai Royal Guard and knew the area, the offer of their services was gratefully accepted. In the event the airliner left Dubai before action could be taken and flew on to Aden, where the aircraft carrying GSG-9 and SAS was refused permission to land. Eventually both aeroplanes landed at Mogadishu, where the terrorists flung on to the tarmac the body of the pilot whom they had murdered. Until then the Germans were fully prepared to negotiate – they had £9 million on board – but as in London three years later murder sealed the fate of the terrorists.

By now the GSG-9 backup force had arrived and the plan, a bold one, was quickly worked out by the SAS team and the Germans. The two SAS men were to fling their percussion grenades from each side of the aircraft, and this was to be the signal for the immediate assault by the Germans, who would bash in the emergency doors above the wings. The entry into the airliner went according to plan, and there ensued an eight-minute gun battle against terrorists in the front and rear of the machine; bullets hummed over the heads of the seventy-nine passengers still strapped in their seats, who suffered no worse fate than the harmless explosion of two terrorist grenades beneath their seats, while the quick-shooting Germans killed three of the four terrorists and made fast the fourth. This fruitful piece of international co-operation enhanced the reputation of both special forces.

Contrary to what is sometimes thought, and indeed to what has appeared in print, neither the SAS, nor any individual member of it, had any commitment whatever in Northern Ireland before the then Prime Minister, Harold Wilson, announced in January 1976 that a squadron was to be sent, in a combatant role, to the troublesome and virtually uncontrolled border area of South Armagh. The only previous visit had been when a squadron was sent to Northern Ireland for ten days to practise emergency deployment. Their absence until 1976 was in some part due to the heavy commitments they had at the time elsewhere – principally South Arabia – and the fact that propaganda put out by the IRA had effectively stopped their use, because politicians had previously denied their presence, even though no one believed that.

When they were sent to the Province it was in the normal role being carried out by other regiments there, in other words surveillance, patrols, ambushes and so on; at no time did they engage in undercover work, nor did they work with the 'counter-gang' Military Reconnaissance Force, known as 'Freds', nor at any time with Military Intelligence – which later was perhaps a pity, for during the early 1970s the whole intelligence network in Northern Ireland was shrouded in Cimmerian gloom and general confusion, with MI5 and MI6 in close competition and rivalry.

As the Dhofar campaign had only recently been concluded at the time of the Prime Minister's statement, it was a little while before a full squadron could be assembled in the Crossmaglen area, but an advance party was early on the scene and very soon satisfactory results were achieved in that dark district. Only the more sensational actions reach the newspapers, and many successes by British soldiers and the police – often bloodless – in the field of ambuscade, finding of arms caches and co-operation with the Royal Ulster Constabulary frequently occur, but are seldom reported.

The SAS skills in well-concealed observation work, perhaps extending for long periods, the speedy transmission of vital intelligence, fast and accurate shooting, and the siting of ambushes soon won for them both respect and obloquy from the IRA. Confusion and calumny have occasionally caused them to suffer adverse publicity. As a declared force they have sometimes been used as the stalking horse for other highly-secretive operatives; on other occasions they have been blatantly accused of atrocities that never occurred; and of course at times there have been mistakes which might perhaps have been avoided.

When such mistakes do occur – and it is seldom enough – they usually stem from the very difficult position in which every soldier finds himself while serving in Northern Ireland. He is at one and the same time acting in aid of the civil power and fighting an undeclared war; a whole mishmash of hand-tying rules and regulations bind him which, when violated or disregarded in the slightest degree, are immediately seized upon by his opponents, who in their turn recognize no law but their own caprice.

Northern Ireland has been for some time, and presumably will continue to be, a regular stamping ground for SAS squadrons – as for other units of the Army. It cannot be a pleasant assignment, for it is an unsatisfactory type of fighting, but it is a job that has to be done, and is being done immensely well. There would appear to be no prospect of eliminating those who practise violence while they continue to command the sympathy of even a small section of the population, and sadly there seems little hope at present of ending the confrontation through the winning of 'hearts and minds'. But surely this has to be the ultimate solution.

At the beginning of April 1982 the Argentines invaded the Falkland Islands, which are some 8,000 miles across the Atlantic from Britain. The British government, and in particular its Prime Minister, Margaret Thatcher, upon whom the principal burden of decision lay, had been taken by surprise and were in an unpleasant predicament. The Prime Minister may well have recalled the words Drake wrote to the first Queen Elizabeth, 'The advantage of time and place in all martial actions is half a victory, which being lost is irrecoverable.' As it happened in this particular 'martial action' the advantage lost by the Task Force in time and place did not prove irrecoverable, but it very easily might have done so.

After agonizing days of shuttle diplomacy, and the eirenical role so assiduously played by Alexander Haig against the background of General Galtieri's gasconades, Mrs Thatcher and her advisers decided that naked aggression, against which Britain has been for so long a sheet-anchor for mankind, could not go unpunished and the country blundered into a war that could well have been avoided.

Two squadrons of the SAS, and to a lesser degree a third, were to play a prominent part from the retaking of South Georgia on 25 April to the end of hostilities on 14 June. Much of what they were called upon to do was reminiscent of the days behind the enemy lines in the Second World War, but the climatic and ground conditions the men had to contend with were much more unpleasant than those experienced by their predecessors in France and Germany, and on a par with those encountered in northern Italy.

As soon as the news became known that a land force was being prepared for possible action Brigadier de la Billière, the current Director, and Lt-Colonel Michael Rose, then commanding 22 SAS, were certain the Regiment must be involved, and Rose alerted his standby squadron. On 5 April sixty-six men of D Squadron with support personnel and 50,000 lb of equipment took off for Ascension Island, and the next day G Squadron accompanied by Rose and Regimental Headquarters were also on their way there.

Towards the end of April, while political negotiations were still dragging on, although moving towards a close, the British government decided to retake South Georgia, which lies some 800 miles to the east of the main objectives. It was thought not to be strongly held, and its capture would demonstrate a strength of purpose. Accordingly a battle fleet sailed from Ascension Island, and an assault force consisting of M Company Royal Marines, D Squadron SAS and about twenty-five men from the Royal Marines Special Boat Squadron, all under Major Sheridan, RM, prepared to tackle the Argentine garrison and the appalling weather conditions. In the event it was the latter which nearly aborted this finely-balanced operation.

A preliminary reconnaissance by air and submarine reported favourably, and it was decided (after considerable discussion as to its feasibility) to adopt the plan of D Squadron's commander, Major Delves, to land the Mountain Troop on the Fortuna Glacier. From there two patrols were to operate round Stromness, Husvick and Leith, while a third reconnoitred a possible beach landing site in Fortuna Bay pending the arrival of the main force of Royal Marines. The SBS men were to go ashore at Hound Bay to observe Grytviken, which was to be the main objective.

Captain Hamilton's Mountain Troop, which took off in three helicopters from HMS *Antrim* on 21 April, met the most appalling weather conditions of blizzards and driving sleet with needles of ice. The helicopter pilots managed to get them down, but ground conditions made chances of survival, let alone any hope of reconnaissance work, totally impossible. The men were blasted by 100 mph snow-laden gales, which caused 'whiteouts', ripped tents from frozen hands and clogged weapons. Moreover, there were found to be 100-ft deep crevasses every 15 yards which made travel impossible. After one night it was clear that the troop had to be evacuated. This proved a dangerous and costly business with two Wessex V helicopters wrecked through 'whiteouts', before a third, brilliantly flown by Lt-Commander Stanley, RN, managed to pick up the SAS men and the pilots of the two crashed machines, and – grossly overloaded – land them safely on *Antrim*'s deck.

It had been a most unpropitious start. Furthermore, the next attempt at reconnaissance on the following night (23rd) was almost as disastrous. D Squadron's Boat Troop in five Gemini inflatable craft got into every sort of difficulty in the gale-whipped seas, and although eventually all crews and boats were recovered, only the men who managed to visit Leith had anything to report. And No. 2 SBS, which had been landed by helicopter at a point in Cumberland East Bay, had its Geminis punctured by glacier ice and could not cross the bay.

So far no lives had been lost, but an intended political prize had not been gained, and M Company was still some 200 miles away. But the very fact that there had been absolutely no interference to these unfortunate attempts to put troops ashore seemed to imply that the garrison was not particularly stout-hearted. And it was probable that they had been somewhat demoralized when the Argentine submarine *Santa Fé* had been attacked and completely disabled by *Antrim*'s helicopters while landing reinforcements at Grytviken early on the 25th. Captain Young (*Antrim*'s commander) and Majors Sheridan and Delves therefore decided to take a chance and put every man they could muster (about seventy-five) ashore by helicopter then, supported by naval gunfire, to make a spirited sortie against Grytviken. The gamble came off with virtually no fighting, and only one casualty – an Argentine sailor. By the evening of 25 April, through several happy turns of Fortune's wheel, South Georgia had been regained without loss.

It was on 8 May that the point of no return was reached, for on that date the decision was taken to send the landing force from Ascension Island. The risks were enormous, and any sort of failure, or even undue delay, could have worldwide unfavourable repercussions. If success was to be achieved it was of paramount importance that a very exact knowledge of the ground and the opposition should be obtained prior to the landings, and this was tailor-made for the SAS and SBS, who commenced patrolling on and around East and West Falkland at the beginning of May.

During the first three nights of May eight patrols from G Squadron were flown in by Sea King helicopter from HMS *Hermes*. The flight of 120 miles by night was a remarkable feat in itself, and made possible only by the use of the new American passive night goggles (PNG), which were to play a winning part in the war. The pilots, with perfect night vision, were able to skim low over the sea and put the patrols down with great accuracy on the pre-selected sites. Accuracy in landing was importantt, so that the patrols could get an exact fix for future navigation. On East Falkland patrols were landed in the Port Stanley, Bluff Cove and Darwin areas. Across Falkland Sound the SAS held a watching brief on Port Howard and Fox Bay, while SBS teams covered, among many other places, Ajax Bay.

Once on the ground these patrols were very much on their own; unlike in Northern Ireland there were no back-up squads within quick helicopter reach, for the nearest friendly troops were many hundreds of miles away. The ground conditions may not have been so bad as those encountered by the Mountain Troop in South Georgia, but they were quite bad enough. Patrols would have to lie up for a long time, with a ration pack that was geared to an inadequate eight days, in squelching bog (which precluded much digging), enduring rain, sleet, snow and wind. At this season the deadly neutrality of deepening cold lay over these bleak islands.

As soon as they landed, these patrols of G Squadron set off on a long approach march on a compass bearing to their pre-arranged OP positions, selected from what scanty information was available as to the whereabouts of the main enemy posts. Then for days on end, and sometimes at unnervingly close quarters, they watched and noted the behaviour of the Argentine soldiers, the coming and going of aircraft, and generally the enemy's offensive and defensive preparations. They lived constantly in the shadow of death, for detection was always close; especially dangerous was the routine wireless transmission. These patrols lacked 'burst transmission'* facilities, and so even brief reports were vulnerable to enemy direction-finding devices. Nevertheless, they managed to send accurate and timely information; the picture they built up was of a fairly low-calibre, young and inexperienced opposition which was poorly led although superbly armed. This proved to be broadly accurate, for only a small proportion of the Argentine force comprised well-trained, seasoned troops.

While the SAS were engaged on collecting data on Argentine land forces, SBS reconnaissance patrols were busy examining beaches on both islands to assess their suitability for the main landing. Their four-man patrols had much the same heavy burden to hump as the SAS men, and a similar formidable armoury – which included grenades, anti-tank missiles, lightweight rifles, night-sight binoculars and the invaluable 9 mm Browning pistol. Their numerous teams scoured most of the bays and inlets with the considerable help of an excellent guide carefully compiled by a Royal Marine officer (Major Southby-Tailyour) who in happier

---

* A highly ingenious method whereby a long message can be pre-recorded and the recording speeded up and transmitted almost instantaneously, thereby greatly reducing the risk of detection.

times had sailed these coasts. On land they concealed themselves for days on end to spy out likely opposition to a landing on any particular beach. The team set out to watch San Carlos Water gave the welcoming news of good and seemingly unguarded landing sites. A few days later (21 May), after some last-minute anxieties had been dispelled, the Royal Navy, with a combination of traditional *élan*, great skill and reasonable fortune, landed an amphibious force of some 2,500 men, which lacked full air cover, intact on a hostile shore.

Once the land battle had begun the principal areas of engagement for the SAS were Pebble Island, Darwin/Goose Green, Mount Kent and Port Howard. Pebble Island guarded the entrance to Falkland Sound, and besides a garrison (later learnt to be 114 strong) there was an airfield in constant use. On the night of 14 May eight men of D Squadron's Boat Troop, who had been landed in the area previously, guided in two helicopters carrying Major Delves and 45 men of the Squadron together with Captain Brown's naval gunfire support team from 148 Battery, 29 Commando Gunners, who were to direct fire from HMS *Glamorgan*.

The original plan was to eliminate both the garrison and the aircraft, but owing to a miscalculation of time by the naval planners only the aircraft could be dealt with. This task was allotted to Captain Hamilton's Mountain Troop, while another troop sealed the approaches to the settlement and a third was kept in reserve. This was an old-time Western Desert-type raid, and carried out with the same degree of efficiency. There were eleven aircraft on the field and, with *Glamorgan*'s guns keeping the garrison's heads well down, the Mountain Troop ran on to the strip and in sight of the enemy trenches proceeded to destroy all eleven aeroplanes with high explosives and missiles, before falling back to the outfield. A remote-controlled charge and a very feeble counter-attack, which petered out almost before it began, were the only attempts at retaliation, and the Squadron got back to the ships with just two men wounded in this very successful operation.

On 19 May, two days before the landing of Brigadier Julian Thompson's 3 Commando Brigade, the SAS suffered a grievous loss. One of G Squadron's reconnaissance patrols having reported a strong Argentine presence in the Goose Green area, it was decided to despatch D Squadron to mask this force while the main landing took place. In the cross-decking manoeuvre between *Hermes* and the amphibious warfare ship *Intrepid* one of the Sea King helicopters plummeted into the sea, killing twenty SAS and

313

attached specialists. The majority of the men lost were from the Mountain Troop, veterans from South Georgia and Pebble Island, and the Regiment also lost two squadron sergeant-majors in this catastrophic accident.

A depleted D Squadron was landed some miles east of the Goose Green area, and then set off on an exceptionally tough twenty-hour forced march to their objective. As one of the purposes of this operation was to bluff the enemy into thinking they were being attacked by a force of battalion strength, ammunition for every form of light and heavy weapon had to be humped over particularly treacherous going. The approach march itself was a fine feat, and the subsequent manoeuvre entirely successful. The Squadron dispersed fairly widely and put down a withering fire from all weapons; the enemy did not venture from their lines, and the Argentine commander later asseverated that he felt certain he was under attack from at least a battalion.

On 21 May the great gamble had come off, but a day or two earlier there was cause for alarm. A small Argentine observation post, recently established on Fanning Head, had been discovered, and its removal in the few hours remaining before the landing was essential. During the dark hours of 20/21 May, as the Assault Group of ships was sailing along the north coast, a strong SBS party, an SAS mortar team and a naval gunfire support officer were landed (necessitating five helicopter journeys in dark and dirty weather conditions) at a point a little distant from the enemy OP. A call to surrender either could not be heard above the naval bombardment or was ignored; but after a brisk firefight, in which the Argentine officer was killed, the enemy made off into the nearby hills, and the SBS were in time to set up landing lights on the beach.

After the beachhead had been consolidated, and no move out of it – other than SAS and SBS patrols – made in five days, the War Cabinet became restless, and from prompting turned to directing Brigadier Thompson to take the offensive. The enemy force at Darwin/Goose Green seemed an obvious target to those in London, although Thompson was inclined to consider it a time-consuming and foolish manoeuvre and would have preferred to mask that force, and go east in strength. Nevertheless, the attack was undertaken by the 2nd Parachute Battalion of the Parachute Regiment and ended in a blaze of glory. Meanwhile the 3rd Parachute Battalion and 45 Commando were sent on a long and arduous march across East Falkland. The march had been made necessary by the sinking on 25 May of the *Atlantic Conveyor*, and the consequent loss of three Chinook helicopters each capable of carrying 70 men. By the end of May these intrepid 'yompers' were within striking distance of the main enemy force in the Port Stanley area.

There was, however, a void in the centre and as part of the movement against Port Stanley it was deemed necessary to take and consolidate the dominant feature of Mount Kent. A patrol from G Squadron had been observing this feature from the beginning of May, and now it fell to D Squadron to clear the mountain of enemy. Some of the Argentine troops in the immediate area had been flown, a week previously, to reinforce Goose Green, but sufficient remained to give the Squadron (and a few days later K Company, 42 Commando) plenty to do, especially against enemy patrols attempting to infiltrate the position at night. But considering its importance the degree of resistance was surprisingly light, and by 1 June not only Mount Kent but the neighbouring Mount Challenger (deserted by troops who had abandoned their equipment) were in the hands of the SAS and the Marines.

Shortly afterwards D Squadron sent a few four-man patrols back to West Falkland, where they were to remain for the rest of the conflict. Men from G had reported a fairly considerable concentration of the enemy at Port Howard and Fox Bay who might, it was thought, cross the Sound and assault the beachhead. As a further precaution against such a manoeuvre the island was ringed with SBS patrols, some of which successfully directed a punishing naval gunfire on to the enemy positions at Port Howard and Fox Bay.

Sooner or later one of the many daring OPs, established as they were within a very short distance of enemy forces, was bound to be discovered and surrounded. This occurred at Port Howard, where the garrison had excellent direction-finding equipment and were unusually alert. Captain Hamilton – whose steely composure had been such a reassuring example on the Fortuna Glacier – had been sending back a series of vitally-important reports when on 10 June he and his radio operator were surrounded. It was impossible for them both to break through the cordon, and so Hamilton – although wounded – engaged the enemy for sufficient time to allow his signaller to escape. Hamilton was killed, but his brave action enabled the signaller, although captured, to survive the war.

In one of the last actions of the war, on the night of 13/14 June, two troops from D Squadron and one from G with some SBS men carried out a raid in support of the attack on Wireless Ridge by the 2nd Parachute Battalion. Wireless Ridge runs to a point immediately north of Port Stanley, and is divided from it by a narrow strip of water. The assault force of some sixty men planned to attack from the sea, travelling in four Royal Marine craft known as Rigid Raiders. Perhaps not surprisingly, this hazardous operation was unsuccessful. Caught in searchlight beams (directed from what purported to be a hospital ship) while running the gauntlet in Port Stanley harbour, they quickly came under a withering fire from every direction and were forced to beat a hasty retreat; but at least only four men were slightly wounded.

Undoubtedly the raid had a damaging effect on enemy morale, for it appeared that they were being threatened both from the land and the sea, as well as being plastered with an enormous weight of lead. One company of 2 Para had some very stiff fighting, but by the next morning the Argentine soldiers were in disarray, and dispersing across the Ridge like falling leaves in a gale.

The fighting was over, and the SAS had played an important part in it with courage, patience and inflexible resolution. But through their commanding officer they also played a part in arranging the peace. Colonel Rose, with his training and experience in what is called 'Psy War', and Captain Roderick Bell, a Royal Marine who was fluent in the Argentine brand of Spanish, had been working for many days before the end of hostilities on the radio circuit, which had been kept open for hospital purposes under Argentine supervision. At first there was no response to their persuasive attempts to arrange an early surrender so as to avoid unnecessary bloodshed among civilians in Port Stanley. But eventually, through the good offices of their contact in the hospital, Dr Alison Bleaney who had remained as senior medical officer in Stanley Hospital, there came a carefully-guarded response from a senior Argentine officer who said that General Menendez would talk. On the afternoon of 14 June Rose and Bell flew into Port Stanley to begin the talks that led that evening to the signing of the surrender document.

A little over forty years before the Argentine surrender at Port Stanley one man's vision had conceived the idea of a strategic raiding force based on four-man groups operating well behind the enemy lines. Thus was born the Special Air Service, but it is doubtful whether even the percipient genius of David Stirling could have foreseen how the fortunes of his small force would broaden through the years. Always faithful to its founder's principles, the SAS has become a renowned regiment with worldwide commitments and a broadening story of achievement, whose greatness lies not in its tradition – for that will come later – but in the superb training, discipline and spirit of its soldiers.

Bibliography

Chapter 1

BUCKLEY, Christopher, *Norway, the Commandos, Dieppe*, HMSO, 1977.

CLARKE, Dudley, *Seven Assignments*, Jonathan Cape, 1948.

COOK, Graeme, *Commandos in Action*, Hart-Davis, MacGibbon, 1973.

DURNFORD-SLATER, J., *Commando*, William Kimber, 1953.

HAMPSHIRE, A. Cecil, *On Hazardous Service*, William Kimber, 1974.

HEILBRUNN, Otto, *Warfare in the Enemy's Rear*, Allen & Unwin, 1963.

SAUNDERS, Hilary St George, *The Green Beret*, Michael Joseph, 1949.

Imperial War Museum
Commander Sir Geoffrey Congreve, RN: personal papers relating to his service with the Commandos.

Public Record Office papers
ADM 116/5552; DEFE 2/37, 38, 45, 700, 701, 711A; WO 218/3, 11, 19.

Chapter 2

BUCKLEY, Christopher, *Norway, the Commandos, Dieppe*, HMSO, 1977.

CLARKE, Dudley, *Seven Assignments*, Jonathan Cape, 1948.

COOK, Graeme, *Commandos in Action*, Hart-Davis, MacGibbon, 1973.

DURNFORD-SLATER, J., *Commando*, William Kimber, 1953.

FERGUSSON, Bernard, *The Watery Maze*, Collins, 1961.

HAMPSHIRE, A. Cecil, *On Hazardous Service*, William Kimber, 1974.

LADD, James D., *Commandos and Rangers of World War II*, Macdonald & Jane's, 1978.

LADD, James D., *SBS: The Invisible Raiders*, Arms & Armour Press, 1983.

LOVAT, The Lord, *March Past*, Weidenfeld & Nicolson, 1978.

McDOUGALL, Murdoch C., *Swiftly They Struck*, Odhams Press, 1954.

MILLAR, George, *The Bruneval Raid*, The Bodley Head, 1974.

MILLER, Russell, *The Commandos*, Time-Life Books, 1981.

SAUNDERS, Hilary St George, *The Green Beret*, Michael Joseph, 1949.

YOUNG, Peter, *Storm from the Sea*, William Kimber, 1958.

Imperial War Museum

Commander Sir Geoffrey Congreve, RN: personal papers relating to his service with the Commandos.

'The Commandos and Combined Operations HQ 1940–43': Brigadier Haydon's report.

Public Record Office papers

ADM 116/5552; DEFE 2/1, 2, 3, 37, 38, 45, 694, 697, 700, 701, 710, 711A, 787, 815, 1093; WO 218/3, 11, 14, 19, 23, 34, 42, 51, 54, 58, 65, 68, 73, 167.

Chapter 3

DURNFORD-SLATER, J., *Commando*, William Kimber, 1953.

LADD, James D., *Commandos and Rangers of World War II*, Macdonald & Jane's, 1978.

LADD, James D., *SBS: The Invisible Raiders*, Arms & Armour Press, 1983.

SAUNDERS, Hilary St George, *The Green Beret*, Michael Joseph, 1949.

YOUNG, Peter, *Storm from the Sea*, William Kimber, 1958.

Public Record Office papers

ADM 116/5552; DEFE 2/37, 38, 45, 700, 701, 711A, 827; WO 218/3, 19, 23, 34, 51, 65.

Chapter 4

BOWEN, John, *Undercover in the Jungle*, William Kimber, 1978.

LADD, James D., *Commandos and Rangers of World War II*, Macdonald & Jane's, 1978.

LADD, James D., *SBS: The Invisible Raiders*, Arms & Armour Press, 1983.

PHILLIPS, C.E. Lucas, *The Raiders of Arakan*, Heinemann, 1971.

SAUNDERS, Hilary St George, *The Green Beret*, Michael Joseph, 1949.

STRUTTON, Bill, and PEARSON, Michael, *The Secret Invaders*, Hodder & Stoughton, 1958.

TURNBULL, Patrick, *Battle of the Box*, Ian Allan, 1979.

WRIGHT, Bruce S., *The Frogmen of Burma*, William Kimber, 1970.

YOUNG, Peter, *Storm from the Sea*, William Kimber, 1958.

Imperial War Museum
Notebook of Lieutenant G. Galway, RN, and Captain N. Clogstoun-Willmott, RN.

'COPP'S Ten's Boxes': George Talbot's typescript.

'Journal of COPP 10': handwritten by Lieutenant Townson, RN, with introduction by Nigel Clogstoun-Willmott.

Public Record Office papers
ADM 116/5552; DEFE 2/37, 38, 45, 700, 701, 711A, 827; WO 218/3, 19, 23, 34, 51, 65.

Chapter 5

BARKER, Colonel A.J., *Eritrea, 1941*, Faber & Faber, 1966.

CHURCHILL, Winston S., *The Second World War, Vols 2 & 3*, Cassell, 1950.

CUNNINGHAM OF HYNDHOPE, Admiral of the Fleet Viscount, *A Sailor's Odyssey*, Hutchinson, 1951.

LAYCOCK, Major-General R.E., 'Raids in the Late War and Their Lessons', *Journal of the Royal United Services Institute*, Vol. XCII, p.528, October 1947.

PITT, Barrie, *Crucible of War: Western Desert, 1941*, Jonathan Cape, 1980.

PLAYFAIR, Major-General I.S.O., *History of the Second World War: the Mediterranean and Middle East*, Vol. I, HMSO, 1954.

Imperial War Museum
'Middle East Commandos Historical Research Group Document No. 67108': editors Colonel G.A.D. YOUNG and Lt-Colonel S.M. Rose, 1 April 1983.

National Army Museum
Private papers of Captain F.R.J. Nicholls 78/I/IT.

Public Record Office papers
ADM 1/11056; DEFE 2/711A, 711B, 787; WO 218/158, 159, 162, 163, 166, 168, 169, 170, 172.

Chapter 6

LANDSBOROUGH, Gordon, *Tobruk Commando*, Cassell, 1956.
MAUND, Rear-Admiral L.E.H., *Assault from the Sea*, Methuen, 1949.

Public Record Office papers
DEFE 2/711B; WO 24/943; WO 201/2624; WO 204/7303, 7876; WO 218/97, 158, 159, 160, 161, 165, 171.

Chapter 7

COURTNEY, G.B., *SBS In World War Two*, Robert Hale, 1983.
LADD, James D., *SBS: The Invisible Raiders*, Arms & Armour Press, 1983.
LODWICK, John, *The Filibusters*, Methuen, 1947.
WRIGHT, Bruce S., *The Frogmen of Burma*, William Kimber, 1970.

Imperial War Museum
Diary of S. Weatherall.

Public Record Office papers
ADM 202/311; DEFE 2/740, 927, 970, 1035, 1061; WO 218/103, 104, 106, 112, 113.

Chapter 8

LADD, James D., *SBS: The Invisible Raiders*, Arms & Armour Press, 1983.
STRUTTON, Bill, and PEARSON, Michael, *The Secret Invaders*, Hodder & Stoughton, 1958.

Imperial War Museum
Notebook of Lieutenant G. Galway, RN, and Captain N. Clogstoun-Willmott, RN.
'COPP'S Ten's Boxes': George Talbot's typescript.
'Journal of COPP 10': handwritten by Lieutenant Townson, RN, with introduction by Nigel Clogstoun-Willmott.

Public Record Office papers
DEFE 2/971, 1035, 1101, 1116, 1192.

Chapter 9

CONSTABLE, Trevor, *Hidden Heroes*, Arthur Barker, 1971.
CRICHTON-STUART, Michael, *G Patrol*, William Kimber, 1958.
KENNEDY SHAW, W.B., *Long Range Desert Group*, Collins, 1945.
LLOYD OWEN, David, *Providence Their Guide*, Harrap, 1980.
LLOYD OWEN, David, *The Desert My Dwelling Place*, Cassell, 1957.
WOOLCOMBE, Robert, *The Campaigns of Wavell, 1939-1943*, Cassell, 1959.

Public Record Office papers
WO 24/939; WO 218/89.

Chapter 10

CONSTABLE, Trevor, *Hidden Heroes*, Arthur Barker, 1971.
CRICHTON-STUART, Michael, *G Patrol*, William Kimber, 1958.
KENNEDY SHAW, W.B., *Long Range Desert Group*, Collins, 1945.
LLOYD OWEN, David, *Providence Their Guide*, Harrap, 1980.
LLOYD OWEN, David, *The Desert My Dwelling Place*, Cassell, 1957.

Public Record Office papers
WO 24/939, 943; WO 201/807-819, 2200; WO 218/90, 94, 95.

Chapter 11

BUCKLEY, Christopher, *Greece and Crete, 1941*, HMSO, 1952.
LASSEN, Suzanne, *Anders Lassen, VC*, Muller, 1965.
LLOYD OWEN, David, *Providence Their Guide*, Harrap, 1980.

Public Record Office papers
WO 201/807-819; WO 218/91, 92, 93.

Chapter 12

PENIAKOFF, Vladimir, *Private Army*, Jonathan Cape, 1950.
WILLETT, John, *Popski: A Life of Vladimir Peniakoff*, MacGibbon & Kee, 1954.
YUNNIE, R. Park, *Warriors on Wheels*, Hutchinson, 1959.

Public Record Office papers
WO 106/2332; WO 170/833, 3962B.

Chapter 13

COWLES, Virginia, *Phantom Major*, Collins, 1958.
JAMES, Malcolm, *Born of the Desert*, Collins, 1945.
MACLEAN, Fitzroy, *Eastern Approaches*, Jonathan Cape, 1949.
SERGENT, Pierre, *Histoire mondiale des parachutistes*, Société de production littéraire, Paris, 1974. Contains an essay by David Stirling on the Special Air Service.
WARNER, Philip, *The Special Air Service*, William Kimber, 1972.

Public Record Office papers
CO 1022/1, 8; DEFE 2/7118; DEFE 11/37-46; DEFE 163/115; WO 218/97, 117.

Chapter 14

LASSEN, Suzanne, *Anders Lassen, VC*, Muller, 1965.
PITT, Barrie, *Special Boat Squadron*, Century Publishing, 1983.
WARNER, Philip, *The Special Boat Squadron*, Sphere, 1983.

Ministry of Defence Library
'Raiding Forces – the story of Independent Command compiled from official sources and reports by Observer Officers': edited by Captain G.W. Read.

Public Record Office papers
WO 201/2202, 2342, 2515, 2519; WO 218/98.

Chapter 15

HAMPSHIRE, A. Cecil, *On Hazardous Service*, William Kimber, 1974.
HAMPSHIRE, A. Cecil, *The Secret Navies*, William Kimber, 1978.
LADD, James D., *SBS: The Invisible Raiders*, Arms & Armour Press, 1983.
PHILLIPS, C.E. Lucas, *Cockleshell Heroes*, Heinemann, 1956.

Public Record Office papers
DEFE 2/952, 1035, 1038.

Chapter 16

FARRAN, Roy, *Operation Tombola*, Collins, 1960.
FARRAN, Roy, *Winged Dagger*, The Elmfield Press, 1973.
HARRISON, D.I., *These Men Are Dangerous*, Cassell, 1957.
HILLS, R.J.T., *Phantom Was There*, Edward Arnold, 1951.

HISLOP, John, *Anything But a Soldier*, Michael Joseph, 1965.
LOVAT, The Lord, *March Past*, Weidenfeld & Nicolson, 1978.
McLUSKEY, J. Fraser, *Parachute Padre*, SCM Press, 1951.
STANHOPE, Henry, *Soldiers: An Anatomy of the British Army*, Hamish Hamilton, 1979.
WARNER, Philip, *The Special Air Service*, William Kimber, 1972.

Public Record Office papers
WO 215/1–63.

Chapter 17

DICKENS, Peter, *SAS: The Jungle Frontier*, Arms & Armour Press, 1983.
GERAGHTY, Tony, *Who Dares Wins*, Arms & Armour Press, 1983.
WARNER, Philip, *The Special Air Service*, William Kimber, 1972.

Chapter 18

AKEHURST, John, *We Won a War: The Campaign in Oman, 1965-75*, Michael Russell, 1982.
DEANE-DRUMMOND, Lt-Colonel A.J., *Operations in Oman*, British Army Review, 1959.
GERAGHTY, Tony, *Who Dares Wins*, Arms & Armour Press, 1983.
JEAPES, Colonel A.S., *SAS: Operation Oman*, William Kimber, 1980.
KITSON, Frank, *Bunch of Five*, Faber & Faber, 1977.
PAGET, Julian, *Last Post . . . Aden, 1964–1967*, Faber & Faber, 1969.
SMILEY, David, with KEMP, Peter, *Arabian Assignment*, Leo Cooper, 1975.
WARNER, Philip, *The Special Air Service*, William Kimber, 1972.

Chapter 19

FOX, Robert, *Eyewitness Falklands*, Methuen, 1982.
GERAGHTY, Tony, *Who Dares Wins*, Arms & Armour Press, 1983.
HASTINGS, Max, and JENKINS, Simon, *Battle for the Falklands*, Michael Joseph, 1983.
LADD, James D., *SBS: The Invisible Raiders*, Arms & Armour Press, 1983.

Index

Achnecarry (Commando depot), 8, 11, 42, 98
Aden, 290, 291, 293, 307
Agnone, Sicily, 36
Ah Hoi, 276
Akyab, Burma, 56, 57, 60, 62, 107, 122
Alamein, battle of, 145
Alban Hills, 178
Albanian Partisans, 53, 55, 157, 162, 218
Alethangyaw, Burma, 58, 59, 106
Alexander, General Sir Harold, 47, 154, 200, 230, 231, 232
Alexander, Captain Herbert, RM, 229
Algiers, 31, 32, 99, 111, 114, 174, 251
Allied Force Headquarters (AFHQ), 50, 173
Allied Military Government in Occupied Territories (AMGOT), 182
Allott, Captain R.K.B., 102, 206
Alston, Lieutenant, 203
Amba Alagi, Abyssinia, 73, 75, 76
Amer, Lieutenant D., RNR, 110
Andartes (Greek guerrillas), 215, 223
Anderson, Captain M.E., 214
Anderson, General, 173
Anti-Japanese Force, 124
Antrim, HMS, 310, 311
Anzio, Italy, 38, 42, 179, 248
Aosta, Duke of, 65, 75
Appleyard, Major. J.G., 22, 23
Arakan, Burma, 56, 58, 103, 120, 228, 233, 248
Armstrong, Captain W.L., 163
Army Commandos: recruitment, 8, 9; organization, 9, 10, 13; training, 10, 11, 13; Commando depot, 11; administration, 12, 13
Arsa Channel, 165, 225
Arya Shay, 76
Asbery, Corporal, 214
Ascension Island, 310
Astor, Major the Hon J.J., 253
Atbara, River, 71

Athens, 55, 220, 221
Atlantic Conveyor (ship), 314
Auchinleck, General Sir Claude, 85, 137, 143, 189, 192, 195, 200
Australian Forces, see under British and Commonwealth Armies

Bagnara Calabria, Italy, 37
Bagnold, Colonel R.A., 85, 129, 130; arrives in Egypt, 126; his ideas for mobile patrols, 126; plans approved by GHQ, 126; enrols pre-war desert explorers, 127; receives permission to enlist New Zealanders, 127; obtains Chevrolet trucks, 127; envisages Patrols operating for up to three weeks from base, 130; confers with Colonel Leclerc, 132; decides on Kufra and Siwa as bases, 133; promoted Colonel and transferred to staff, 136; offers advice to Lloyd Owen, 155, 156
Balkan Air Force, 158, 164, 165
Ballantyne, Captain L.B., 132
Balsillie, Lieutenant Keith, 214, 221
Barce, Libya, 89, 145, 146, 170
Bardia, Libya, 77, 78
Bari, Italy, 39, 156, 157, 161, 175, 177, 223
Barker, Lieutenant M.W., 163
Barker, Trooper, 135
Barnes, Captain G., 102, 105
Barr, Corporal E., 102, 193, 194
Bassens South, France, 240, 241
Beautyman, Sergeant J.E., 184
Bell, Captain Roderick, RM, 316
Benghazi, Libya, 89, 96, 139, 140, 141, 145, 190, 194, 195
Bennett, Sergeant-Major, 189
Beresford-Peirse, Major-General, 74
Bergé, Commandant, 192, 196, 197
Bernal, Professor J.D., 17
Berneval, France, 21
Bhadur Mia, 106
Biddulph, Colonel, 232
Billière, Lt-Colonel Peter de la Cour

de la, 275, 276, 291, 309
Bimrose, Lieutenant Charles, 219, 220, 223
Bir Hakeim, Libya, 143
Bleaney, Dr Alison, 316
Boldrini, Arrigo 'Bulow', 103
Bonaventure, HMS, 102
Bond, Major, 263
Boom Patrol Boat (BPB), 234, 236
Bordeaux, France, 237, 240, 241
Border Scouts, 279, 280, 281
Bourmont, Corporal, 196
Bourne, General Sir Alan, RM, 9, 14
Brac, Dalmatian island, 49, 50, 51, 52, 53
Bramley, Lieutenant J.B., 157, 158
Bremner, Lance-Corporal, 96
Brettesnes, Lofoten Islands, 16
Briggs, General Sir Harold, 270, 273
Brinkworth, Captain, 210
British and Commonwealth Armies
   Armies: 1st, 173, 202, 204; 2nd, 266; 8th, 35, 38, 137, 138, 143, 144, 157, 173, 175, 183, 190, 200, 202, 207, 225; 14th, 57, 105
   Army Groups: 15th, 259, 261; 21st, 117
   Corps: Army Air Corps, 268, 277; Royal Army Medical Corps, 213; Royal Army Ordnance Corps, 128, 137; Royal Corps of Signals, 213, 252, 287; Royal Electrical and Mechanical Engineers, 213; 1st Airborne (British), 251; 8th, 266; 10th, 37, 40, 42, 43; 13th, 249; 15th, 57, 58, 60, 103, 122
   Divisions: New Zealand Expeditionary Force, 127; Royal Marine Division, 228; 1st Airborne British, 173, 175, 176, 177; 1st Armoured, 174; 1st Canadian, 262, 263; 2nd Canadian, 21, 262; 4th Armoured Canadian, 177, 263, 264; 5th British, 35; 5th Indian, 58, 71; 6th Airborne British, 27, 265; 7th

Armoured British, 266; 7th
Australian, 83; 11th Armoured
British, 266; 17th Indian, 229,
230, 232; 46th British, 43; 50th
Northumbrian, 35, 36; 56th
London, 46; 78th British, 39
  Brigades: 3rd Commando Royal
Marines, 313; 5th New Zealand,
79; 6th Guards Armoured, 265,
266; 7th Indian, 106; 9th Indian,
71; 15th British, 37; 16th British,
77; 22nd Guards, 77; 24th Guards,
46; 29th Armoured British, 262;
36th British, 32, 33; 48th Gurkha,
232; 74th Indian, 61; 201st Guards
British, 40, 150, 180
  Regiments: Argyll & Sutherland
Highlanders, 33, 89, 184;
Coldstream Guards, 46;
Derbyshire Yeomanry, 174;
Goorkha Rifles 2/2nd, 281;
Gurkha Rifles 1/10th, 281;
Highland Light Infantry, 51, 53,
219; Inns of Court, 266; Kings
Own, 152; The Life Guards, 287;
Parachute, 23, 210, 221, 275, 291,
314, 316; Queen's Royal Irish
Hussars, 279; Royal Air Force
Regiment, 219, 220, 221, 222;
Royal East Kents (The Buffs),
152; Royal Irish Fusiliers, 152;
Royal Malay Regiment, 281;
Royal West Kents, 154; Scots
Guards, 46; 8/19th Hyderabad,
Indian, 61; 11th Hussars, 266;
13th/18th Hussars, 287; 14th
Canadian Army Tank Regiment,
21; 18th Indian Cavalry, 84; 19th
Lancers, 61, 62; 27th Lancers, 184,
185; 56th Reconnaissance, 39; 61st
Reconnaissance, 262; 111th Royal
Artillery, 54
  Other Units: Guards
Independent Parachute Company,
279, 280, 281; Gurkha
Independent Parachute Company,
279, 280; Indian Long Range
Squadron, 148, 149
Bromilow, Colonel, 169
Brooke, Lt-Colonel Oliver, 274, 275
Browne, Captain L.H., 166
Bruce, Major the Hon Bernard, 147
Brunei, revolt, 278
Bruneval, France, 23
Buck, Captain, 89, 196
Bucketforce, 219
Burbridge, Captain G., 114
Burrough, Rear-Admiral H.M., 18,
Bury, Lieutenant Robert, 222

Cabinet Office Briefing Room
(COBRA), 305, 306
Cafa Krabs, Albania, 163
caique (boat), 153, 217, 221
Calvert, Brigadier J.M., 274, 277;
  commands 2 Burma Commando,
230; succeeds Brigadier McLeod
in command of SAS Brigade, 262;
called to Malaya by General
Harding, 269; recommends
infiltration methods, 270; raises
Malayan Scouts, 270; training at
Johore Bahru, 271; pioneer of

'hearts and minds', 271; leaves
Malaya, 271
Camerino, Italy, 182
Cameron, Corporal W., 174, 176,
181, 184
Campbell, Major C.L., 86, 87, 88
Campbell, Captain J.D., 184, 186
Campbell, Major R.F., 88, 90, 91
Campbeltown, HMS, 19, 20
Campioni, Admiral, 211
Canadian Forces, *see under* British
and Commonwealth Armies
Caneri, Major J.M., 171, 172, 174,
177, 179, 183, 185, 186
Castelorizzo, Dodecanese island, 68,
70, 152, 243, 245
Casulli, Lieutenant Stefan, 214
catamaran, Mk VI rigid canoe, 103,
122
Cator, Lt-Colonel J.J.: commands
No 1 Company PAMPC, 73;
urges their employment as a
fighting unit, 73; forms 51 (ME)
Commando, 73; wounded at
Keren, 75; commands Raiding
Forces/1 SAS Regiment, 207, 249
Cave, Lieutenant Peter, RM, 229
Central Mediterranean Force, 179
Ceylon (now called Sri Lanka), 56,
60, 102, 103, 121, 123, 228
Chavasse, Lt-Colonel, 39
Chetniks (Royalist Yugoslav
guerrillas), 218
Chindwin, River, 60, 103, 230, 231,
232, 233
Chin Peng, 269
Christison, Lt-General Sir Philip, Bt,
57, 103
Churchill, Lt-Colonel J.M.T.F., 49,
51, 52
Churchill, Randolph, 193, 195
Churchill, Brigadier T.B.L., 40, 48,
54, 55
Churchill, Rt Hon Sir Winston, 14,
15, 65, 79, 85, 152, 154, 174, 195,
200
Civil Action Teams, 295, 296, 297,
302
Clandestine Communist
Organization (CCO), 278, 279
Clark, General Mark, 98, 99
Clarke, Brigadier Dudley, 7, 8, 9,
43n, 189
Clarke, Captain K.G., 214, 215, 221,
224
Clayton, Major P.A., 127, 130, 131,
132
Clogstoun-Willmott, Captain Nigel,
RN, 114; reconnoitres Rhodes
beaches with Courtney, 94–6, 109;
organizes a Beach Pilotage
School, 109; trains navigators for
Torch, 110; raises, trains and
equips COPPs, 111, 112; sends
two teams to the Mediterranean,
113, 114; insists that men should
trained men should operate, 115;
aims to train a COPP team in four
to five months, 115; training with
X-craft on Loch Striven, 116,
117;heads team on reconnaissance
off Normandy coast, 117, 118;
second reconnaissance in an X-

craft, 118, 119; insists COPP
service should be strictly limited,
121
Clynes, Captain Charles, 223
COBRA, *see* Cabinet Office Briefing
Room
Cockle (boat): Mk I, 12, 97, 236, Mk
1★★, 103, 112; Mk II, 12, 234,
236, 237, 238, 239; Mk II★★, 243
Collins, Lt-Colonel I.G., 252
Comacchio, Lake, Italy, 38, 44, 46,
185, 226, 248
Combined Operations Development
Centre (CODC), 233, 235
Combined Operations Headquarters
(COHQ), 14, 15, 17, 20, 26, 97,
103, 233
Combined Operations Headquarters
Zara (COZA), 164, 165
Combined Operations Pilotage
Parties (COPPs), 45, 96, 99, 100,
103, 104, 131, 245; training for
North African landings (Party
Inhuman), 110; landings at
Algiers, 111; demand for fifty
teams, 111; composition of a
team, 111, 112; specialist
equipment, 112; requirements of a
Coppist, 112, 113; six teams
training at Hayling Island, 113;
COPPs 3 and 4 in Mediterranean
action, 113–15; serious losses, 114;
COPPs 5 and 6 to Mediterranean,
115, 116; COPPs 7 and 8 to Far
East, 116; reconnaissance work
for Operation Overlord, 117–19;
COPPs 1, 6 and 9 in Overlord,
119, 120; COPPs 4 and 10 busy in
Adriatic and Aegean, 120; COPP
operations in Far East, 60, 120–4;
use of flying boats, 122; landing
on Phuket, 123; landing on west
coast of Malaya, 124
Combined Training Centre (CTC),
10, 93, 109
Commando Brigades (formerly
Special Service Brigades):
formation, 27
  1st: composition, 27; role on D-
Day, 27; subsequent fighting, 28;
casualties, 28; withdrawn to
England, 28; returns to Europe,
29; river crossings, 29, 30; reaches
Neustadt, 30
  2nd: 42, 56, 63, 226;
composition, 40; at Garigliano,
40; deployment of Commandos,
January 1944, 44; at Lake
Comacchio, 44, 45; casualties, 47;
disbanded, 47; in the Adriatic, 48,
50, 51; in Albania, 54, 55
  3rd: 60, 61, 122, 123;
composition, 56; sails for Far
East, 56; operations in Arakan,
56–9; moved to India and Hong
Kong, 63; disbanded, 63
  4th: composition, 27; role on
D-Day, 27, 28; subsequent
fighting, 28; attack on Walcheren,
28, 29
Commandos (units mentioned)
  1: 10; emergence from
Independent Companies, 9n; St

Nazaire raid, 20; St Cécily Plage raid, 24; lands in North Africa, 31, 32; Operation Bizerta, 32, 33; casualties and contraction, 33; sails for home, 34; sails for Far East, 56; attack on Hill 170, 61, 62; disbanded, 63

2: 10, 40, 48; designated (Para) Commando, 9n; Vaagso raid, 18, 19; St Nazaire raid, 20; Glomfjord raid, 23; at Gibraltar, 34; raid in Sicily, 37; fighting in Italy, 37, 38; in 2nd SS Brigade at Vis, 44; Lake Comacchio, 44, 45, 226; Argenta, 46; raid on Hvar, 49, 50; raid on Solta, 50; inspection by Tito, 52; operations in Albania, 53, 54, 55

3: 10, 60; first into the field, 9; raid on Guernsey, 9; Lofoten Islands raid, 15, 16; Vaagso raid, 18, 19; St Nazaire raid, 20; Dieppe raid, 21; in Special Service Brigade, 27, 28; preparations for Sicily, 34; Sicily fighting, 35, 36; invasion of Italy, and subsequent fighting, 37; Termoli, 38, 39; returns to UK, 40

4: 10; formed, 9; Lofoten Islands raid, 15, 16; Vaagso raid, 18, 19; St Nazaire raid, 20; Dieppe raid, 21, 22; in 1st SS Brigade, 27; D-Day landings, 27, 28; at Walcheren, 29

5: 10, 60; formed, 9; St Nazaire raid, 20; sails for Far East, 56; Madagascar, 56; training at Teknaf, 57; Operation Screwdriver, 59; in defence of mountain artillery, 59; attack on Hill 170, 61, 62; disbanded, 63

6: 10, 34; formed, 9; Vaagso raid, 18, 19; in 1st SS Brigade, 27; D-Day landing, 28; lands in North Africa, 31; attack on Green Hill, 33; casualties and contraction, 33; sails for home, 34

7 (A Battalion Layforce): 10, 64; formed, 9; sails for Middle East, 25, 31; known as Layforce, 65, 76, 77; earmarked for Operation Cordite, 76; raid on Bardia, 77, 78; fighting in Crete, 78, 82; most of Commando left on Crete, 78, 82; disbanded with Layforce, 85

8 (B Battalion Layforce): 10, 64, 94, 252; formed, 25; sails for Middle East, 25, 31; known as Layforce, 65, 76, 77; earmarked for Operation Cordite, 76; raiding from Tobruk, 84; disbanded with Layforce, 85

9: 10, 34, 40, 44, 53, 180; formed, 9; St Nazaire raid, 20; in 2nd SS Brigade, 40; Garigliano crossing, 40, 41; Anzio, 42, 43; Operation Darlington II, 43, 44; Lake Comacchio, 44, 45, 226; Fossa Marina, 46; lands on Kithera, 55, 163; part of Foxforce, 55; returns to Italy, 55

10 (Inter-Allied): 10, 27, 40, 48; formed, 10, 25; organization, 25

11 (C Battalion Layforce): 10,

64, 86; sails for Middle East, 25, 31; known as Layforce, 65, 76, 77; earmarked for Operation Cordite, 76; sent to Cyprus, 77; landing and assault at River Litani, Syria, 83, 84; Rommel raid, 86-8; disbanded with Layforce, 85

12: 10, 19; formed, 10; St Nazaire raid, 20; Bruneval raid, 23

14: 25

40 (Royal Marines): 53, 219, 228; originally RM A Commando, 26; all volunteers, 26; severe casualties at Dieppe, 26, 34; Sicily landings, 34; Operation Baytown, 37; Termoli, 39; with 2nd SS Brigade in Mediterranean, 40; at Anzio, 42, 43; on Vis, 50; Lake Comacchio, 45, 46; attack on Brac, 51, 52; taking of Sarande in Albania, 54; reformed in 1946, 63

41 (Royal Marines): part of 4th SS Brigade, 27; demolishes underground radar station, 28; Sicily landings, 34, 35; land in Italy, 37; Salerno casualties, 38; return to UK, 40

42 (Royal Marines): sail for Far East, 56; Hill 170, 61, 62; reformed 1946, 63

43 (Royal Marines): 40; with 2nd SS Brigade in Mediterranean, 40; at Anzio, 43; at Monte Ornito, 43; on Vis, 44; Lake Comacchio battle, 43, 45; Argenta battle, 46; raid on Solta, 50; attack on Brac, 51, 52, 53

44 (Royal Marines): 57, 60; sail for Far East, 56; action at Alethangyaw, 58, 59; Kangaw and the Myebon Peninsula, 61

45 (Royal Marines): part of 1st SS Brigade, 27; D-Day landings, 28; reformed 1946, 63

46 (Royal Marines): part of 4th SS Brigade, 27; returns to UK, 28

47 (Royal Marines): part of 4th SS Brigade, 27;

48 (Royal Marines): part of 4th SS Brigade, 27, 228

50 (Middle East): 85; formed, 64; recruits for, 65, 66; strength, 66; training, 66, 67; raid on Bomba cancelled, 67, 68; sent to Crete, 68; Kasos raid, 68; Castelorizzo raid, 68-71; amalgamates with 52, forms fourth battalion of Layforce, 76; new organization, 76, 77; fighting in Crete, 78-82; battle at Babali Hani, 81; left on Crete, 78

51 (Middle East): 66, 85, 86; formed, 64; needs longer period to train, 67; early history, 73; composition, 73; moves to Alexandria, 73; seaborne raids cancelled, 74; at Sollum, 74; attached to 4th Indian Division at Keren, 74; fighting at Keren, 74, 75; part of Fletcher Force, 75; at Amba Alagi, 75, 76; at Gondar, 76; disbanded, 76

52 (Middle East): 77, 85; formed, 64; recruits for, 65, 66; strength, 66; training, 66, 67; arrives Tuklein, Abyssinia, 71; part of 9th Indian Infantry Brigade, 71; kindergarten patrols, 72; raid on Metemma–Gondar road, 72; move to Gedaref, 73; amalgamates with 50, and forms fourth commando of Layforce, 76; new organization, 76, 77; fighting in Crete, 78-82; battle of Babali Hani, 81; left in Crete, 78

62, see Small Scale Raiding Force

Commonwealth Forces, see British and Commonwealth Armies
Congreve, Commander Sir Geoffrey, 17n
Conway, James, RM, 239, 241
Cook, Lieutenant Guy, 87, 88
Cooper, Major John, 189, 193, 204, 275, 288
Cooper, Major L.C., 70
Cooper, Lieutenant, RN, 114
COPPs, see Combined Operations Pilotage Parties
Cornthwaite, Private, 223
Cos, Sporades Islands, Greece, 152, 153, 211
Courtney, Major G.B., 98, 99
Courtney, Major R.J.A., 98, 110, 150, 206; with 7 Commando on Bardia raid, 77; pre-war occupations, 93; suggests the use of collapsible Folbots, 93; forms first Special Boat Section, 94; operations on Dutch coast, 94; reconnaissance off Rhodes with Clogstoun-Willmott, 94-6, 109; returns to England to form 2 SBS, 96; favours work in Mediterranean, 100; leaves SBS, 103; death of, 107
Coventry, Major Dudley, 275
Coventry, HMS, 90, 91
Cowan, Admiral Sir Walter, 78
Cox's Bazar, Bangladesh, 56
Cox, Lieutenant David, RM, 242
Coxon, Lt-Colonel, 221
Crete, 66, 67, 96, 101, 102, 208, 243
Crete, battle of, 78-82, 155, 187
Crichton-Stuart, Captain M.D., 131, 132, 135, 139
Crouch, Trooper, 226
Croucher, Captain C.H.B., 166
Crowley, Corporal, 259
Cunningham, Admiral Sir Andrew, 68, 71
Curtis, Sergeant C.H., 174, 184
Cyclades Islands, 212, 213, 214
Cyprus Commando, 84
Cyrenaica, Libya, 138, 147, 195
Cyrene, Libya, 88

Dalby, Major, 152, 210, 211
Davidoff, General, 6
Davies, Sergeant Barry, 307
Davy, Brigadier George, 158, 218
Dawson, Lt-Colonel R.W.P. 27
Deane-Drummond, Lt-Colonel Anthony, 287, 288, 289
Decoy, HMS, 69, 70
de Gaulle, General Charles, 193

Index

de Guingand, Major-General Francis, 179
Delves, Major C.N.G., 310, 313
Dempsey, Lt-General M.C., 35, 36, 249, 250
Denniff, Captain A.F., 159
Dennis, Flying Officer, 222
Dennis, Sergeant J., 146, 147
Dennison, Captain, 280
Derby, HMS, 68
Detachment 385, 104, 123, 228, 233, 245,
Dhofar, Oman, 247, 285, 294, 295, 296, 303
Dieppe, France, 11, 17, 20, 26, 248
Dill, Field-Marshal Sir John, 7
Djebel Azag, Tunisia, 33
Dodecanese Islands, 65, 68, 212, 213, 243
Donald, Lt-Colonel A.A., 58
D'Ornano, Lt-Colonel, 131, 132
dory (boat), 12
Drapsin, General, commanding 4th Yugoslav Army, 165
Druce, Major, 263
Dubrovnik, Yugoslavia, 160
Du Cane, Commander, 234
Duggan, Marine, 206
Dugi Otok, Dalmatian island, 159
DUKW (amphibious vehicle), 41, 183, 184, 248
Duncan, Captain G.I.A., 102, 193, 194
Dunning-White, Lt-Colonel J.M., 55
Duplex Drive (swimming tanks), 119
Durnford-Slater, Brigadier J.F., 40, 250, 252; raises and commands 3 Commando, 9; commands troops ashore on Vaagso Island, 18, 19; on Dieppe raid, 21; assault on Sicily, 35; the fight for Ponte dei Malatti, 36; given a brigade command, 37; lands in Italy, 37; praises performance of 3 Commando, 39

EAM (Greek National Liberation Front), 220
Easonsmith, Lt-Colonel J.R., 138, 150, 154; action in command of H Patrol, 134, 135; leads the attack on Barce, 145-7, 170; commands LRDG, 153; killed on Leros, 155
East Falkland Island, 311, 314
Eastwood, Captain S.N., 157, 162, 163, 165
EDES (Hellenic National Democratic Army), 220, 222
Edwardes, Major John, 279
Edwards, Captain Robin, 291, 292, 293
ELAS (Hellenic People's Army of Liberation), 220, 222, 223
Elbe, River, 29, 30, 120
Elizabeth Island, Burma, 121
Ellery, W.A., RM, 239
Ettrick, HMS, 100
Eureka (boat), *see under* landing craft
Evett, Major-General, 77
Ewart, Robert, RM, 239
Eyston, Captain J., 260

Farran, Major Roy: commands SAS

squadron sent to Italy, 258; leads Operation Tombola, 259-61; raises fifth brigade of Reggio Commando Unico, 260; equipping and training Battaglione Alleato, 260; attacks HQ German 51 Corps, 260, 261; in action along Highway 12, 261
Fayle, Lieutenant Douglas, RM, 229
Feeberry, Sergeant C., 102
Feisal, King of Saudi Arabia, 290
Ferri, Major, 182
Ferri, Professor Giuseppe, 182
Fezzan, Libya, 131
Fisher, Eric, RM, 239, 244
Fleming, Lieutenant S.D., 157
Fletcher Force, 75, 76
Folbot (boat), 12, 93, 99, 105
Foot, Lieutenant J.P., 99
Force Viper, 236; call for volunteers, 228; personnel and equipment, 229; training for first assignment, 229; engagement at Hinzada, 230; betrayal at Padaung, 231; ferrying troops across Irrawaddy and Chindwin, 231, 232; and at Kalewa and Shwegyin, 232; arrival in India, 233; end of mission, 233
Force 133, 49, 50
Force 136, 102, 269, 270
Force 266, 50, 157
Fortuna Glacier, South Georgia, 310
Fox-Davies, Lt-Colonel H.E., 6, 7, 126
Fox Force, 55
Frankforce, 264, 266
Franks, Lt-Colonel B.M.F., 252, 264, 268
Fraser, Major W., 190, 191, 192, 265
Freeberry, Sergeant, 102
Freyberg, Lt-General Sir Bernard, 79, 80, 127
Frost, Captain H.S., 75
Frost, Major J.D., 23
Fynn, Lt-Colonel E., 53

Gabes, Tunisia, 148, 149, 202, 203, 204
Gallabat, Sudan, 71
Galloway, Captain, 202
Galtieri, General, 309
Gargano Peninsula, Italy, 156, 177
Garigliano, River, 38, 40, 42, 43
Garland, Lieutenant, 84
Garnons-Williams, Captain G.A., RN, 9
Garonne, River, 240
Geraghty, Tony, 271, 290
German Army
Corps: Afrika, 90, 133, 147, 171; 11th Air, 79; 51st, 260, 261
Divisions: Hermann Goering, 34; 1st Parachute, 176; 5th Tank, 79; 5th Mountain, 81; 16th Panzer, 39, 178; 118th Jäger, 49
Regiments: Hermann Goering Parachute, 36
Ghalib bin Ali, 286
Gibson, Captain, RAMC, 89, 160
Gideon Force, 71, 72
Giles, Lt-Commander Morgan, RN, 49

Gillies, Lt-Colonel H.S., 269
Giraud, General Henri, 99
Gironde, River, 237, 239
Glamorgan, HMS, 313
Glengyle, HMS, 11, 77, 83, 93
Glen Ships, 77, 78
Glomfjord, Norway, 23, 24
Glynn-Evans, Lieutenant, 265
Goatley (boat), 12, 22, 226
Goatley, Fred, 12, 234
Gondar, Abyssinia, 73, 76
Gothic Line, 183
Graham, Lt-Colonel, J.M., 86
Grand Sea Erg, Algeria, 203
Graziani, Marshal, 65
Great Sand Sea, Egypt, 126, 130, 131
Greaves, Corporal S., 209
Greek Sacred Regiment, 55, 200, 202, 207, 211, 212, 216, 217
Green Hill, Tunisia, 33
Greenwood, Captain A.M., 155, 157, 158
Greville-Bell, Major A., 270
Gubbins, Lt-Colonel Colin, 7
Guernsey, 8
Guild, Major A.I., 151
Gurdon, Captain R.B. 144, 198
Gustav Line, 42

Hackett, Colonel J.W., 145, 170, 201
Haig, General Alexander, 309
Hall, Lieutenant G., RN, 120
Hamilton, Captain G.J., 310, 313, 315
Hamilton, Admiral Sir Louis, 19
Hampshire, A. Cecil, 230
Hanaya, General, 57
Hansell, Signalman, 159
Harding, Field-Marshal the Lord, 257, 269, 274n
Harding-Newman, Colonel Rupert, 127
Hardy, Brigadier C.R., RM, 56, 60, 62
Harris, Sub-Lieutenant Peter, 100
Harrison, Lt-Colonel S.S., 19
Hart, Lt-Colonel L.E.D.T., 268
Hart, Major Tony, 288
Haselden, Lt-Colonel John, 89-92, 141
Hasler, Lt-Colonel H.G., RM, 103, 237; joins team at CODC, 233; submits paper to COHQ, 233; works on Boom Patrol Boat, 234, 235; arranges parachute course, 236; initial plan for Operation Frankton, 238; trains teams for Frankton, 238; elaborates plan at sea, 238; journey up the Gironde with Marine Sparks, 239; attacks shipping in Bordeaux docks, 240, 241; lands north of Blaye and escapes through Spain, 241; posted to Far East, 242
Hastings, Lieutenant N., RN, 110
Hawkins, Private L., 166
Hay, Captain A.M., 139
Haydon, Major-General J.C., 10, 15, 18
Hayes, Captain G., 22, 23
Head, Major L.G.S., 281
Henningsvaar, Lofoten Islands, 16
Henshaw, Lieutenant J.C., 160, 218,

222, 223, 225
Hereward, HMS, 69, 70
Hermes, HMS, 311, 313
Heywood, Major G.B., 136
Hickman, Corporal, 105
Hill 170, Burma, 61, 62
Hills, R.J.T., 252n
Hislop, Captain J.L., 253
Hitler, Adolf, 256
Holden-White, Major H.V., 106
Holland, Captain, 263
Holland, Major J.F.C., 6, 7
Holliman, Captain C.A., 140
Holmes, Major D.C.B., 57, 58
Hopkinson, Major-General G.F., 175, 252
Hore-Ruthven, Captain the Honourable Patrick, 201
Horner, Corporal, RM, 243, 244
Horsburgh-Porter, Brigadier Sir A.M., 184
Horton, Lt-Colonel Cyril, RM, 58, 59
Hoxha, Enver (Albanian partisan leader), 162
Hughes-Hallett, Vice-Admiral John, 10, 109
Hunter, Captain Anthony, 145, 170, 193, 194
Hunter, Corporal, VC, 45
Hurst, Captain S.G., RM, 241
Hussey, Captain T.A., RN, 233
Hvar, Yugoslavia, 49, 50

Ilot de la Marine, island off Algeria, 31, 32
Imbert-Terry, Captain Edward, 210
Independent Companies, 7, 9
Indian Forces, *see under* British and Commonwealth Armies
Indraled Channel, 18
Inter-Services Training and Development Centre, 4
Irrawaddy River, 103, 104, 230, 231
Irwin, Major A.S., 58
Istrian Peninsula, 161, 165, 225
Italian special and partisan forces:
    Auto-Saharan Company, 132;
    Battaglione Alleato, 260, 261;
    Commando Unico, 259, 260;
    Garibaldini Brigade, 183, 185
Ivan, Russian PoW, 177

Jackson, Lieutenant C.J.D., 157
Jalo, Libya, 140, 145, 190, 192, 193
Jaquier, Lieutenant, 197
Jeapes, Lt-Colonel A.S., 295
Jebel Akhdar, Libya, 87, 138, 141, 169, 170, 171
Jebel Akhdar, Oman, 285, 286, 287, 288
Jellicoe, Lt-Colonel Earl, 153, 160, 196, 197, 202, 214; commands Special Boat Squadron, 37n, 206, 207; arranges parachute drop into Sicily, 210; attempts negotiations with Admiral Campioni on Rhodes, 152, 210, 211; deploys troops to take over islands in Aegean, 211; advocates co-ordinating headquarters, 212; commands Bucketforce, 219; has need for diplomatic skill, 220;

enters Athens in triumph, 221; put in command of Pompforce, 221; leaves SBS for Staff College, 224
Jenson, Lieutenant, 265
Johnsen, Captain P.B., 253
Johnston, Major Duncan, RM, 228, 231, 232, 233
Jones, Gunner, 209
Jones-Parry, Lieutenant, 224
Jordan, Captain Augustin, 196, 202, 203

Kalansho Sand Sea, 131
Kalinnos, 153, 211, 244, 245
Kalpaks, 212
Kangaw, Burma, 61, 62
Karasovici, Yugoslavia, 160, 218
Kasos, Dodecanese Islands, 68, 69
Kastelli Airfield, 101, 102, 208
Kealy, Captain M.J.A., 299, 300
Kealy, Major M.R.B., 84, 98, 103, 206
Keren, battle of, 73, 74, 75, 76
Kerr, Captain, 59
Kesselring, Field-Marshal A. von, 38, 44, 183
Kesterton, Sergeant, 210, 211
Keyes, Admiral of the Fleet Lord, 10, 14, 15, 16, 17, 26, 94
Keyes, Lt-Colonel Geoffrey, VC, 84, 87, 88
King, Sergeant, RM, 243, 244
Klopper, General, 178
Knight, Captain, 106
Knowland, Lieutenant G.A., VC, 62
Komrower, Major A.G., 39
Kufra, Libya, 126, 128, 132, 133, 137, 144, 145, 148, 170, 171, 201
Kufra, MVF, 159, 164

Labalaba, Trooper, 300
Ladybird, HMS, 69
LAF, *see* Libyan Arab Force
Lamonby, Lieutenant Keith, 208, 209
Lanark, Lieutenant David, 92
Land Force Adriatic (LFA), 53, 54, 55, 158, 218
landing craft: Assault (LCA), 12, 23, 32, 248; Infantry – Large (LCI[L]), 11; Infantry – Small (LCI[S]), 12; Mechanized (LCM), 32; Navigation (LCN), 117, 118; Personnel – Large (LCP[L] – Eureka), 12, 21; Support (LCS), 12; Tank (LCT), 44, 180, 184
landing ships: Infantry – Large (LSI[L]), 21
Landon Lane, Captain R.J., 166
Langley, Lt-Colonel, 235
Langton, Lieutenant T.B., 89, 91, 92, 207, 208, 210
La Palma, MVF, 159
Lapraik, Colonel J.N., 67, 210, 211, 212, 215, 216, 217, 218, 222, 268
Lash, Captain, 35
Lassen, Captain Anders, VC, 218; enlists in British Army, 160n; blows up bridge at Karasovici, 160; posted to Special Boat Squadron, 208; attacks Kastelli airfield, 208, 209; with S detachment on Simi, 211, 212; commands two patrols in attack

on Santorini, 214, 215; appointed to command M detachment, 222; investigates islands in the Sporadhes, 222; operations in Salonika, 222, 223; in Crete December 1944, 223; locates channels on Lake Comacchio, 226; leads attacks on five strongpoints, 226; killed by treachery, 226; awarded posthumous VC, 227
Laver, Corporal A.F., RM, 239, 240, 241
Lawrence, T.E., 6
Laws Island, 107
Lawson, Captain R.P., RAMC, 145, 146
Laycock, Lt-Colonel Peter, 25
Laycock, Major-General R.E., 10, 92, 112, 121, 187, 208, 242; becomes Chief of Combined Operations, 25, 39; anxious that commandos should be employed in their proper role, 26; permitted to form commando brigade in Sicily, 34; splits the brigade, 37; with two commandos spearheads 10th Corps' landing at Salerno, 37; arrives in Egypt with Layforce, 76; anger at Bardia raid, 78; makes initial plan for Layforce in Crete, 80; ordered to evacuate his headquarters, 82; accompanies Keyes on Rommel raid, 87, 88; regains British lines, 88
Layforce, *see* Commandos, 7, 8 and 11
Layforce II, 25, 117
Lazarus, Major K.H., 156, 161, 172
Lea, Major, 202
Lea, Major-General George, 275, 284
Leclerc, Colonel J., 132, 133, 148
Lees, Major Michael, 259, 260, 261
Leicester, Brigadier B.W., 27
Leigneglia, Italy, 101
Leros, Sporadhes Islands, 152, 153, 154, 155, 211, 213, 243, 244
Levita, Sporadhes Islands, 153, 154
Lewis, Captain J.S., 140, 187, 189, 190, 191, 192
Lewis, Trooper, 263
Libyan Arab Force (LAF), 169, 171
Libyan Arab Force Commando, 169
Lilley, Sergeant, 189, 191
Lillico, Sergeant, 280, 283
Lister, Lt-Colonel Dudley, 25
Littlejohn, Captain Ross, 259
Livingstone, Major R.P., 99, 101, 107
Lloyd Owen, Lt-Colonel David, 144, 151, 154, 156, 157, 158, 161; in command of LRDG Yeomanry Patrol, 138; meets up with David Stirling, 138; carries out first of Road Watches, 140-2; Tobruk raid, 88, 90; Barce raid, 146, 147; commands B Squadron in Lebanon, 151; ordered to Leros, 152; sets up base on Dugi Otok, 159; appointed second-in-command, 153; in command of LRDG, 155, 156; parachutes into Albania and injured, 162, 163; in

command of COZA, 164; presses for LRDG service in Far East, 166
Locke, Corporal A.W., 171, 184
Lodwick, Lieutenant John, 214, 225
Lofoten Islands, 15, 18, 19, 248
Long Range Desert Group (LRDG), 85, 93, 109, 167n, 169, 172, 174, 190, 193, 211, 218; the desert, 125; brainchild of Bagnold, 126; founder members, 127; men selected from NZEF, 127; vehicles, 127, 128; the sun compass, 128, 129; first patrols, 129, 130; volunteers from Yeomanry, Rhodesians and Foot Guards, 131, 133; raid into the Fezzan, 131-3; Kufra taken, 133; brought up to establishment, 133; reconnaissance and skirmishing from Siwa, 134, 135; a typical patrol, 134; purchase of aircraft, 135; change of command, 136; change in organization, 136, 137; in support of 8th Army's autumn offensive, 138, 139; danger from air attacks, 139; transporting SAS, 138, 140, 143; Road Watches, 140-4, 147, 148, 159, 201; Tobruk raid, 88, 90, 145; raid on Barce, 145-7; reconnoitring Mareth Line, 148; end of desert campaign, 149 proposed new role, 150; revised organization, 151; parachuting, 151; B Squadron embarks from Haifa for Leros, 151, 152; joins with Raiding Forces, 153, 212; ordered to retake Levita, 153, 154; driven from Leros, 155; commanding officer killed, 155; New Zealanders withdrawn, 156; sail for Italy, 156; operations in Italy, 157, 158; operations in Albania, 157, 158, 162, 163; under command LFA, 53; raids on enemy shipping in Dalmatian islands, 159; shipping watch from Yugoslavia, 159; operations in Yugoslavia, 160, 161, 165; difficulties with Yugoslav partisans, 162, 165; operations in Greece, 55, 163, 164, 219; shipping watch from Istria, 164, 165; disbanded August 1945, 166
Lovat, Brigadier Lord: commands 4 Commando at Dieppe raid, 21, 22; commands 1st Special Service Brigade, 27; severely wounded, 28; deputy to Brigadier Laycock, 35
LRDG, *see* Long Range Desert Group
Lucas, Major-General John P., 43
Lucas Phillips, C.E., 237n
Lyne, Lieutenant L.G., RN, 110

Maaloy Island, Norway, 18
MacArthur, General Douglas, 270
Macdonald, Captain, 259
Macdonald, Lieutenant, 90
MacFie, Captain Norman, 89
Mackenzie, Major Ian, 123, 124
Mackinnon, Lieutenant J.W., RM, 236, 239, 241

Mackintosh, Lt-Colonel A.A., 253
Maclean, Brigadier Fitzroy, 48, 162, 193, 195, 207, 208, 210
Madagascar, 56, 248
Maidstone, HMS, 101
Malayan Scouts, Special Air Service, Brigadier Calvert's report, 270; raised by Calvert, 270; recruiting for squadrons, 270; training at Johore Bahru, 271; early operations make a bad impression, 271; Belum Valley operation, 273
Malaysia, Federation of, 280, 281, 283
Malta, 96, 101, 114
Manfredonia, Italy, 39
Manners, Lt-Colonel J.C., RM, 52
Manningham, Colonel Coote, 6
Maquis, 255, 257
'Marble Arch', Libya, 142, 192
March-Phillips, Major G., 22, 23, 208
Mareth Line, Tunisia, 148, 149, 172, 202, 203
Maungdaw, Burma, 57, 58
Mayne, Brigadier A.G.O.M., 71
Mayne, Major R.B., 140, 197, 201; recruited for SAS, 189; character, 189; success at Tamit airfield, 191; destroys aircraft on Berca airstrip, 194; leads operations based on Kufra, 200, 202; appointed to command newly created Special Raiding Squadron, 37n, 207; trains SRS from camp at Azzib, 249; operations in Sicily with SRS, 250; in Italy with Brigadier Durnford-Slater's brigade, 37n; returns to UK and commands 1 SAS Regiment, 251; commands two squadrons in Operation Howard, 263, 264;
McCallum, Lieutenant I.W., 185
McCoy, Major S.V., 148
McDermott, Lieutenant, 204
McGonigal, Lieutenant Ambrose, 218, 224, 225
McHarg, Lt-Commander N.N., 110, 113
McLean, Lt-Colonel N.L.D., 296
McLellan, Lieutenant, 265
McLeod, Brigadier R.W., 252, 262
Medjez-el-Bab, Tunisia, 34
Menendez, General Mario, 316
Micklethwait, Captain St John A., RN, 91
Middle East Commando (1st Special Service Regiment): raised, 85; composition, 86; raid on Marua Fort, 86; Rommel raid, 87, 88; raid on Tobruk (Operation Daffodil), 88-92; ceases to exist, 92
Miller, Lt-Colonel S.D., 75
Mills, W.H., RM, 239, 240, 241
Mills-Roberts, Brigadier Derek, 21, 28, 34
Milne-Barry, Captain Walter, 221, 222
Minghelli, Ateo, 184
Mirbat, Oman, 295, 297, 298, 299, 300

Mitford, Major E.C., 128, 133
Mobile Naval Base Defence Organization (MNBDO), 228
Moffat, David, RM, 239
Montanaro, Captain G.C.S., 97, 98
Monte St Angelo, Italy, 216, 218, 223
Montgomery, General Sir Bernard, 35, 36, 39, 147, 172, 173, 201
Moore, Captain C.R., 253
Morib beaches, Malaysia, 124
Morley, Sergeant L., 158
Morrison, Major Alastair, 307
Motor Gun Boat (MGB), 25, 44, 117, 118
Motor Launch (ML), 20, 107, 217
Motor Submersible Canoe (MSC), 235, 236
Motor Torpedo Boat (MTB), 12, 23, 44, 89-92, 94
Mountain Warfare School, Italy, 164
Mountain Warfare School, Lebanon, 151, 156
Mounbatten, Vice-Admiral Lord Louis, 15, 22, 111, 120, 121, 123; becomes Chief of Combined Operations, 17; promoted, 20; becomes 'Supremo' SEAC, 25; asks for LRDG in SEAC, 166; approves formation of RMBPD, 235; asks that Hasler be given command, 236; involved in Operation Frankton, 238, 239
Mount Challenger, East Falkland, 315
Mount Kent, East Falkland, 315
Mubarak, Salim, 296
Myebon Peninsula, Burma, 60, 61, 122

Naf, River, 57, 106, 121
Naples, Italy, 42, 43
Nerejisce, Brac, Dalmatian island, 51
Newman, Lt-Colonel A.C., VC, 20
New Zealand Forces, *see under* British and Commonwealth Armies
Nicholson, Sergeant J., 209
Nikolai, Russian PoW, 177
Nizam, HMS, 82
Nonweiler, Brigadier W.I., RM, 56, 58, 60
Northern Ireland, 247, 304, 307, 308

Ogden Smith, Sergeant B., 117, 118, 119
Olivey, Captain J.R., 154, 155, 164, 165
Ollerenshaw, Sergeant, 147
'Omaha' beach, 119
Oman, 285, 286, 287, 294, 303
Operations and Operational Bases Abstention, 69, 70, 180, 181; Amherst, 262, 263; Anklet, 19; Archway, 264-6; Astrolabe, 44; Baytown, 37; Bizerta, 32; Claret, 282, 283; Cold Comfort, 259; Cordite, 65, 76; Daffodil, 89-92, 195; Darlington II, 43; Fabian, 254, 261; Franklin, 262; Frankton, 237-41; Galia, 258, 259; Gobbo, 261, 262; Houndsworth, 254; Howard, 263, 264; Husky, 34;

Keystone, 262; Kipling, 254; Larkswood, 262, 263; Loyton, 254; Overlord, 116, 119; Partridge, 40; Portcullis, 243; Regent, 262; Screwdriver, 58; Shingle, 42; Snowdrop, 195; Termite, 275, 276; Tombola, 259–61; Torch, 25, 31, 98–100, 111; Wallace, 255

Oran, Algeria, 99, 100, 111

O'Reilly, Guardsman Shaun, 226

Osborne, Lt-Colonel Michael, 275

O'Sullivan, Captain, 202

Ouistreham, France, 27

Pagnum, Captain Colin, 100

Palestinian Auxiliary Military Pioneer Corps (PAMPC), 73

Palmer, Lt-Colonel Alan, 162

Parsons, Captain Michael, RAMC, 163

Patras, Greece, 219, 220

Patterson, Major Ian, 210, 219, 220, 221, 223, 224

Peacock, Lieutenant Michael, RN, 121

Pedder, Lt-Colonel R.R.H., 83

Peniakoff, Vladimir (Popski): with 9 Commando on Operation Astrolabe, 44; with LRDG at Barce, 145; origins, 167, 168; character, 168, 169; obtains commission on General List, 169; commands detachment of Libyan Arab Force Commando, 169, 170; recruits men for private army, 170, 171; leaves Cairo at head of PPA, 171; too late for operations in Tripolitania, 171; reconnoitres Mareth Line, 172; transfers his unit from 1st to 8th Army, 173; plans for invasion of Sicily and recruits new men, 174, 175; takes PPA to Sicily, 175; arrives Italy with 1st Airborne Division, 175; obtains complete ration strength of German 1st Parachute Division, 176; leaves 1st Airborne Division, 176; on long distance recce to Alban Hills, 178; works out new and larger establishment, 179; blames Guards for minefield disaster, 180; takes jeeps across Chienti, 181, 182; distressed at death of friend and driver, 181; joins forces with Ferri brothers, 182; assumes command of PPA–partisan force, 182; combines with 'Bulow' and 28th Garibaldini Brigade, 183, 184; under command Porter Force, 184; commandeers and operates DUKWs, 183, 184; severely wounded, 185

Penman, Lieutenant Guthrie, RNVR, 229

Phantom (GHQ Liaison Regiment): role, 252; origins, 252, 253; organization, 253; F Squadron to serve with SAS Brigade, 252, 253; work quite invaluable, 253; training and parachuting, 253, 254; rapid communication to

headquarters enables targets to be pinpointed and attacked, 255, 256; Operation Archway, 264, 265

Phuket Island, Thailand, 123

Pinckney, Captain Philip, 208, 259n

Pitt, Lieutenant G.V., 165

Platt, Lt-General W., 74n, 75, 76

Poat, Major H., 264, 265, 266

Pompforce, 221, 222

Ponsonby, Lieutenant F., RN, 120

Ponte dei Malatti, Sicily, 35, 36

Pooley, Major J.B.V., 36

Popski's Private Army, 44, 167 et seq, 250

Porter Force, 184

Portolago Bay, Leros, 243, 244

Power, Major P.L.J. Le Poer, 264, 265

Preece, Trooper F., 98

Prendergast, Lt-Colonel G.L., 127, 140, 149, 150; joins LRDG as 2 i/c, 135; purchases two aeroplanes, 135; assumes command of LRDG, 136; difficulty in withdrawing Patrols to El Alamein, 144; not suited for co-ordinating role, 145; arranges parachute course, 151; becomes 2 i/c Raiding Forces, 153; reverts to command LRDG temporarily, 156; decides to remain with Raiding Forces, 156

Primasole, Sicily, 35

Pritchard-Gordon, Lieutenant W.H.A., RM, 236, 243

Qaboos bin Said, Sultan of Oman, 294, 295

Qattara Depression, Egypt, 144, 198

Queen Elizabeth, HMS, 107

Radfan, South Arabia, 290, 291, 293

Raiding Forces, 65, 153, 156, 214, 218, 243, 245; formed October 1943, 212; constituent units, 212, 213; task after fall of Leros, 213; ordered to concentrate on destruction of enemy shipping, 214; adopt policy of large-scale raids, 215; raid on Simi July 1944, 215, 216; fighting on Samos, 216, 217; large-scale raid on Lemnos, 217; administration of islands, 217, 218

Raiding Support Regiment, 48, 50, 53, 54, 164, 212

Ramree Island, Burma, 107

Redfern, Major Alan, 153

Reid, Brigadier Denys, 140, 190, 191

Renouf, Rear-Admiral E. de F., 70, 71

Reynolds, Lieutenant M., 164, 165

Rhine, River, 29, 120, 265

Rhodes, 65, 68, 94, 95, 152, 206, 207, 211, 218

Ribiana Sand Sea, 131

Richards, Lieutenant J.F., RM, 243, 244

Rickwood, Major J.E.W., 181

Riddiford, Captain Daniel, 225

Riley, Corporal, 101

Riley, Lieutenant, 265

Ritchie, General Sir Neil, 137, 188

Roberts, Major-General J.H., 21

Rodney, Lieutenant J., 106

Rome, 42, 43, 157

Rommel, Field-Marshal, 79, 86, 87, 88, 133, 138, 143, 145, 147, 170, 171, 195, 197, 198, 202, 204, 256

Ronald, Major A.S., 31

Rose, Lt-Colonel Michael, 309, 310, 316

Roussos, Lt-Colonel, 217

Rowbottom, Captain G.F., 157, 158

Rowe, Lieutenant R.G., 208, 209

Royal Air Force Levies, 54

Royal Marines Amphibious School, 246, 247

Royal Marine Boom Patrol Detachment (RMBPD), 100, 108, 124, 212, 228; date of formation, 234, 235; establishment, 235; training, 236; special force raised to perform a particular task, 236; Operation Frankton, 238–41; Boom Patrol boat trials, 241, 242; Motor Submersible Canoe Section, 242; Earthworm Detachment sent to Middle East, 243; destruction of enemy shipping in Portolago Bay, 215, 243–5; operations from Malta, 243, 245; Earthworm Detachment return to England, 245; become, with other units, Small Raids Wing of Amphibious School RM, 245, 246

Royal Marines Special Boat Squadron, 108; operational Special Boat Section units formed, 246; redesignated Special Boat Squadron, 246; special skills required, 246, 247; training exercises, 247; in action in South Georgia, 310, 311; patrols in and around Ajax Bay, 312; four-man patrols examine beaches for main landing, 312, 313; enemy cleared from Fanning Head, 314; landing lights for invasion fleet San Carlos Bay, 314; patrol West Falkland, 315; attack on Wireless Ridge, 316

Royal Naval Beach Commandos, 247, 248

Royal Ulster Constabulary, 308

Ruff, Marine, 244

Ryder, Commander R.E.D., VC, 19

Saddler, Major Michael, 193, 199, 204

Sadoine, Captain R.J. McC., 253

Said bin Taimur, Sultan of Muscat, 294

St Honorine, France, 23

St Nazaire, France, 17, 19

St Vaast, France, 13

Salerno, Italy, 37, 42, 248

Salih bin Isa, Sheikh, 286

Samos, Sporadhes Islands, 152, 154, 211, 216

Sanders, Sergeant E., 184

Sandford, Colonel D.A., 71, 72

Sandy Point, 112, 115, 116

Santa Fé (Argentine submarine), 311

Sarande, Albania, 54, 55

Sarawak Rangers, 276

SAS, *see* Special Air Service
SBS, *see* Special Boat Section *and*
   Special Boat Section
School of Combined Operations
   Beach and Boat Section
   (SCOBBS), 246
Scott, Pilot Officer A.L., 89, 91
Scott-Bowden, Major L., 117, 118,
   119
Sea Reconnaissance Unit (SRU),
   104, 245
Seleri, Major P.A., 86
Senussi, 169
Seraph, HM Submarine, 99
Services Reconnaissance
   Department, 102
Shakespeare, HM Submarine, 115
Shaw, Lt-Colonel David, 57
Shaw, Captain Tony, 295
Shaw, Captain W.B. Kennedy, 127,
   128, 130, 142
Sheard, Corporal C.J., RM, 239
Sheridan, Major Guy, RM, 310
Shute, Captain L.A.J., 160, 161
Sibyl, HM Submarine, 99
Sidders, Major, 103, 105
Sidi Haneish, Libya, 199
Sidi Rezegh, Libya, 138
Sikh, HMS, 90, 91
Silca, Brac, Dalmatian island, 51
Sillito, Lieutenant David, 90
Simi, Sporadhes Islands, 153, 211,
   212, 215, 216
Simmonds, Lt-Colonel R.W.B., 52
Sinclair, Lieutenant George, RN, 110
Siwa, Egypt, 133, 134, 135, 137, 139,
   143, 170
Skipwith, Captain David, 160, 218
Skorzeny, Otto, 5
Sloane, Lt-Colonel John, 271
Small Operations Group (SOG),
   103, 104, 121, 123, 228, 242, 245
Small Scale Raiding Force (SSRF) (62
   Commando), 22, 23, 208, 250
Smiley, Colonel D. de C., 287, 288,
   290
Smith, Lieutenant P.R., RN, 114
Smith, Lieutenant S., 97
Smuts, Field Marshal, 257
Smyth, Major-General J.G., VC, 229
SOE, *see* Special Operations
   Executive
Solomon, Lieutenant Martin,
   RNVR, 222
Solta, Dalmatian island, 49, 50, 53
Southby-Tailyour, Major Ewen, 312
South East Asia Command (SEAC),
   25, 120, 121
South Georgia, 309, 310, 311, 312,
   314
Spakhia, Crete, 80, 81
Sparks, W.E., RM, 239, 240, 241,
   243
Special Air Service (SAS)
   1 SAS Regiment, 85, 93, 130,
   138, 140, 143, 169, 207, 249, 250,
   253; as L Detachment Special Air
   Service Brigade, 189; early
   recruits, 189; training at Kabrit,
   189; Lewis bomb, 189, 190; failure
   of first operation, 190; airfield
   raids December 1941, 190-2;
   enlargement of force, 192;

requirements for a recruit, 192;
   Free French parachutists
   recruited, 192, 193; Bouerat raid,
   192, 193; Operation Snowdrop,
   145, 195; attack on airfields June
   1941, 195-7; French patrol in
   Crete, 196, 197; obtain their own
   jeeps, 144, 197, 198; jeep raids on
   Bagush airfield, 198; jeep raid at
   Sidi Haneish, 199, 200; given
   official place in roll of regiments,
   144, 200; operations in support of
   General Montgomery's advance,
   200-4; posted and actual strength
   January 1943, 201, 202; operations
   in connection with
   Montgomery's attack at Mareth,
   202, 203; loss of Colonel Stirling,
   204, 205, 207; absorbs Special
   Boat Section and troop from
   Greek Sacred Regiment, 206, 207;
   formed into two new units, 207;
   re-formed as 1 SAS, 251; part of
   SAS Brigade, 252; A Squadron
   sent to France, 254; selection of
   operational bases, 254; work with
   French maquisards, 255; German
   attack on Houndsworth bases,
   255;B squadron surprised, 256;
   resupply drop that went wrong,
   257; achievements up to end of
   1944, 258; Operation Howard,
   263, 264; Operation Archway,
   264-6; work with 11th Hussars,
   266; across the Elbe and on to
   Kiel, 266; success of Archway,
   266; results of operations in
   North-West Europe, 267;
   occupational duties in Norway,
   267; disbanded, 267
   2 SAS Regiment, 23, 202, 253,
   268; training at Philippeville, 174,
   249, 250; early operations in
   North Africa and Sicily, 210, 250,
   251; operations in Italy, 250, 251;
   new commanding officer, 252;
   part of SAS Brigade, 252;
   selection of operational bases, 254;
   work with French maquisards,
   255; type of work performed
   from operational bases, 254, 255,
   256; resupply by parachute, 257;
   achievements up to end of 1944,
   258; squadron sent to Italy, 258;
   Operation Galia, 258, 259;
   Operation Cold Comfort, 259;
   Operation Tombola, 259-61;
   Operation Keystone, 262;
   Operation Archway, 264-6;
   administrative and operational
   changes, 266; advance to the Elbe,
   266; success of Archway, 266;
   casualties suffered in North-West
   Europe, 267; occupational duties
   in Norway, 267; disbanded, 267
   3 SAS Regiment (2ème
   Regiment de Chasseurs
   Parachutistes), 252, 254, 258, 263,
   267
   4 SAS Regiment (3ème
   Regiment de Chasseurs
   Parachutistes), 252, 254, 258, 262,
   263, 267

Belgian Independent Parachute
   Squadron, 252, 258, 261, 267
   21 SAS (Artists), Territorial
   Army, 268
   22 SAS Regiment, 246, 247,
   269, 273; receives official title
   May 1952, 270; training and
   selection for the Regiment, 272,
   273; changes in command, 275;
   Rhodesians replaced by Kiwi
   Squadron, 275; Operation
   Termite, 275, 276; taking of An
   Hoi, 276; included in permanent
   Order of Battle – less two
   squadrons, 277; return from
   Malaya, 277; A Squadron arrive in
   Brunei, 278; task in Borneo and
   type of country, 278, 279;
   squadrons relieved after four
   months, 279; training Border
   Scouts, 279, 280; Indonesian
   incursions, 281, 282; two
   squadrons restored, 281;
   Operation Claret, 282, 283;
   training in South Arabia, 283; D
   Squadron to Oman and Jebel
   Akhdar, 286-9; Radfan
   operations, 290-3; undercover
   work in Aden, 290, 293, 294;
   trouble in Dhofar, 294, 295; SAS/
   BATT teams on Dhofar, 295-302;
   training of firquats, 296, 297;
   action in the jebel, 298, 299; the
   fight at Mirbat, 299, 300; clearing
   the jebel, 301; last squadron leaves
   Dhofar, 302; organization, role
   and training post-Arabia, 303-5;
   Iranian Embassy, 305, 306;
   Mogadishu hijack, 306, 307;
   Northern Ireland, 307-9; D and G
   Squadrons leave for Ascension
   Island, 309, 310; action in South
   Georgia, 310, 311; patrols landed
   on East Falkland for observation
   work, 311, 312; raid on Pebble
   Island, 313; serious loss in
   helicopter accident, 313, 314; D
   Squadron at Goose Green, 313,
   314; action on Mount Kent, 315;
   Captain Hamilton killed at Port
   Howard, 315; last action on
   Wireless Ridge, 316; faithful to its
   founder's principles, 316, 317
   23 SAS Regiment, Territorial
   Army, 269
   63 SAS Signal Squadron, 269
Special Air Service Brigade, 251-3,
   267
Special Boat Section (SBS), 85, 88,
   89, 93, 121, 130, 137, 150, 160,
   161, 193, 194, 202, 206, 227;
   formed as Folbot Troop, 94; type
   of work envisaged, 94; sails with 8
   Commando for Middle East, 94;
   training at Kabrit, 94, 95;
   demolition raid on Sicily, 96;
   evacuation of troops from Crete,
   96; 2 SBS formed, 96, 97; initial
   war establishment, 97; training in
   Scotland, 97, 98; raid on shipping
   in Boulogne harbour, 98; 1 SBS
   attached to SAS, 98; boating with
   Generals Mark Clark and Henri

Giraud, 98, 99; 2 SBS in North Africa landings, 99; Z SBS works independently in Mediterranean, 101; coastal raid on Leigneglia railway tunnel, 101; raid on airships in Crete, 101, 102 parachute training, 102; war establishment for Groups in Far East, 102; Z SBS leaves for Far East, 102; Section becomes split, 102; A and B Groups arrive in Far East, 102; attack on enemy motorboat River Chindwin, 105; Donbaik reconnaissance, 105, 106; Alethangyaw reconnaissance, 106; Laws Island reconnaissance, 107; over eighty sorties on west coast of Burma, 107; last raid of 1 SBS, 206

Special Boat Squadron (SBS), 55, 153, 160, 164, 165, 200, 249; formed from 1 SAS, 160; divided into three detachments, 208; S Detachment raid Cretan airfields, 208-10; L Detachment in Sardinia and Sicily, 210; M and S Detachments on Simi, 211, 212; shipping attacked at Stampalia, 214; S Detachment attacks German transmitting stations, 214; participates in Simi raid July 1944, 215, 216; sails to Italy, 216; raid against bridge at Karasovici, 218, 219; difficulties with Yugoslav partisans, 218; L Detachment dropped into Greece, 219; helps clear enemy from Peloponnese, 219-21; successful operation in Patras, 220, 221; attempts to cut off enemy withdrawal from Athens, 220, 221; liberation of Athens, 221; part of Pompforce, 221, 222; driving Germans out of Greece, 222, 223; difficulties with ELAS troops, 222, 223; M Detachment in Crete December 1944, 223; leaves Greece for Italy, 223; island-hopping in Adriatic, 224, 225; attacks on Lussin, 224, 225; operations in and around Lake Comacchio, 226; SBS not sent to Far East, 227

Special Interrogation Group (SIG), 88, 89, 90, 92, 196

Special Operations Executive (SOE), 17, 19, 22, 102, 188, 219, 220, 235, 270

Special Raiding Squadron (SRS), 40, 140, 207; forms part of Durnford-Slater's brigade, 37; seizes Bagnara Calabria, 37; the battle of Termoli, 39; organization, 249; training for Sicily (Operation Husky), 249; fighting in Sicily, 250; sails for UK, 251; reverts to being 1 SAS, 251

Special Service Brigade, 10, 25, 34, 37, 40, 112, 208

Special Service Group, 25, 26, 40

Stampalia, Sporadhes Islands, 153, 211, 214

Stamsund, Lofoten Islands, 16

Stanley, Lt-Commander Ian, 310

Steele, Major D.G., 133

Stevens, Marine, 244

Stewart, Captain J.D., RM, 236, 237, 242

Stirling, Lt-Colonel David, 6n, 85, 98, 140, 144, 145, 197, 198, 249, 275, 316; injured in parachute descent, 187; character, 137, 187, 188; SAS philosophy, 188; presents paper to General Ritchie, 188; gets authority to recruit sixty-five men, 189; first parachute descent and meeting with LRDG, 138; Sirte raid, 191; obtains permission to recruit Free French parachutists, 193; leads Bouerat raid, 193, 194; jeep raid on Sidi Haneish, 199, 200; summoned to British Embassy Cairo, 200; promoted Lt-Colonel, 200; submits plan in support of 8th Army's advance, 201; reconnoitres going conditions in northern Tunisia, 202-4; captured, 204; proposes SAS for service in Far East, 267

Stirling, Lt-Colonel W.S., 174; forms 2 SAS, 202; training and operations North Africa and Sicily, 249, 250; advocates dropping small parties well behind lines, 251, 252; in dissension over D-Day role, 251; resigns command, 252

Stokes, Captain Arthur, 159, 160

Stormonth-Darling, Major M.P., 156, 163, 164

Street, Major Vivian, 201, 212, 249

Stuart, Major Robin, 62

Student, General, 79

Sturges, Major-General R.G., RM, 26, 40

Sudan Defence Force, 134, 145

Suharto, General, 283

Sukarno, President, 277, 280, 281, 282, 283

Suleiman bin Himya, 286

Sultan of Oman's Air Force (SOAF), 299, 300, 301

Sultan of Oman's Armed Forces (SAF), 287, 295, 296, 297

Sutherland, Lt-Colonel D.G.C., 101, 164, 206, 207, 214, 218, 222, 268; attempts destruction of aircraft on Rhodes, 206, 207; commands S Detachment SBS on Crete raid, 208-10; succeeds Jellicoe in command of SBS, 224; turns his attention to Istria, 225; faced with difficult decisions and explosive situations on Istria, 225

Sutherland, Lieutenant J., 154

Swinburn, SSM Arthur, 86, 88

Taigantis, Colonel, 216

Talib bin Ali, 286

Talisman, HM Submarine, 87

Taxis, Sergeant, 204

Taylor, Lieutenant G., 90, 91

Teacher, Lt-Commander Norman, 110, 113, 114

Teknaf, Burma, 60, 103, 105, 106, 107, 121

Templer, General Sir Gerald, 270n

Tenna, River, 44

Termoli, Italy, 38, 250

Terry, Sergeant, 88

Thatcher, Margaret, 306, 309

Thesiger, Lieutenant, 203

Thompson, Major Harry, 275, 276

Thompson, Brigadier Julian, RM, 313, 314

Thomson, Trooper, 283

Timbaki, Crete, 101, 102, 208, 209

Timpson, Captain J.A.L., 140, 141, 145, 146, 1547, 148, 198

Tinker, Captain R., 148, 166, 172

Tito, Marshal, 48, 50, 52, 159

Tobin, Trooper, 300

Tobruk: Operation Daffodil, 88-92; fall of, 143

Tod, Brigadier R.J.F., 40, 41, 43, 44, 45, 55, 226

Tollemache, Colonel H.T., RM, 103

Tamatave, Madagascar, 56

Tonkin, Major J., 265

Torbay, HM Submarine, 87, 88

Tourneret, Corporal, 196

Trevor, Major K.R.S., 31

Trevor, Lt-Colonel T.H., 31

Trieste, Italy, 158, 165, 225

Trucial Oman Scouts, 286, 287

Tuna, HM Submarine, 239

Turnbull, Brigadier D.J.T,: appointed to command Raiding Forces, 153, 212; ordered to concentrate on destruction of enemy shipping, 213, 214; evolves different type of operation, 214; leads raid on Simi, 215, 216, 245; partakes in Lemnos raid, 217; faces difficult administrative task, 217, 218; hands over to UNRRA, 218

Ulversund, Norway, 18

United Nations Relief and Rehabilitation Administration (UNRRA), 218

United States Army
Armies: 5th, 37, 175, 177, 225; 7th, 35, 38
Corps: 2nd, 42, 172, 173; 6th, 43; 18th, 265, 266
Divisions: 17th Armoured, 262; 87th Infantry, 262
Regiments: 168th Infantry Regiment Combat Team, 31; 1st Battalion, Rangers, 21, 42; 3rd Battalion, Rangers, 42; 4th Battalion, Rangers, 42
Other Units: Special Operations Group, 48, 50

Unruly, HM Submarine, 243

Unwin, Lt-Colonel, RM, 89

Unsparing, HM Submarine, 245

Ursula, HM Submarine, 100

Ustachi (pro-German Yugoslavs), 160, 219

Uweinat, Libya, 126, 130

Vaagso, Norway, 17, 18, 248

Valetta Canal, Italy, 45

Varengeville, France, 21, 29

Vaughan, Lt-Colonel C.E., 11

Index

Verney, Captain John, 210
Vernon, HMS, 234
V Force (British), 57, 106
V Force (Japanese), 106
Vis, Adriatic island, 44, 48, 49, 50, 51, 159

Walker, Major Muir, 280
Walker, Major-General Walter, 278, 279, 280, 281, 282, 284
Walker, Captain, 288
Walker-Brown, Major R., 258, 260
Wallace, Sergeant Samuel, RM, 239
Warner, Philip, 195n
Waterson, SSM G., 171, 184
Watler, Private, 89n
Watts, Lt-Colonel John, 281, 288, 295, 298
Waugh, Evelyn, 71
Wavell, Field-Marshal Earl, 6, 64, 65, 71, 73, 79, 94, 133
Weatherall, CSM S.J., 100, 101, 107
Wedderburn, Lt-Colonel E.A.M., 25
Wesley, Lieutenant, 105
West Falkland, 311, 315
Wilder, Captain N.P., 143, 145, 146, 147, 148
Wildman-Lushington, Brigadier G.E., RM, 17
Willett, John, 168
Williams, Sergeant, 105

Wilson, Harold, 307
Wilson, General Sir Maitland, 83, 154, 155, 207
Wilson, Driver W.J., 171
Wingate, Major O.C., 6, 72, 76, 262
Wingate-Gray, Lt-Colonel Michael, 283, 292
Wonfor, Colour-Sergeant Harry, RM, 229
Woodhouse, Corporal C., 97
Woodhouse, Lt-Colonel J.M., 275; joins Calvert in Malaya, 271; previous service, 271; organizes SAS training course, 272, 273; on Belum Valley operation, 273; demands high standard for new squadron, 281; advocates use of four-man patrols, 282; leaves the army, 283
Wright, Lieut-Commander Bruce, RCNVR, 104
Wynne, Squadron-Leader, 219, 220

X-craft (midget submarine), 118-19, 241

Yemen, People's Democratic Republic of, 290, 291, 293, 294, 301
Young, Captain Brian, RN, 311
Young, Lt-Colonel G.A.D., 77, 81, 82
Young, Brigadier Peter: on Dieppe raid, 21; assaults beach defences Sicily, 35; in command of 3 Commando, 37; carries out raids on toe of Italy, 37; contracts jaundice, 39; deputy commander 3 Commando Brigade, 60; takes command, 60; describes slaughter on Hill 170, 62; returns to UK to command 1 Commando Brigade, 63; suggests Westminster Abbey for Commando Memorial, 63
Yugoslav Army of National Liberation, 165, 225
Yugoslav Partisans, 48, 50, 51, 52, 120, 159, 162, 163, 218, 224, 225, 255
Yunnie, Captain R.P., 168; joins PPA, 171; loses vehicles at Qaret Ali, 172; reconnoitres Gargano Peninsula, 177, 178; in charge of Patrol organization and training, 179; extricates patrol from minefield, 180; on Operation Astrolabe, 180, 181; obtains compassionate home posting, 185

Zara, Yugoslavia, 164, 165, 224, 225
Zirnheld, Captain André, 197, 200
Zulu, HMS, 90, 91